Waiting for Spring

10

Anashin

Waiting
for Spring
vol.10

Presented by
Anashin

CONTENTS

WAITING FOR SPRING
Harumatsu Bokura

Character & Story

To be like her role model Aya-chan, Mitsuki is determined to make some real friends in high school. One day, the school celebrities—the Elite Four Hotties of the basketball team—appear at the café where she works! Mitsuki gets caught up in their silly hijinks, but as she gets to know the four of them, she manages to make new friends, and begins to crush hard on her classmate Towa. But when Mitsuki is reunited with Aya-chan, she is stunned to learn that her best friend was actually a boy! What's more, he really wants to date her! Towa realizes how he feels about Mitsuki and tells her he likes her, but she puts her answer on hold, especially since there's a team rule against dating. To change the rule, the team must defeat Aya-chan's school Hōjō and win the New Team Tournament! But Aya-chan gets injured protecting Mitsuki...

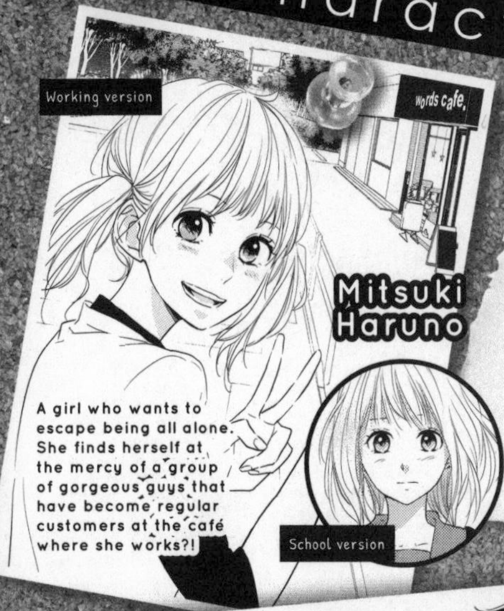
Working version
words cafe.
School version

Mitsuki Haruno

A girl who wants to escape being all alone. She finds herself at the mercy of a group of gorgeous guys that have become regular customers at the café where she works?!

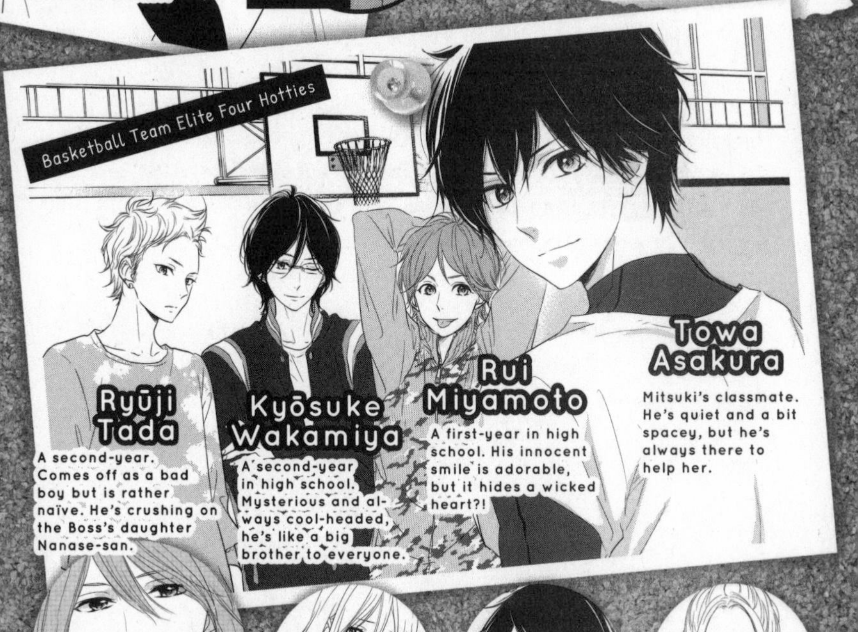
Basketball Team Elite Four Hotties

Towa Asakura

Mitsuki's classmate. He's quiet and a bit spacey, but he's always there to help her.

Rui Miyamoto

A first-year in high school. His innocent smile is adorable, but it hides a wicked heart?!

Kyōsuke Wakamiya

A second-year in high school. Mysterious and always cool-headed, he's like a big brother to everyone.

Ryūji Tada

A second-year. Comes off as a bad boy but is rather naïve. He's crushing on the Boss's daughter Nanase-san.

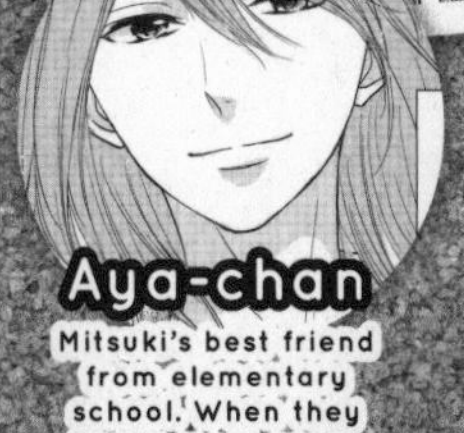

Aya-chan

Mitsuki's best friend from elementary school. When they finally meet again, she discovers he was a boy!

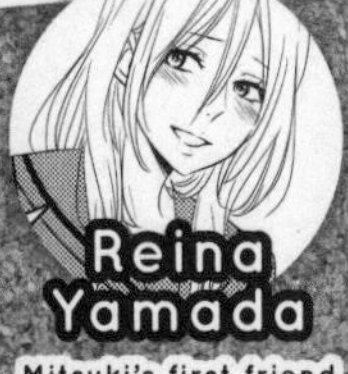

Reina Yamada

Mitsuki's first friend from her class. She has somewhat eccentric tastes?!

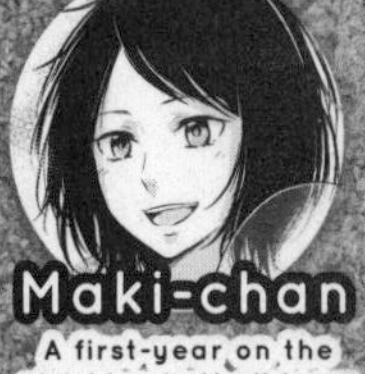

Maki-chan

A first-year on the girls' basketball team who gets along with Mitsuki. Apparently she has a crush on Towa?!

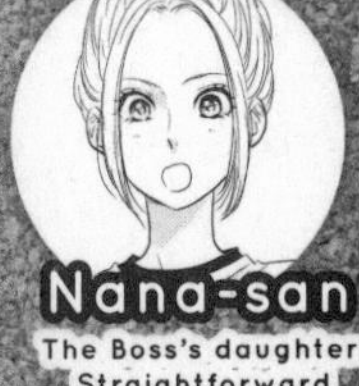

Nana-san

The Boss's daughter. Straightforward and resolute, she is a reliable, big sister type.

Hello!! Anashin here.

Thank you so much for picking up volume 10! ✧

Wow, volume 10! It really is thanks to all of you that I was able to make it this far. I'm happy, but it was so hard! Ha ha (and it's not even over yet!)

It wasn't until I was drawing the last chapter of this volume, Chapter 44, that I finally, *finally* started to feel like I had gotten the hang of drawing pictures of the characters (their faces). ...Took me long enough!! Ha ha

It's been the same with every series I've done. In the second half or in the last arc, I finally get used to drawing everyone, and then I get even more sad about it ending, because I wish I could draw them even more. It's one of my own personal "happens all the time" things.

But since I **have** gotten the hang of it, I want to make good use of that for the rest of the series, and work as hard as I can until we make it to the end. I hope you continue to enjoy it!

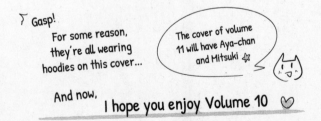

Gasp!
For some reason, they're all wearing hoodies on this cover...

The cover of volume 11 will have Aya-chan and Mitsuki ✧

And now, I hope you enjoy Volume 10 ♡

period 41: "All Together at the 'HOT' Spring Part 1"

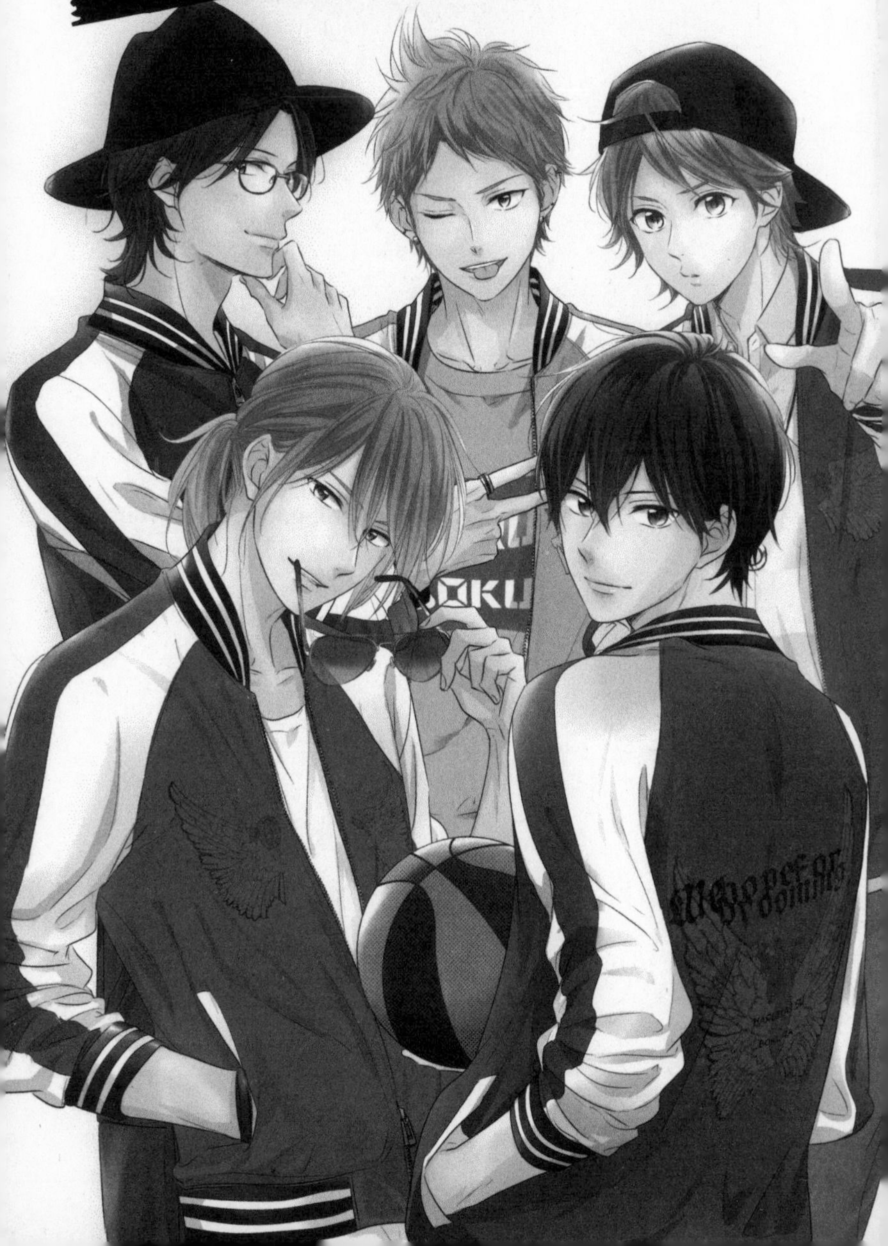

Thank you so much for all the letters, questionnaire answers, and social media messages giving me your opinions and encouragement. I read every word of all of them.

They're my biggest support!

ARIGATO—

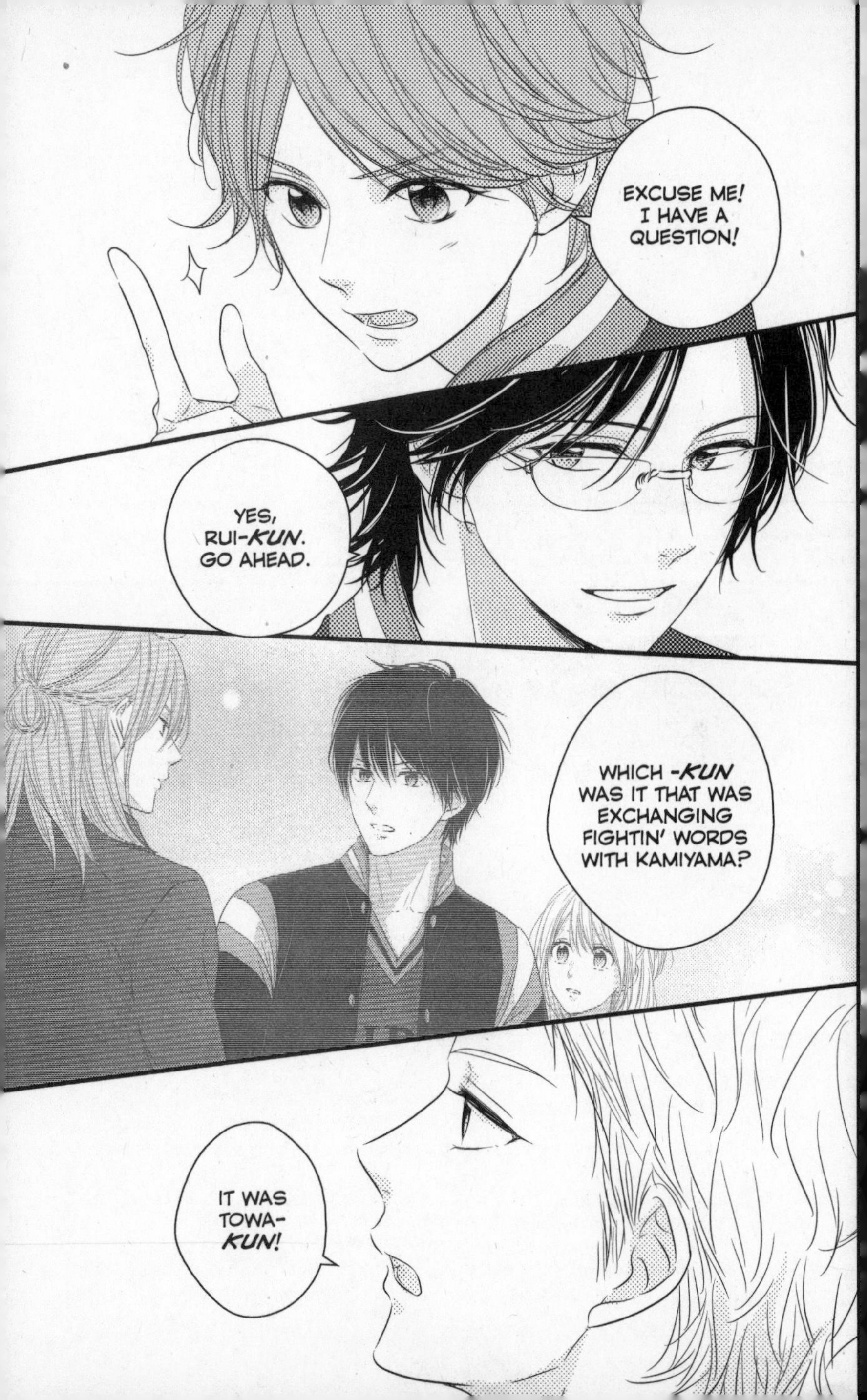
EXCUSE ME! I HAVE A QUESTION!
YES, RUI-*KUN*. GO AHEAD.
WHICH -*KUN* WAS IT THAT WAS EXCHANGING FIGHTIN' WORDS WITH KAMIYAMA?
IT WAS TOWA-*KUN*!

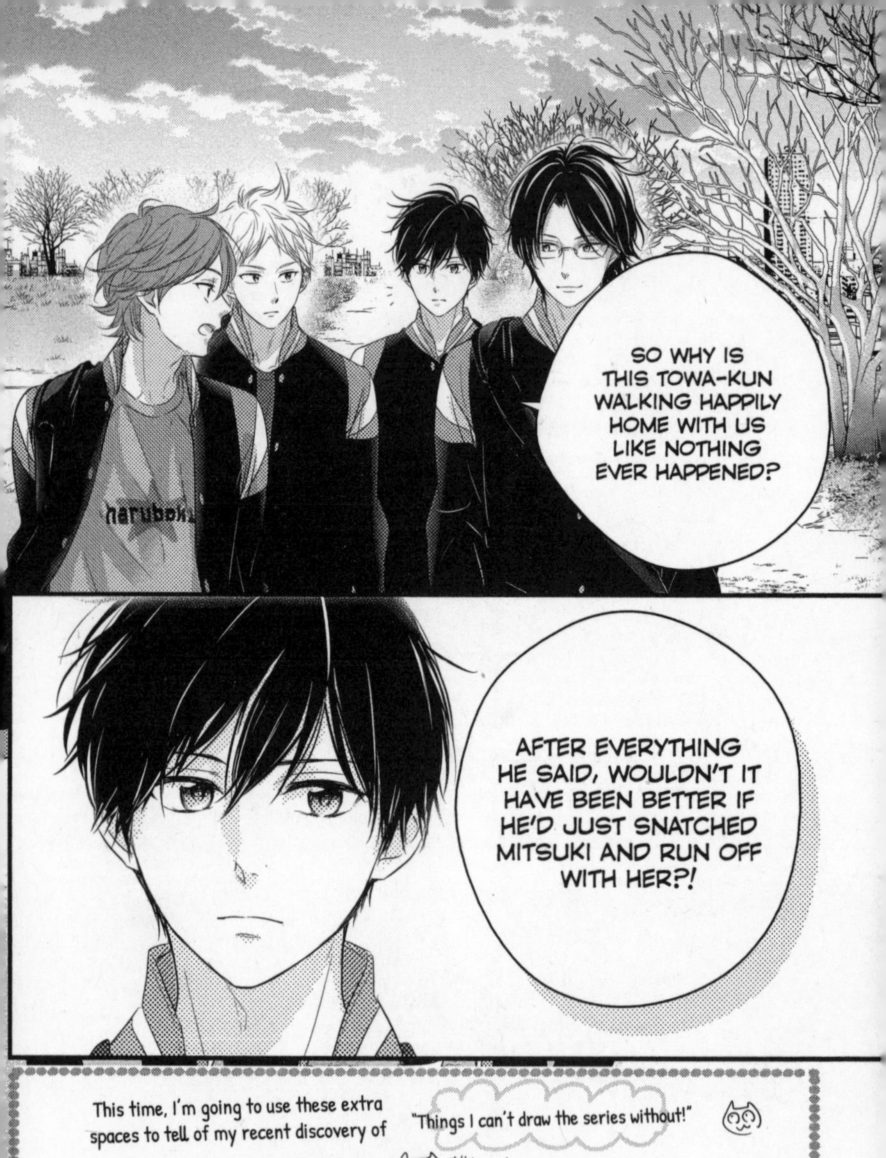
SO WHY IS THIS TOWA-KUN WALKING HAPPILY HOME WITH US LIKE NOTHING EVER HAPPENED?
AFTER EVERYTHING HE SAID, WOULDN'T IT HAVE BEEN BETTER IF HE'D JUST SNATCHED MITSUKI AND RUN OFF WITH HER?!

This time, I'm going to use these extra spaces to tell of my recent discovery of "Things I can't draw the series without!"

The first is something to chew on! ガオー! Rar!

Apparently I just have to be chewing on something when I'm drawing or planning manga (because of the stress? Ha ha). I used to chew on dried squid like there was no tomorrow, but all the excess salt hurt my stomach, so lately I'd switched to gum. But the other day, I chewed too much gum and I hurt my teeth...

(It happened when I went through three bottles of gum in one go. That was too much.) What should I chew on next...?

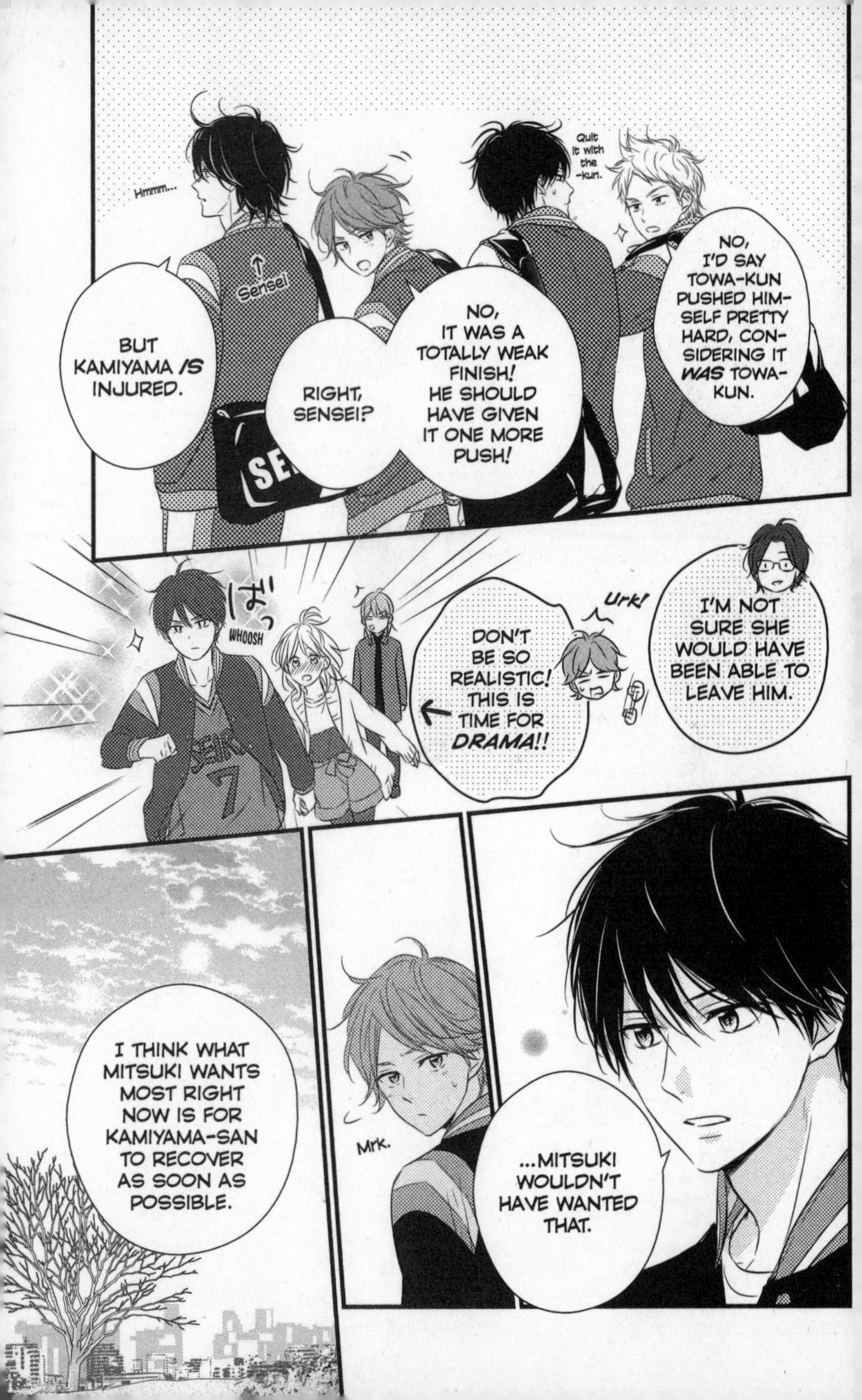
NO, I'D SAY TOWA-KUN PUSHED HIMSELF PRETTY HARD, CONSIDERING IT *WAS* TOWA-KUN.
Quit it with the -kun.
NO, IT WAS A TOTALLY WEAK FINISH! HE SHOULD HAVE GIVEN IT ONE MORE PUSH!
RIGHT, SENSEI?
Hmmm...
Sensei
BUT KAMIYAMA *IS* INJURED.
I'M NOT SURE SHE WOULD HAVE BEEN ABLE TO LEAVE HIM.
Urk!
DON'T BE SO REALISTIC! THIS IS TIME FOR *DRAMA*!!
ばっ
WHOOSH
...MITSUKI WOULDN'T HAVE WANTED THAT.
Mrk.
I THINK WHAT MITSUKI WANTS MOST RIGHT NOW IS FOR KAMIYAMA-SAN TO RECOVER AS SOON AS POSSIBLE.

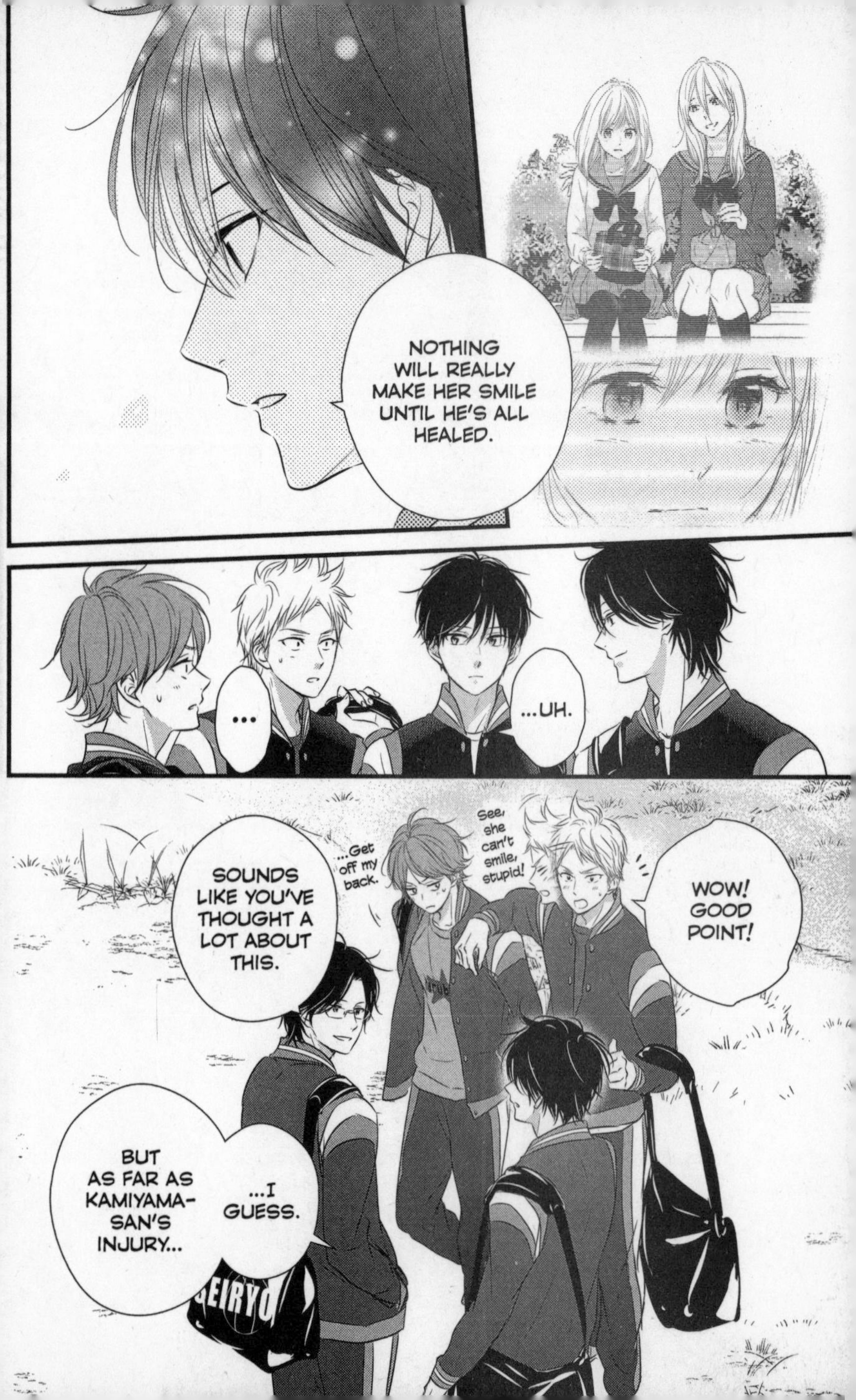
NOTHING WILL REALLY MAKE HER SMILE UNTIL HE'S ALL HEALED.
...UH.
...
WOW! GOOD POINT!
See, she can't smile, stupid!
...Get off my back.
SOUNDS LIKE YOU'VE THOUGHT A LOT ABOUT THIS.
...I GUESS.
BUT AS FAR AS KAMIYAMA-SAN'S INJURY...

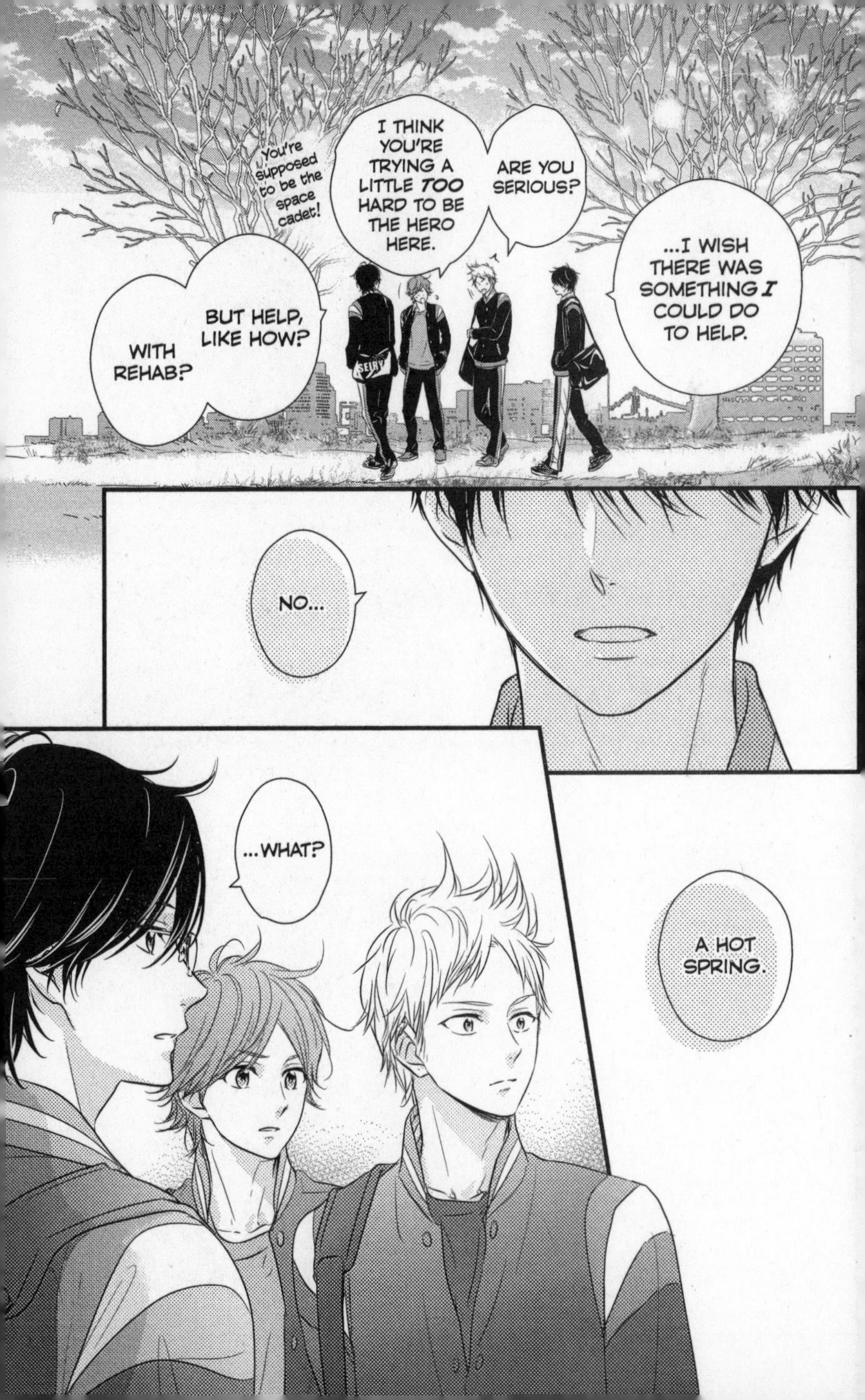
...I WISH THERE WAS SOMETHING I COULD DO TO HELP.
ARE YOU SERIOUS?
I THINK YOU'RE TRYING A LITTLE TOO HARD TO BE THE HERO HERE.
You're supposed to be the space cadet!
BUT HELP, LIKE HOW?
WITH REHAB?
NO...
A HOT SPRING.
...WHAT?

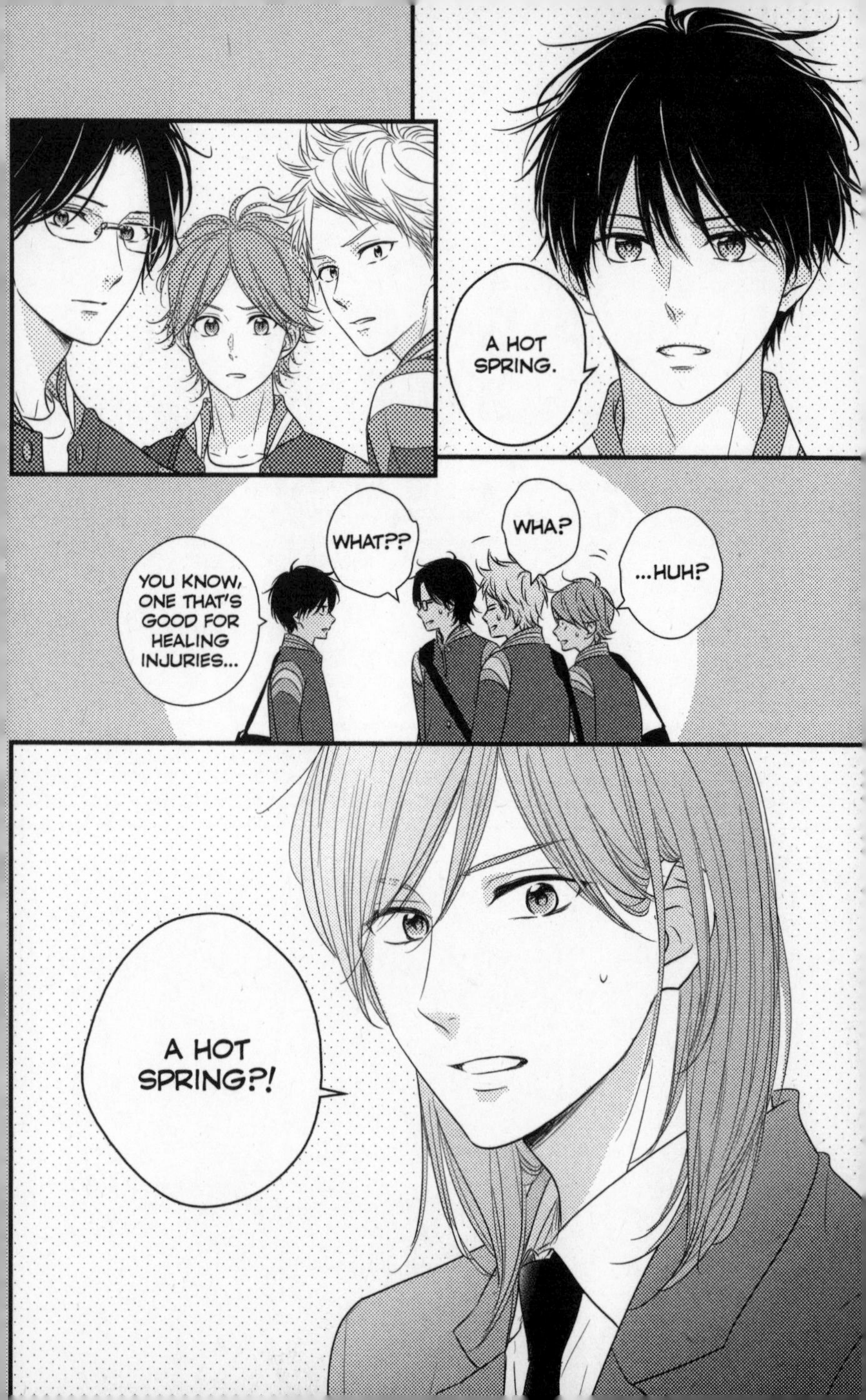
A HOT SPRING.
...HUH?
WHA?
WHAT??
YOU KNOW, ONE THAT'S GOOD FOR HEALING INJURIES...
A HOT SPRING?!

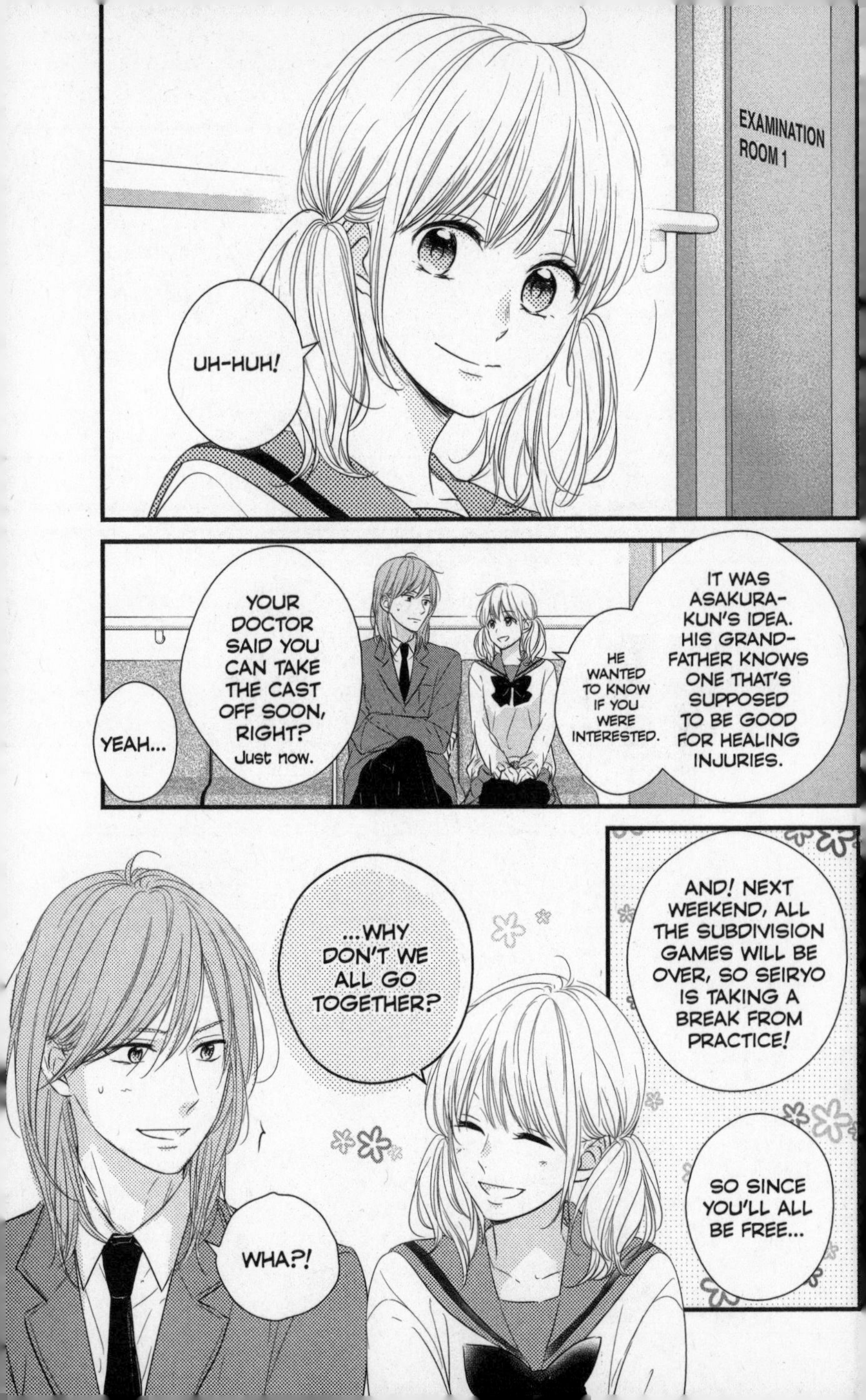
EXAMINATION ROOM 1
UH-HUH!
IT WAS ASAKURA-KUN'S IDEA. HIS GRAND-FATHER KNOWS ONE THAT'S SUPPOSED TO BE GOOD FOR HEALING INJURIES.
HE WANTED TO KNOW IF YOU WERE INTERESTED.
YOUR DOCTOR SAID YOU CAN TAKE THE CAST OFF SOON, RIGHT?
Just now.
YEAH...
AND! NEXT WEEKEND, ALL THE SUBDIVISION GAMES WILL BE OVER, SO SEIRYO IS TAKING A BREAK FROM PRACTICE!
SO SINCE YOU'LL ALL BE FREE...
...WHY DON'T WE ALL GO TOGETHER?
WHA?!

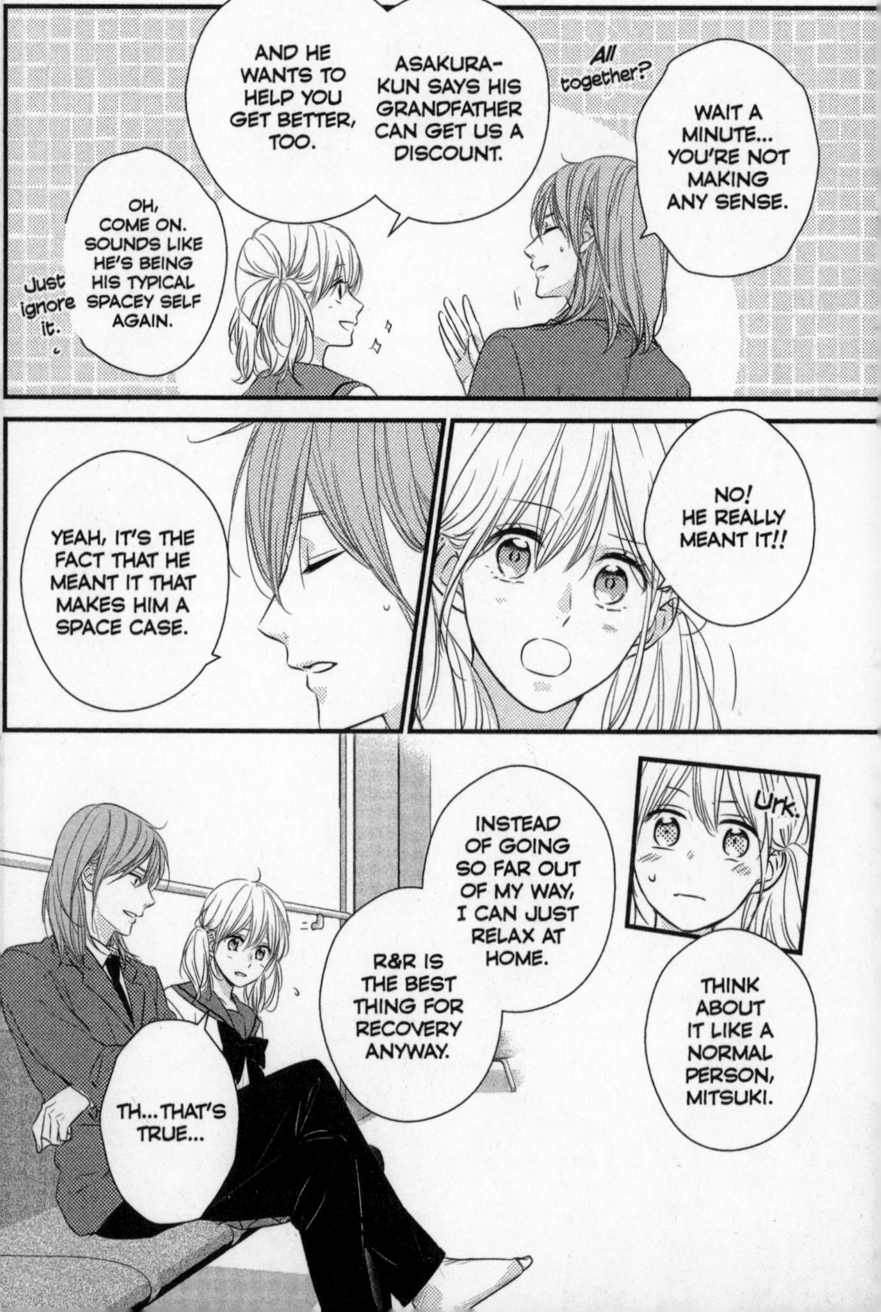

All together?
WAIT A MINUTE... YOU'RE NOT MAKING ANY SENSE.
ASAKURA-KUN SAYS HIS GRANDFATHER CAN GET US A DISCOUNT.
AND HE WANTS TO HELP YOU GET BETTER, TOO.
OH, COME ON. SOUNDS LIKE HE'S BEING HIS TYPICAL SPACEY SELF AGAIN.
Just ignore it.
NO! HE REALLY MEANT IT!!
YEAH, IT'S THE FACT THAT HE MEANT IT THAT MAKES HIM A SPACE CASE.
Urk.
THINK ABOUT IT LIKE A NORMAL PERSON, MITSUKI.
INSTEAD OF GOING SO FAR OUT OF MY WAY, I CAN JUST RELAX AT HOME.
R&R IS THE BEST THING FOR RECOVERY ANYWAY.
TH...THAT'S TRUE...

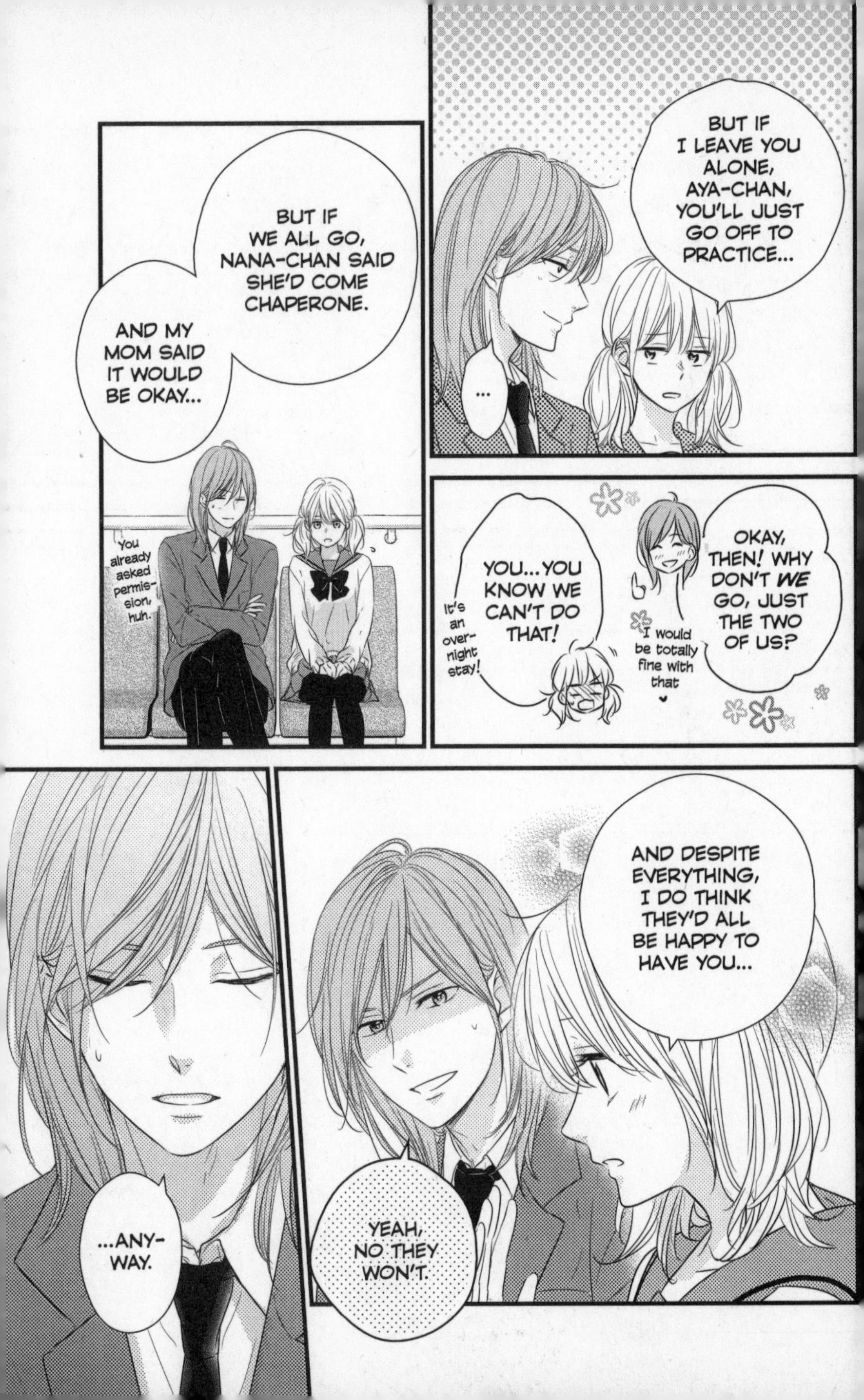
BUT IF I LEAVE YOU ALONE, AYA-CHAN, YOU'LL JUST GO OFF TO PRACTICE...
...
OKAY, THEN! WHY DON'T *WE* GO, JUST THE TWO OF US?
I would be totally fine with that ♥
YOU...YOU KNOW WE CAN'T DO THAT!
It's an over-night stay!
BUT IF WE ALL GO, NANA-CHAN SAID SHE'D COME CHAPERONE.
AND MY MOM SAID IT WOULD BE OKAY...
You already asked permis-sion, huh.
AND DESPITE EVERYTHING, I DO THINK THEY'D ALL BE HAPPY TO HAVE YOU...
YEAH, NO THEY WON'T.
...ANY-WAY.

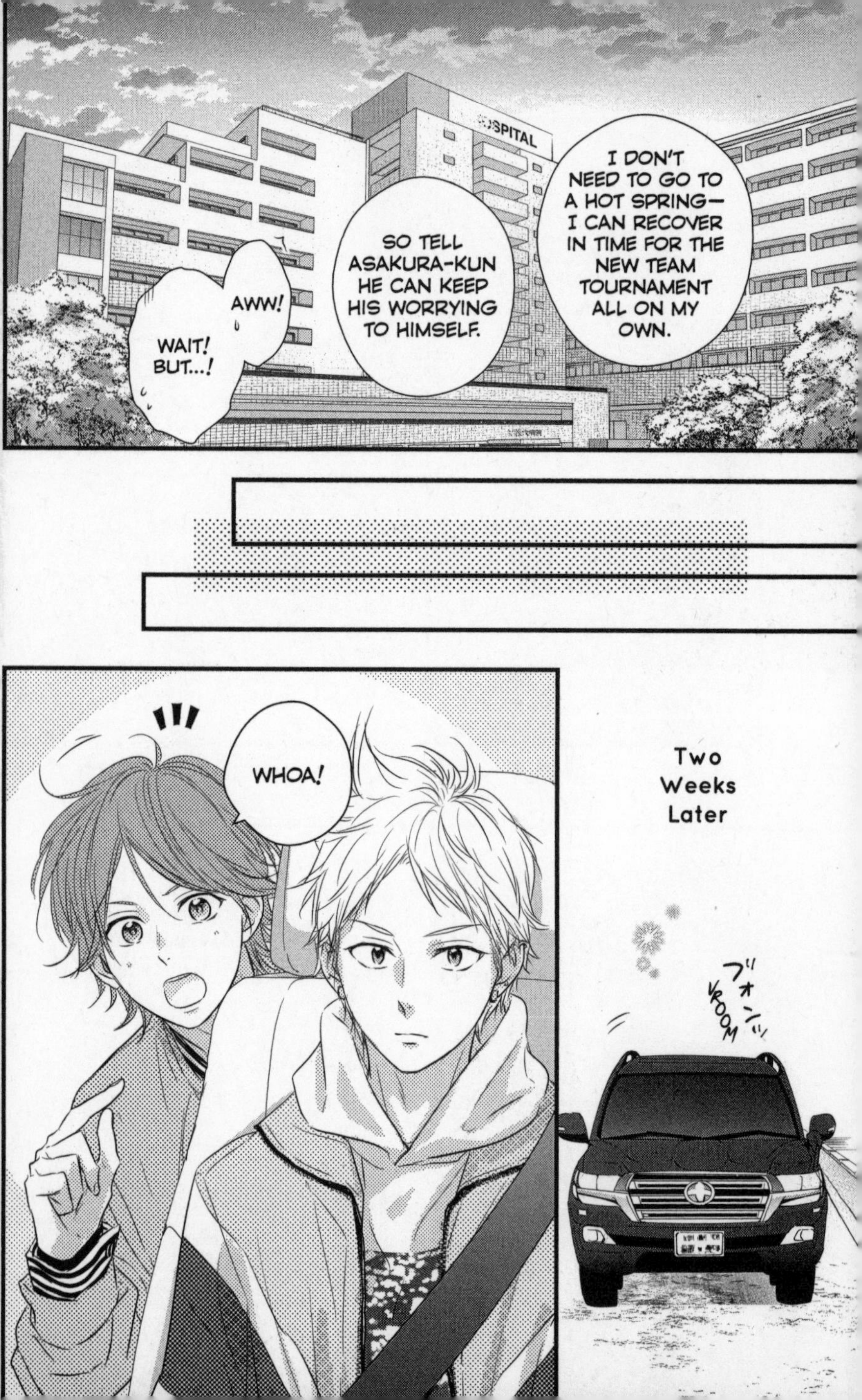
I DON'T NEED TO GO TO A HOT SPRING— I CAN RECOVER IN TIME FOR THE NEW TEAM TOURNAMENT ALL ON MY OWN.
SO TELL ASAKURA-KUN HE CAN KEEP HIS WORRYING TO HIMSELF.
AWW!
WAIT! BUT...!
Two Weeks Later
VROOM
WHOA!

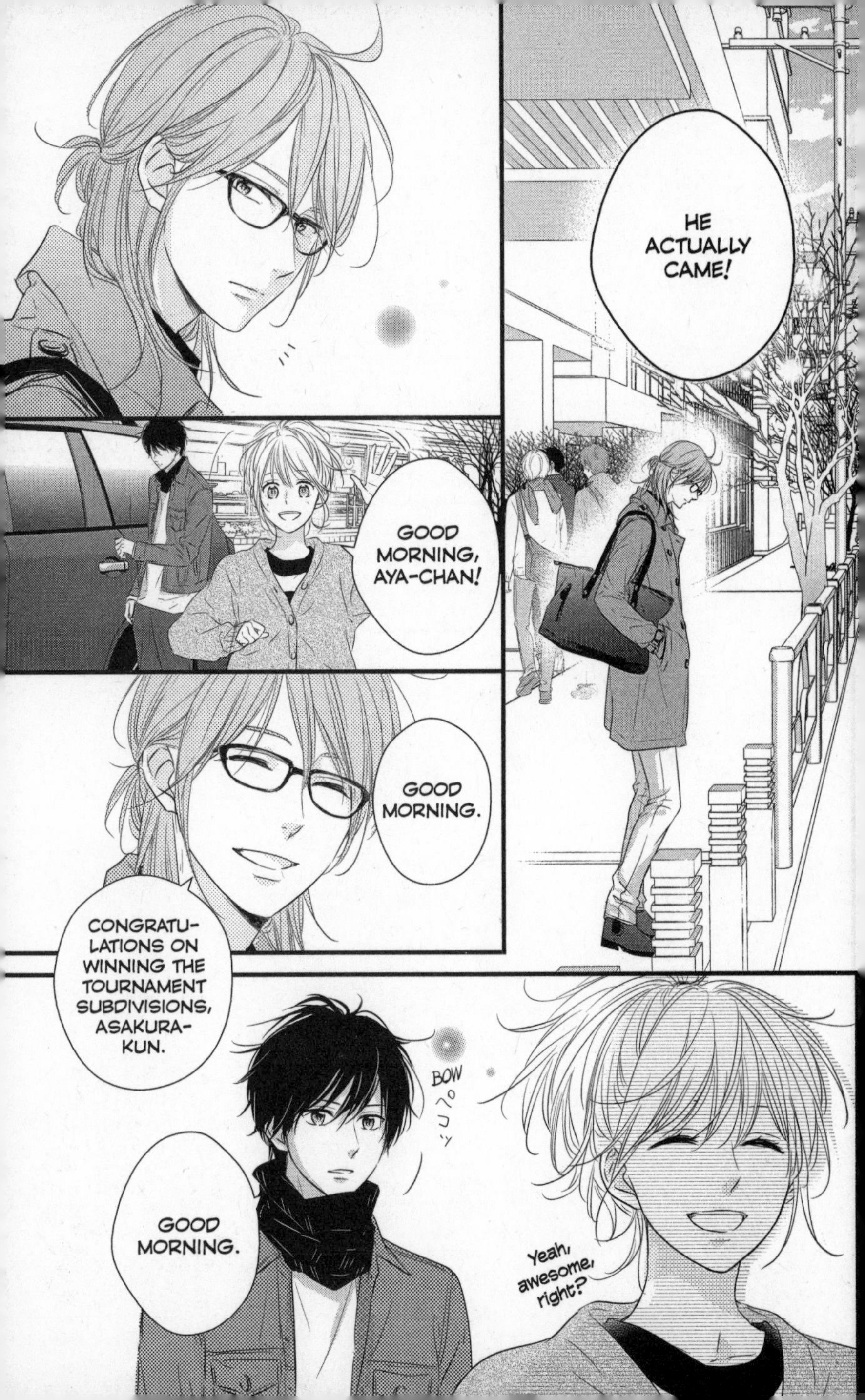
HE ACTUALLY CAME!
GOOD MORNING, AYA-CHAN!
GOOD MORNING.
CONGRATULATIONS ON WINNING THE TOURNAMENT SUBDIVISIONS, ASAKURA-KUN.
GOOD MORNING.
BOW
Yeah, awesome, right?

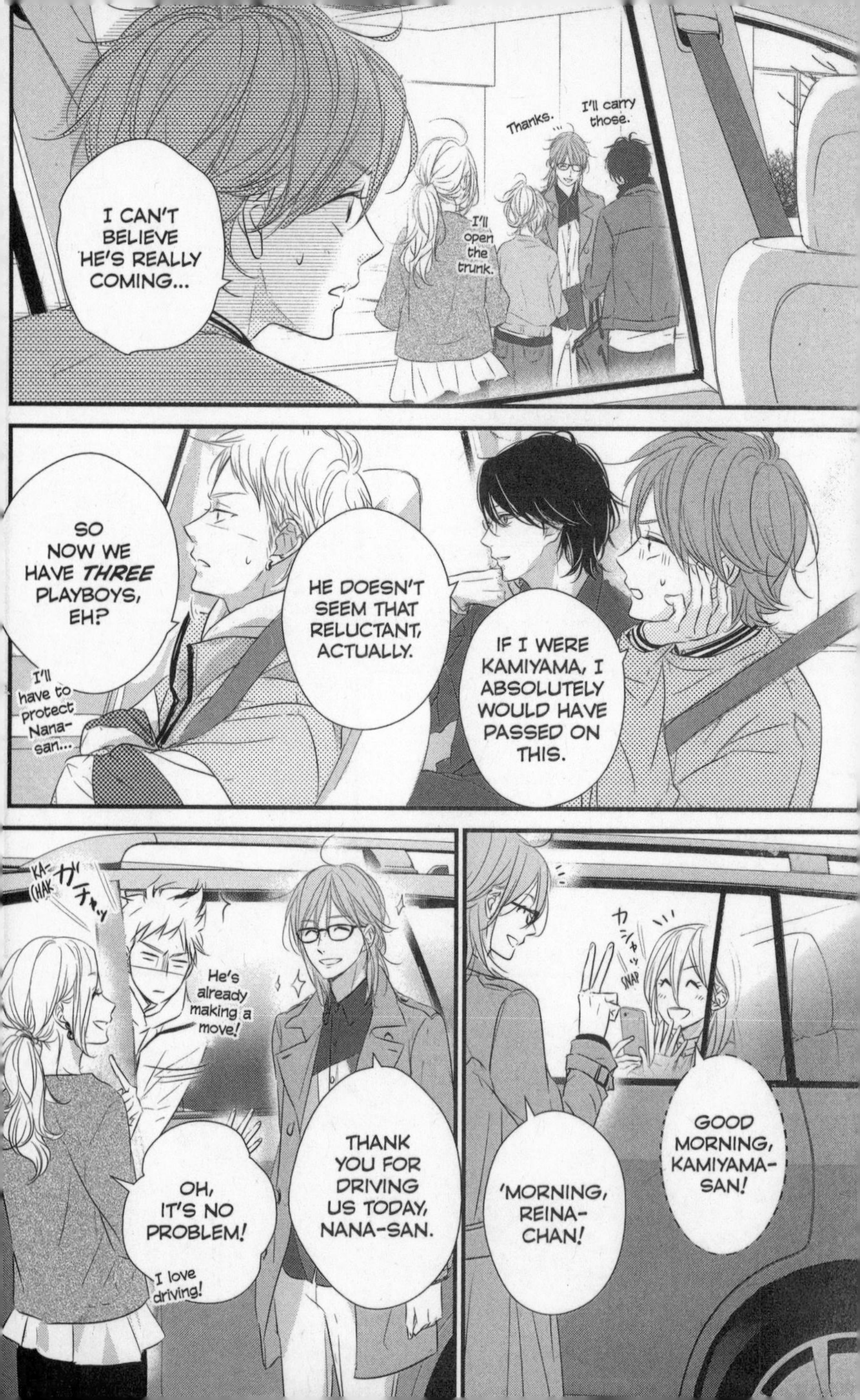
I'll carry those.
Thanks.
I'll open the trunk.
I CAN'T BELIEVE HE'S REALLY COMING...
IF I WERE KAMIYAMA, I ABSOLUTELY WOULD HAVE PASSED ON THIS.
HE DOESN'T SEEM THAT RELUCTANT, ACTUALLY.
SO NOW WE HAVE *THREE* PLAYBOYS, EH?
I'll have to protect Nana-san...
カシャッ SNAP
GOOD MORNING, KAMIYAMA-SAN!
'MORNING, REINA-CHAN!
KA-CHAK ガチャッ
He's already making a move!
THANK YOU FOR DRIVING US TODAY, NANA-SAN.
OH, IT'S NO PROBLEM!
I love driving!

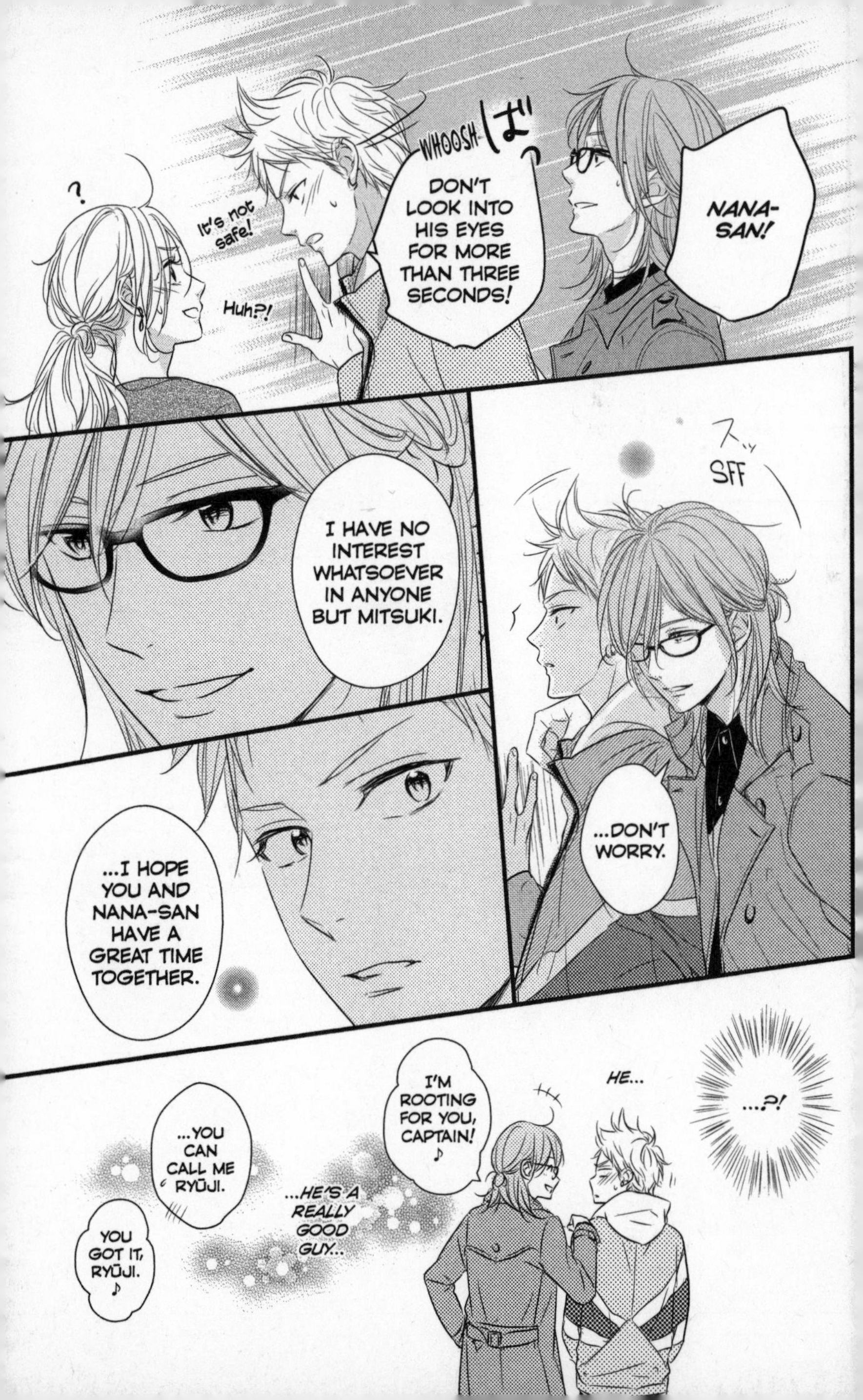
NANA-SAN!
WHOOSH
ばっ
DON'T LOOK INTO HIS EYES FOR MORE THAN THREE SECONDS!
It's not safe!
Huh?!
?
スッ
SFF
...DON'T WORRY.
I HAVE NO INTEREST WHATSOEVER IN ANYONE BUT MITSUKI.
...I HOPE YOU AND NANA-SAN HAVE A GREAT TIME TOGETHER.
...?!
HE...
I'M ROOTING FOR YOU, CAPTAIN! ♪
...HE'S A REALLY GOOD GUY...
...YOU CAN CALL ME RYŪJI.
YOU GOT IT, RYŪJI. ♪

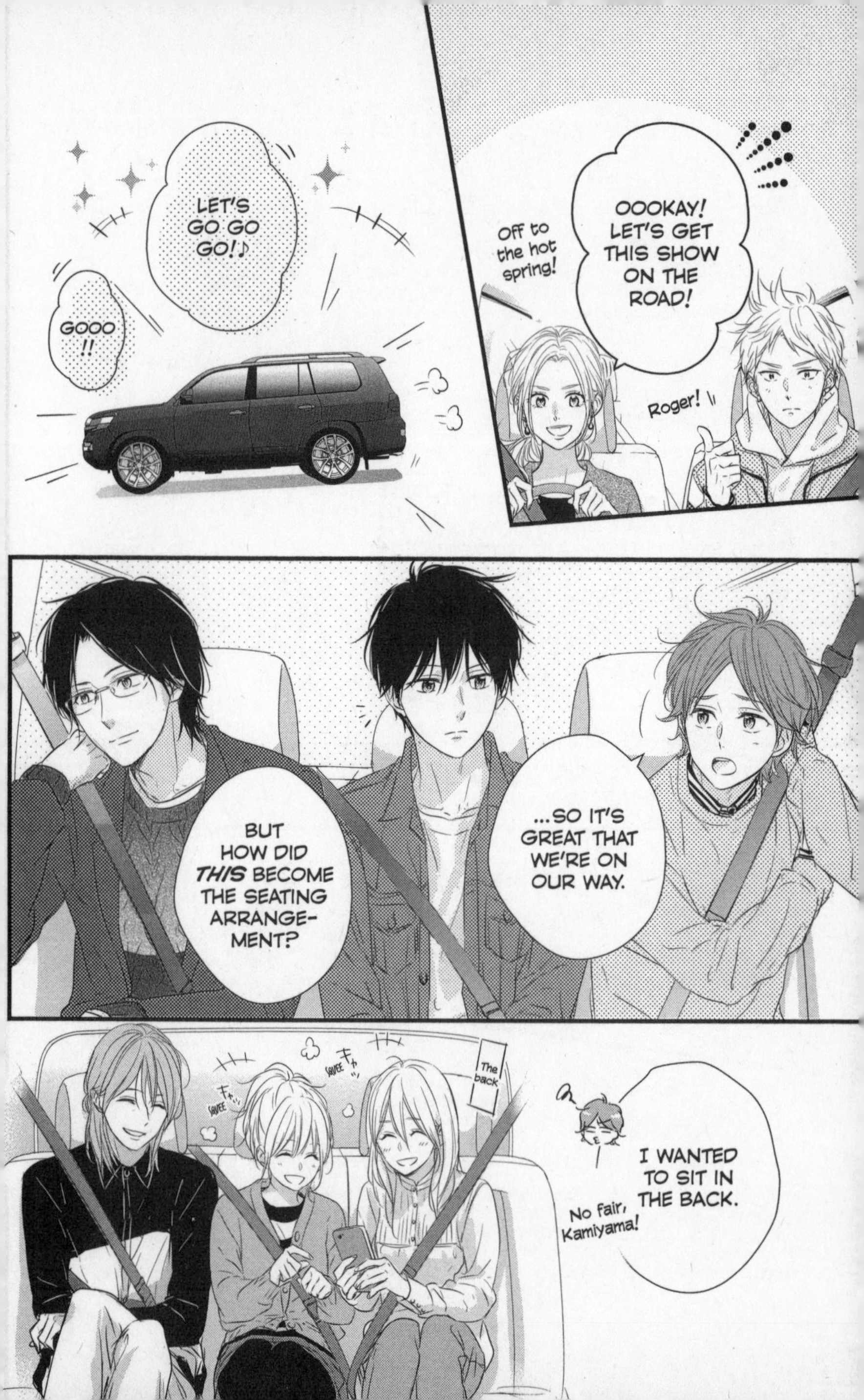
OOOKAY! LET'S GET THIS SHOW ON THE ROAD!
Off to the hot spring!
Roger!
LET'S GO GO GO!♪
GOOO !!
...SO IT'S GREAT THAT WE'RE ON OUR WAY.
BUT HOW DID *THIS* BECOME THE SEATING ARRANGE-MENT?
I WANTED TO SIT IN THE BACK.
No fair, Kamiyama!
The back
SQUEE
SQUEE

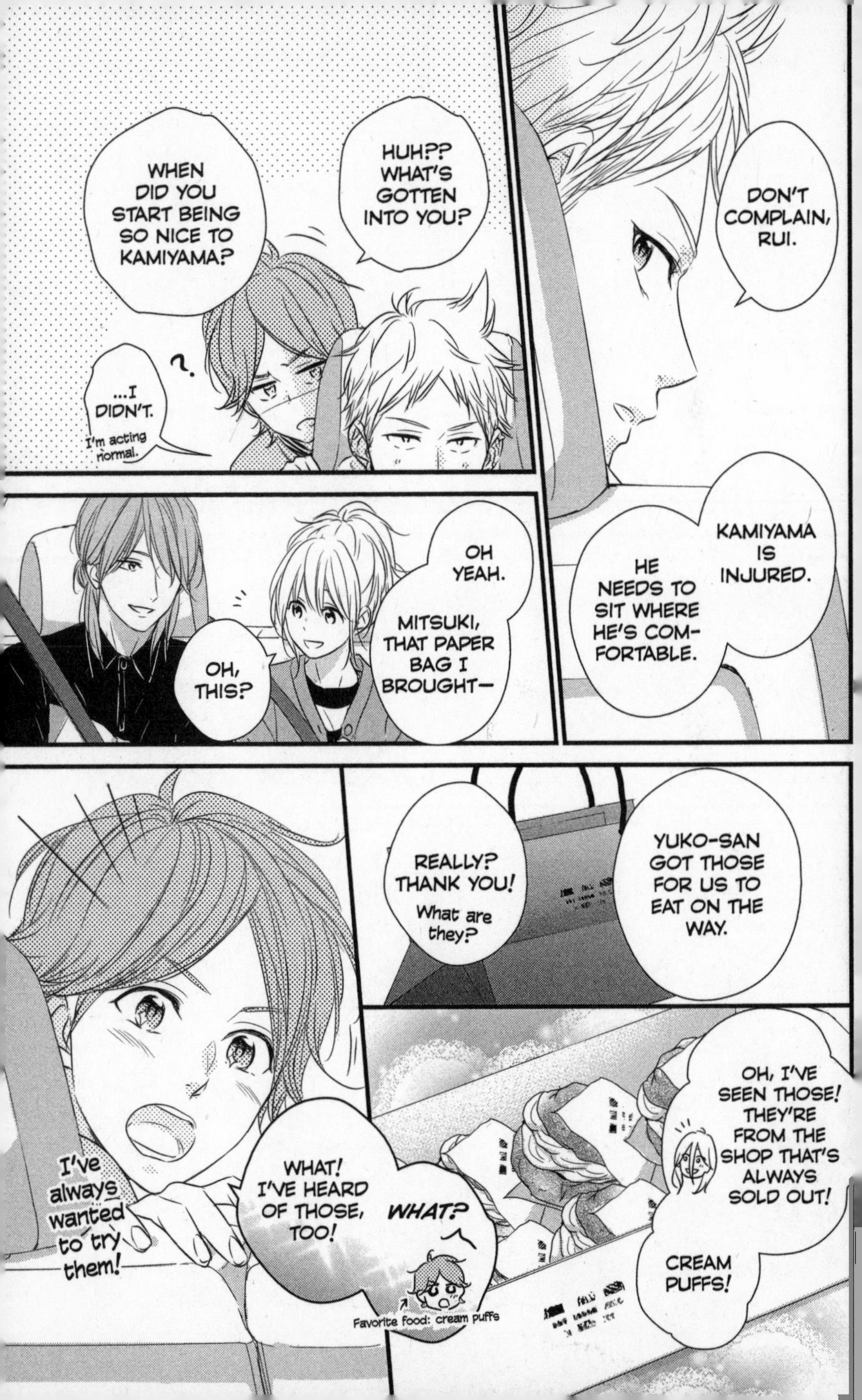

DON'T COMPLAIN, RUI.
KAMIYAMA IS INJURED.
HE NEEDS TO SIT WHERE HE'S COM-FORTABLE.
HUH?? WHAT'S GOTTEN INTO YOU?
WHEN DID YOU START BEING SO NICE TO KAMIYAMA?
?
...I DIDN'T.
I'm acting normal.
OH YEAH.
MITSUKI, THAT PAPER BAG I BROUGHT—
OH, THIS?
YUKO-SAN GOT THOSE FOR US TO EAT ON THE WAY.
REALLY? THANK YOU!
What are they?
OH, I'VE SEEN THOSE! THEY'RE FROM THE SHOP THAT'S ALWAYS SOLD OUT!
CREAM PUFFS!
WHAT?
Favorite food: cream puffs
WHAT! I'VE HEARD OF THOSE, TOO!
I've always wanted to try them!

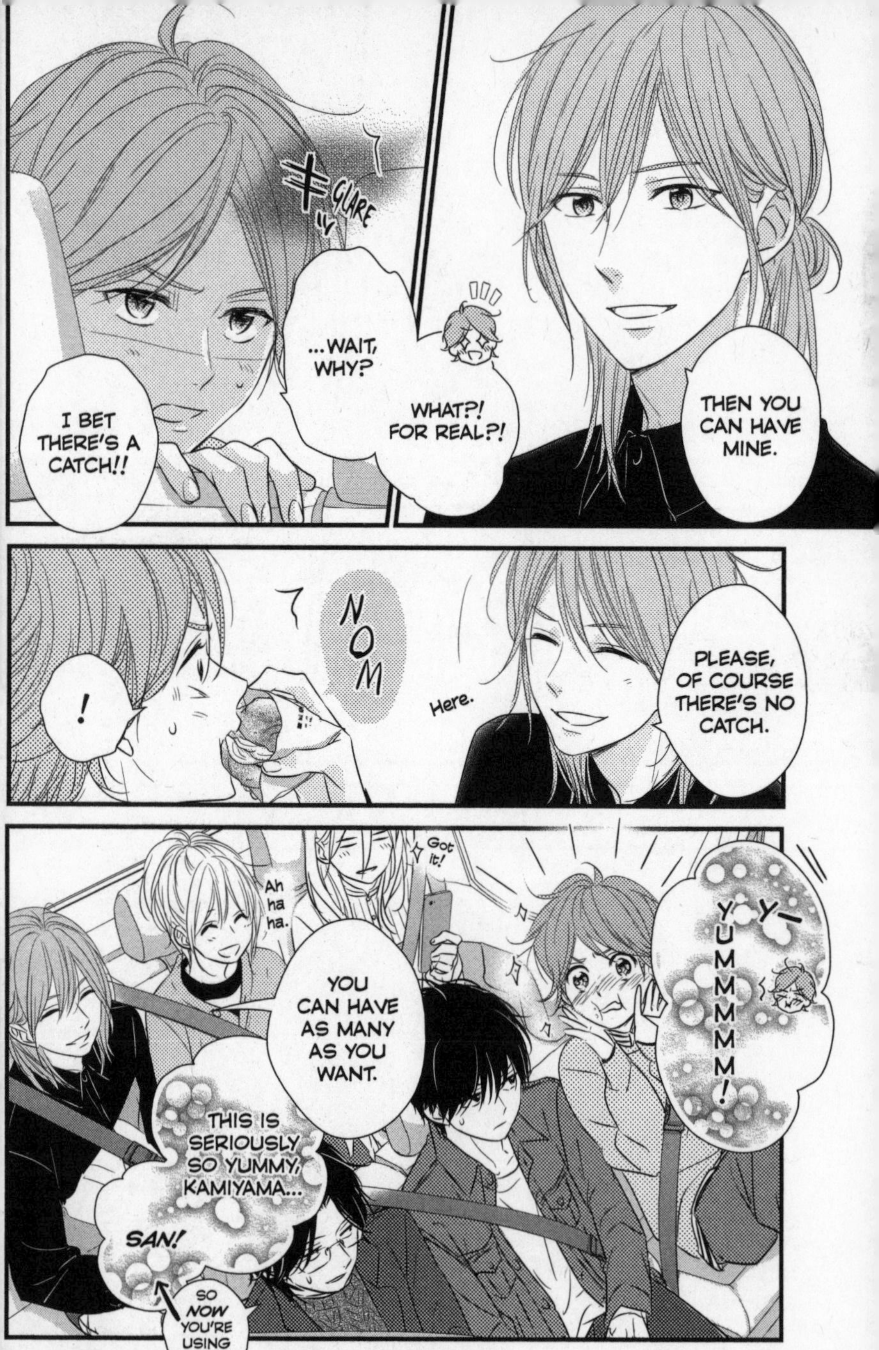
THEN YOU CAN HAVE MINE.
WHAT?! FOR REAL?!
GLARE
...WAIT, WHY?
I BET THERE'S A CATCH!!
PLEASE, OF COURSE THERE'S NO CATCH.
Here.
NOM
!
Y-Y—YUMMMMM!
Got it!
Ah ha ha.
YOU CAN HAVE AS MANY AS YOU WANT.
THIS IS SERIOUSLY SO YUMMY, KAMIYAMA...
SAN!
SO NOW YOU'RE USING "-SAN."

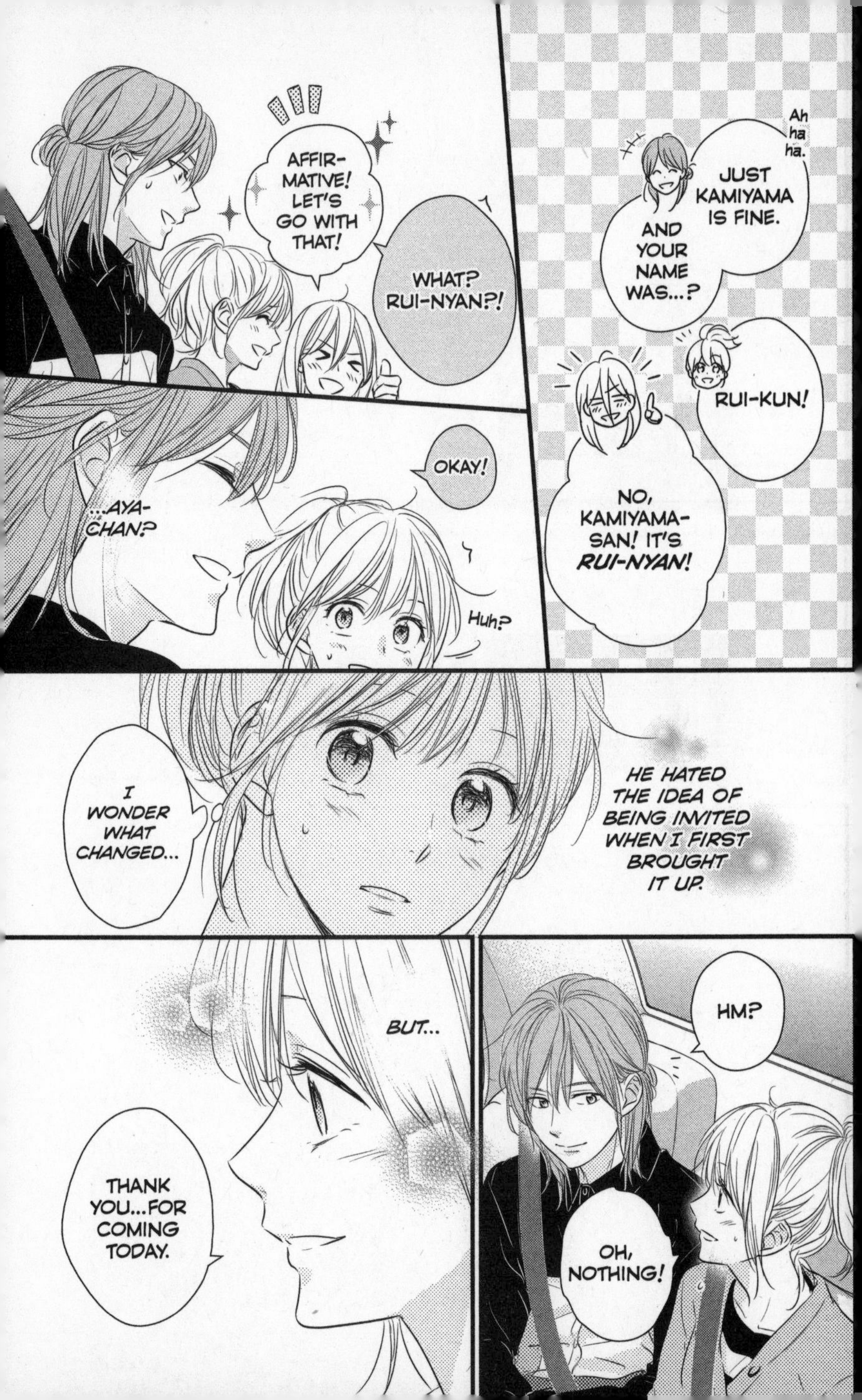
Ah ha ha.
JUST KAMIYAMA IS FINE.
AND YOUR NAME WAS...?
RUI-KUN!
NO, KAMIYAMA-SAN! IT'S *RUI-NYAN*!
WHAT? RUI-NYAN?!
AFFIRMATIVE! LET'S GO WITH THAT!
OKAY!
...AYA-CHAN?
Huh?
HE HATED THE IDEA OF BEING INVITED WHEN I FIRST BROUGHT IT UP.
I WONDER WHAT CHANGED...
HM?
OH, NOTHING!
BUT...
THANK YOU...FOR COMING TODAY.

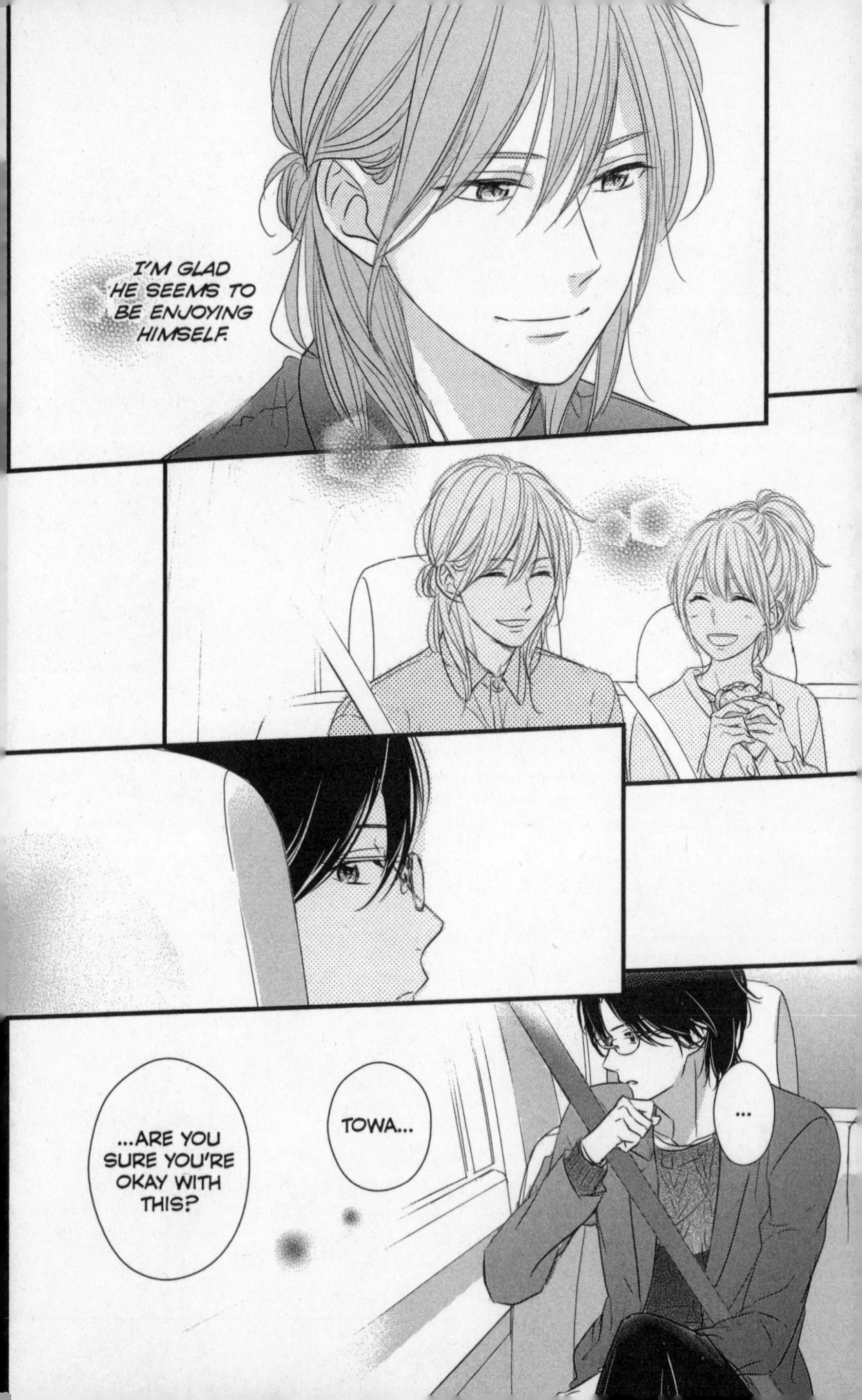
I'M GLAD HE SEEMS TO BE ENJOYING HIMSELF.
TOWA...
...
...ARE YOU SURE YOU'RE OKAY WITH THIS?

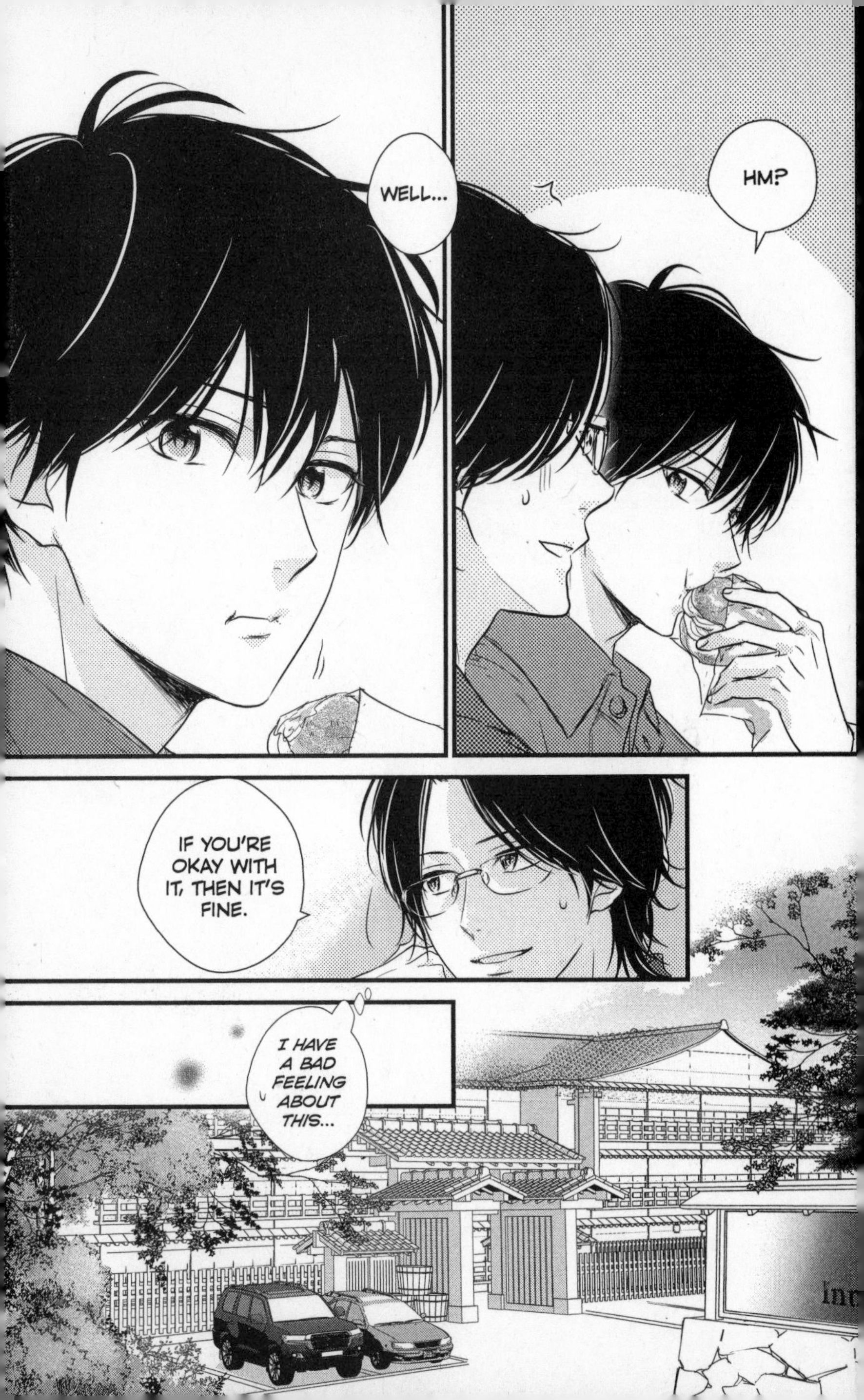
HM?
WELL...
IF YOU'RE OKAY WITH IT, THEN IT'S FINE.
I HAVE A BAD FEELING ABOUT THIS...

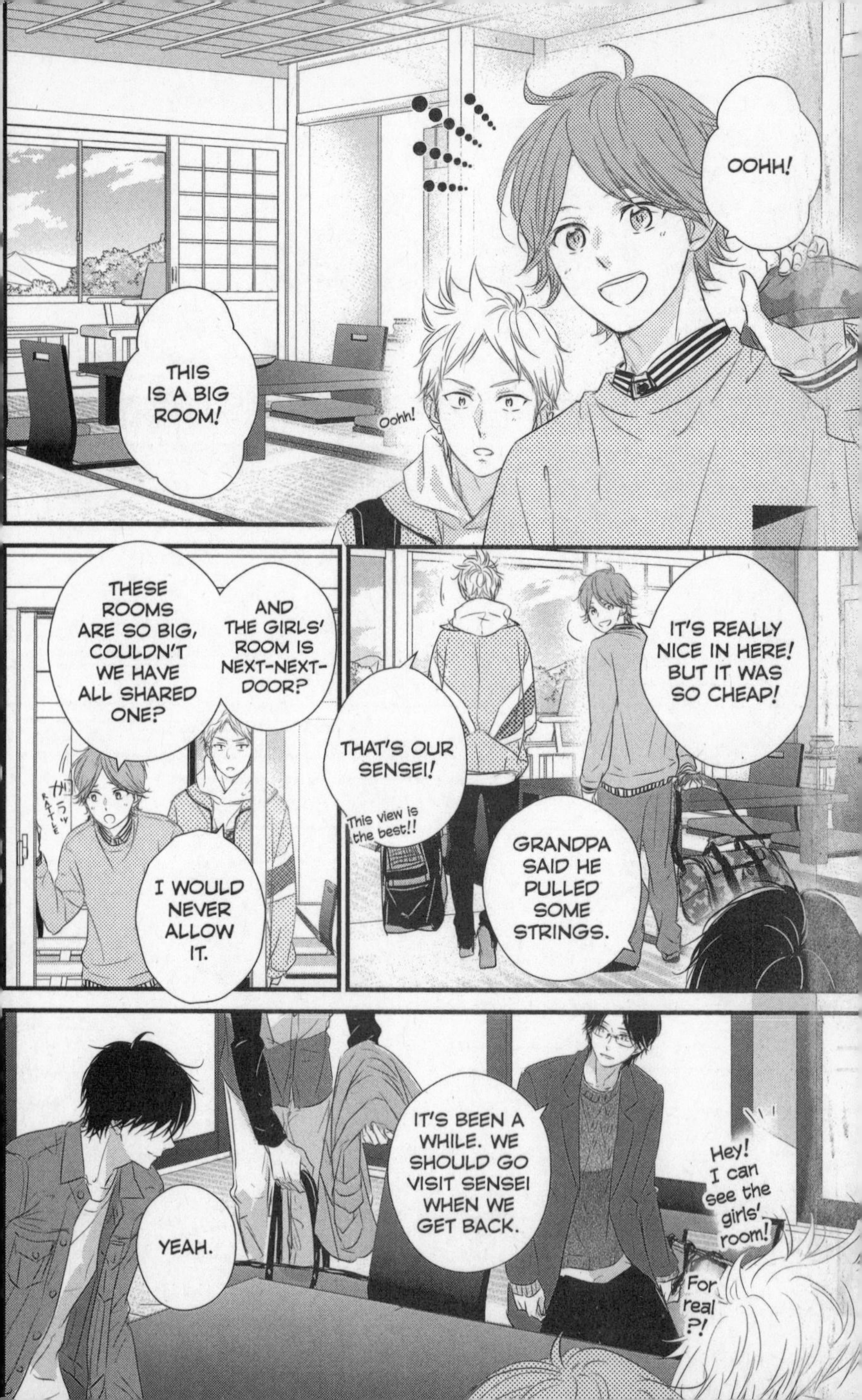
OOHH!
Oohh!
THIS IS A BIG ROOM!
IT'S REALLY NICE IN HERE! BUT IT WAS SO CHEAP!
GRANDPA SAID HE PULLED SOME STRINGS.
THAT'S OUR SENSEI!
This view is the best!!
AND THE GIRLS' ROOM IS NEXT-NEXT-DOOR?
THESE ROOMS ARE SO BIG, COULDN'T WE HAVE ALL SHARED ONE?
RATTLE
I WOULD NEVER ALLOW IT.
Hey! I can see the girls' room!
For real?!
IT'S BEEN A WHILE. WE SHOULD GO VISIT SENSEI WHEN WE GET BACK.
YEAH.

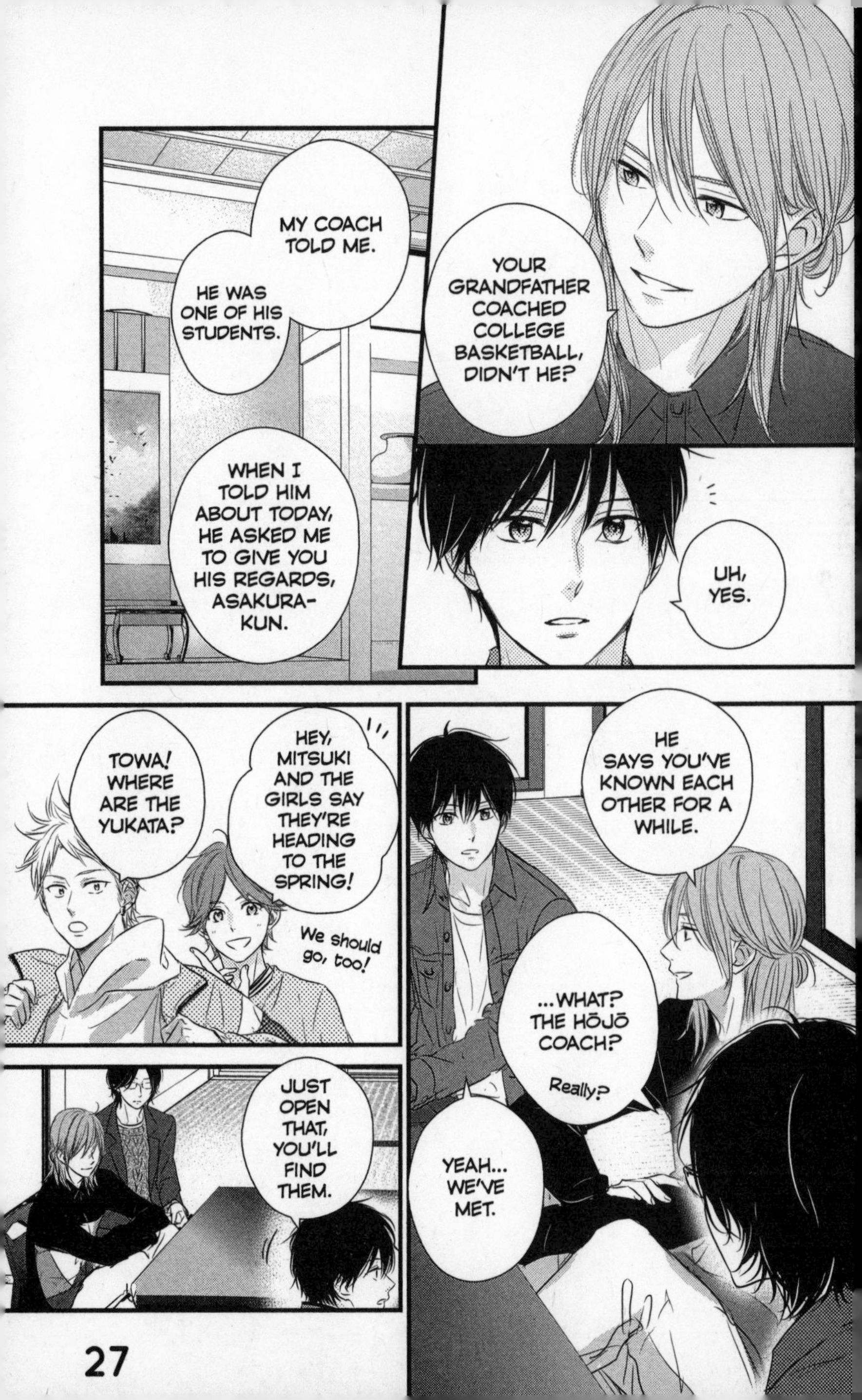
YOUR GRANDFATHER COACHED COLLEGE BASKETBALL, DIDN'T HE?
UH, YES.
MY COACH TOLD ME.
HE WAS ONE OF HIS STUDENTS.
WHEN I TOLD HIM ABOUT TODAY, HE ASKED ME TO GIVE YOU HIS REGARDS, ASAKURA-KUN.
HE SAYS YOU'VE KNOWN EACH OTHER FOR A WHILE.
...WHAT? THE HŌJŌ COACH?
Really?
YEAH... WE'VE MET.
HEY, MITSUKI AND THE GIRLS SAY THEY'RE HEADING TO THE SPRING!
We should go, too!
TOWA! WHERE ARE THE YUKATA?
JUST OPEN THAT, YOU'LL FIND THEM.

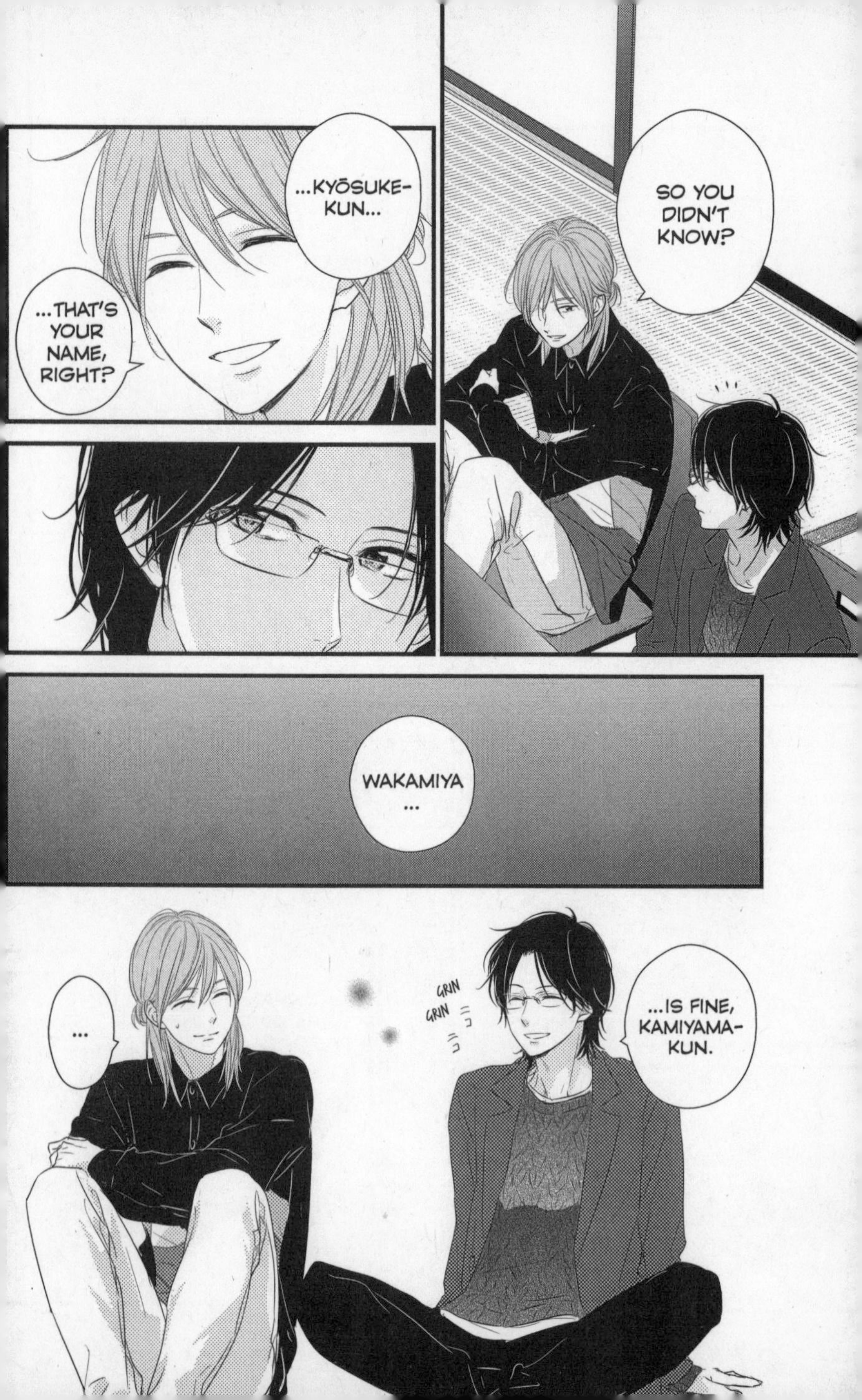
SO YOU DIDN'T KNOW?
...KYŌSUKE-KUN...
...THAT'S YOUR NAME, RIGHT?
WAKAMIYA ...
...IS FINE, KAMIYAMA-KUN.
GRIN GRIN
...

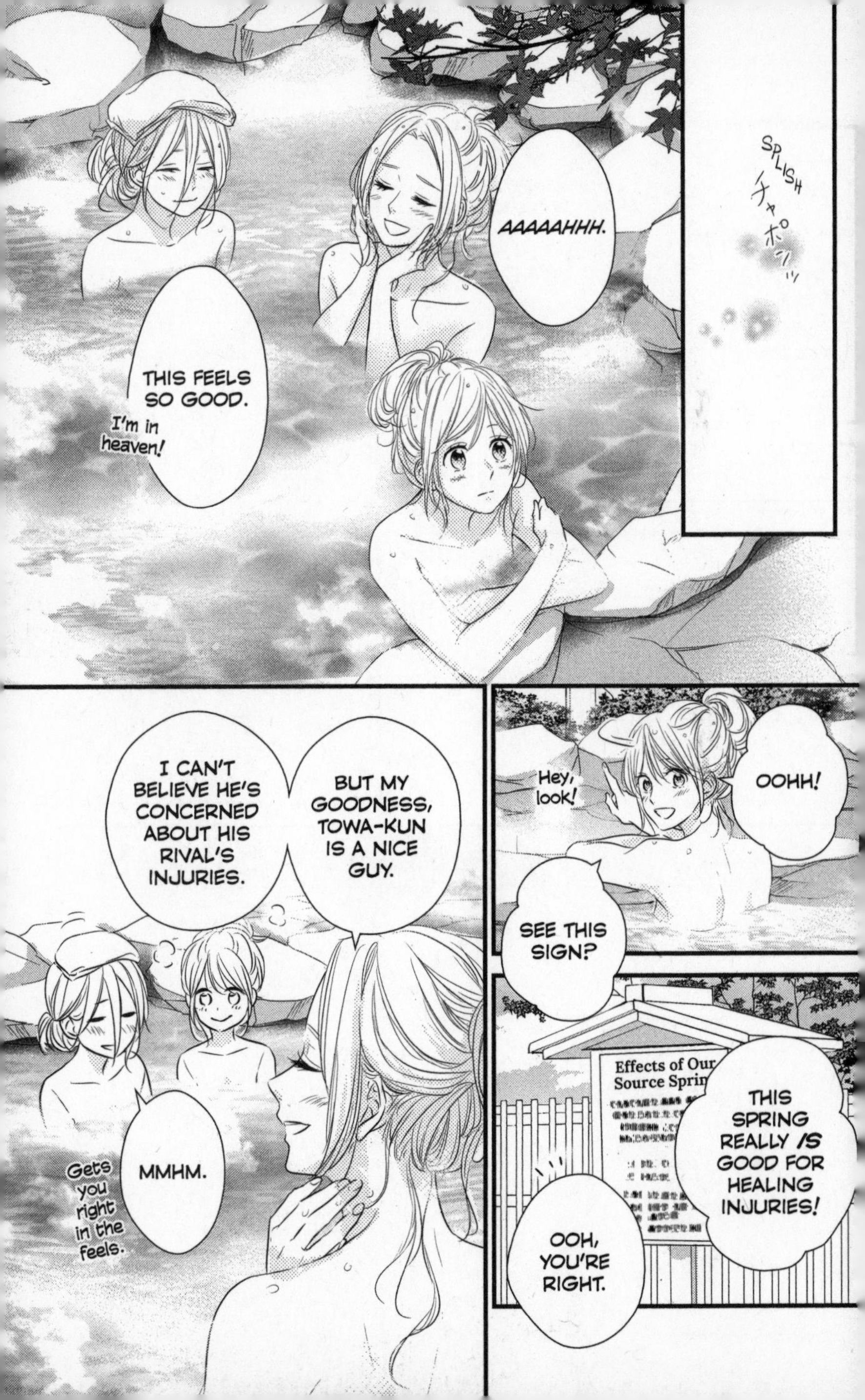
SPLISH
チャポッ
AAAAAHHH.
THIS FEELS SO GOOD.
I'm in heaven!
OOHH!
Hey, look!
SEE THIS SIGN?
Effects of Our Source Sprin
THIS SPRING REALLY *IS* GOOD FOR HEALING INJURIES!
OOH, YOU'RE RIGHT.
BUT MY GOODNESS, TOWA-KUN IS A NICE GUY.
I CAN'T BELIEVE HE'S CONCERNED ABOUT HIS RIVAL'S INJURIES.
MMHM.
Gets you right in the feels.

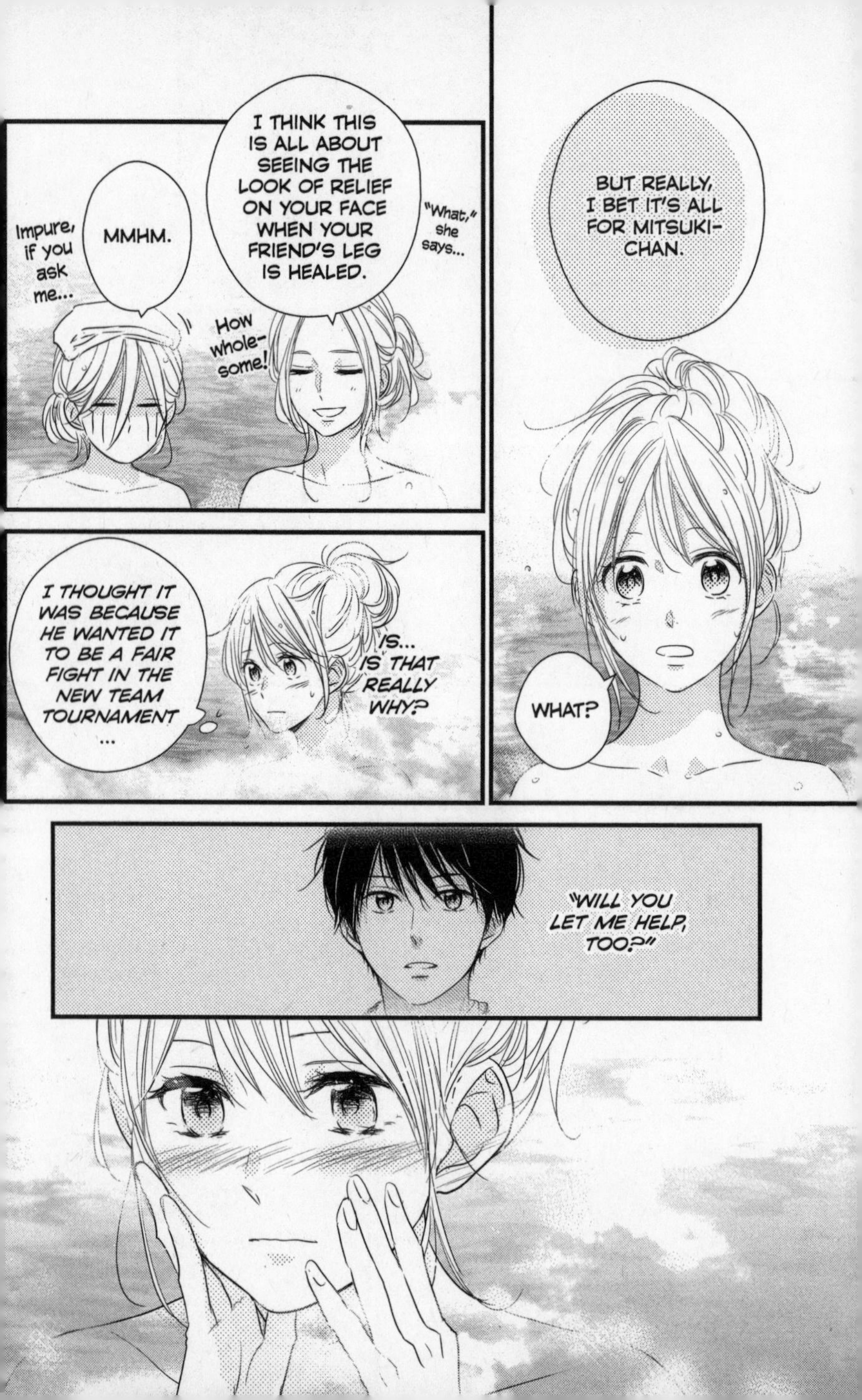
BUT REALLY, I BET IT'S ALL FOR MITSUKI-CHAN.
WHAT?
"What," she says...
I THINK THIS IS ALL ABOUT SEEING THE LOOK OF RELIEF ON YOUR FACE WHEN YOUR FRIEND'S LEG IS HEALED.
How whole-some!
MMHM.
Impure, if you ask me...
IS... IS THAT REALLY WHY?
I THOUGHT IT WAS BECAUSE HE WANTED IT TO BE A FAIR FIGHT IN THE NEW TEAM TOURNAMENT...
"WILL YOU LET ME HELP, TOO?"

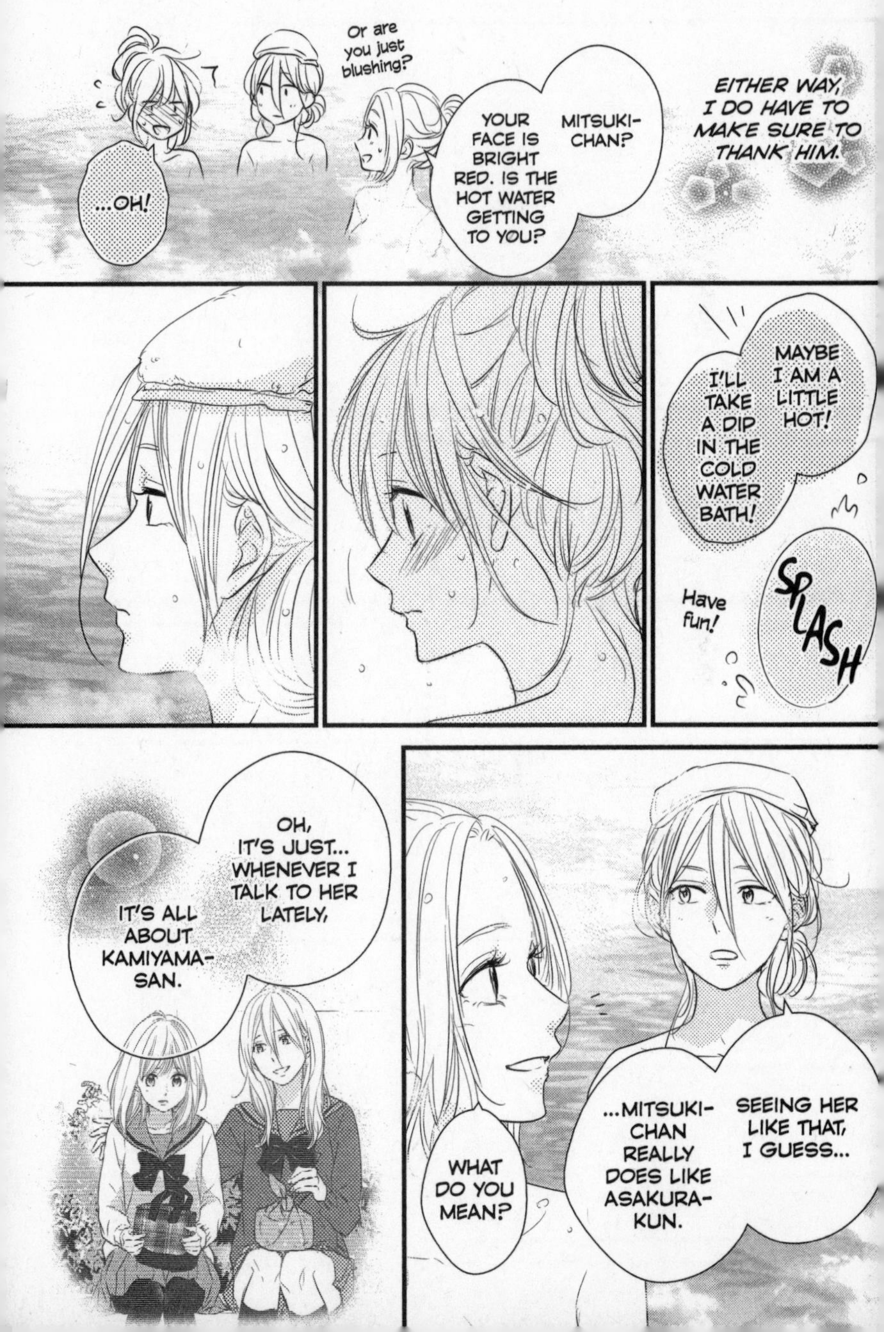
EITHER WAY, I DO HAVE TO MAKE SURE TO THANK HIM.
MITSUKI-CHAN? YOUR FACE IS BRIGHT RED. IS THE HOT WATER GETTING TO YOU?
Or are you just blushing?
...OH!
MAYBE I AM A LITTLE HOT! I'LL TAKE A DIP IN THE COLD WATER BATH!
SPLASH
Have fun!
SEEING HER LIKE THAT, I GUESS... ...MITSUKI-CHAN REALLY DOES LIKE ASAKURA-KUN.
WHAT DO YOU MEAN?
OH, IT'S JUST... WHENEVER I TALK TO HER LATELY, IT'S ALL ABOUT KAMIYAMA-SAN.

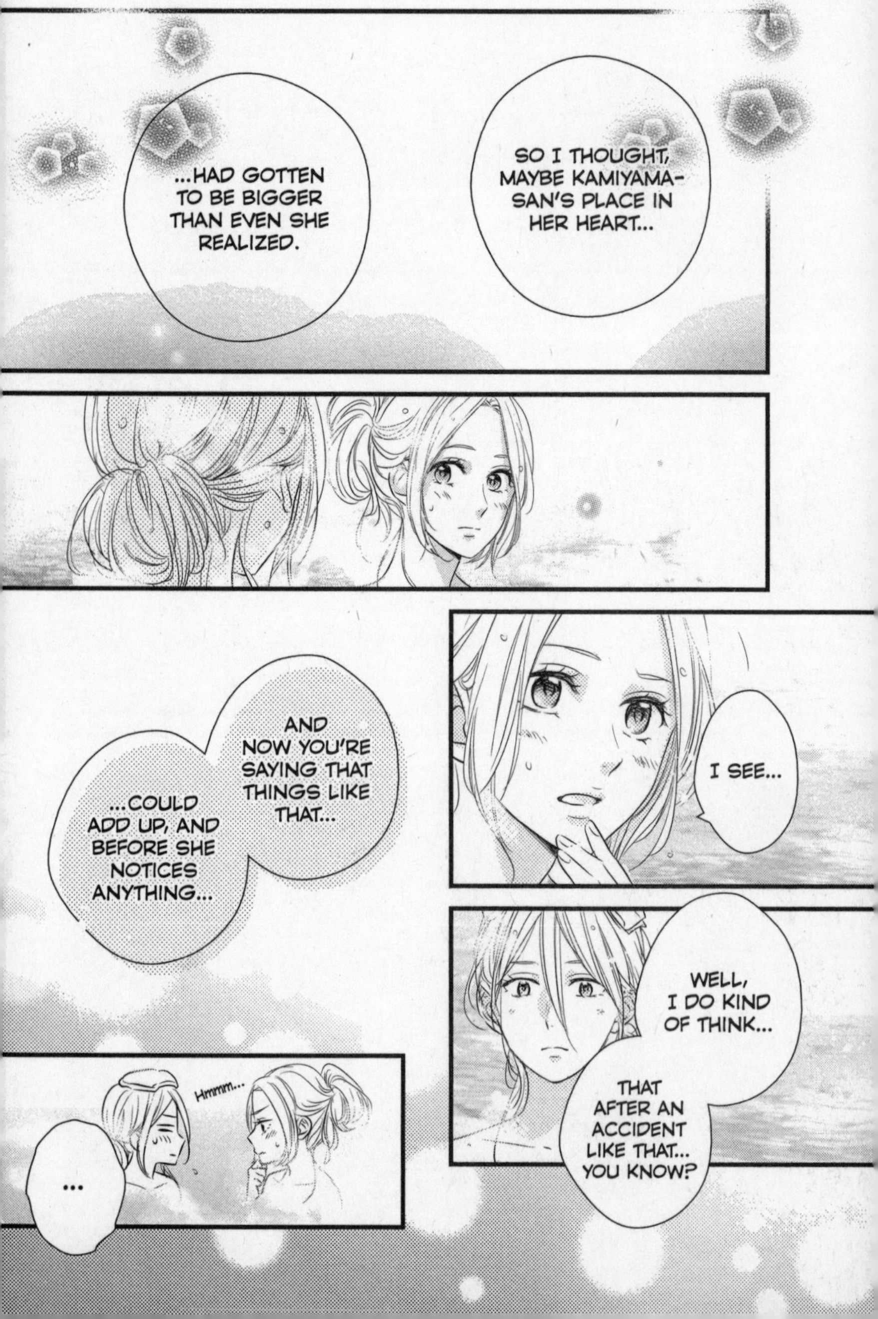
SO I THOUGHT, MAYBE KAMIYAMA-SAN'S PLACE IN HER HEART...
...HAD GOTTEN TO BE BIGGER THAN EVEN SHE REALIZED.
AND NOW YOU'RE SAYING THAT THINGS LIKE THAT...
...COULD ADD UP, AND BEFORE SHE NOTICES ANYTHING...
I SEE...
WELL, I DO KIND OF THINK...
THAT AFTER AN ACCIDENT LIKE THAT... YOU KNOW?
Hmmm...
...

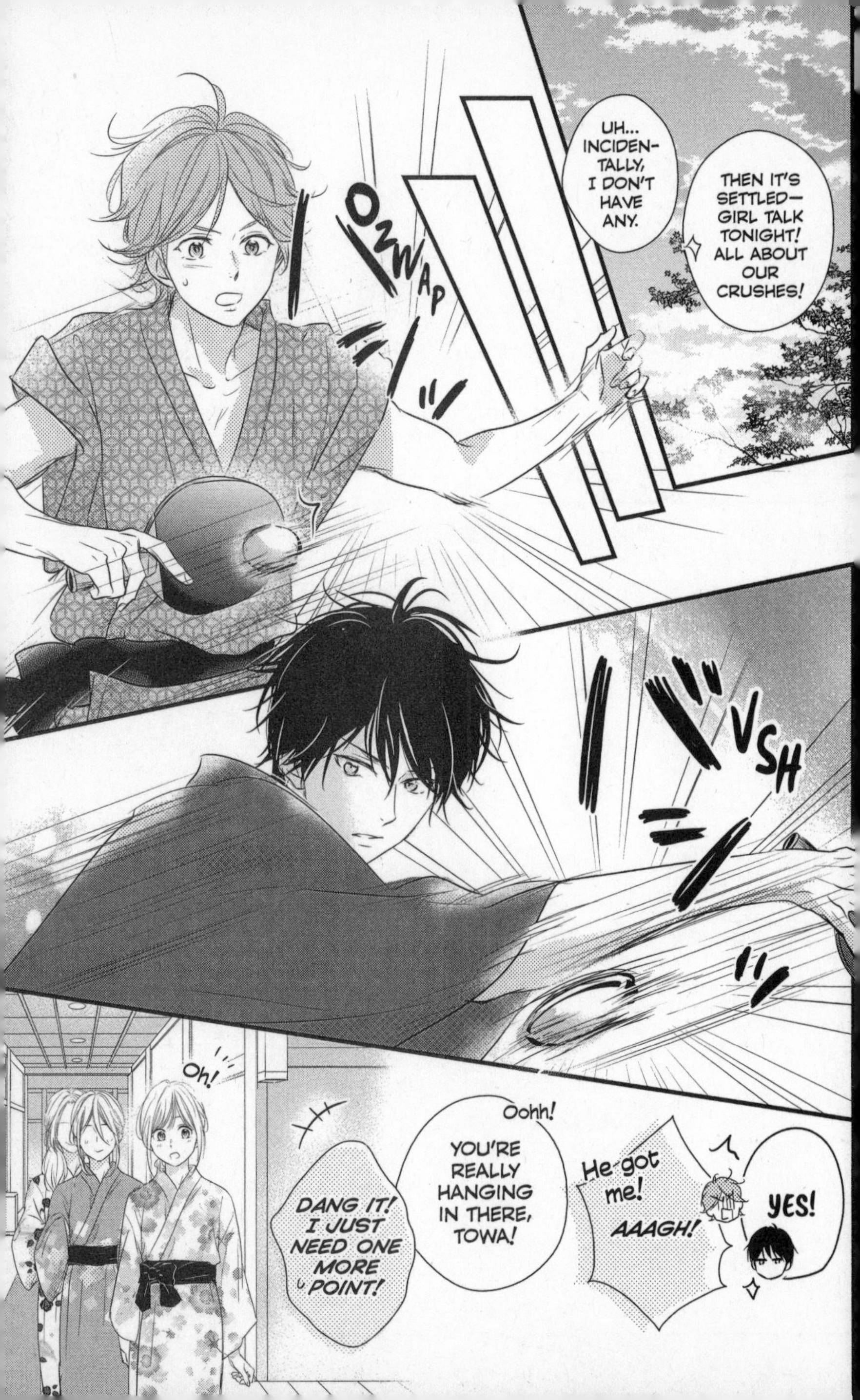
THEN IT'S SETTLED—GIRL TALK TONIGHT! ALL ABOUT OUR CRUSHES!
UH... INCIDEN-TALLY, I DON'T HAVE ANY.
OZWAP
VSH
YES!
He got me!
AAAGH!
Oohh!
YOU'RE REALLY HANGING IN THERE, TOWA!
DANG IT! I JUST NEED ONE MORE POINT!
Oh!

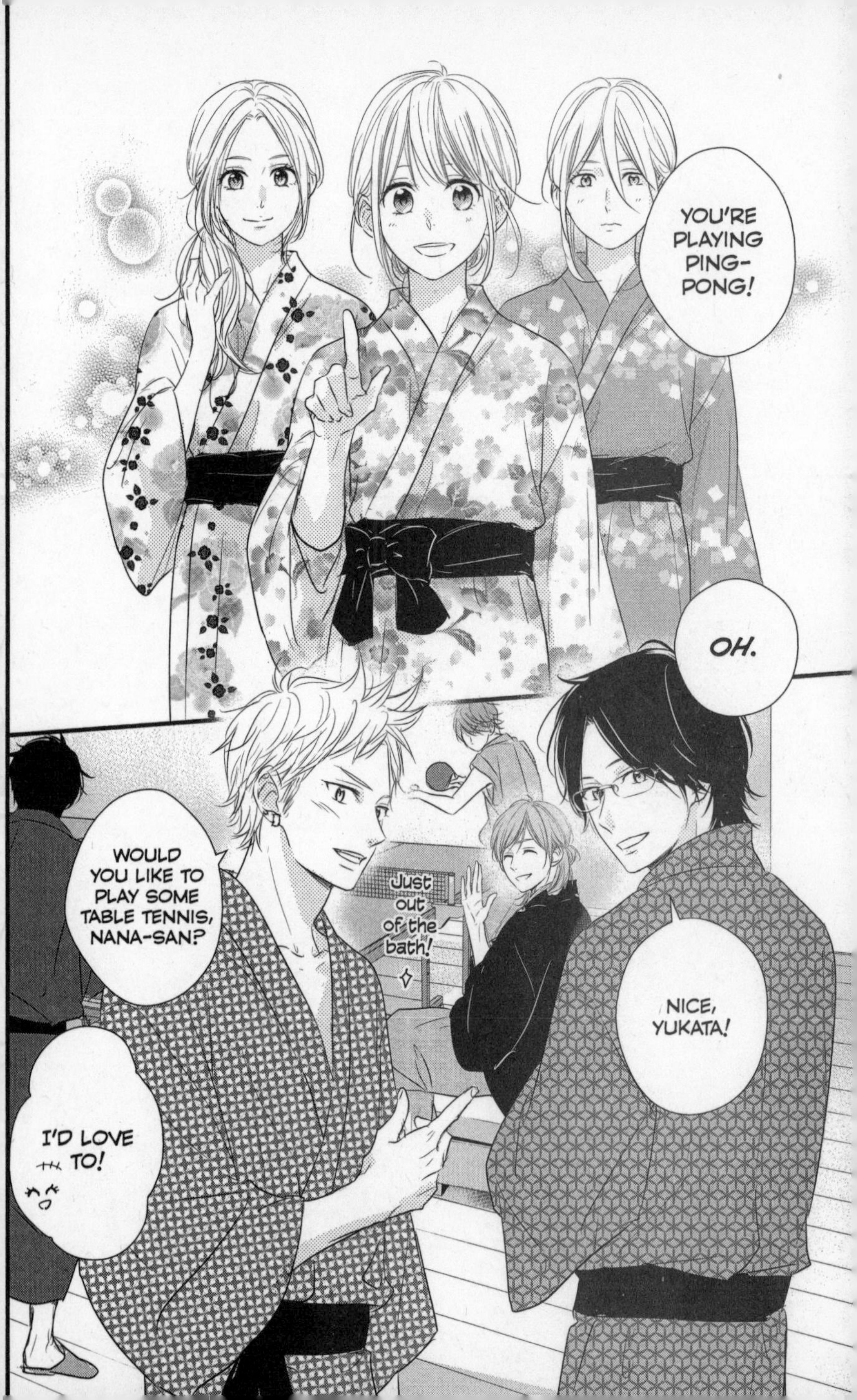
YOU'RE PLAYING PING-PONG!
OH.
NICE, YUKATA!
Just out of the bath!
WOULD YOU LIKE TO PLAY SOME TABLE TENNIS, NANA-SAN?
I'D LOVE TO!

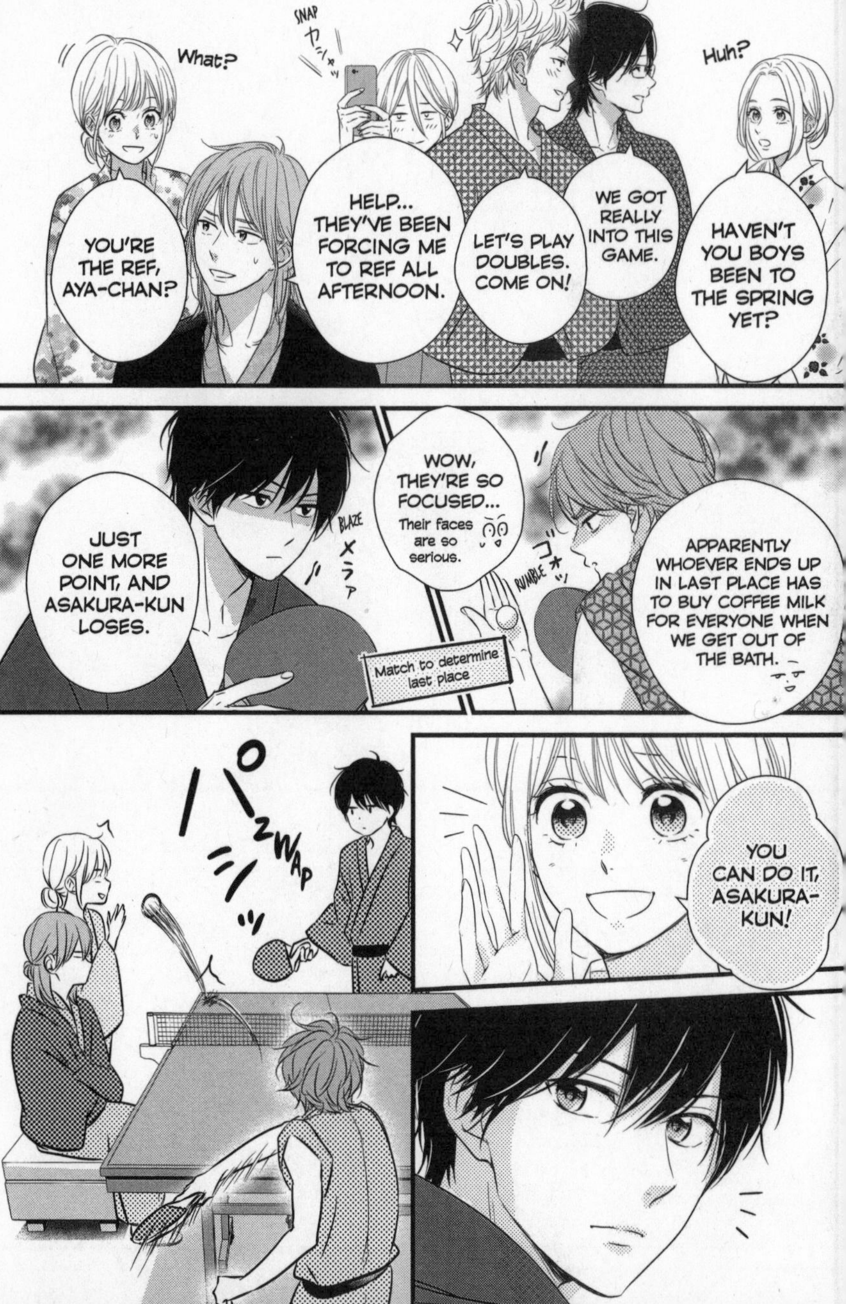
Huh?
HAVEN'T YOU BOYS BEEN TO THE SPRING YET?
WE GOT REALLY INTO THIS GAME.
LET'S PLAY DOUBLES. COME ON!
SNAP カシャッ
HELP... THEY'VE BEEN FORCING ME TO REF ALL AFTERNOON.
What?
YOU'RE THE REF, AYA-CHAN?
APPARENTLY WHOEVER ENDS UP IN LAST PLACE HAS TO BUY COFFEE MILK FOR EVERYONE WHEN WE GET OUT OF THE BATH.
RUMBLE ゴォッ
WOW, THEY'RE SO FOCUSED...
Their faces are so serious.
BLAZE メラァ
JUST ONE MORE POINT, AND ASAKURA-KUN LOSES.
Match to determine last place
YOU CAN DO IT, ASAKURA-KUN!
パシッ ZWAP

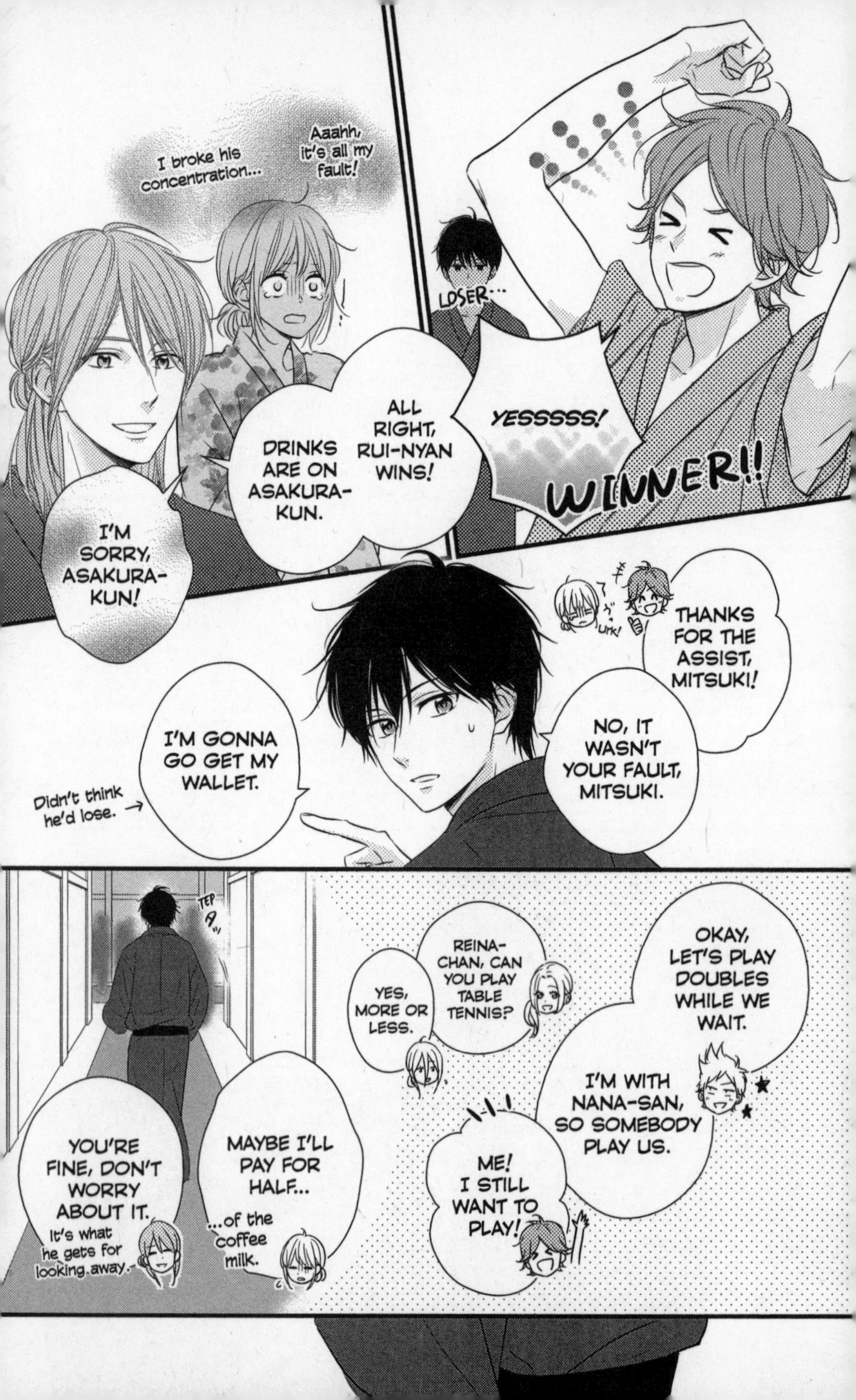
YESSSSS!
WINNER!!
LOSER...
Aaahh, it's all my fault!
I broke his concentration...
ALL RIGHT, RUI-NYAN WINS!
DRINKS ARE ON ASAKURA-KUN.
I'M SORRY, ASAKURA-KUN!
THANKS FOR THE ASSIST, MITSUKI!
Urk!
NO, IT WASN'T YOUR FAULT, MITSUKI.
I'M GONNA GO GET MY WALLET.
Didn't think he'd lose.
OKAY, LET'S PLAY DOUBLES WHILE WE WAIT.
I'M WITH NANA-SAN, SO SOMEBODY PLAY US.
REINA-CHAN, CAN YOU PLAY TABLE TENNIS?
YES, MORE OR LESS.
ME! I STILL WANT TO PLAY!
TEP
MAYBE I'LL PAY FOR HALF...
...of the coffee milk.
YOU'RE FINE, DON'T WORRY ABOUT IT.
It's what he gets for looking away.

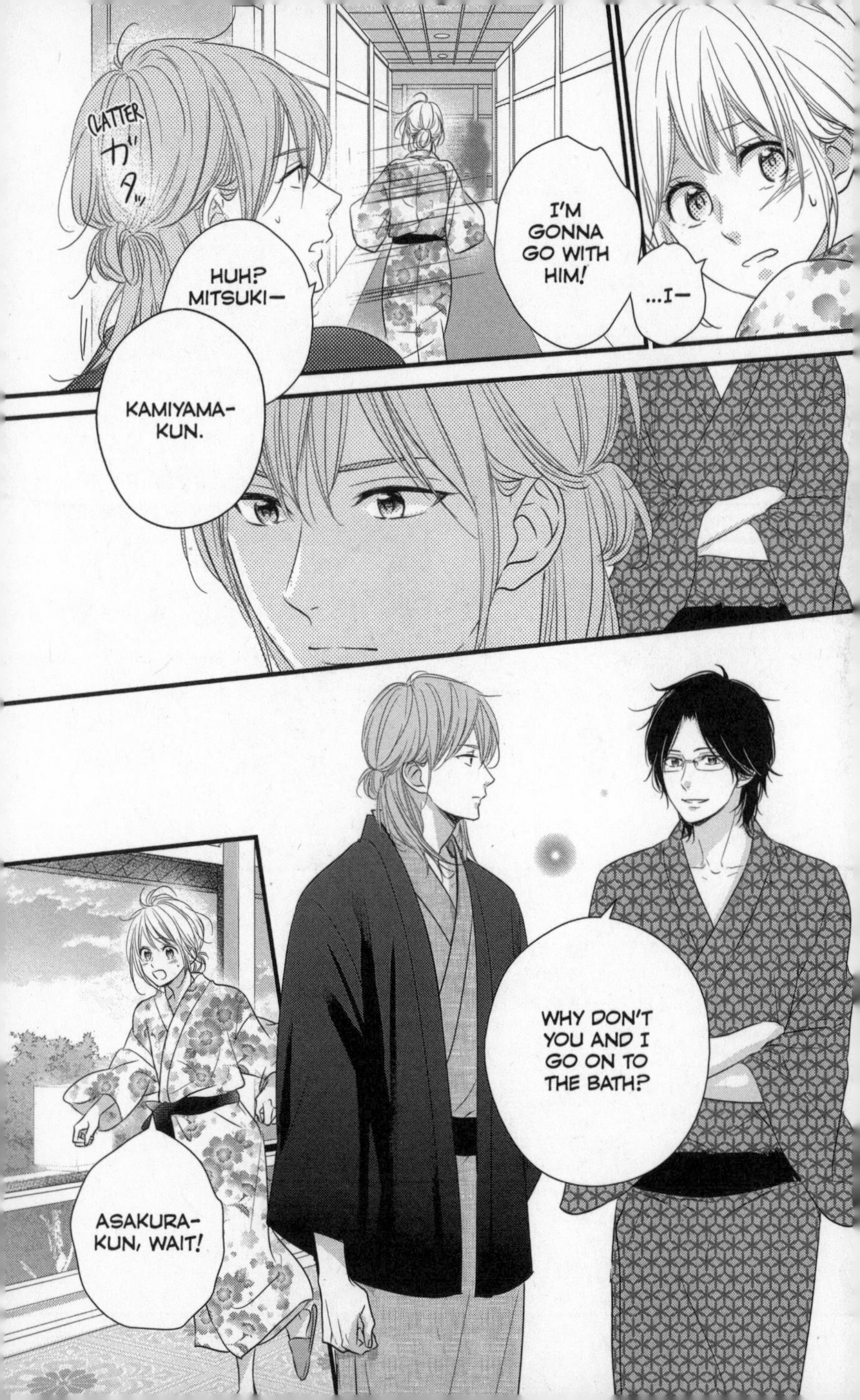
...I—
I'M GONNA GO WITH HIM!
CLATTER
ガタッ
HUH? MITSUKI—
KAMIYAMA-KUN.
WHY DON'T YOU AND I GO ON TO THE BATH?
ASAKURA-KUN, WAIT!

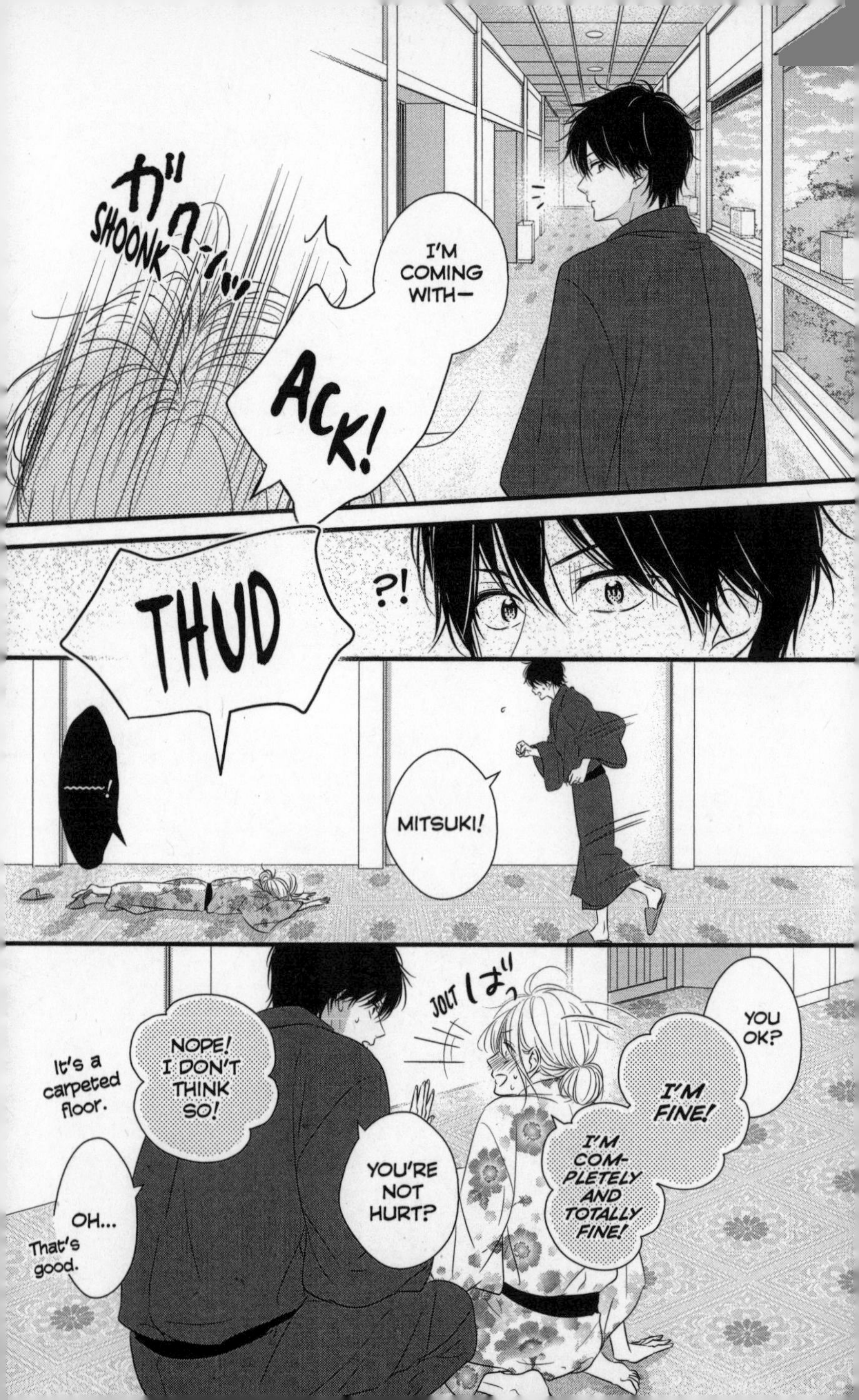

I'M COMING WITH—
ガクーッ
SHOONK
ACK!
THUD
?!
MITSUKI!
~~~~~!
YOU OK?
ばっ
JOLT
I'M FINE!
I'M COMPLETELY AND TOTALLY FINE!
YOU'RE NOT HURT?
NOPE! I DON'T THINK SO!
It's a carpeted floor.
OH...
That's good.
~~~~~

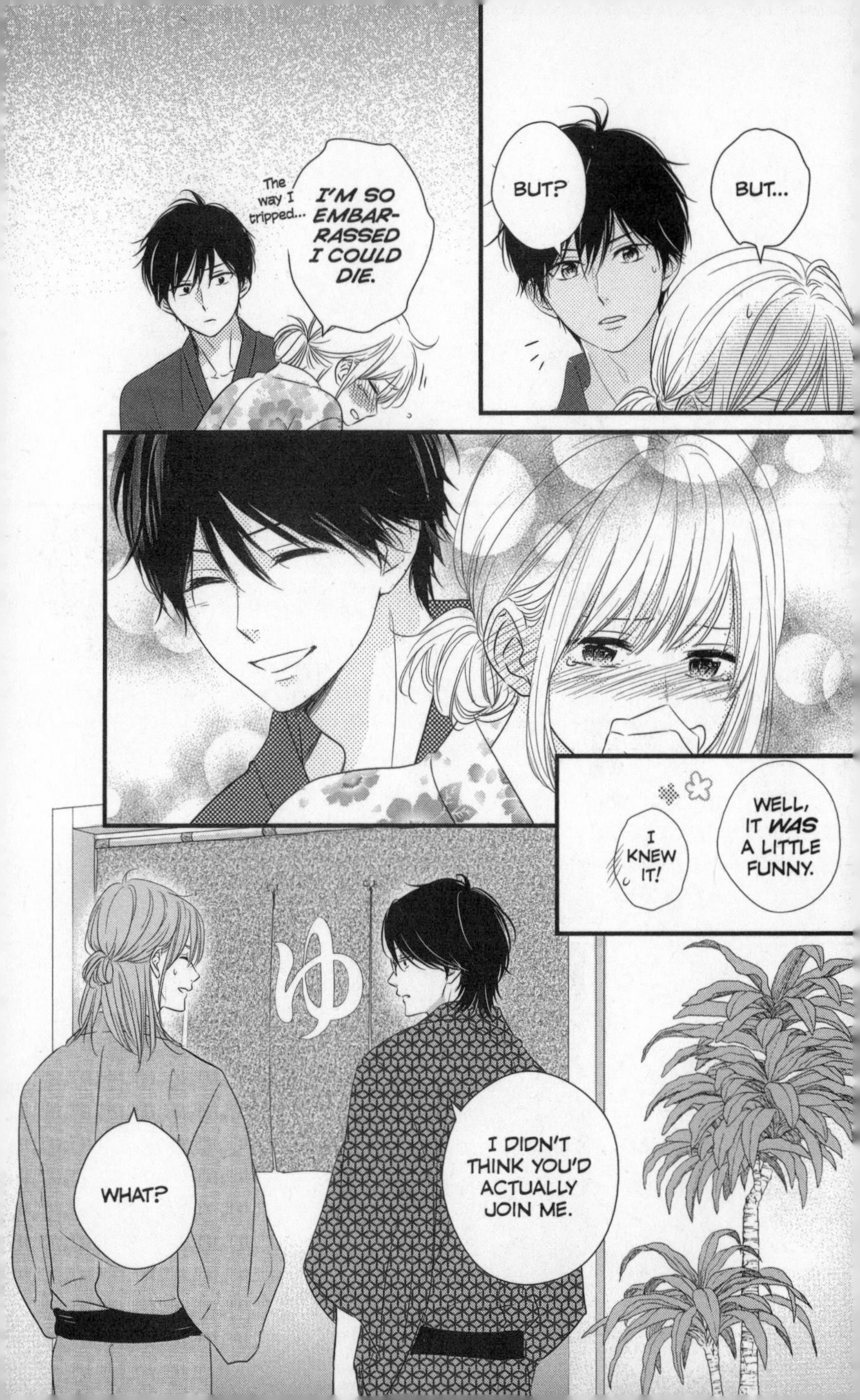
BUT...
BUT?
The way I tripped...
I'M SO EMBARRASSED I COULD DIE.
WELL, IT WAS A LITTLE FUNNY.
I KNEW IT!
ゆ
I DIDN'T THINK YOU'D ACTUALLY JOIN ME.
WHAT?

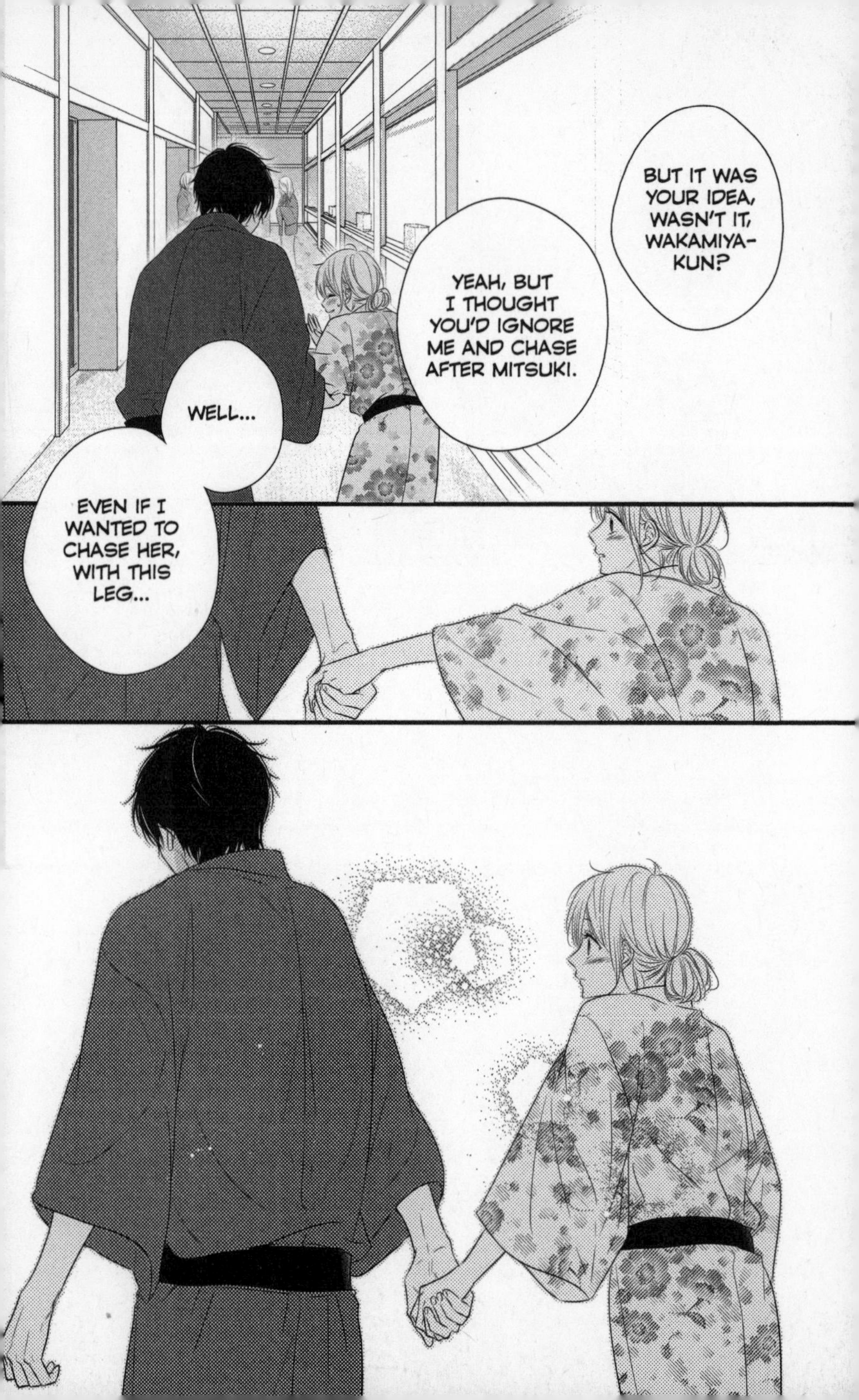
BUT IT WAS YOUR IDEA, WASN'T IT, WAKAMIYA-KUN?
YEAH, BUT I THOUGHT YOU'D IGNORE ME AND CHASE AFTER MITSUKI.
WELL...
EVEN IF I WANTED TO CHASE HER, WITH THIS LEG...

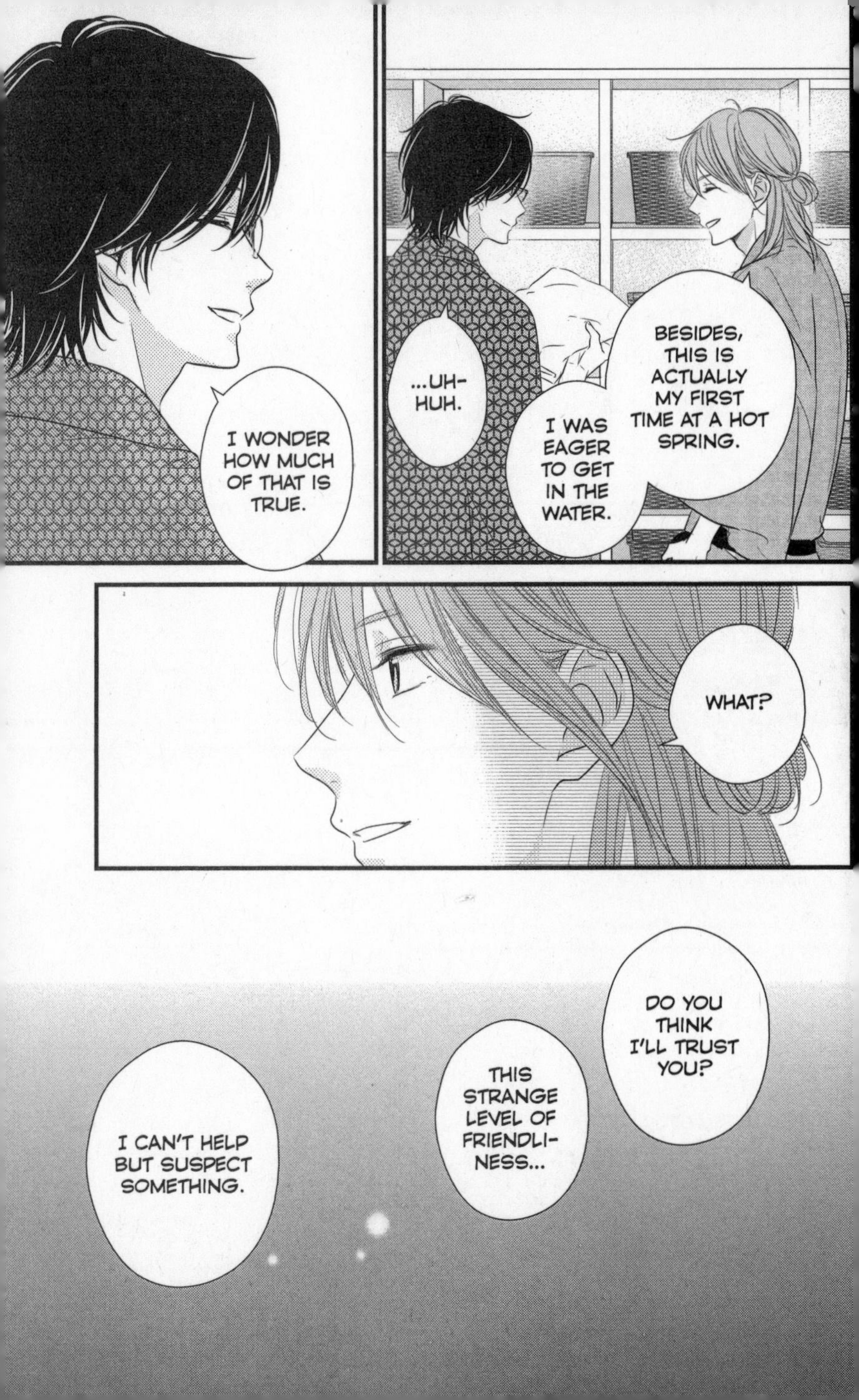
BESIDES, THIS IS ACTUALLY MY FIRST TIME AT A HOT SPRING.
I WAS EAGER TO GET IN THE WATER.
...UH-HUH.
I WONDER HOW MUCH OF THAT IS TRUE.
WHAT?
DO YOU THINK I'LL TRUST YOU?
THIS STRANGE LEVEL OF FRIENDLI-NESS...
I CAN'T HELP BUT SUSPECT SOMETHING.

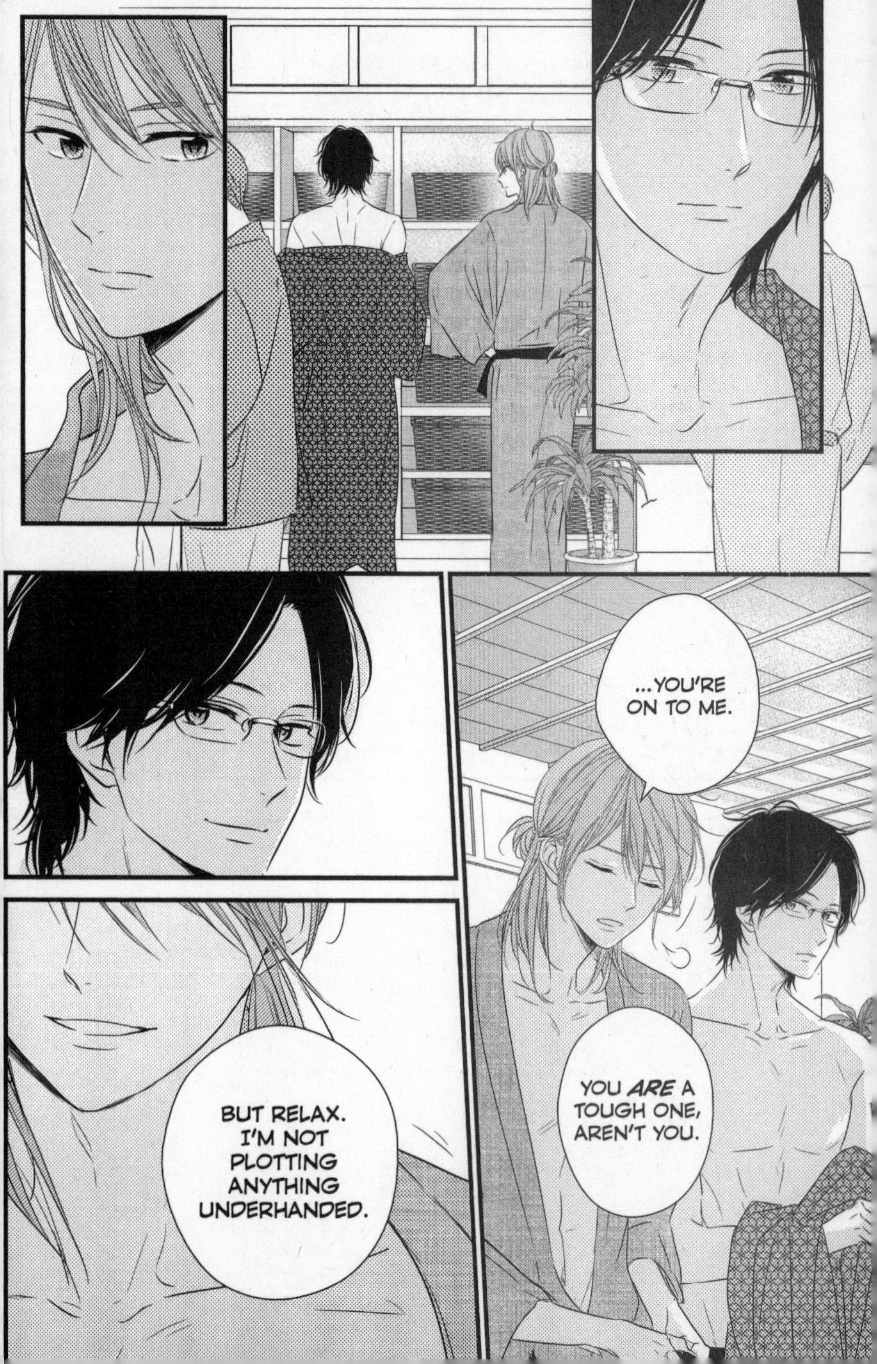
...YOU'RE ON TO ME.
YOU *ARE* A TOUGH ONE, AREN'T YOU.
BUT RELAX. I'M NOT PLOTTING ANYTHING UNDERHANDED.

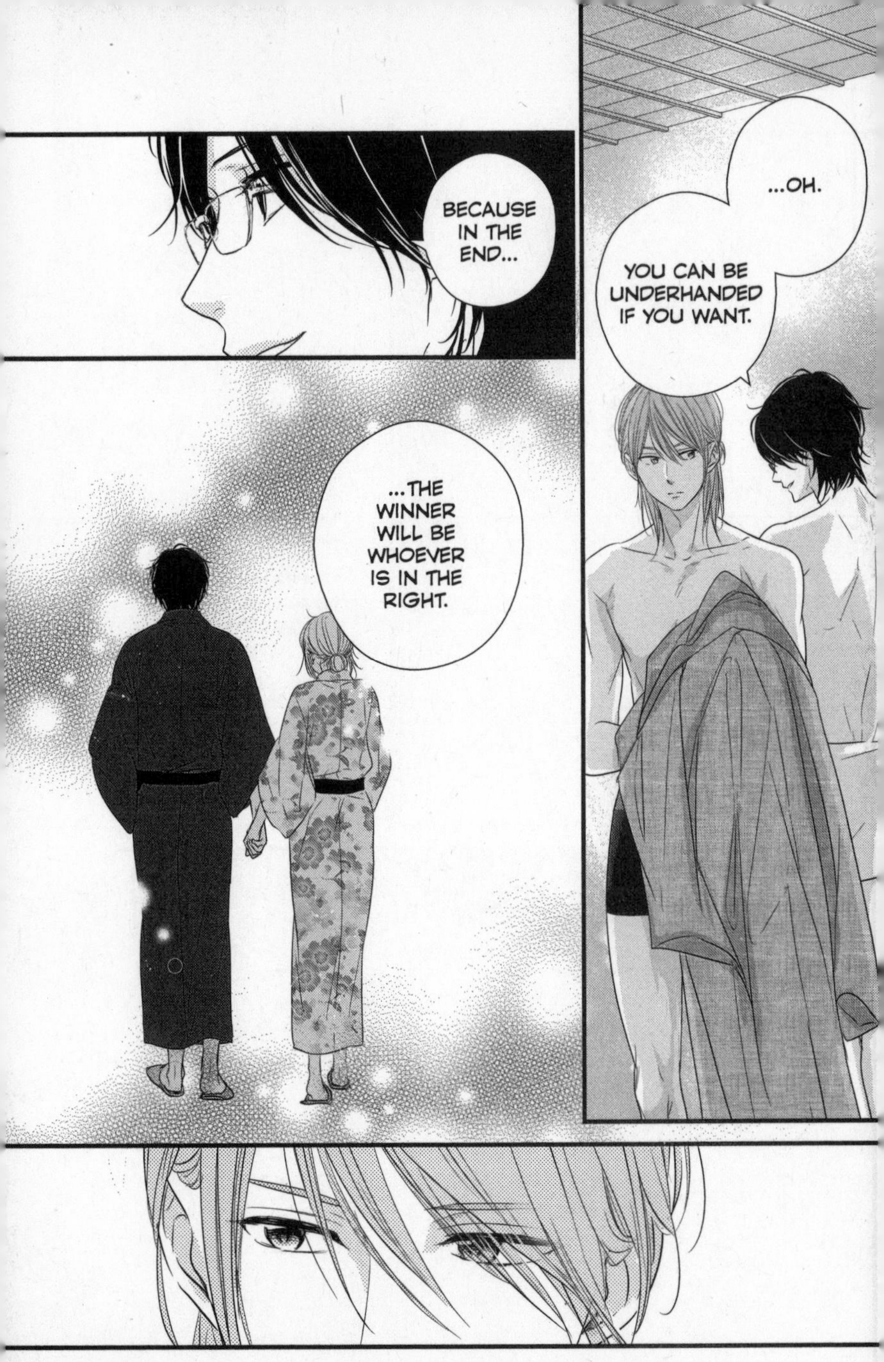
...OH.
YOU CAN BE UNDERHANDED IF YOU WANT.
BECAUSE IN THE END...
...THE WINNER WILL BE WHOEVER IS IN THE RIGHT.

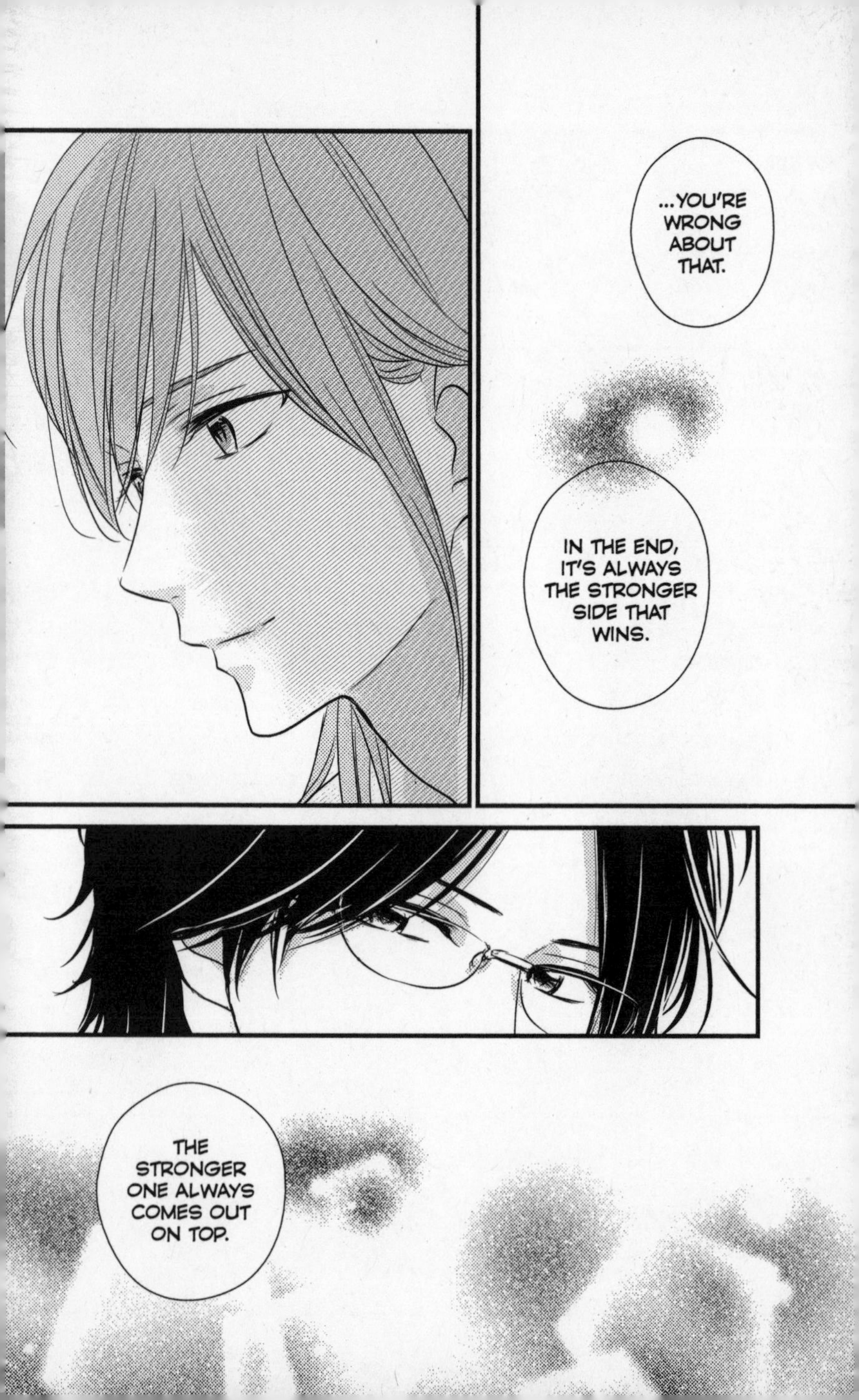
...YOU'RE WRONG ABOUT THAT.
IN THE END, IT'S ALWAYS THE STRONGER SIDE THAT WINS.
THE STRONGER ONE ALWAYS COMES OUT ON TOP.

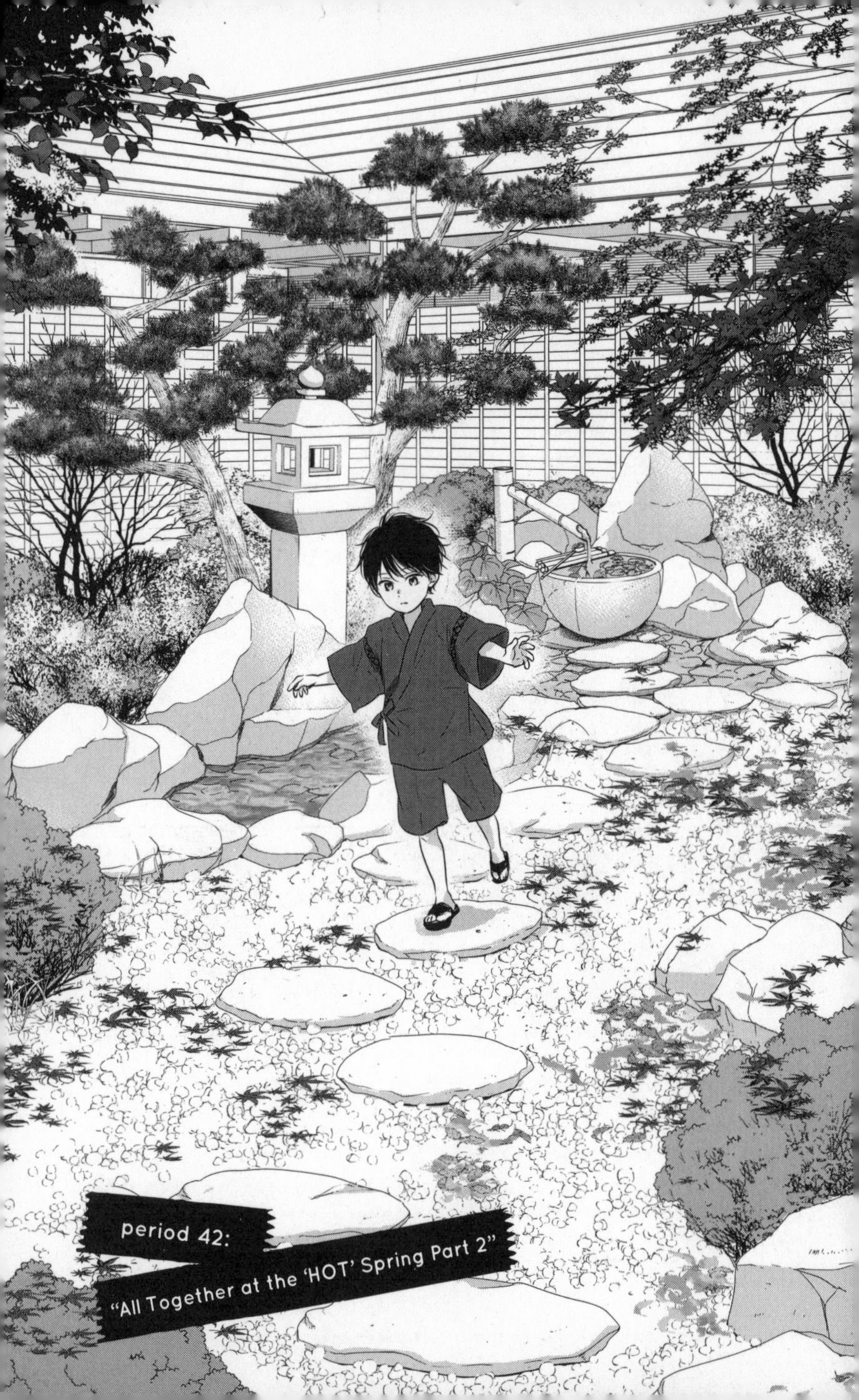
period 42:
"All Together at the 'HOT' Spring Part 2"

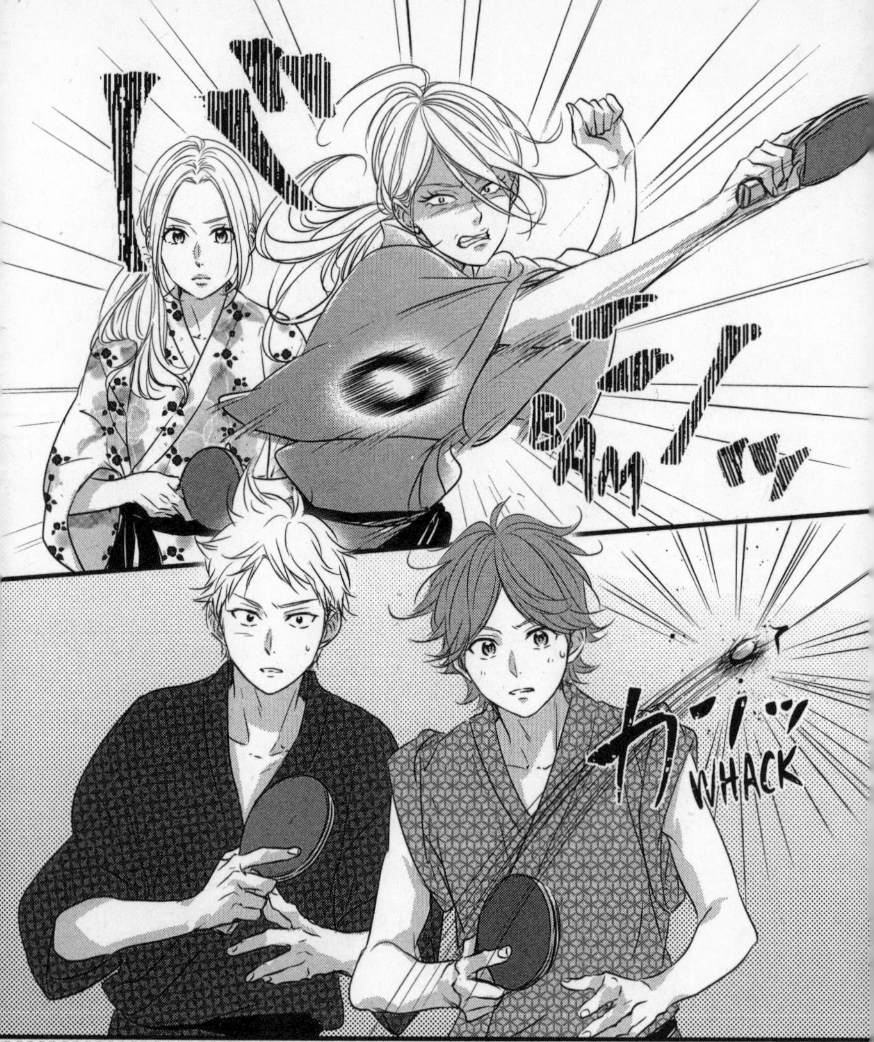
BAM
WHACK

The second thing I can't draw without is Rui, Ryūji, Reina-chan

(I know you didn't expect me to talk about the characters, but no worries! Anything goes here!!)

I guess you could say these three are the ones who make it so anything can go in the story, too. Or like, to be honest they're ~~the butts of the jokes~~ very important people in drawing a fun manga. I could add Kyōsuke to the group, but when Kyōsuke is the punchline, I have a strong tendency to make it dirty, so I have to be careful (ha ha). So I usually use these three.

You're always helping me out!
Thank you ♡

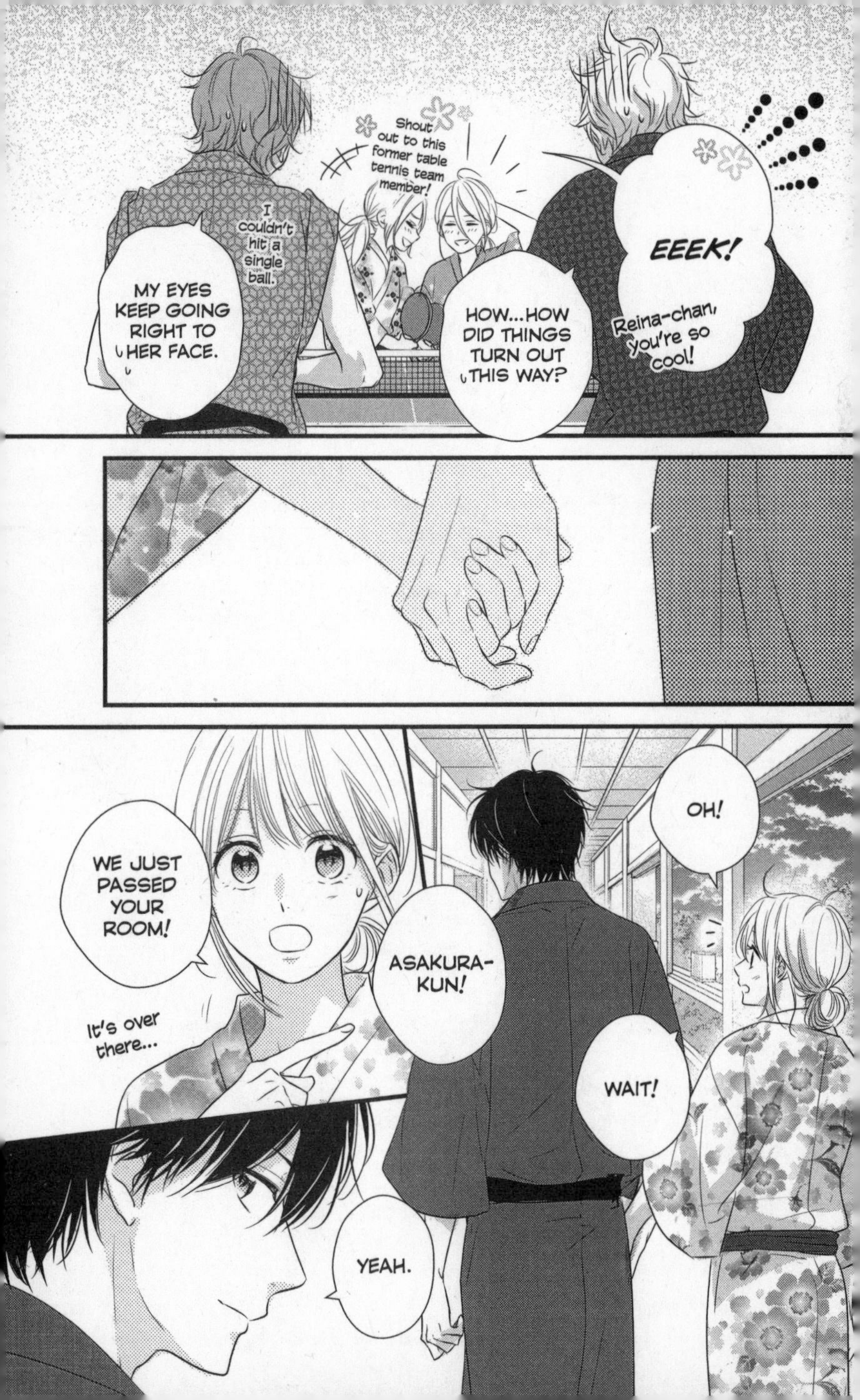
EEEK!
Reina-chan, you're so cool!
Shout out to this former table tennis team member!
HOW...HOW DID THINGS TURN OUT THIS WAY?
I couldn't hit a single ball.
MY EYES KEEP GOING RIGHT TO HER FACE.
OH!
WAIT!
ASAKURA-KUN!
WE JUST PASSED YOUR ROOM!
It's over there...
YEAH.

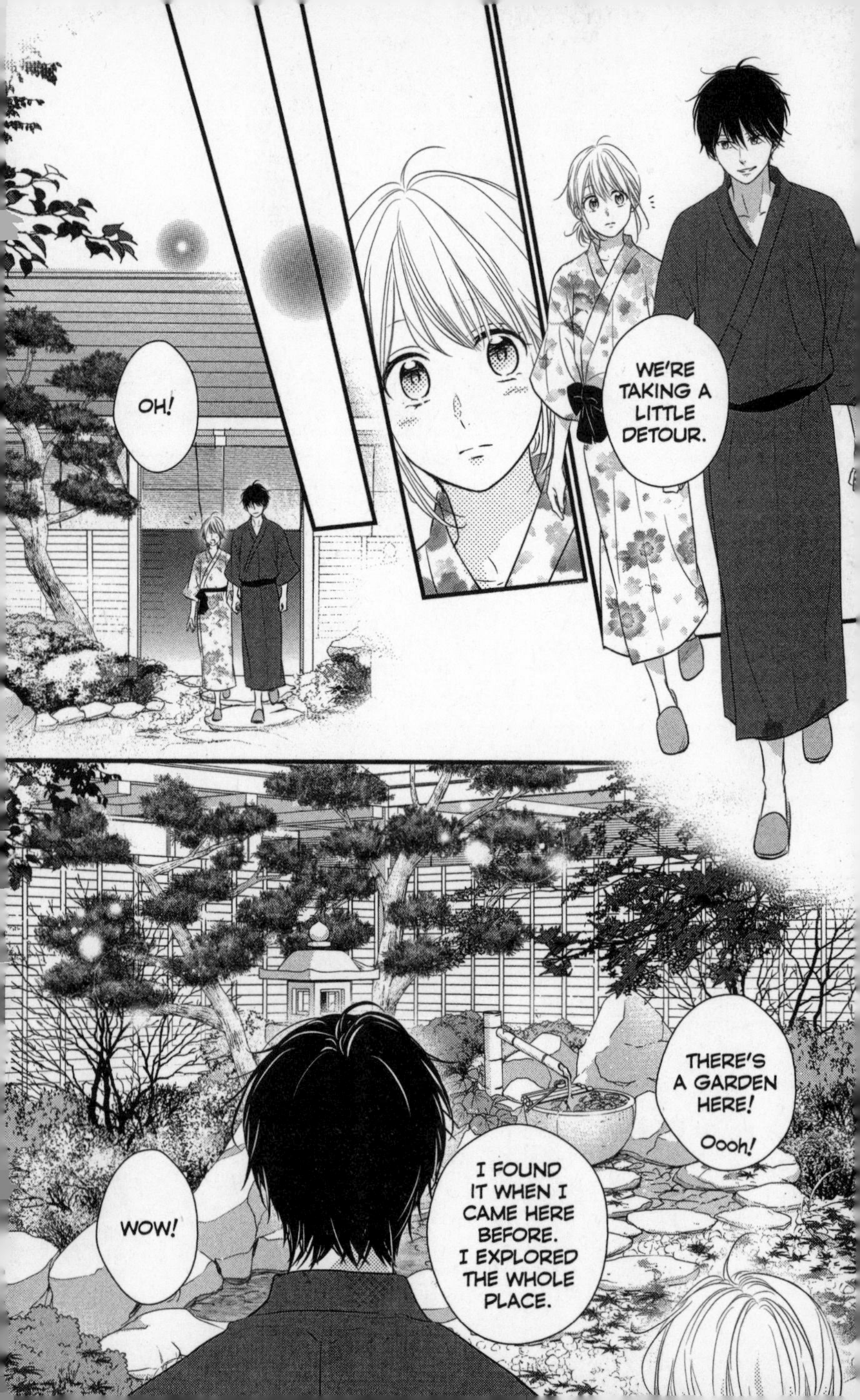
WE'RE TAKING A LITTLE DETOUR.
OH!
THERE'S A GARDEN HERE!
Oooh!
I FOUND IT WHEN I CAME HERE BEFORE. I EXPLORED THE WHOLE PLACE.
WOW!

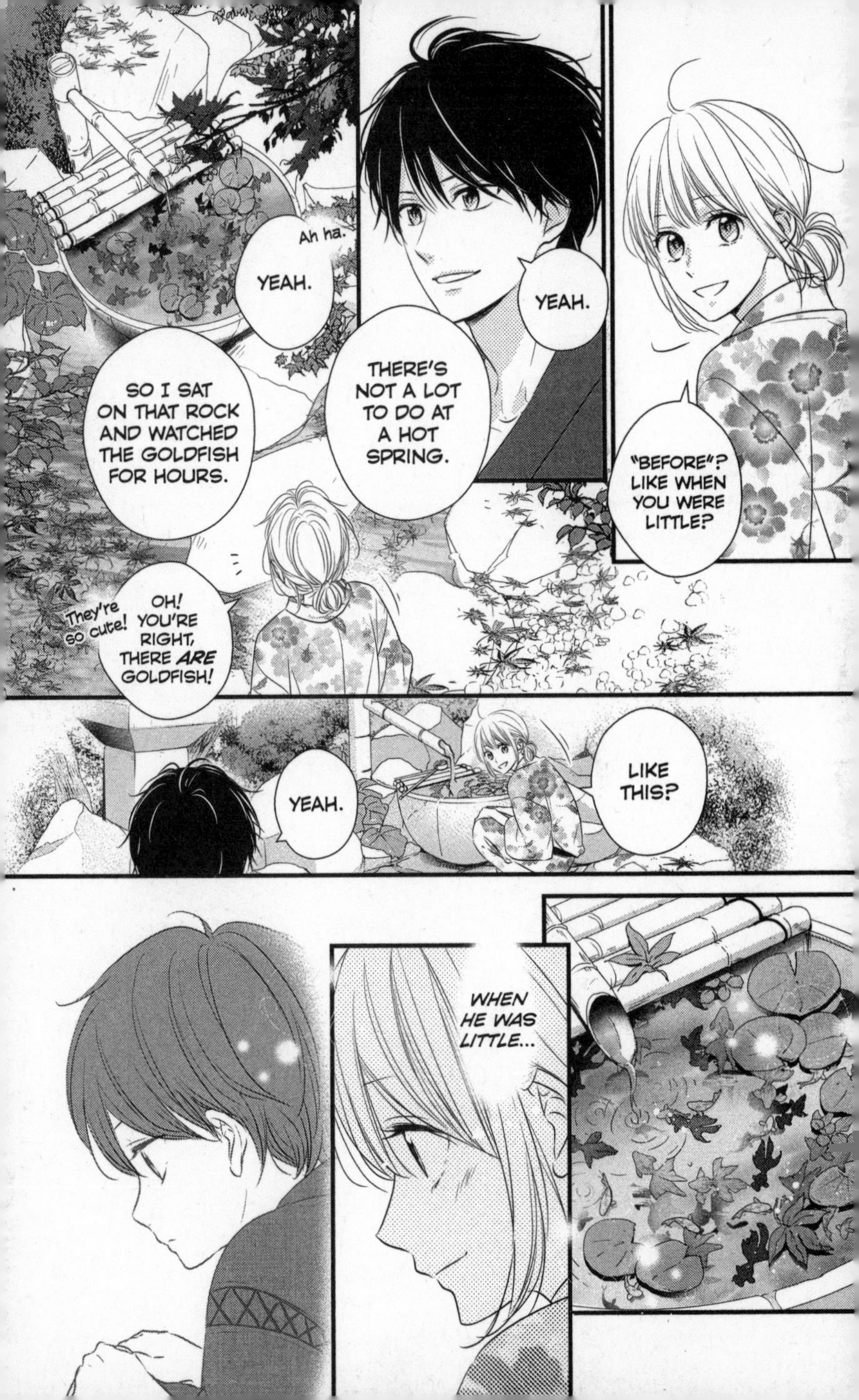
"BEFORE"? LIKE WHEN YOU WERE LITTLE?
YEAH.
THERE'S NOT A LOT TO DO AT A HOT SPRING.
Ah ha.
YEAH.
SO I SAT ON THAT ROCK AND WATCHED THE GOLDFISH FOR HOURS.
OH! YOU'RE RIGHT, THERE ARE GOLDFISH!
They're so cute!
LIKE THIS?
YEAH.
WHEN HE WAS LITTLE...

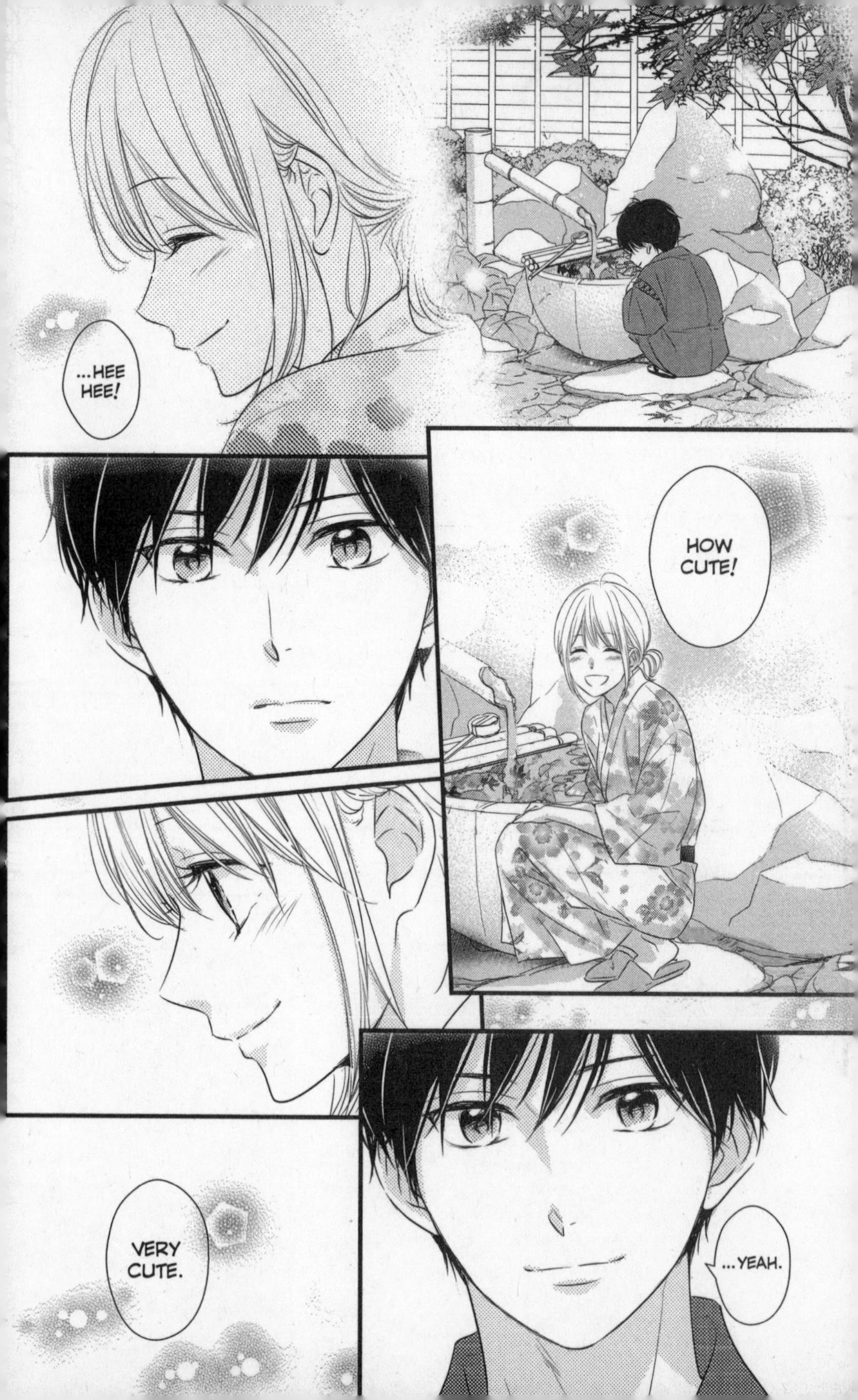
...HEE HEE!
HOW CUTE!
VERY CUTE.
...YEAH.

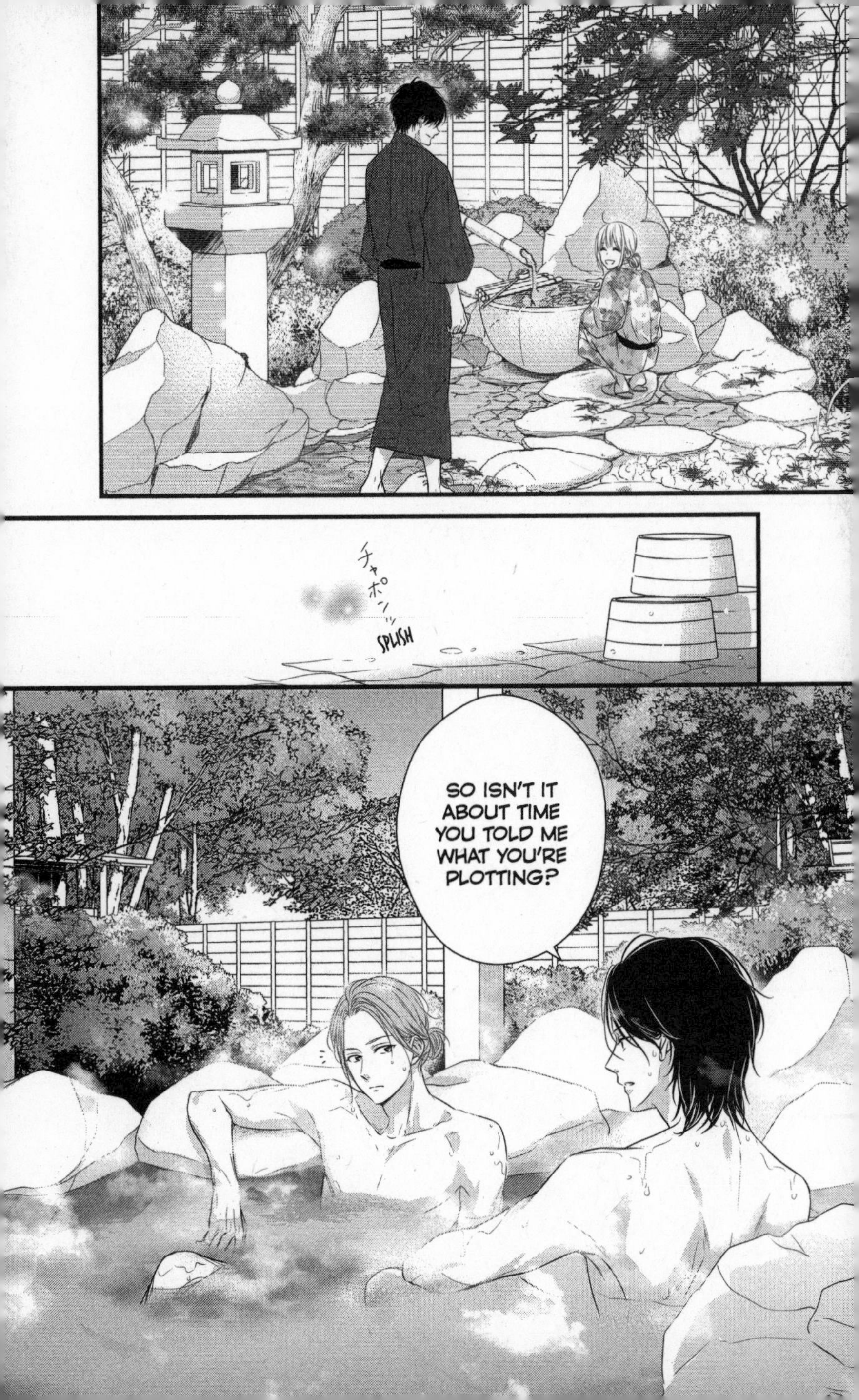
チャポンッ
SPLISH
SO ISN'T IT ABOUT TIME YOU TOLD ME WHAT YOU'RE PLOTTING?

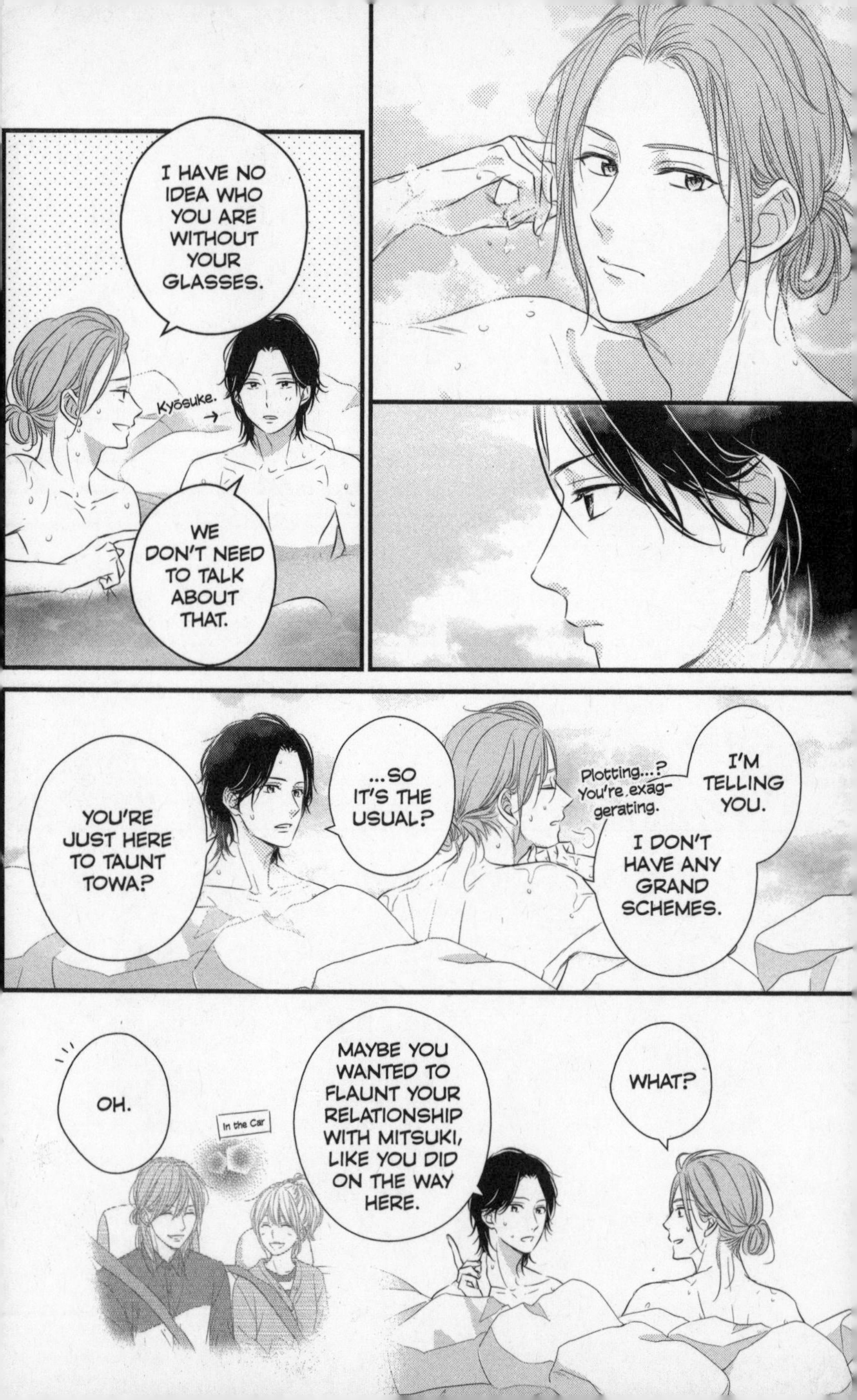
I HAVE NO IDEA WHO YOU ARE WITHOUT YOUR GLASSES.
Kyōsuke. →
WE DON'T NEED TO TALK ABOUT THAT.
I'M TELLING YOU.
Plotting...? You're exag-gerating.
I DON'T HAVE ANY GRAND SCHEMES.
...SO IT'S THE USUAL?
YOU'RE JUST HERE TO TAUNT TOWA?
WHAT?
MAYBE YOU WANTED TO FLAUNT YOUR RELATIONSHIP WITH MITSUKI, LIKE YOU DID ON THE WAY HERE.
In the Car
OH.

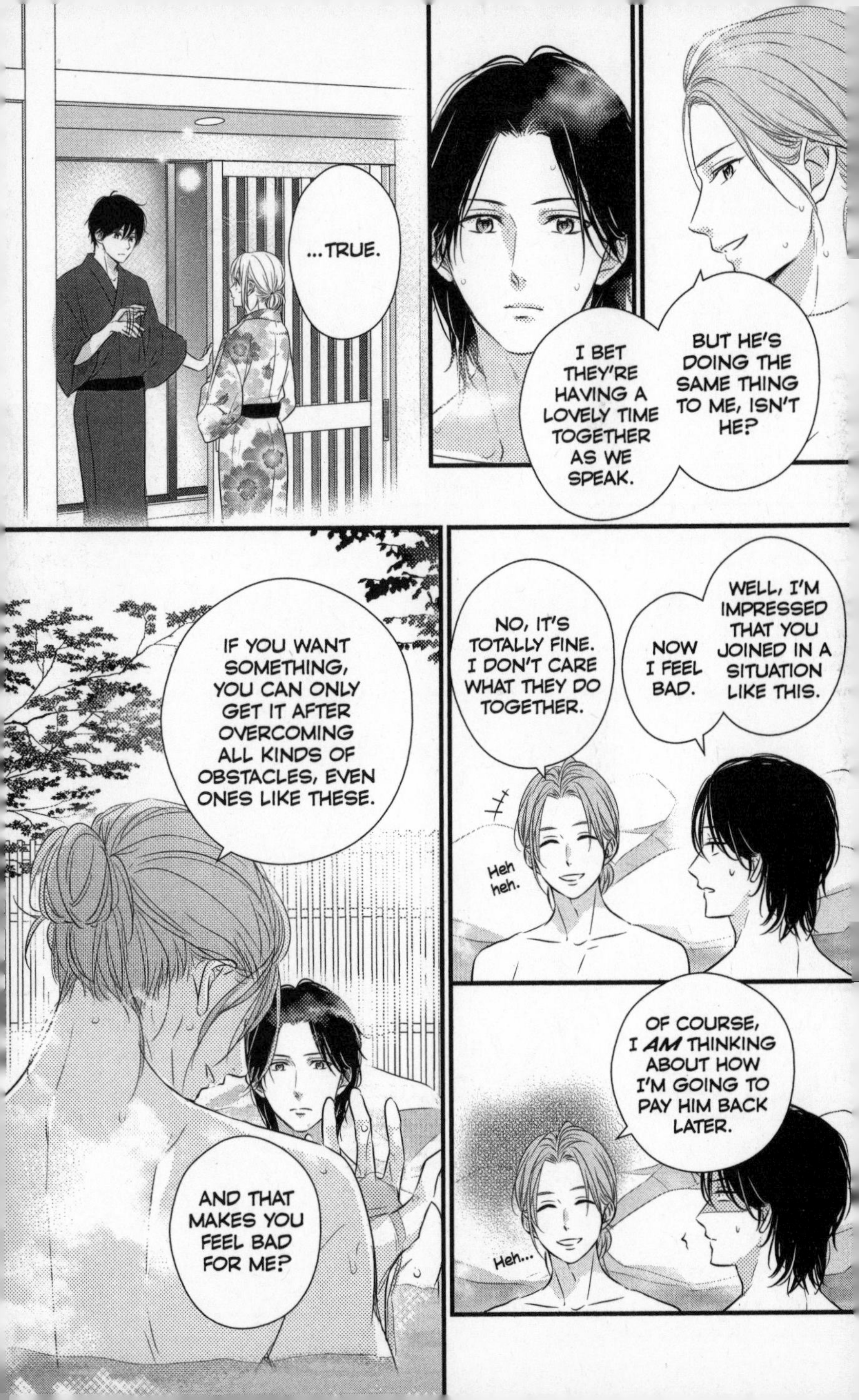
BUT HE'S DOING THE SAME THING TO ME, ISN'T HE?
I BET THEY'RE HAVING A LOVELY TIME TOGETHER AS WE SPEAK.
...TRUE.
WELL, I'M IMPRESSED THAT YOU JOINED IN A SITUATION LIKE THIS.
NOW I FEEL BAD.
NO, IT'S TOTALLY FINE. I DON'T CARE WHAT THEY DO TOGETHER.
Heh heh.
OF COURSE, I *AM* THINKING ABOUT HOW I'M GOING TO PAY HIM BACK LATER.
Heh...
IF YOU WANT SOMETHING, YOU CAN ONLY GET IT AFTER OVERCOMING ALL KINDS OF OBSTACLES, EVEN ONES LIKE THESE.
AND THAT MAKES YOU FEEL BAD FOR ME?

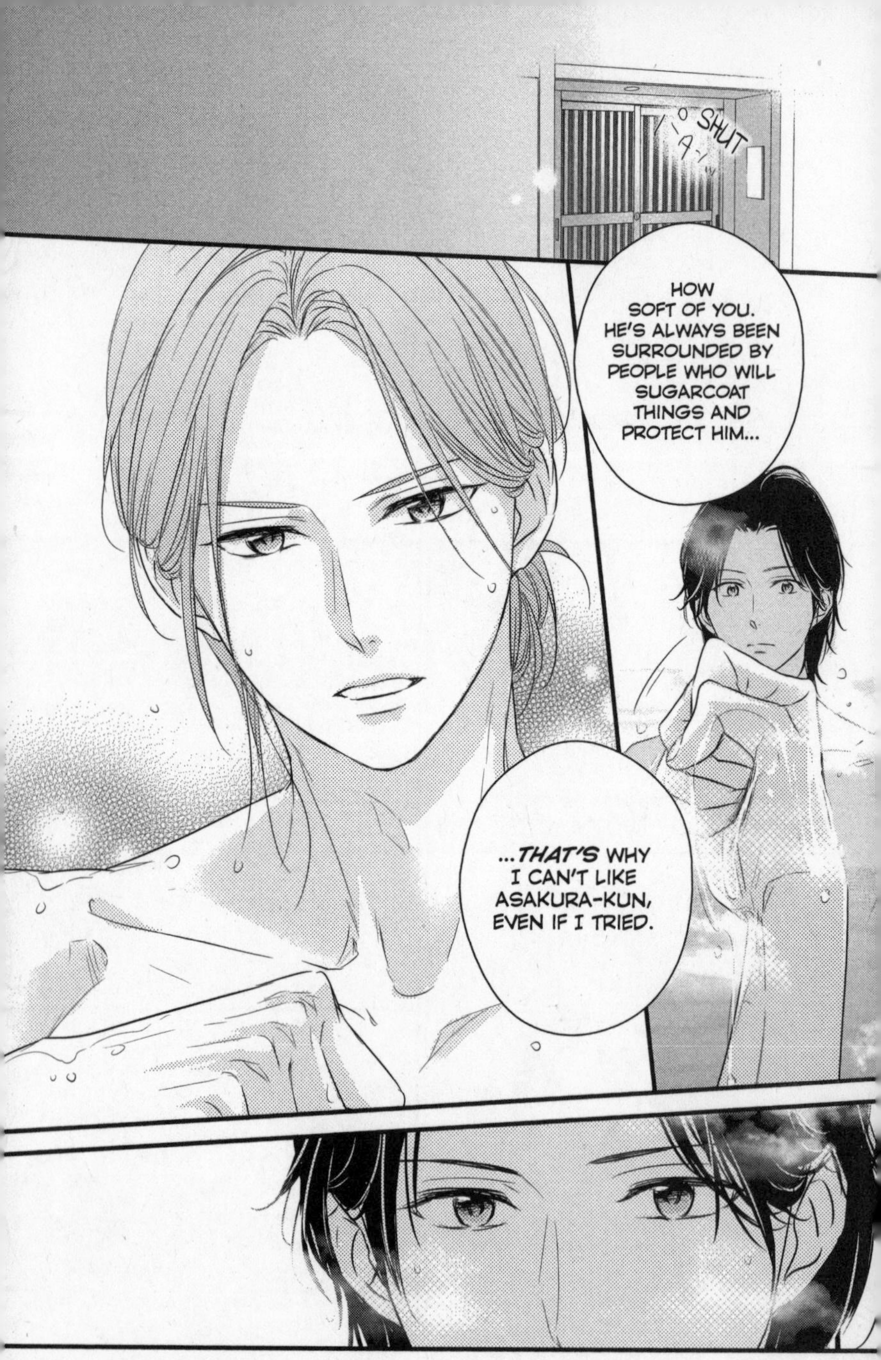
SHUT
HOW SOFT OF YOU. HE'S ALWAYS BEEN SURROUNDED BY PEOPLE WHO WILL SUGARCOAT THINGS AND PROTECT HIM...
...*THAT'S* WHY I CAN'T LIKE ASAKURA-KUN, EVEN IF I TRIED.

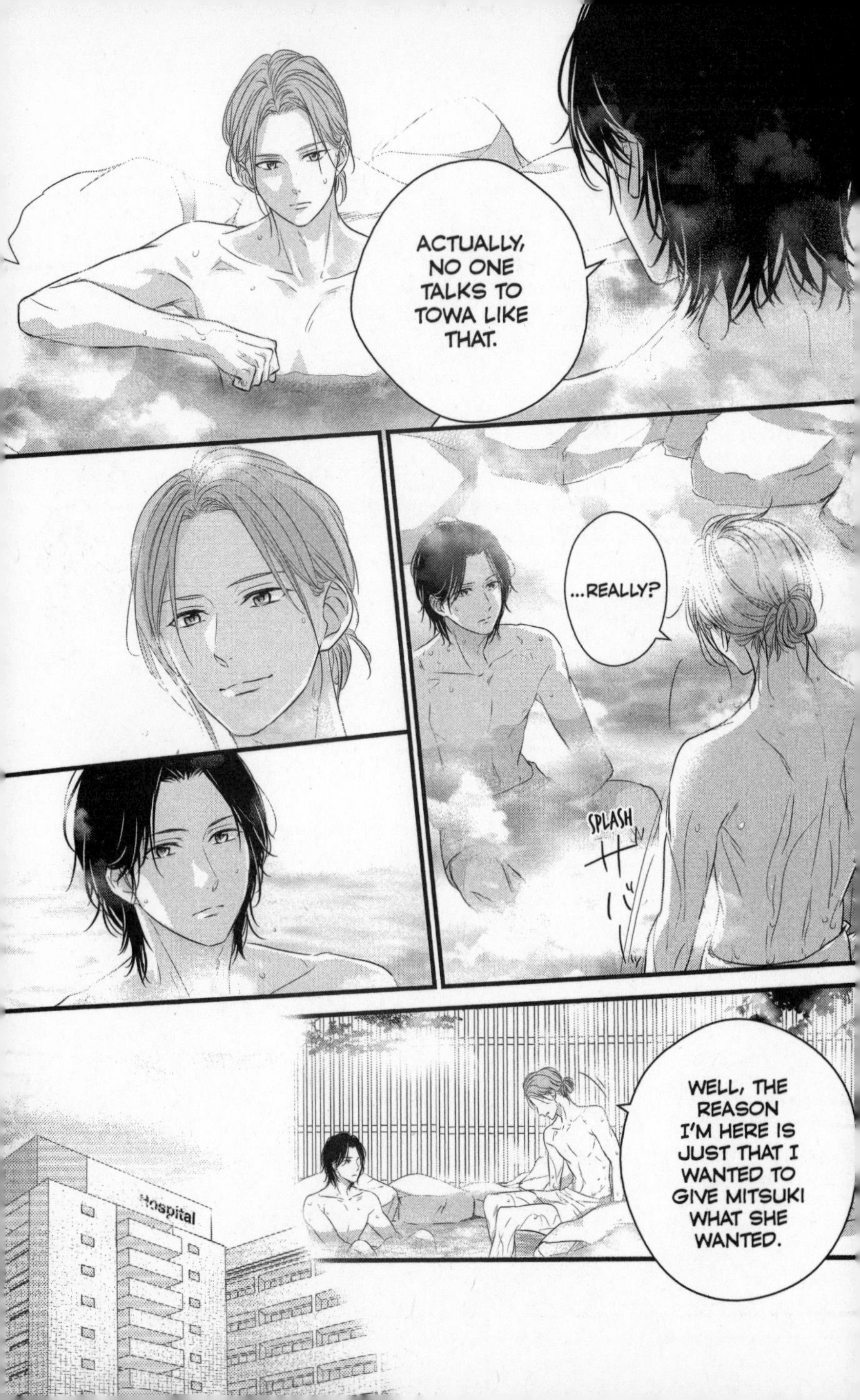
ACTUALLY, NO ONE TALKS TO TOWA LIKE THAT.
...REALLY?
SPLASH
WELL, THE REASON I'M HERE IS JUST THAT I WANTED TO GIVE MITSUKI WHAT SHE WANTED.
Hospital

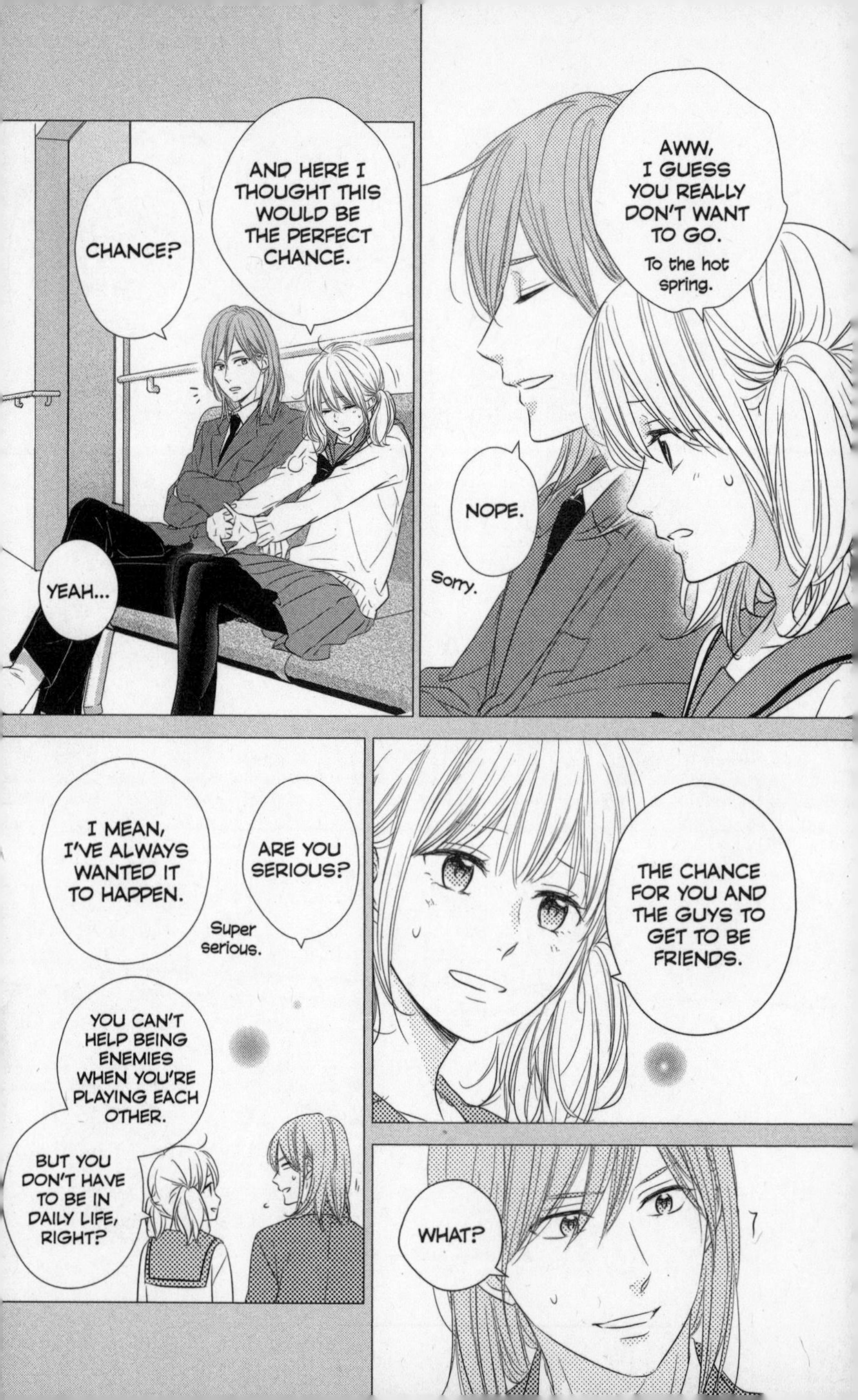
AWW, I GUESS YOU REALLY DON'T WANT TO GO.
To the hot spring.
NOPE.
Sorry.
AND HERE I THOUGHT THIS WOULD BE THE PERFECT CHANCE.
CHANCE?
YEAH...
THE CHANCE FOR YOU AND THE GUYS TO GET TO BE FRIENDS.
WHAT?
ARE YOU SERIOUS?
Super serious.
I MEAN, I'VE ALWAYS WANTED IT TO HAPPEN.
YOU CAN'T HELP BEING ENEMIES WHEN YOU'RE PLAYING EACH OTHER.
BUT YOU DON'T HAVE TO BE IN DAILY LIFE, RIGHT?

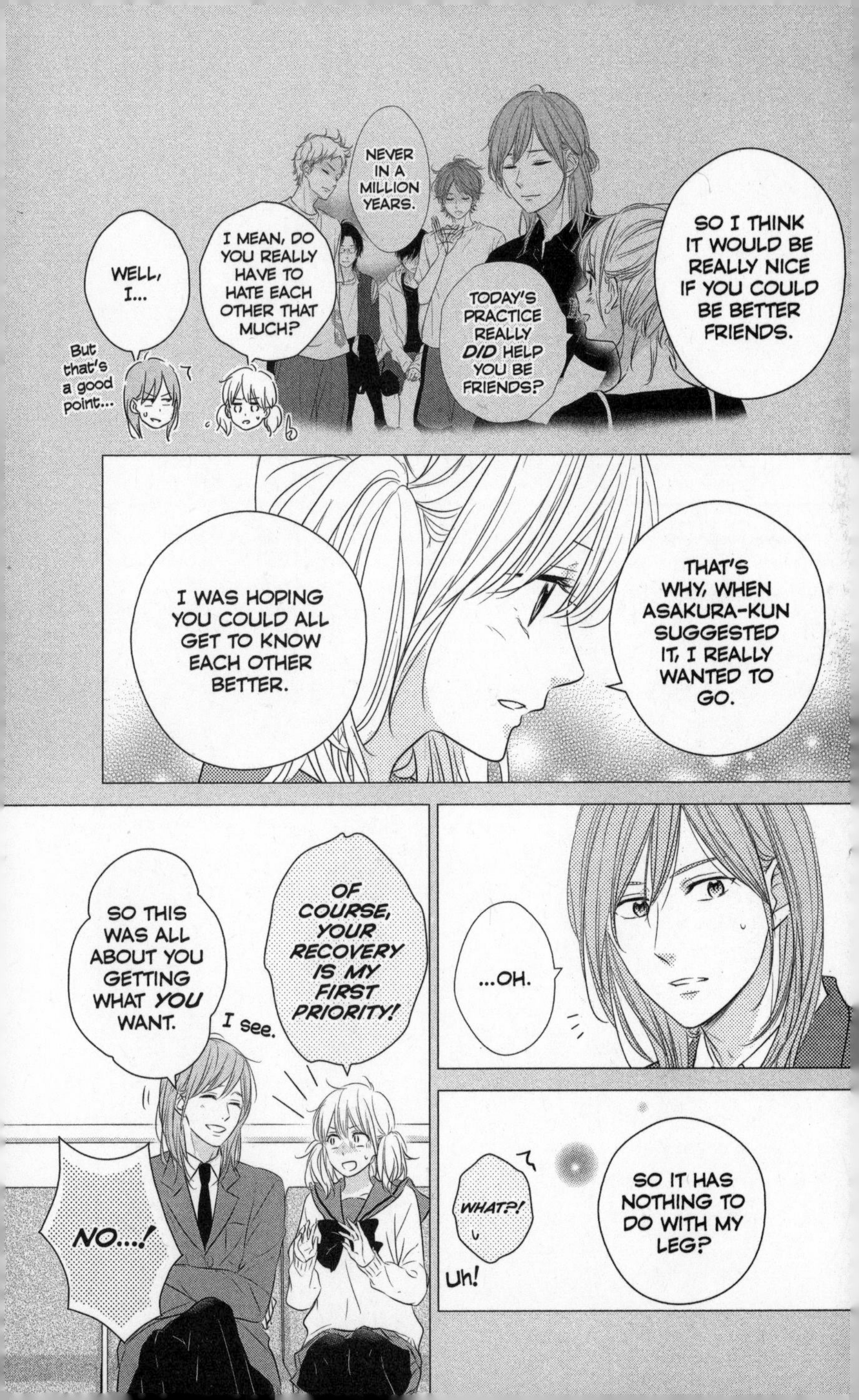
SO I THINK IT WOULD BE REALLY NICE IF YOU COULD BE BETTER FRIENDS.
TODAY'S PRACTICE REALLY *DID* HELP YOU BE FRIENDS?
NEVER IN A MILLION YEARS.
I MEAN, DO YOU REALLY HAVE TO HATE EACH OTHER THAT MUCH?
WELL, I...
But that's a good point...
THAT'S WHY, WHEN ASAKURA-KUN SUGGESTED IT, I REALLY WANTED TO GO.
I WAS HOPING YOU COULD ALL GET TO KNOW EACH OTHER BETTER.
...OH.
SO IT HAS NOTHING TO DO WITH MY LEG?
WHAT?!
Uh!
OF COURSE, YOUR RECOVERY IS MY FIRST PRIORITY!
SO THIS WAS ALL ABOUT YOU GETTING WHAT *YOU* WANT.
I see.
NO...!

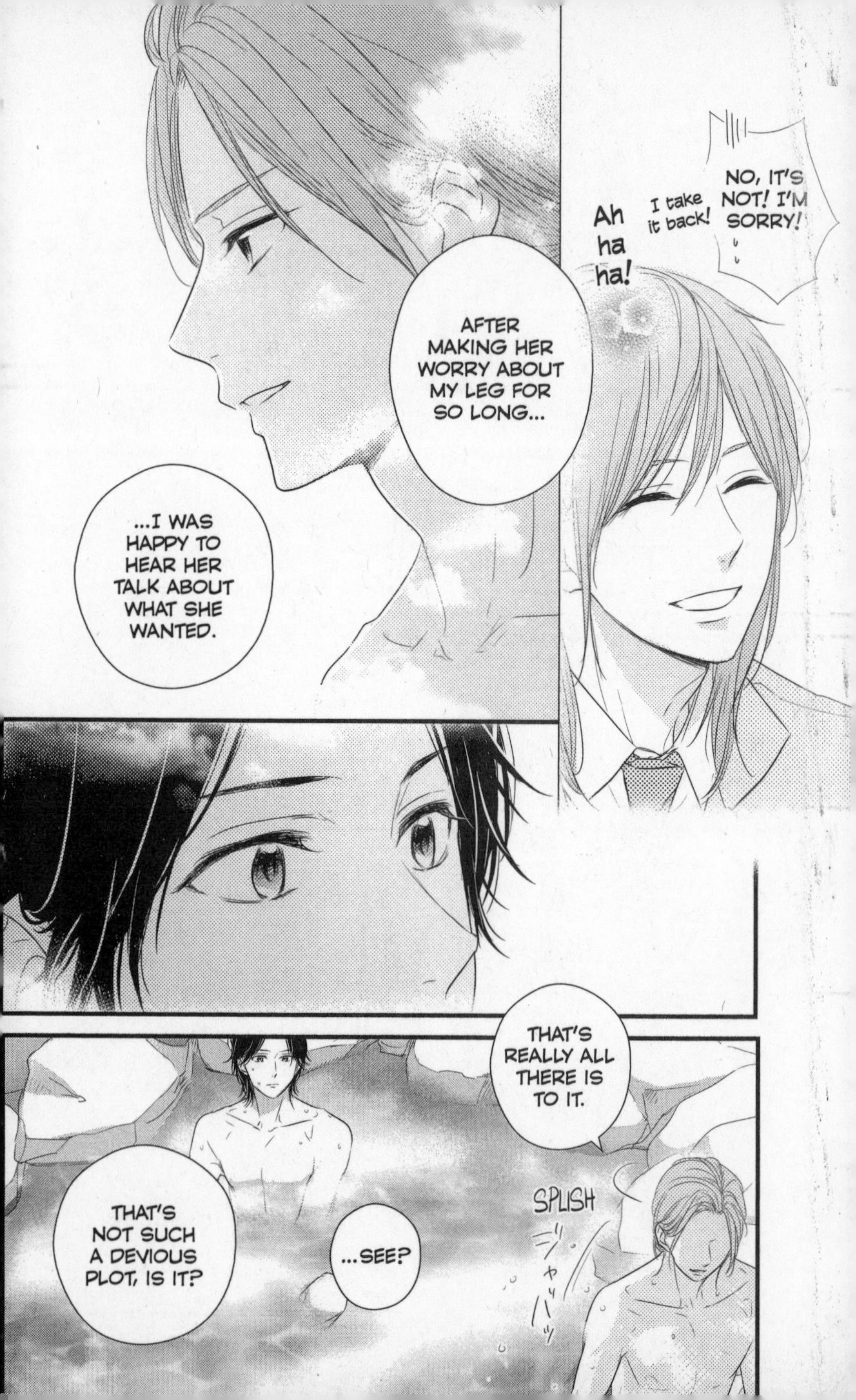
NO, IT'S NOT! I'M SORRY!
I take it back!
Ah ha ha!
AFTER MAKING HER WORRY ABOUT MY LEG FOR SO LONG...
...I WAS HAPPY TO HEAR HER TALK ABOUT WHAT SHE WANTED.
THAT'S REALLY ALL THERE IS TO IT.
SPLISH
...SEE?
THAT'S NOT SUCH A DEVIOUS PLOT, IS IT?

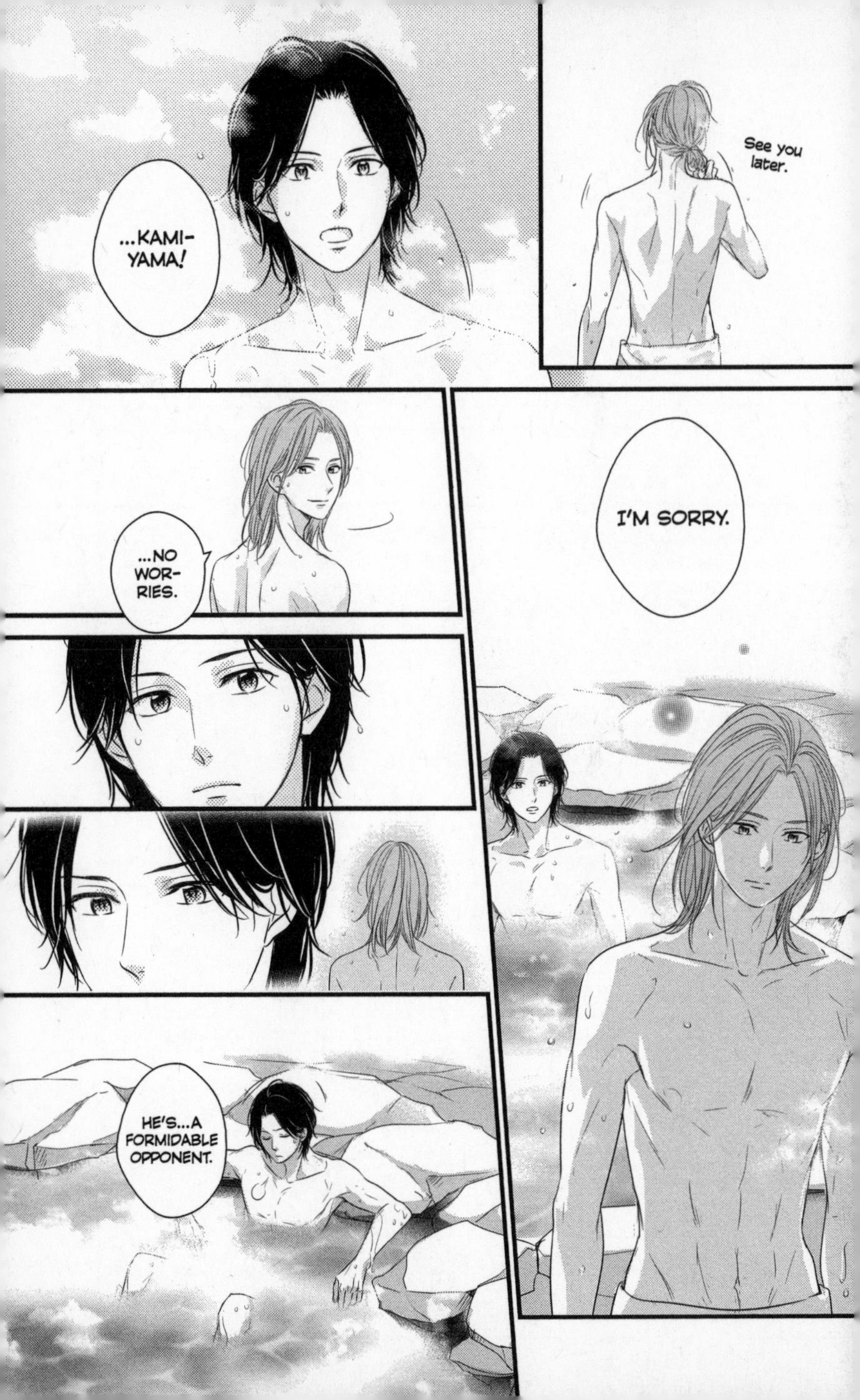
See you later.
...KAMI-YAMA!
I'M SORRY.
...NO WOR-RIES.
HE'S...A FORMIDABLE OPPONENT.

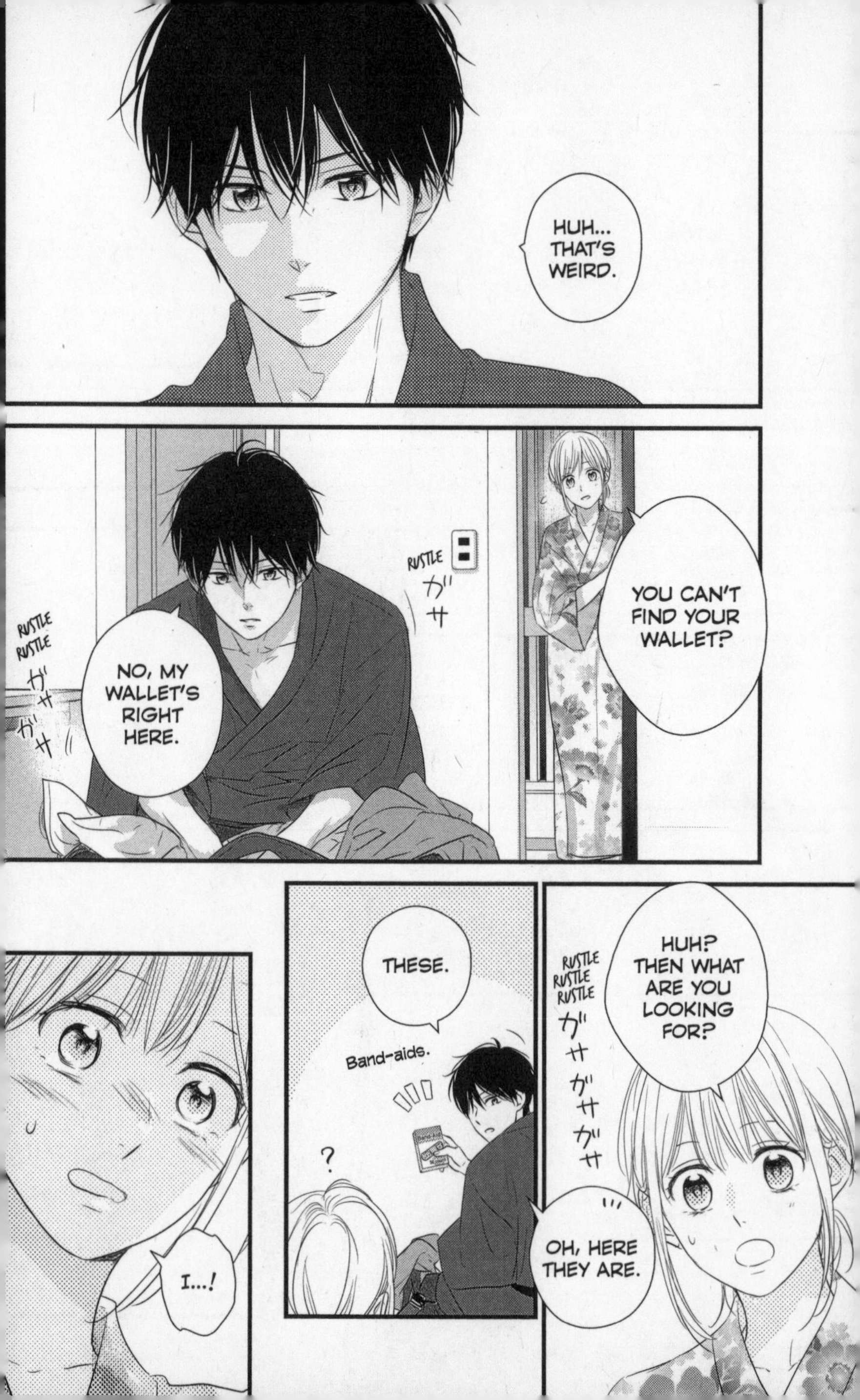
HUH... THAT'S WEIRD.
YOU CAN'T FIND YOUR WALLET?
RUSTLE
ガサ
NO, MY WALLET'S RIGHT HERE.
RUSTLE RUSTLE
ガサガサ
HUH? THEN WHAT ARE YOU LOOKING FOR?
RUSTLE RUSTLE RUSTLE
ガサガサガサ
OH, HERE THEY ARE.
THESE.
Band-aids.
?
I...!

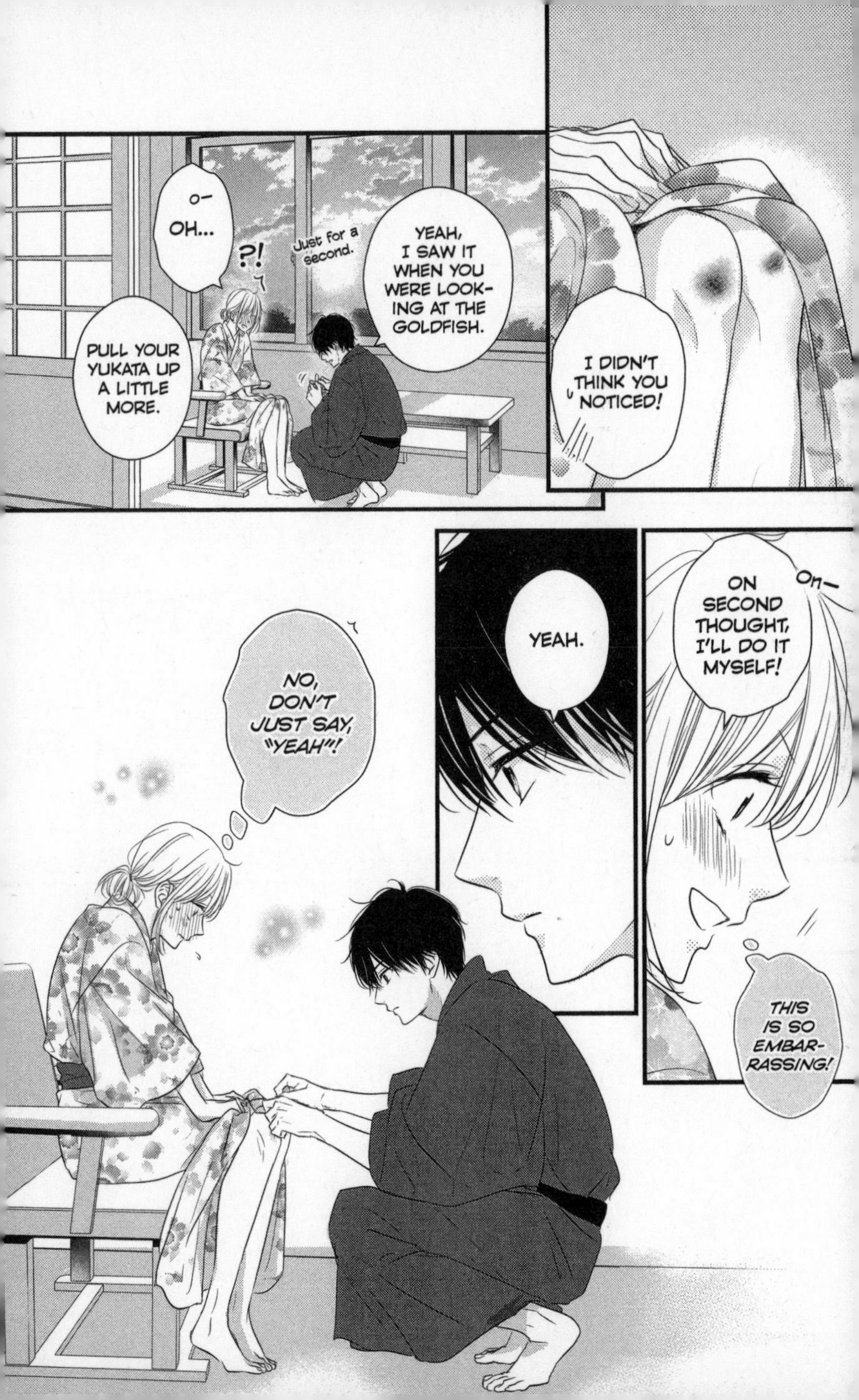
I DIDN'T THINK YOU NOTICED!
YEAH, I SAW IT WHEN YOU WERE LOOK-ING AT THE GOLDFISH.
Just for a second.
O- OH...
?!
PULL YOUR YUKATA UP A LITTLE MORE.
Oh—
ON SECOND THOUGHT, I'LL DO IT MYSELF!
THIS IS SO EMBAR-RASSING!
YEAH.
NO, DON'T JUST SAY, "YEAH"!

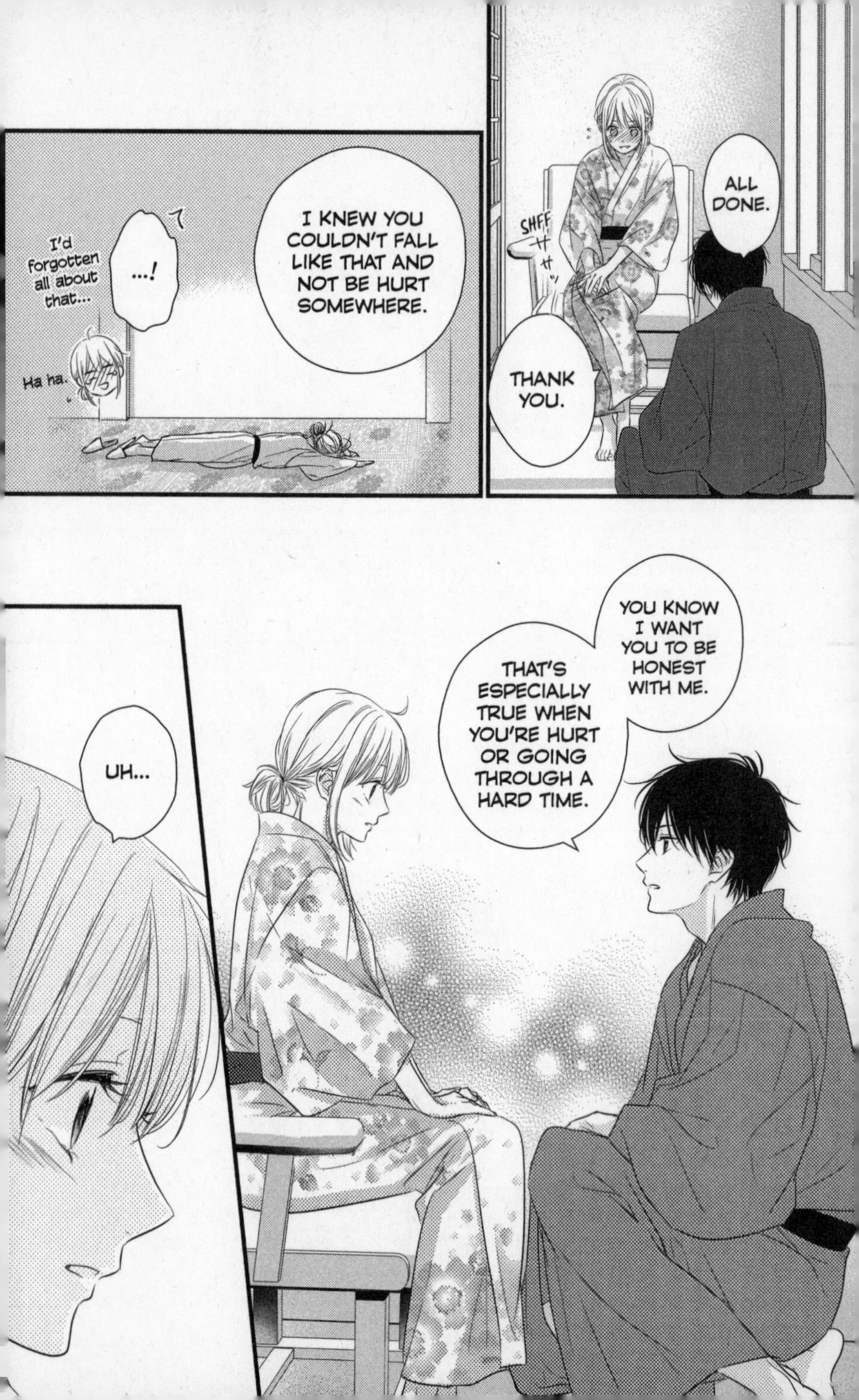
ALL DONE.
SHFF
THANK YOU.
I KNEW YOU COULDN'T FALL LIKE THAT AND NOT BE HURT SOMEWHERE.
...!
I'd forgotten all about that...
Ha ha.
YOU KNOW I WANT YOU TO BE HONEST WITH ME.
THAT'S ESPECIALLY TRUE WHEN YOU'RE HURT OR GOING THROUGH A HARD TIME.
UH...

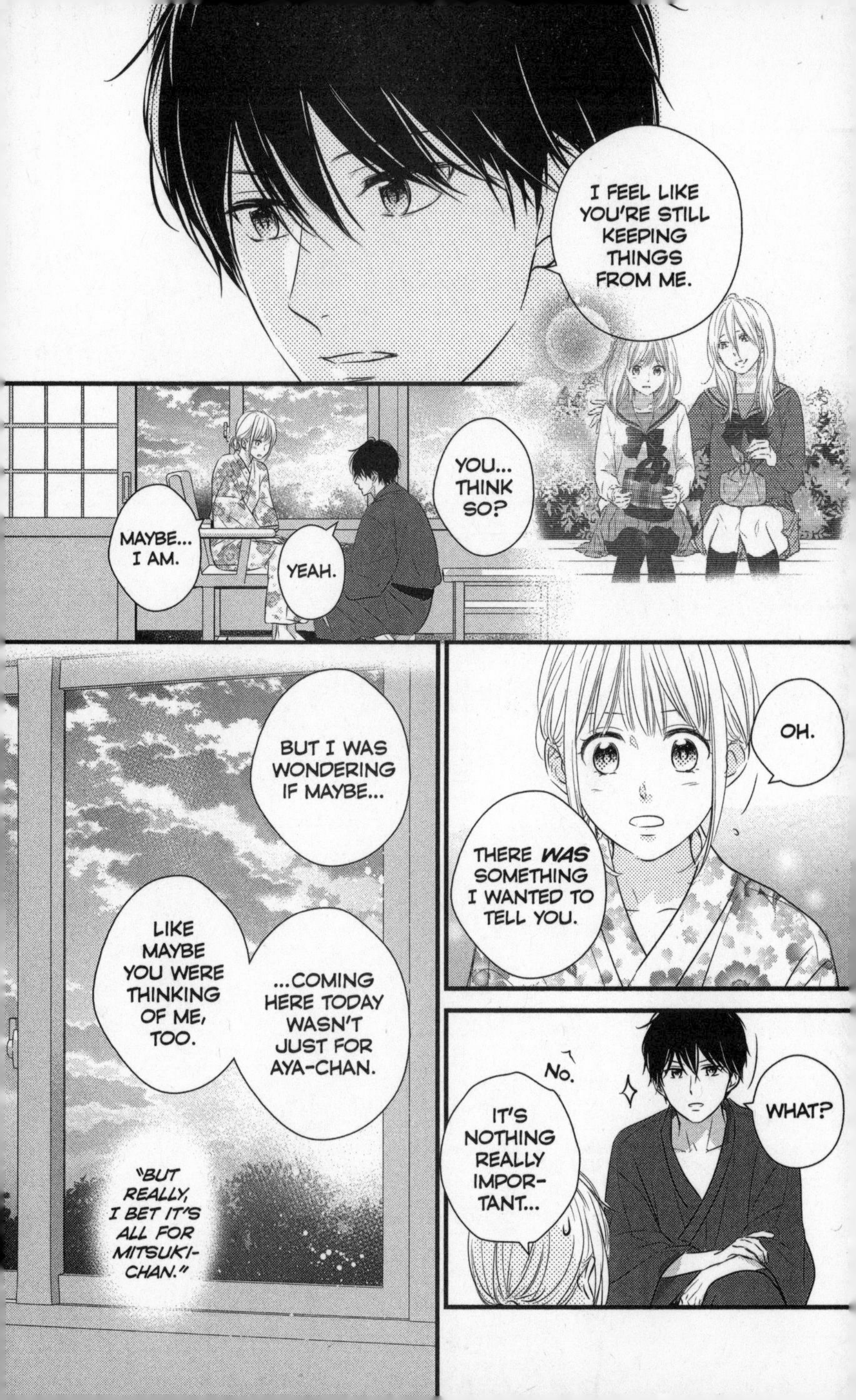
I FEEL LIKE YOU'RE STILL KEEPING THINGS FROM ME.
YOU... THINK SO?
YEAH.
MAYBE... I AM.
OH.
THERE *WAS* SOMETHING I WANTED TO TELL YOU.
WHAT?
No.
IT'S NOTHING REALLY IMPOR-TANT...
BUT I WAS WONDERING IF MAYBE...
...COMING HERE TODAY WASN'T JUST FOR AYA-CHAN.
LIKE MAYBE YOU WERE THINKING OF ME, TOO.
"BUT REALLY, I BET IT'S ALL FOR MITSUKI-CHAN."

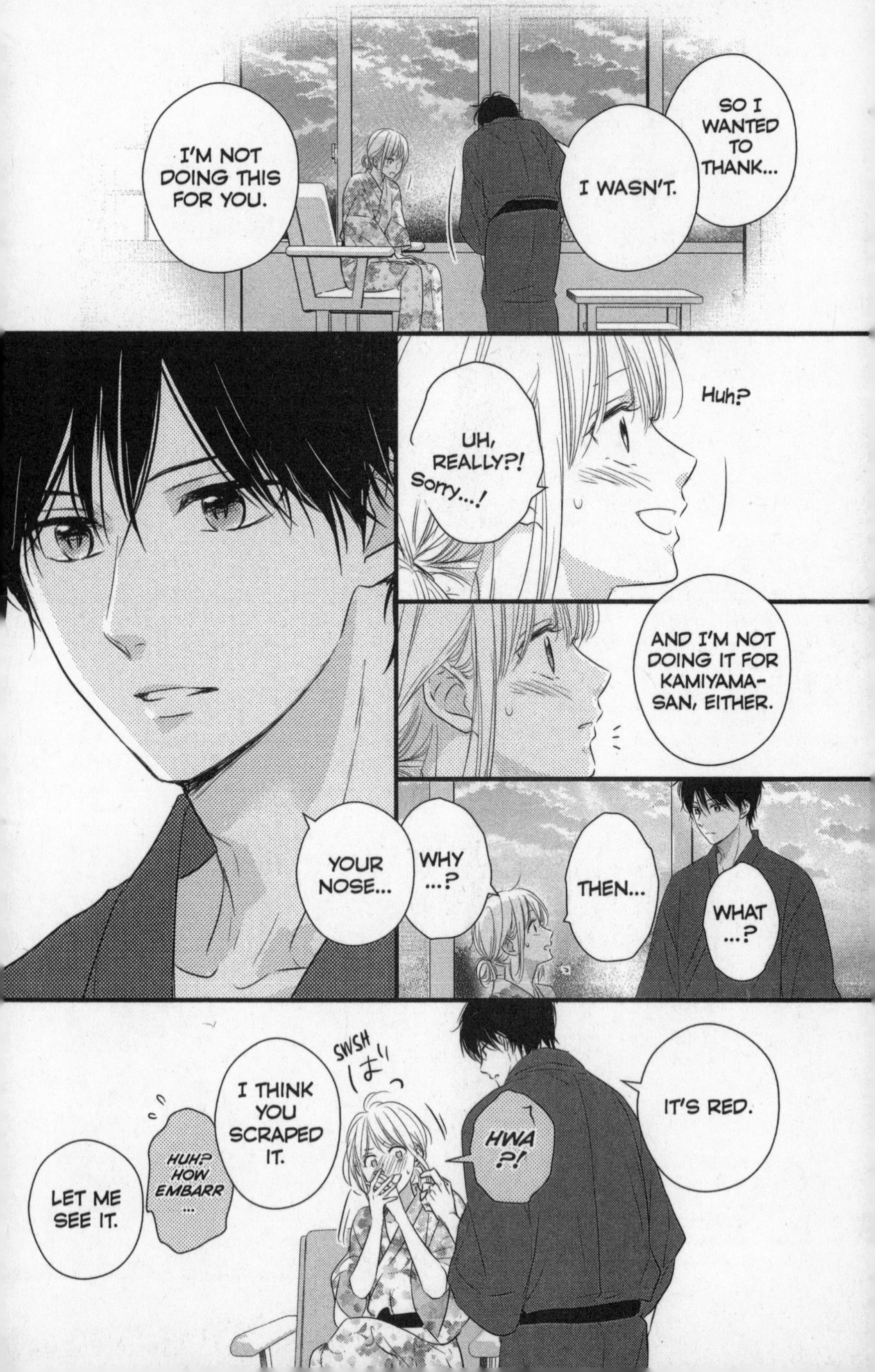
SO I WANTED TO THANK...
I WASN'T.
I'M NOT DOING THIS FOR YOU.
Huh?
UH, REALLY?! Sorry...!
AND I'M NOT DOING IT FOR KAMIYAMA-SAN, EITHER.
WHAT ...?
THEN...
WHY ...?
YOUR NOSE...
IT'S RED.
HWA ?!
SWSH
I THINK YOU SCRAPED IT.
HUH? HOW EMBARR ...
LET ME SEE IT.

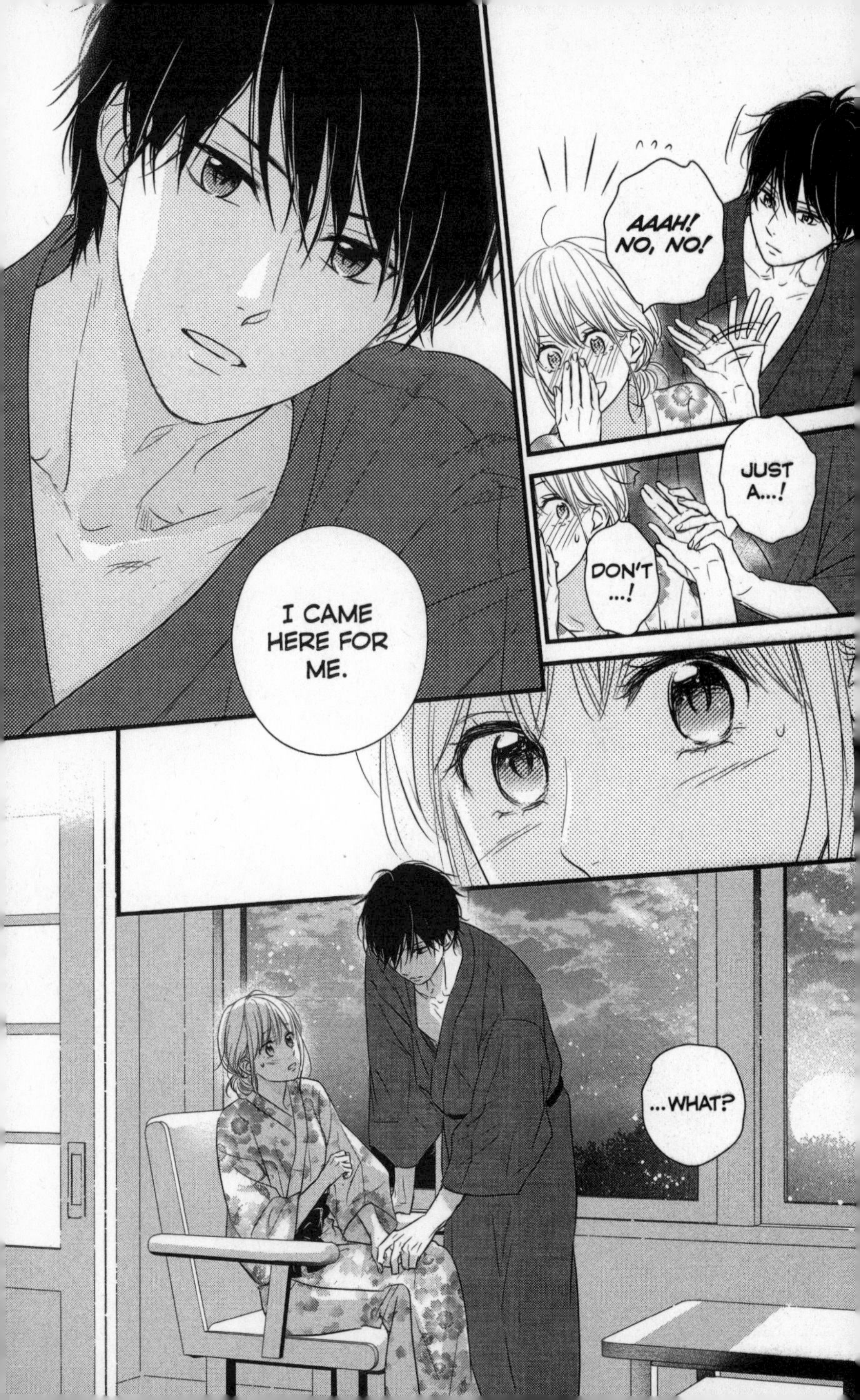
AAAH! NO, NO!
JUST A...!
DON'T ...!
I CAME HERE FOR ME.
...WHAT?

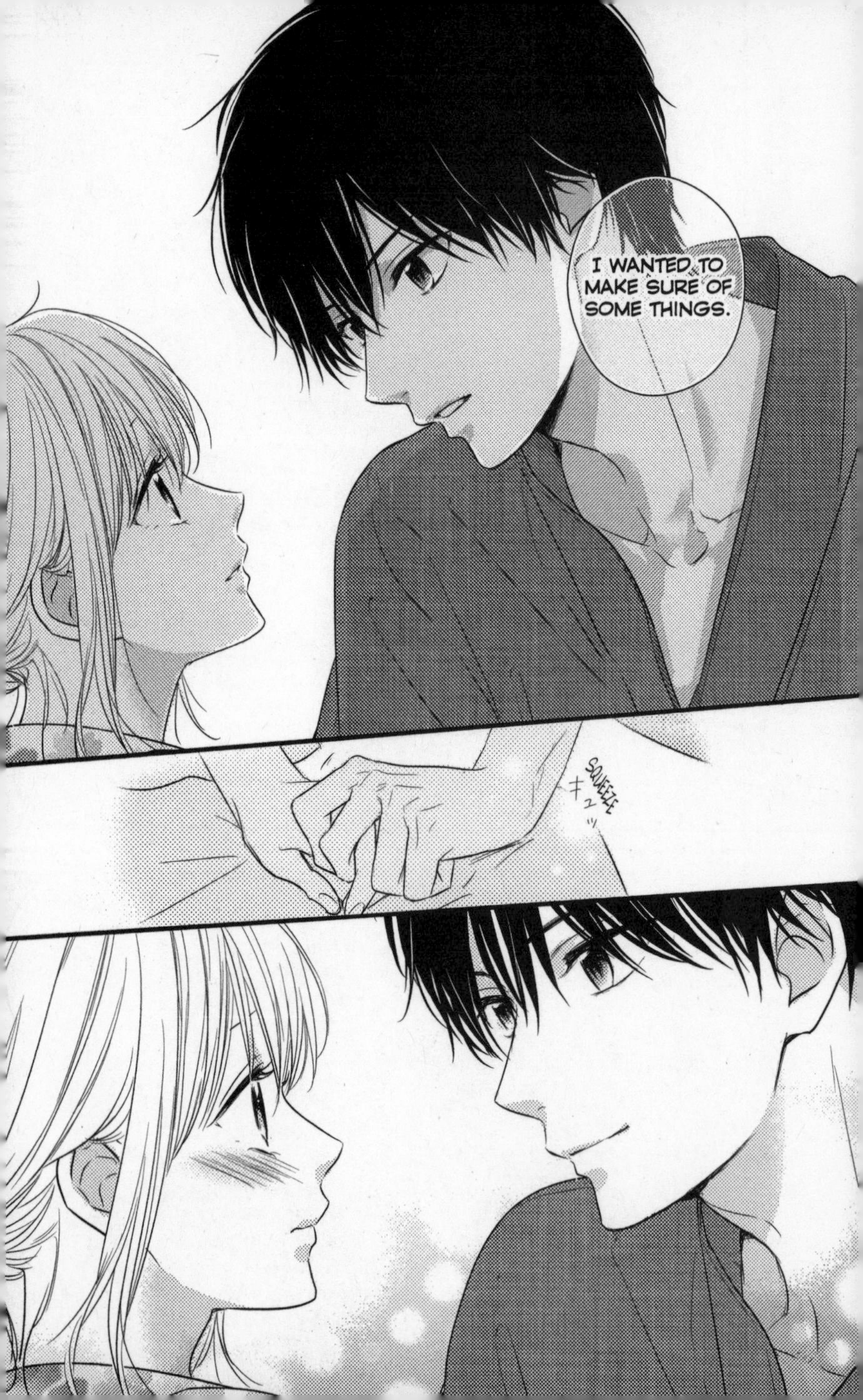
I WANTED TO MAKE SURE OF SOME THINGS.
SQUEEZE
キュッ

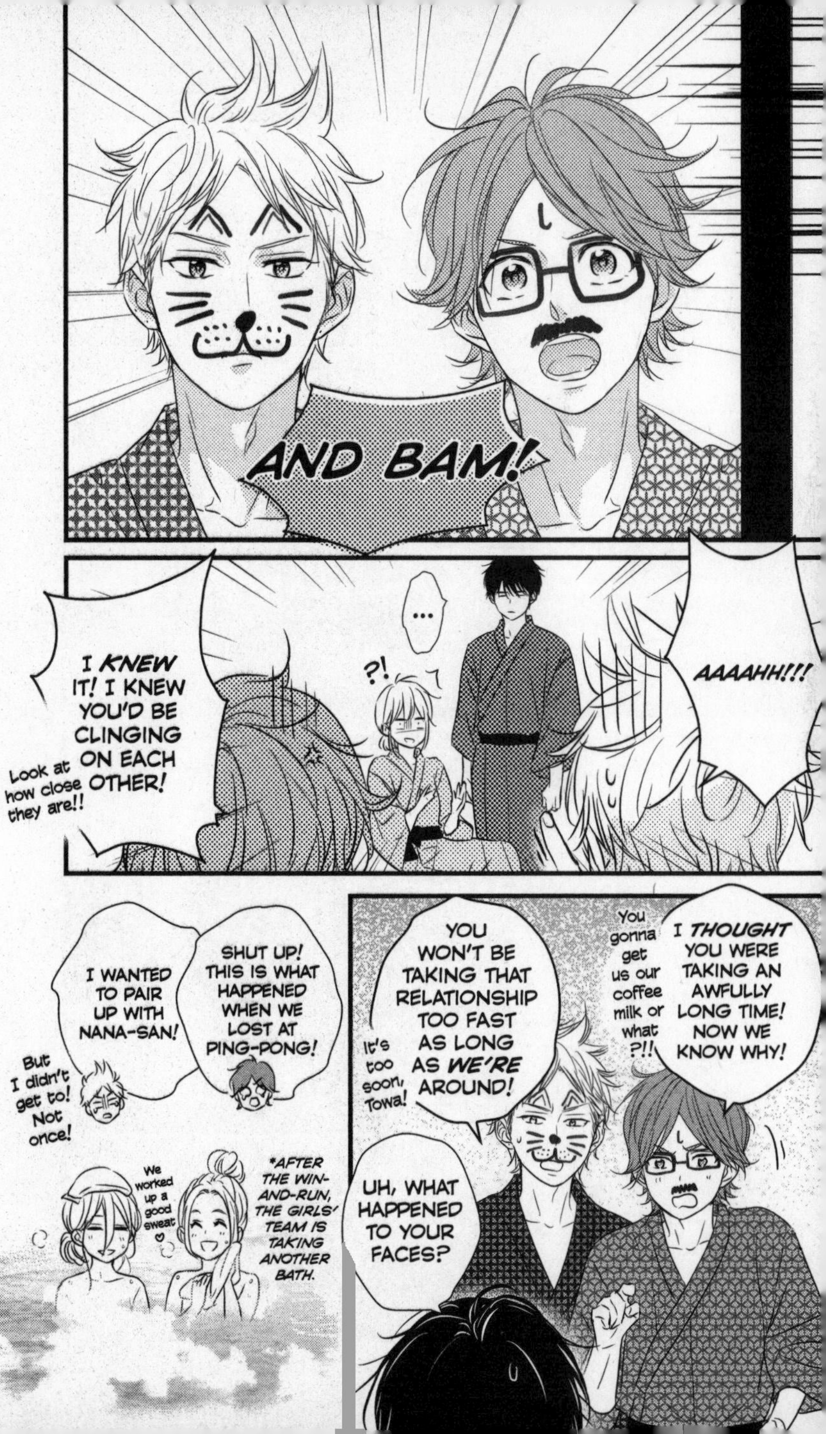
AND BAM!
AAAAHH!!!
...
?!
I KNEW IT! I KNEW YOU'D BE CLINGING ON EACH OTHER!
Look at how close they are!!
I THOUGHT YOU WERE TAKING AN AWFULLY LONG TIME! NOW WE KNOW WHY!
You gonna get us our coffee milk or what?!!
YOU WON'T BE TAKING THAT RELATIONSHIP TOO FAST AS LONG AS WE'RE AROUND!
It's too soon, Towa!
UH, WHAT HAPPENED TO YOUR FACES?
SHUT UP! THIS IS WHAT HAPPENED WHEN WE LOST AT PING-PONG!
I WANTED TO PAIR UP WITH NANA-SAN!
But I didn't get to! Not once!
*AFTER THE WIN-AND-RUN, THE GIRLS' TEAM IS TAKING ANOTHER BATH.
We worked up a good sweat ♡

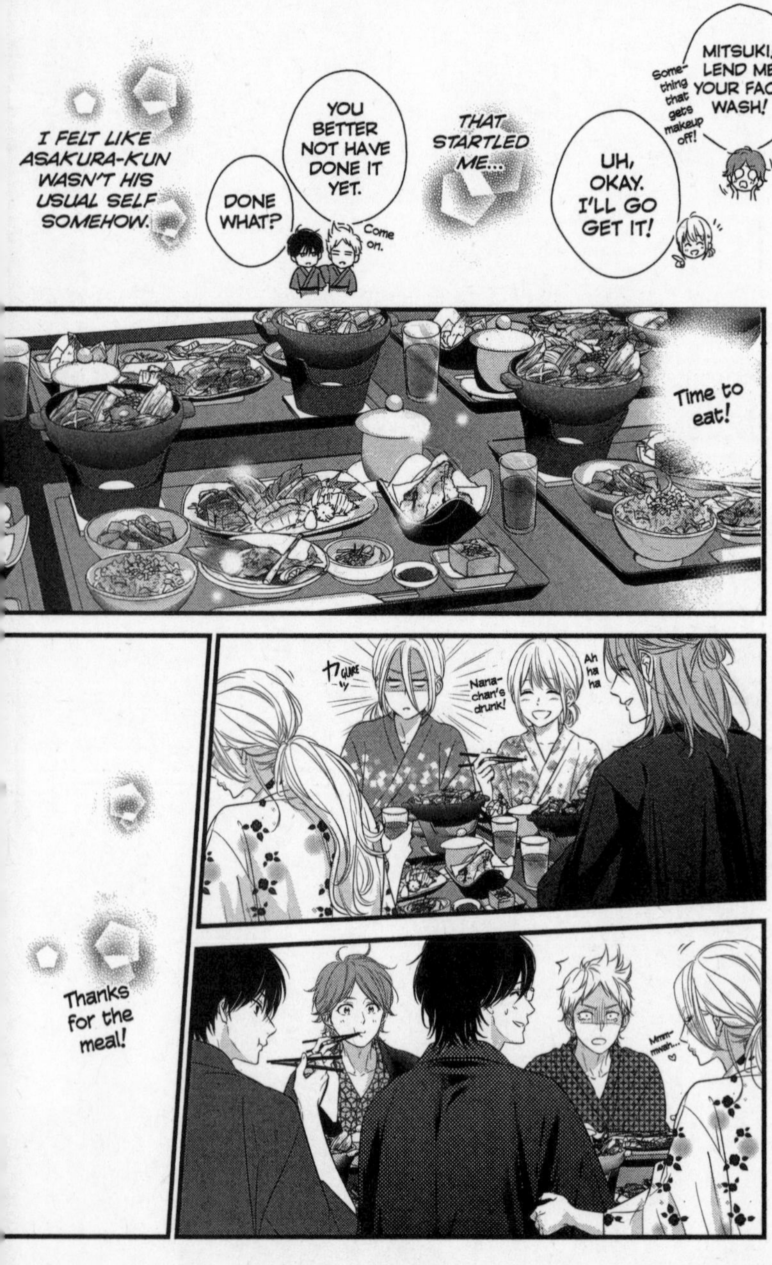
MITSUKI! LEND ME YOUR FACE WASH!
Something that gets makeup off!
UH, OKAY. I'LL GO GET IT!
THAT STARTLED ME...
YOU BETTER NOT HAVE DONE IT YET.
Come on.
DONE WHAT?
I FELT LIKE ASAKURA-KUN WASN'T HIS USUAL SELF SOMEHOW.
Time to eat!
Ah ha ha
Nana-chan's drunk!
GURE
Mmm-mwah♡
Thanks for the meal!

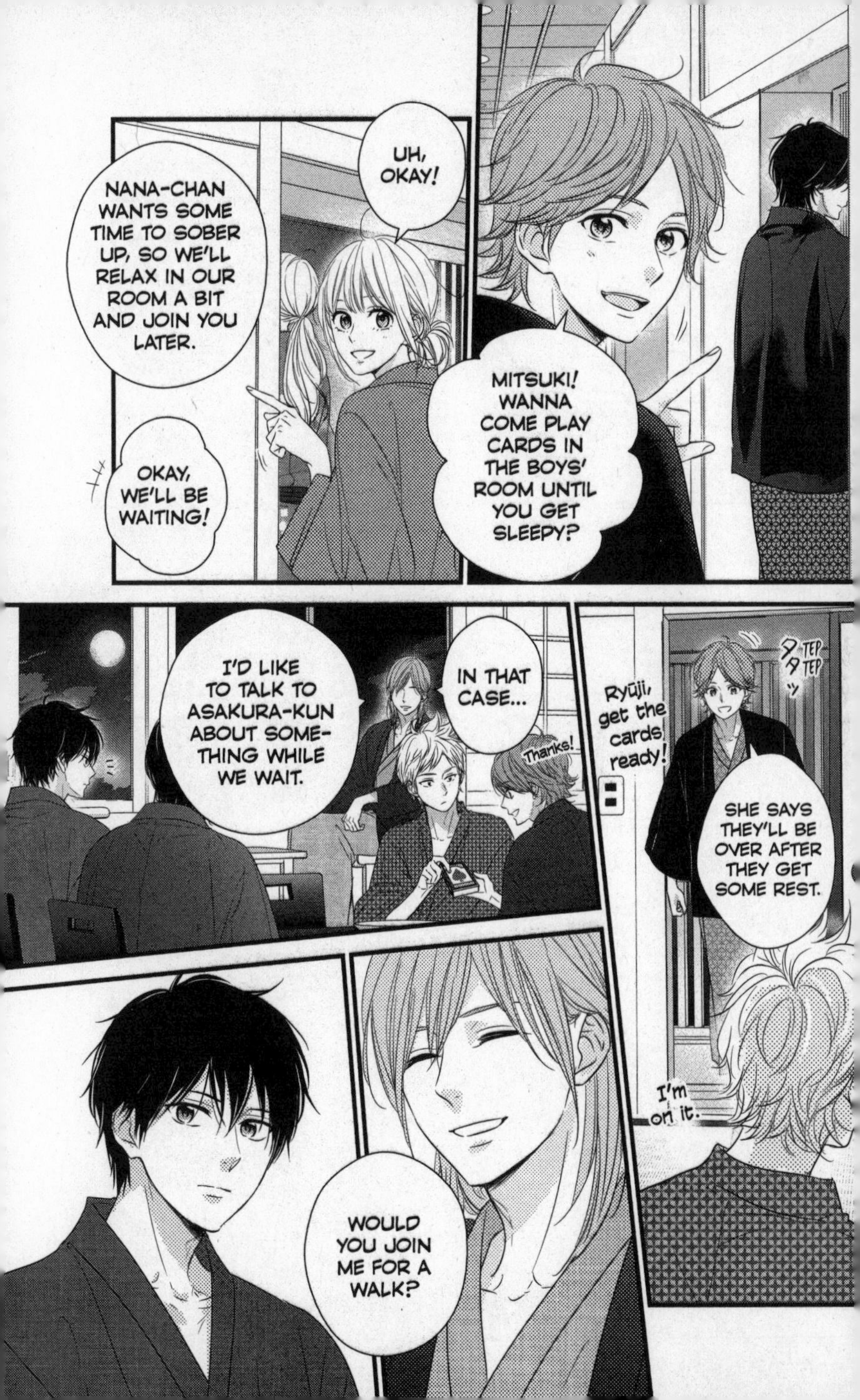
MITSUKI! WANNA COME PLAY CARDS IN THE BOYS' ROOM UNTIL YOU GET SLEEPY?
UH, OKAY!
NANA-CHAN WANTS SOME TIME TO SOBER UP, SO WE'LL RELAX IN OUR ROOM A BIT AND JOIN YOU LATER.
OKAY, WE'LL BE WAITING!
タタッ TEP TEP
Ryūji, get the cards ready!
SHE SAYS THEY'LL BE OVER AFTER THEY GET SOME REST.
I'm on it.
IN THAT CASE...
Thanks!
I'D LIKE TO TALK TO ASAKURA-KUN ABOUT SOME-THING WHILE WE WAIT.
WOULD YOU JOIN ME FOR A WALK?

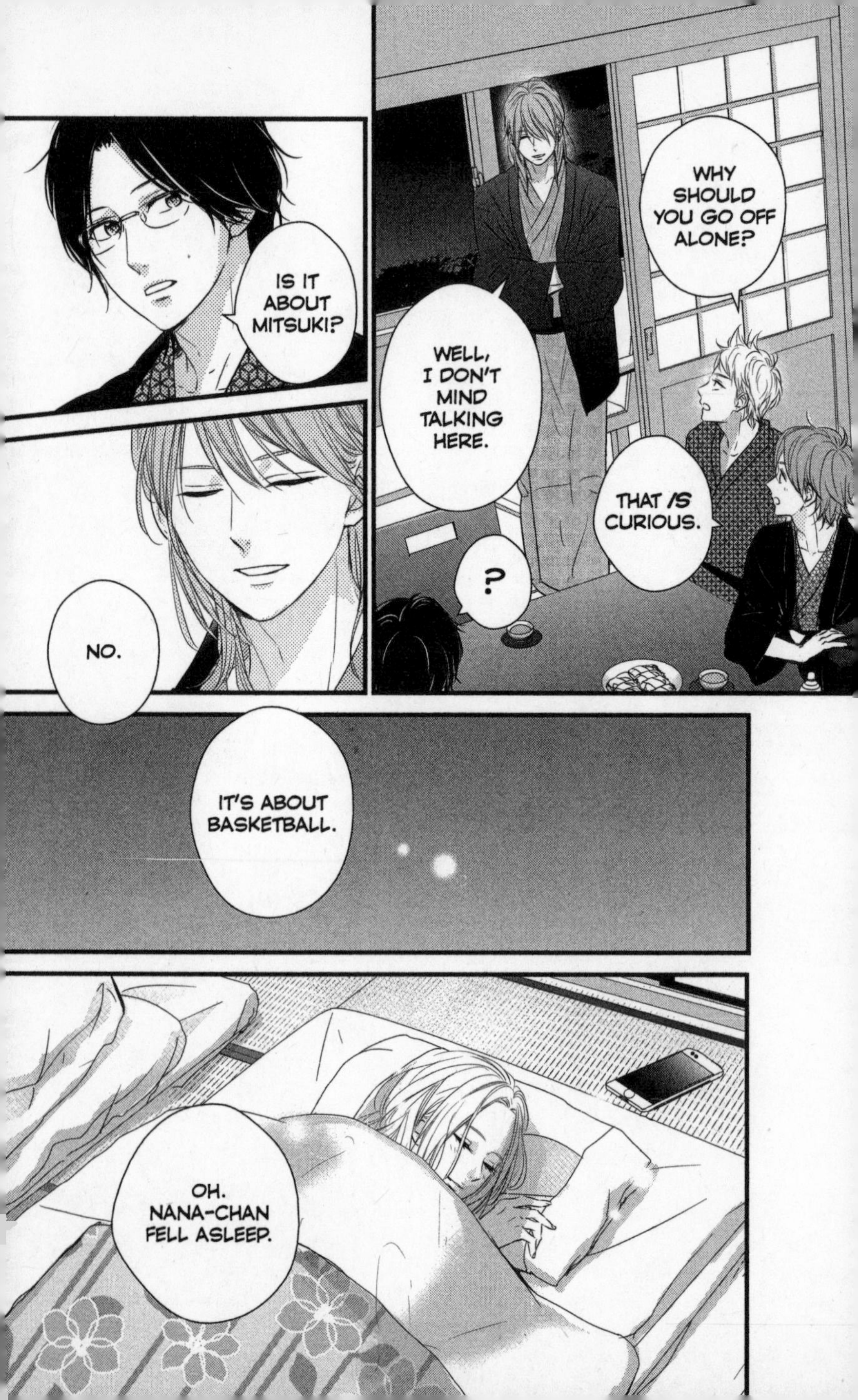
WHY SHOULD YOU GO OFF ALONE?
WELL, I DON'T MIND TALKING HERE.
THAT IS CURIOUS.
?
IS IT ABOUT MITSUKI?
NO.
IT'S ABOUT BASKETBALL.
OH. NANA-CHAN FELL ASLEEP.

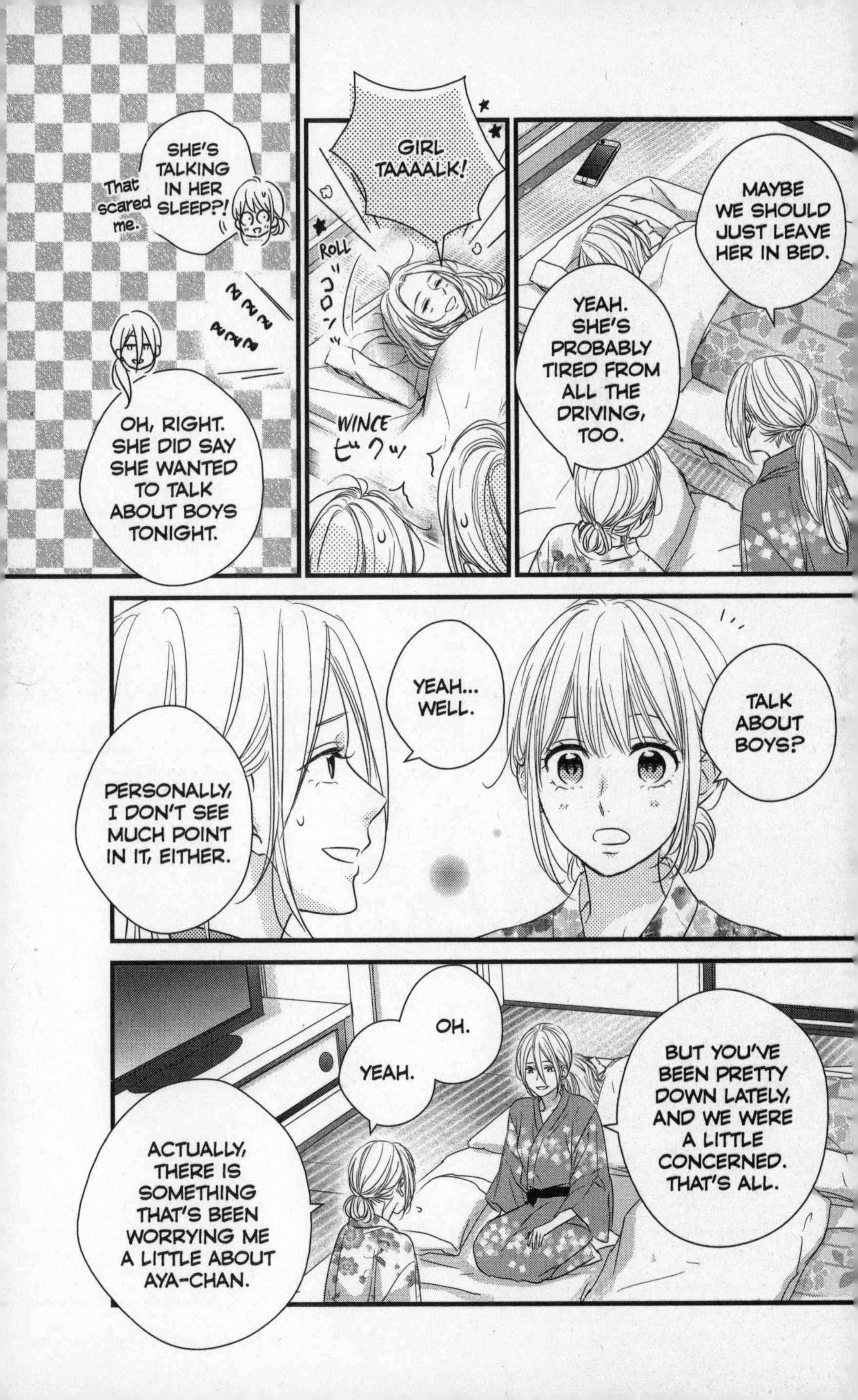
MAYBE WE SHOULD JUST LEAVE HER IN BED.
YEAH. SHE'S PROBABLY TIRED FROM ALL THE DRIVING, TOO.
GIRL TAAAALK!
ROLL
ゴロン
WINCE
ビクッ
SHE'S TALKING IN HER SLEEP?!
That scared me.
OH, RIGHT. SHE DID SAY SHE WANTED TO TALK ABOUT BOYS TONIGHT.
TALK ABOUT BOYS?
YEAH... WELL.
PERSONALLY, I DON'T SEE MUCH POINT IN IT, EITHER.
BUT YOU'VE BEEN PRETTY DOWN LATELY, AND WE WERE A LITTLE CONCERNED. THAT'S ALL.
OH.
YEAH.
ACTUALLY, THERE IS SOMETHING THAT'S BEEN WORRYING ME A LITTLE ABOUT AYA-CHAN.

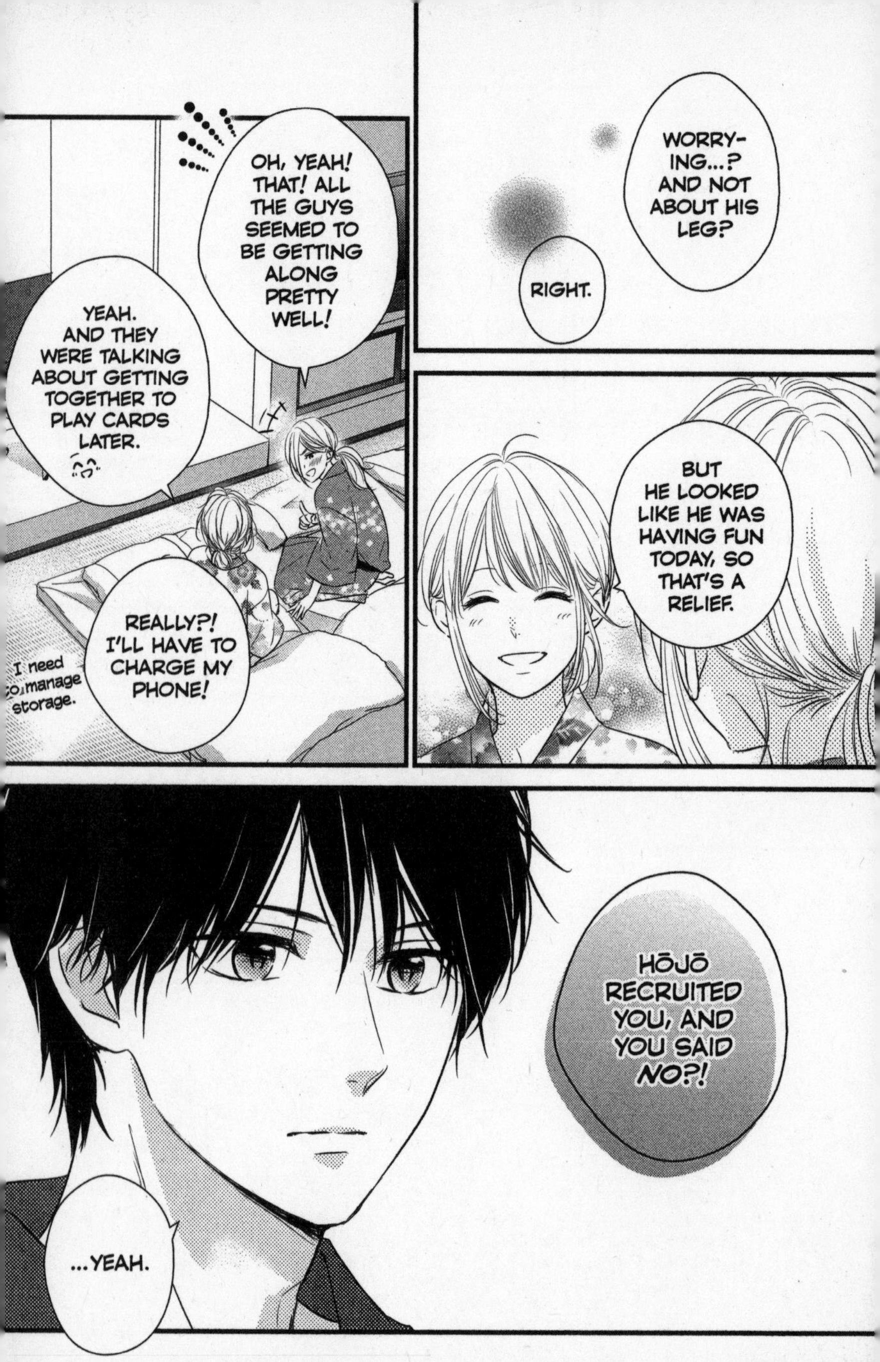
WORRYING...? AND NOT ABOUT HIS LEG?
RIGHT.
BUT HE LOOKED LIKE HE WAS HAVING FUN TODAY, SO THAT'S A RELIEF.
OH, YEAH! THAT! ALL THE GUYS SEEMED TO BE GETTING ALONG PRETTY WELL!
YEAH. AND THEY WERE TALKING ABOUT GETTING TOGETHER TO PLAY CARDS LATER.
REALLY?! I'LL HAVE TO CHARGE MY PHONE!
I need to manage storage.
HŌJŌ RECRUITED YOU, AND YOU SAID NO?!
...YEAH.

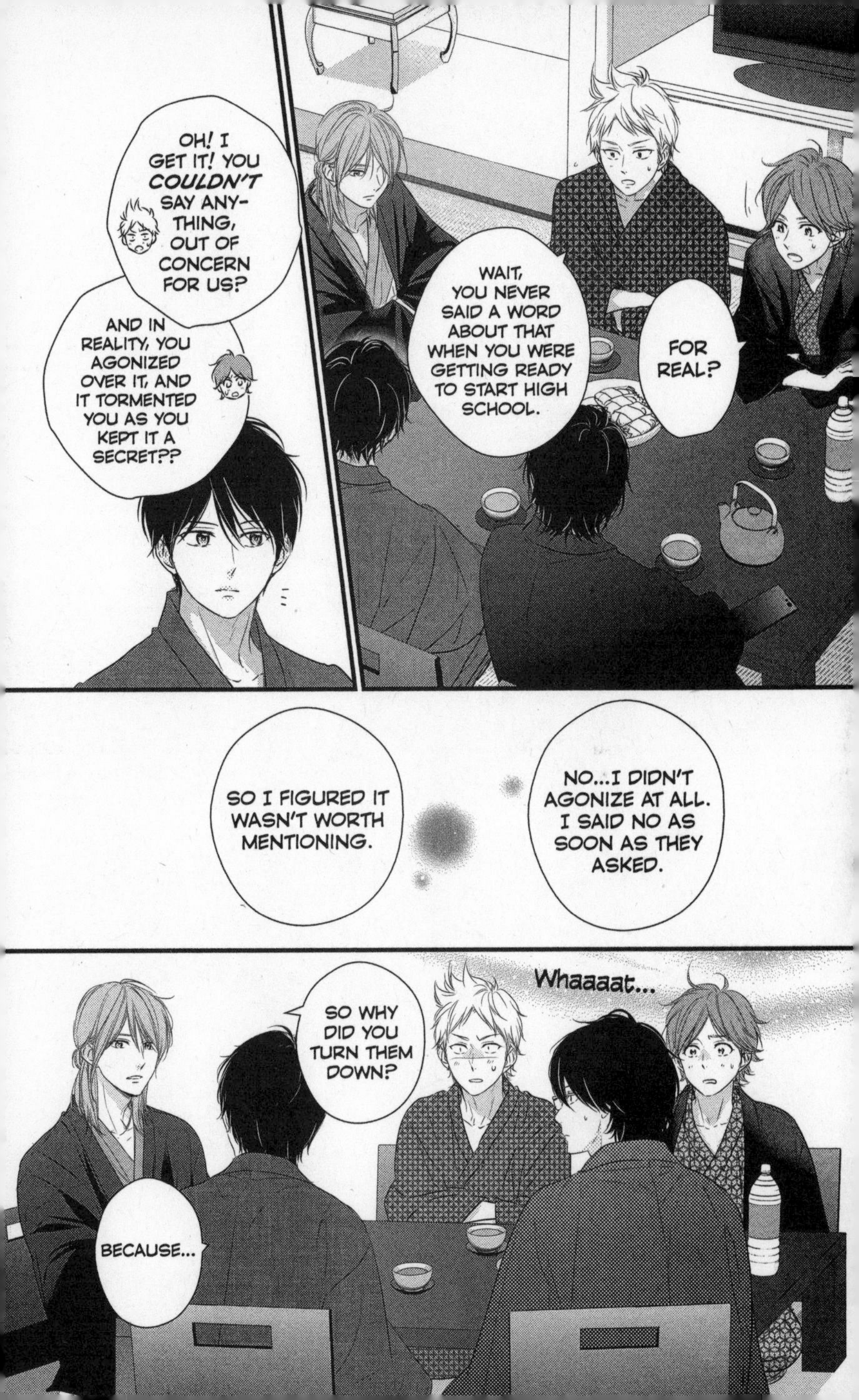
FOR REAL?
WAIT, YOU NEVER SAID A WORD ABOUT THAT WHEN YOU WERE GETTING READY TO START HIGH SCHOOL.
OH! I GET IT! YOU *COULDN'T* SAY ANYTHING, OUT OF CONCERN FOR US?
AND IN REALITY, YOU AGONIZED OVER IT, AND IT TORMENTED YOU AS YOU KEPT IT A SECRET??
NO...I DIDN'T AGONIZE AT ALL. I SAID NO AS SOON AS THEY ASKED.
SO I FIGURED IT WASN'T WORTH MENTIONING.
Whaaaat...
SO WHY DID YOU TURN THEM DOWN?
BECAUSE...

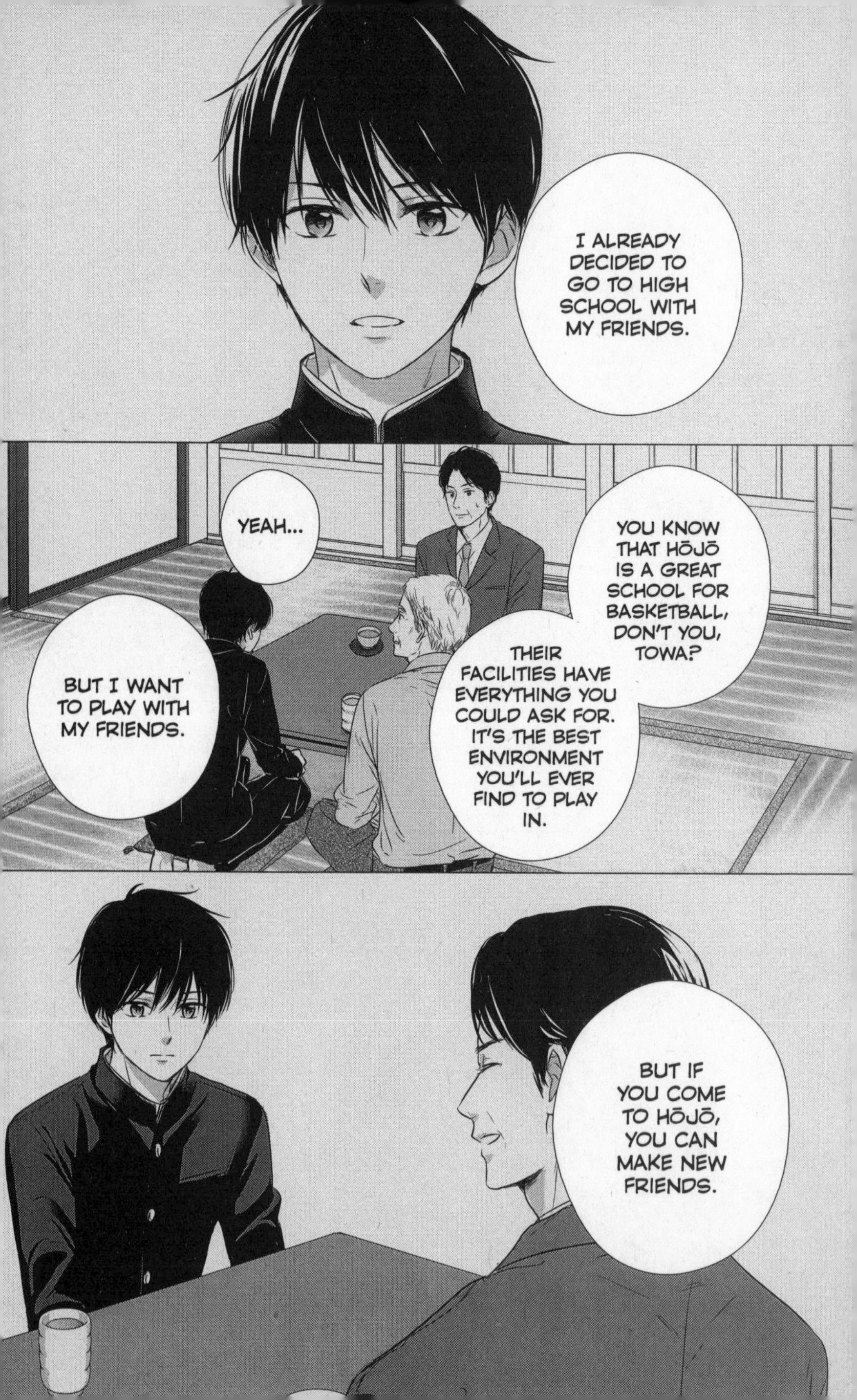
I ALREADY DECIDED TO GO TO HIGH SCHOOL WITH MY FRIENDS.
YOU KNOW THAT HŌJŌ IS A GREAT SCHOOL FOR BASKETBALL, DON'T YOU, TOWA?
YEAH...
THEIR FACILITIES HAVE EVERYTHING YOU COULD ASK FOR. IT'S THE BEST ENVIRONMENT YOU'LL EVER FIND TO PLAY IN.
BUT I WANT TO PLAY WITH MY FRIENDS.
BUT IF YOU COME TO HŌJŌ, YOU CAN MAKE NEW FRIENDS.

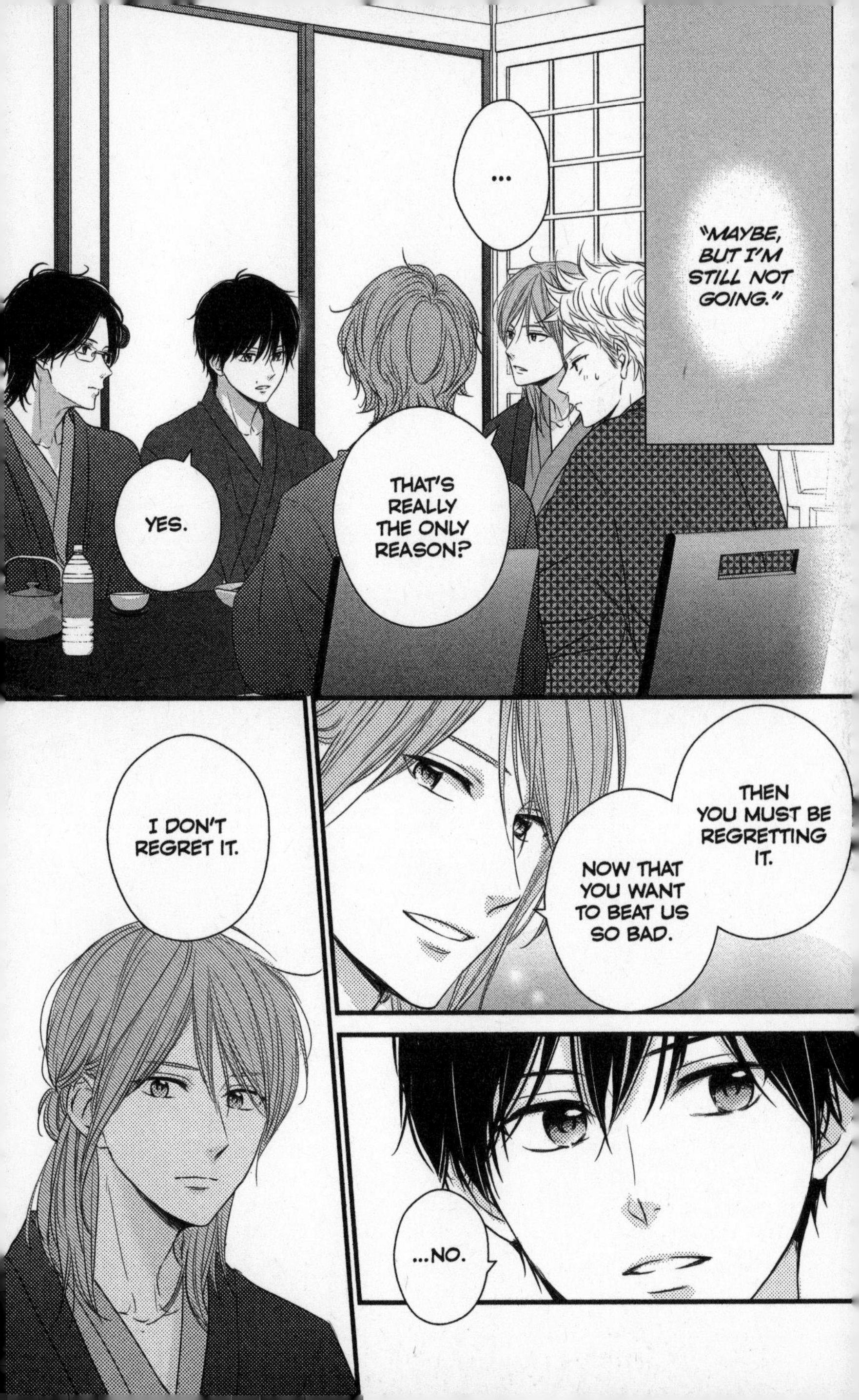
"MAYBE, BUT I'M STILL NOT GOING."
...
THAT'S REALLY THE ONLY REASON?
YES.
THEN YOU MUST BE REGRETTING IT.
NOW THAT YOU WANT TO BEAT US SO BAD.
...NO.
I DON'T REGRET IT.

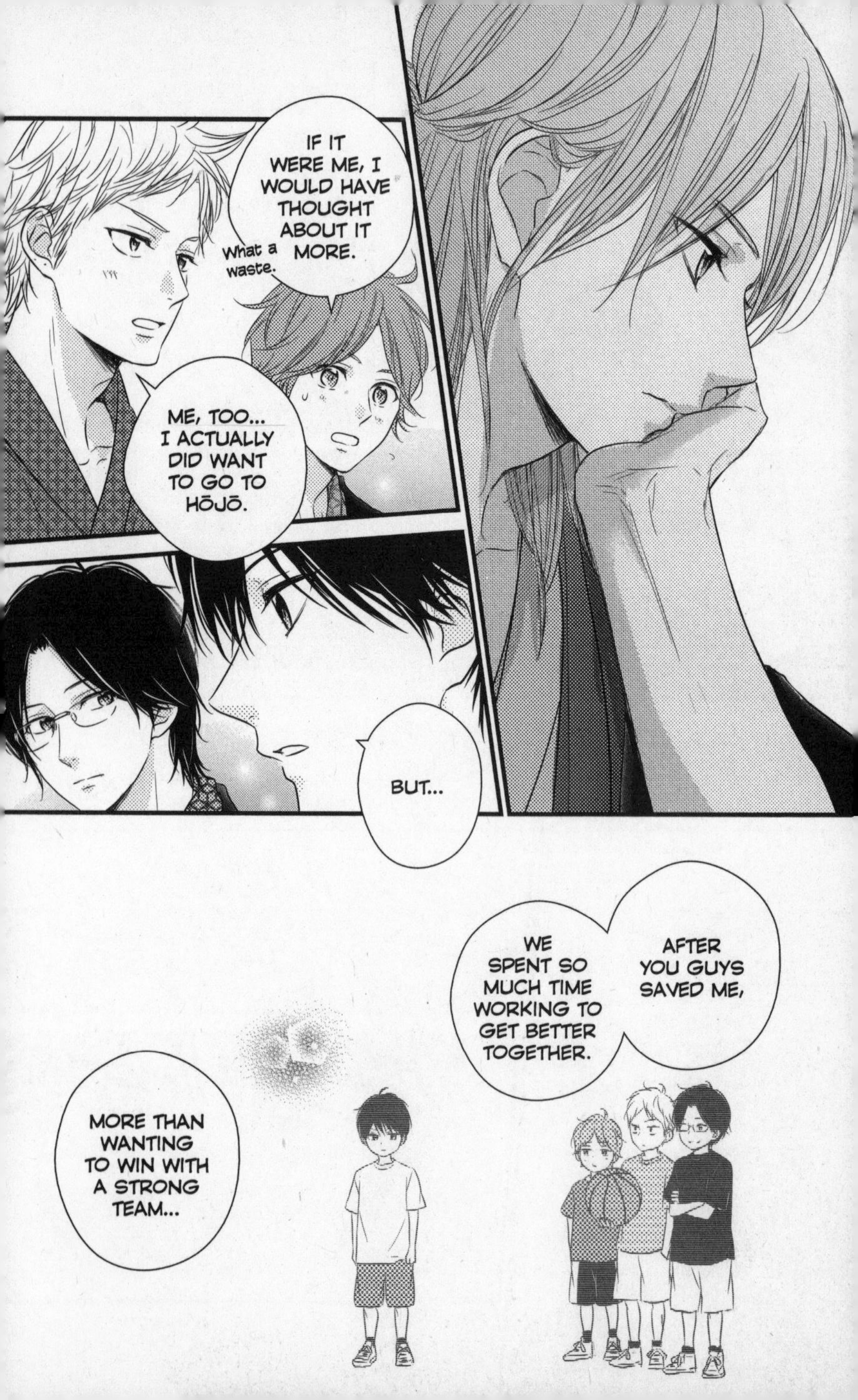
IF IT WERE ME, I WOULD HAVE THOUGHT ABOUT IT MORE.
What a waste.
ME, TOO... I ACTUALLY DID WANT TO GO TO HŌJŌ.
BUT...
AFTER YOU GUYS SAVED ME,
WE SPENT SO MUCH TIME WORKING TO GET BETTER TOGETHER.
MORE THAN WANTING TO WIN WITH A STRONG TEAM...

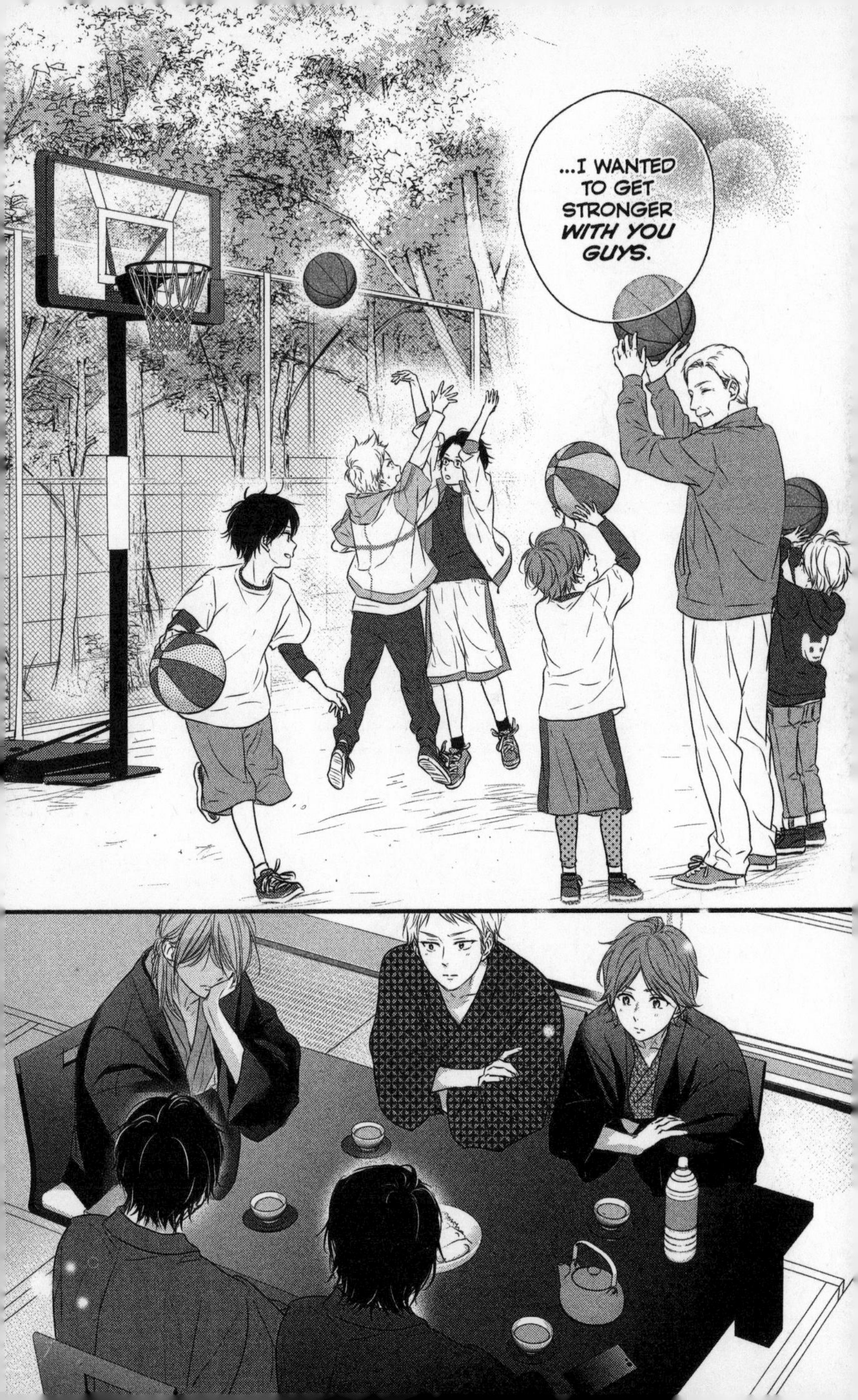
...I WANTED TO GET STRONGER *WITH YOU GUYS.*

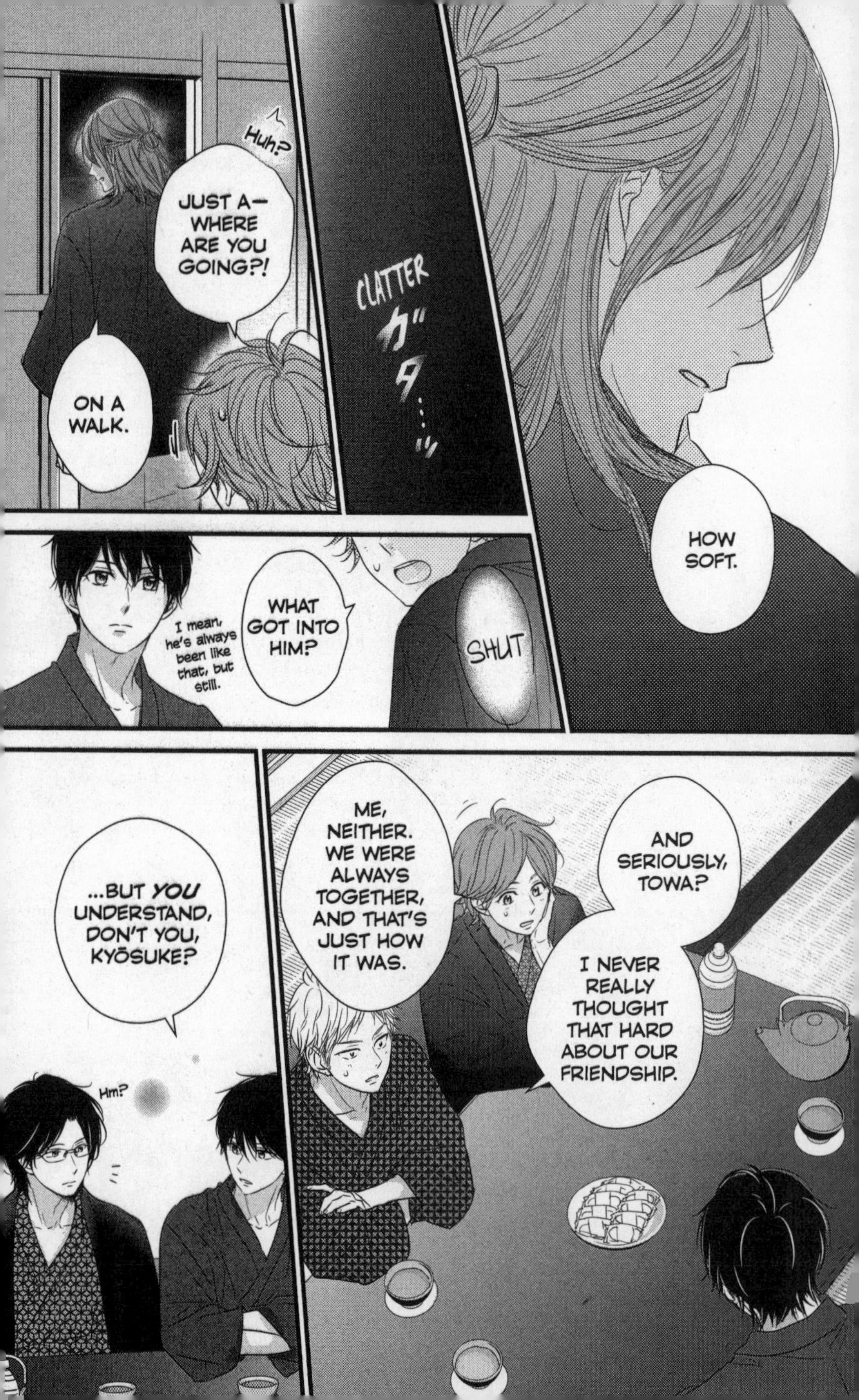

HOW SOFT.
CLATTER
ガタ…ッ
Huh?
へ
JUST A— WHERE ARE YOU GOING?!
ON A WALK.
SHUT
WHAT GOT INTO HIM?
I mean, he's always been like that, but still.
AND SERIOUSLY, TOWA?
I NEVER REALLY THOUGHT THAT HARD ABOUT OUR FRIENDSHIP.
ME, NEITHER. WE WERE ALWAYS TOGETHER, AND THAT'S JUST HOW IT WAS.
...BUT *YOU* UNDERSTAND, DON'T YOU, KYŌSUKE?
Hm?

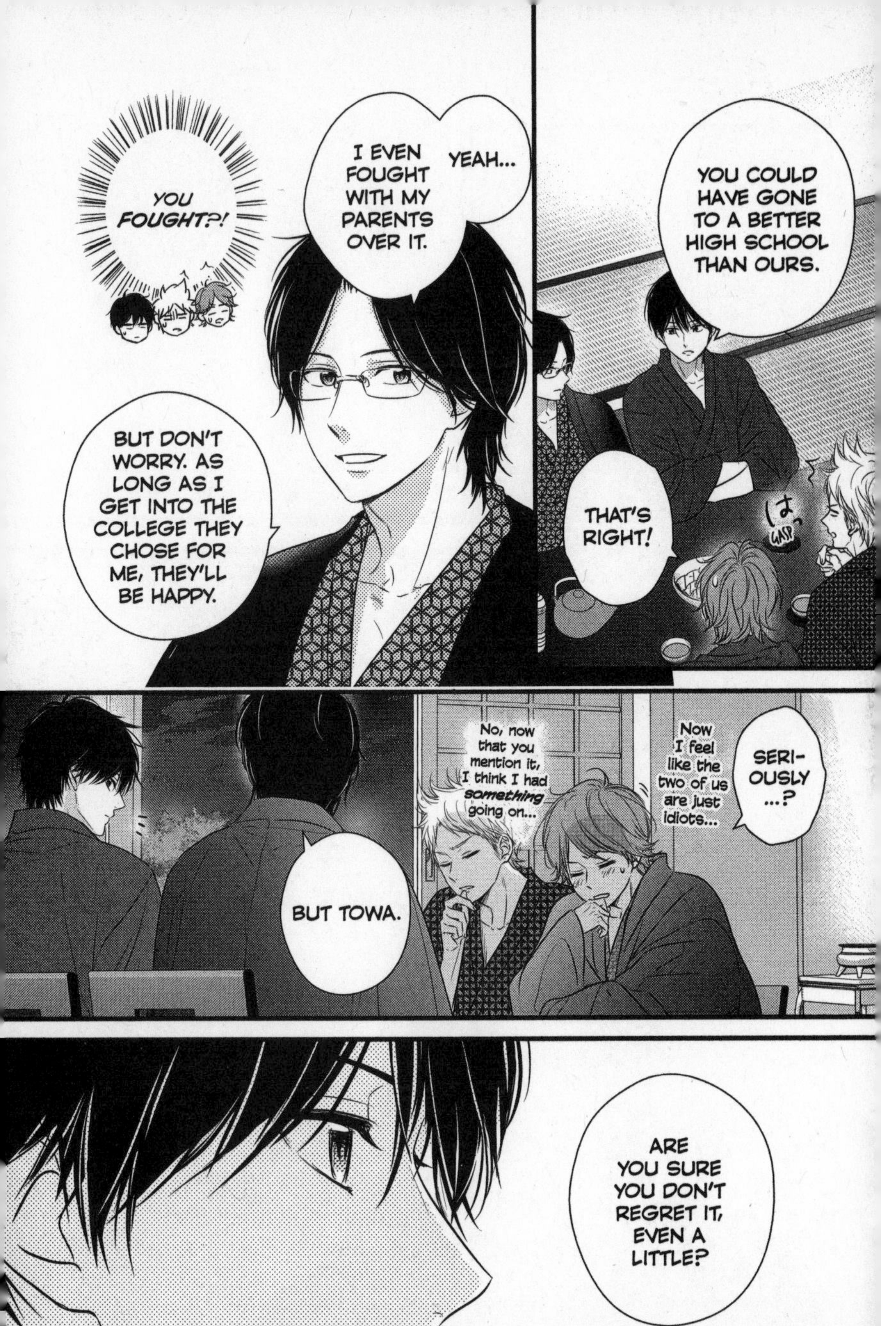
YOU COULD HAVE GONE TO A BETTER HIGH SCHOOL THAN OURS.
THAT'S RIGHT!
は GASP
YEAH...
I EVEN FOUGHT WITH MY PARENTS OVER IT.
YOU *FOUGHT*?!
BUT DON'T WORRY. AS LONG AS I GET INTO THE COLLEGE THEY CHOSE FOR ME, THEY'LL BE HAPPY.
SERI-OUSLY ...?
Now I feel like the two of us are just idiots...
No, now that you mention it, I think I had *something* going on...
BUT TOWA.
ARE YOU SURE YOU DON'T REGRET IT, EVEN A LITTLE?

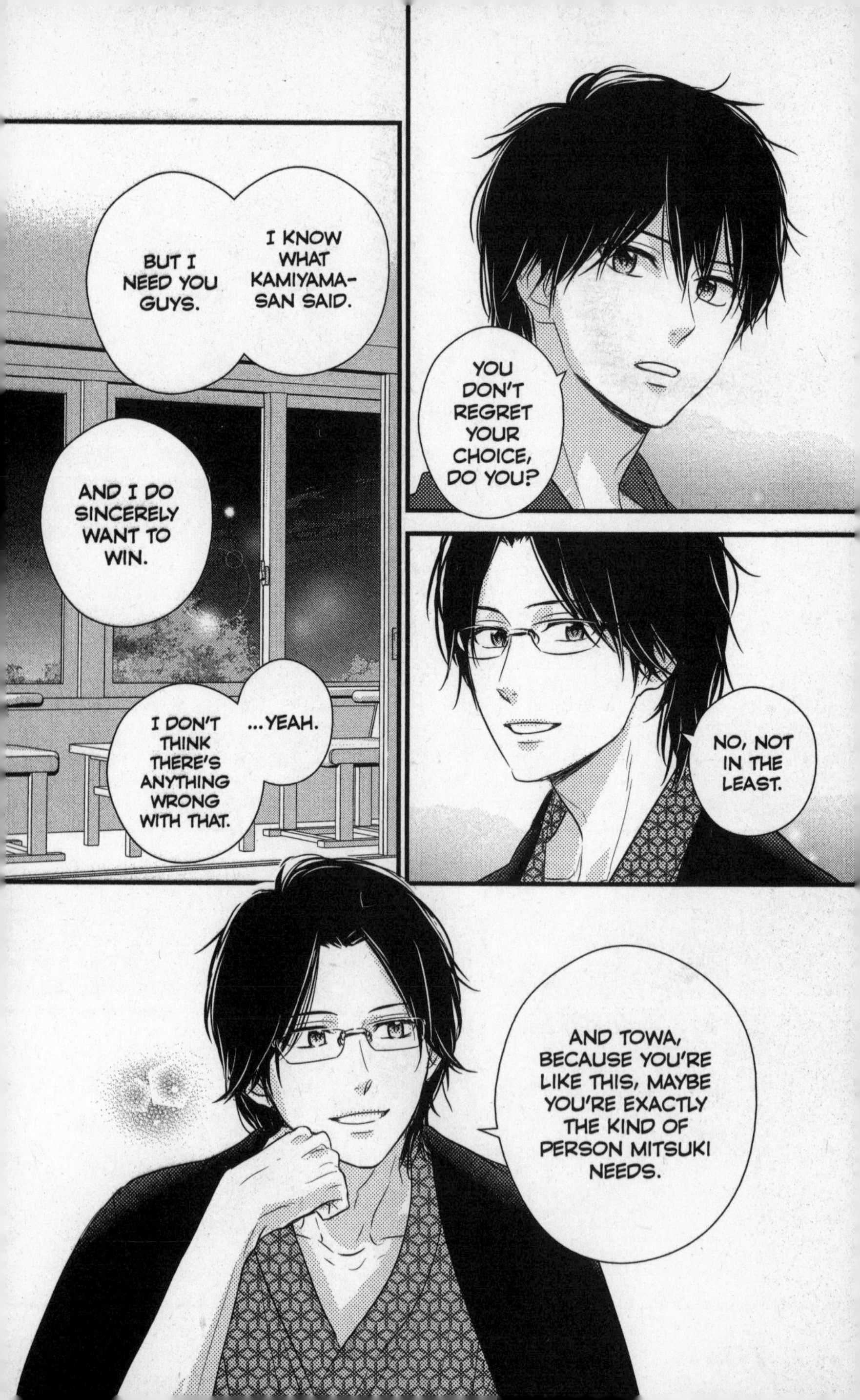
YOU DON'T REGRET YOUR CHOICE, DO YOU?
NO, NOT IN THE LEAST.
I KNOW WHAT KAMIYAMA-SAN SAID.
BUT I NEED YOU GUYS.
AND I DO SINCERELY WANT TO WIN.
...YEAH.
I DON'T THINK THERE'S ANYTHING WRONG WITH THAT.
AND TOWA, BECAUSE YOU'RE LIKE THIS, MAYBE YOU'RE EXACTLY THE KIND OF PERSON MITSUKI NEEDS.

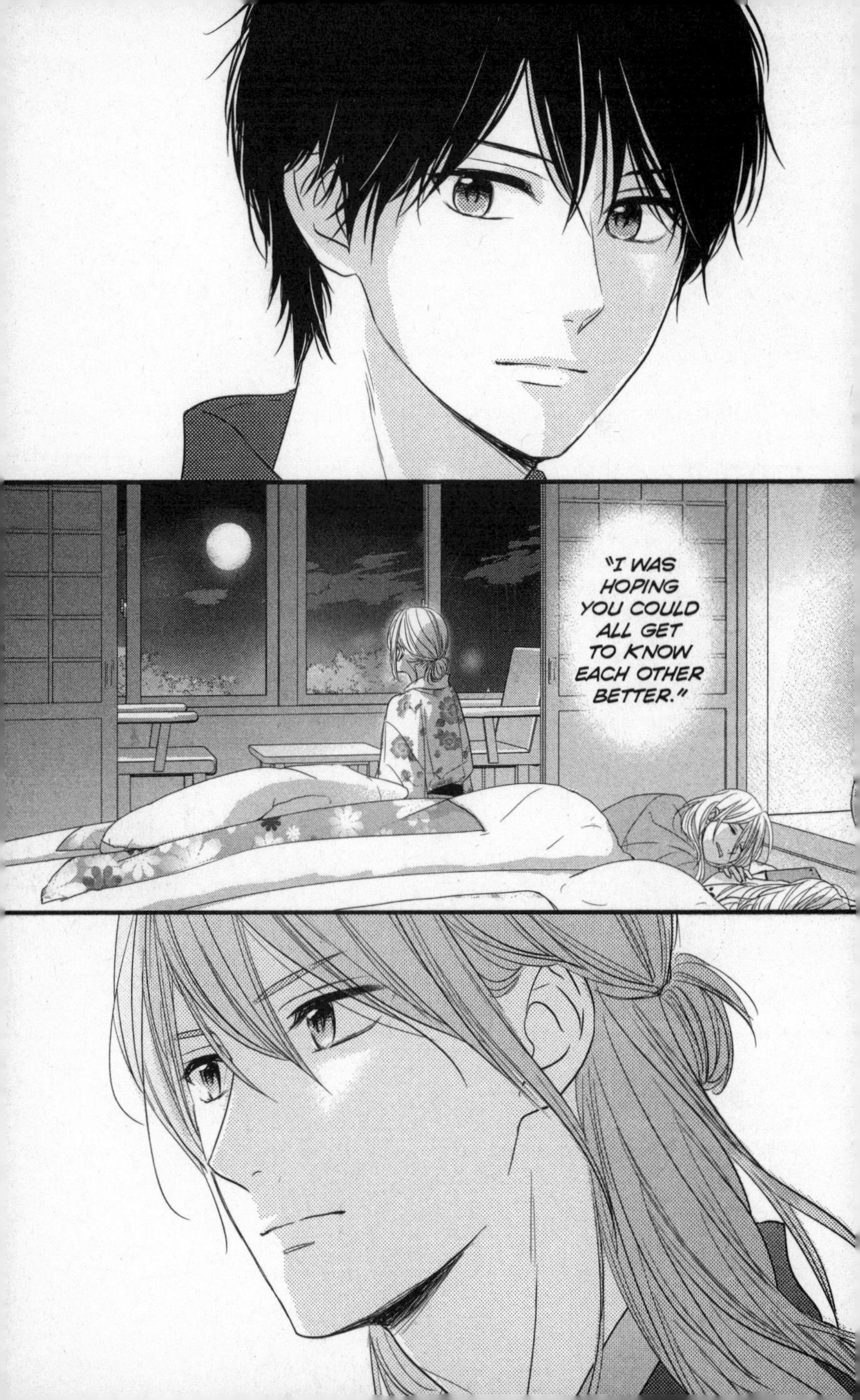
"I WAS HOPING YOU COULD ALL GET TO KNOW EACH OTHER BETTER."

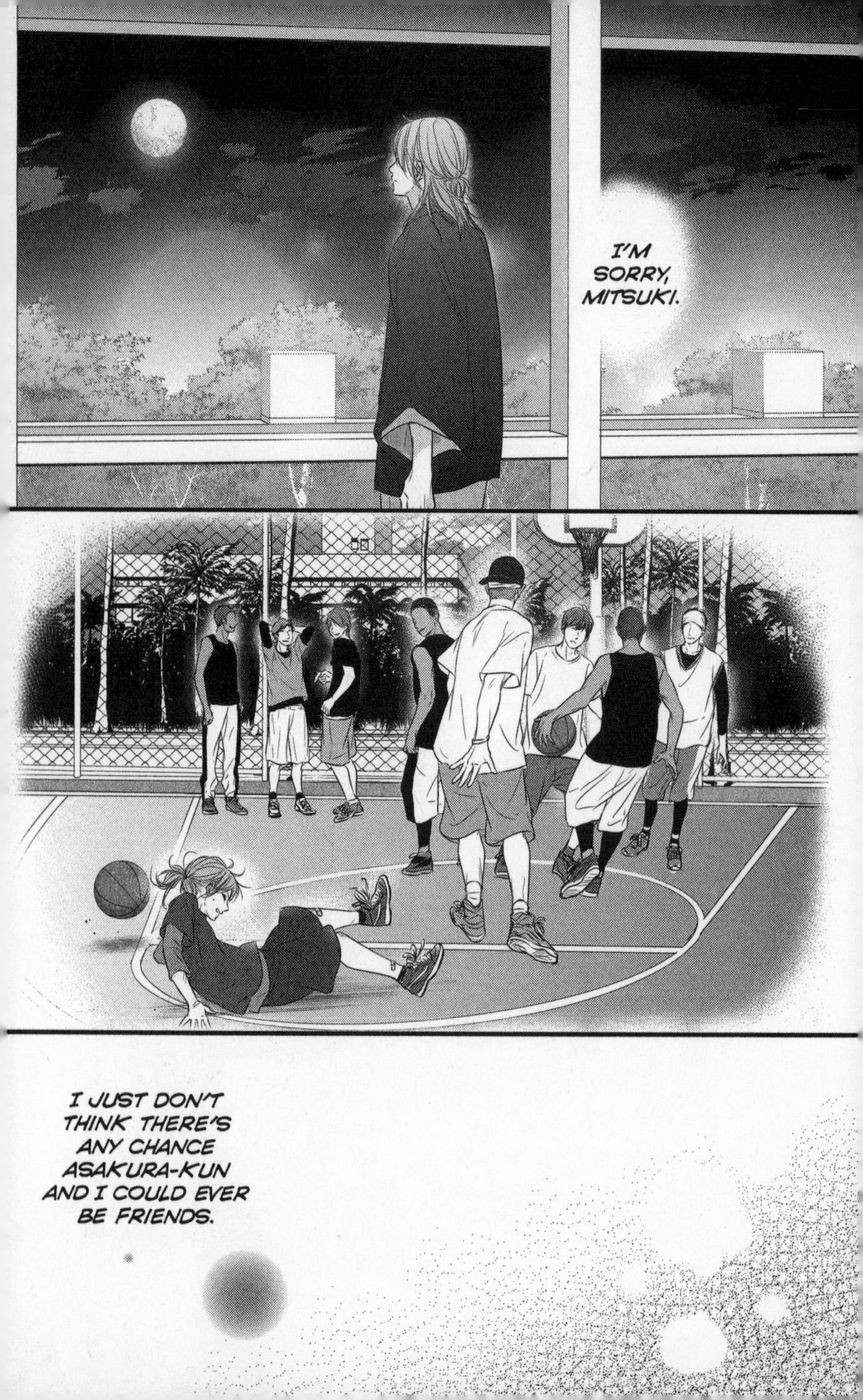
I'M SORRY, MITSUKI.
I JUST DON'T THINK THERE'S ANY CHANCE ASAKURA-KUN AND I COULD EVER BE FRIENDS.

Waiting for Spring in Fairy Tale Land

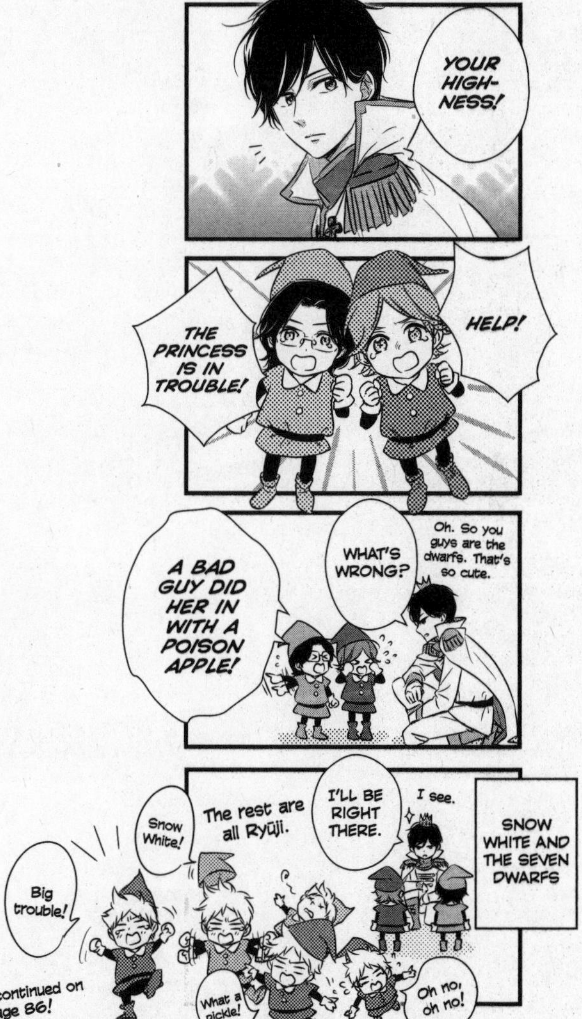
YOUR HIGH-NESS!
HELP!
THE PRINCESS IS IN TROUBLE!
Oh. So you guys are the dwarfs. That's so cute.
WHAT'S WRONG?
A BAD GUY DID HER IN WITH A POISON APPLE!
SNOW WHITE AND THE SEVEN DWARFS
I see.
I'LL BE RIGHT THERE.
The rest are all Ryūji.
Snow White!
Big trouble!
Oh no, oh no!
What a pickle!

To be continued on Page 86!

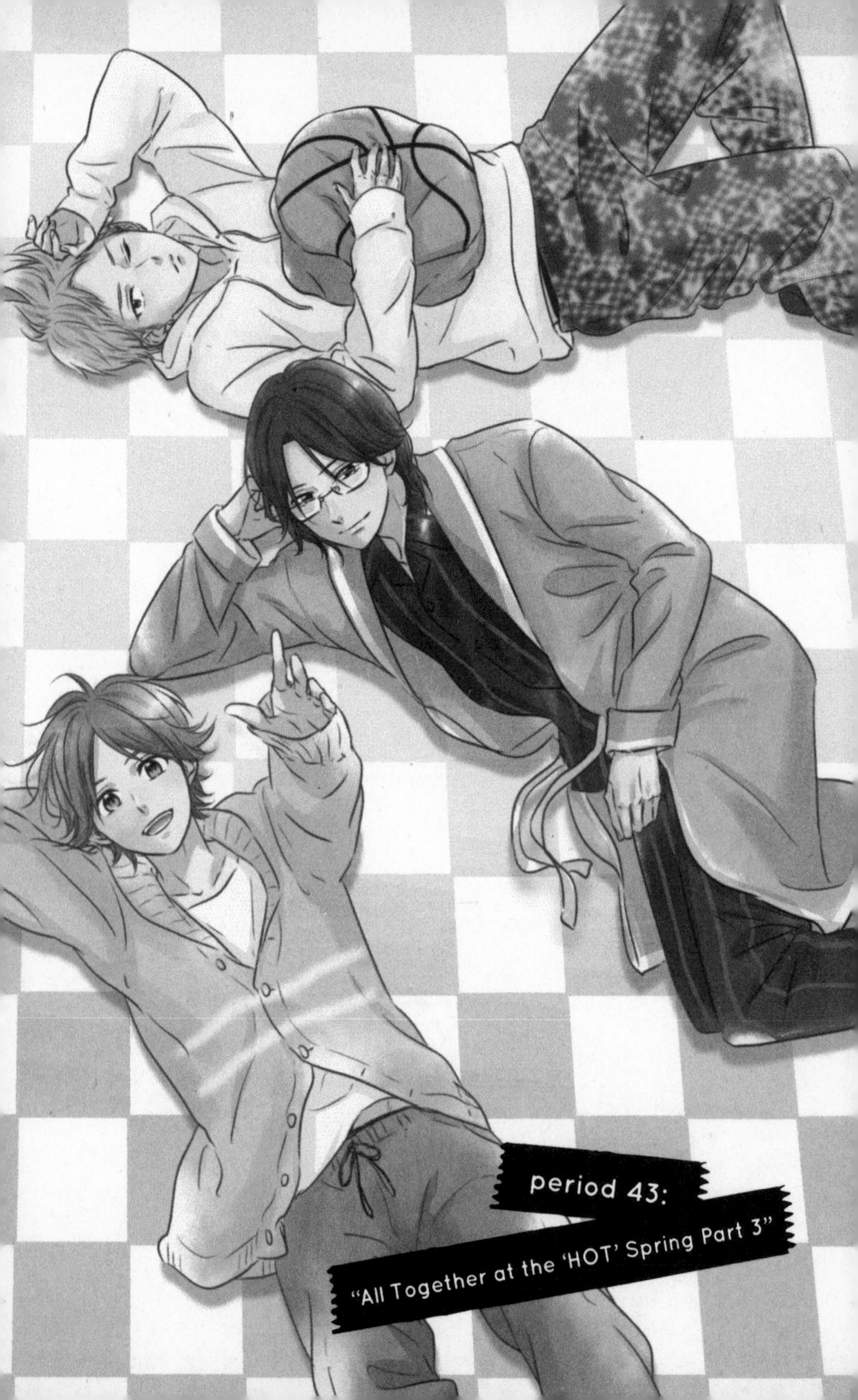
period 43:
"All Together at the 'HOT' Spring Part 3"

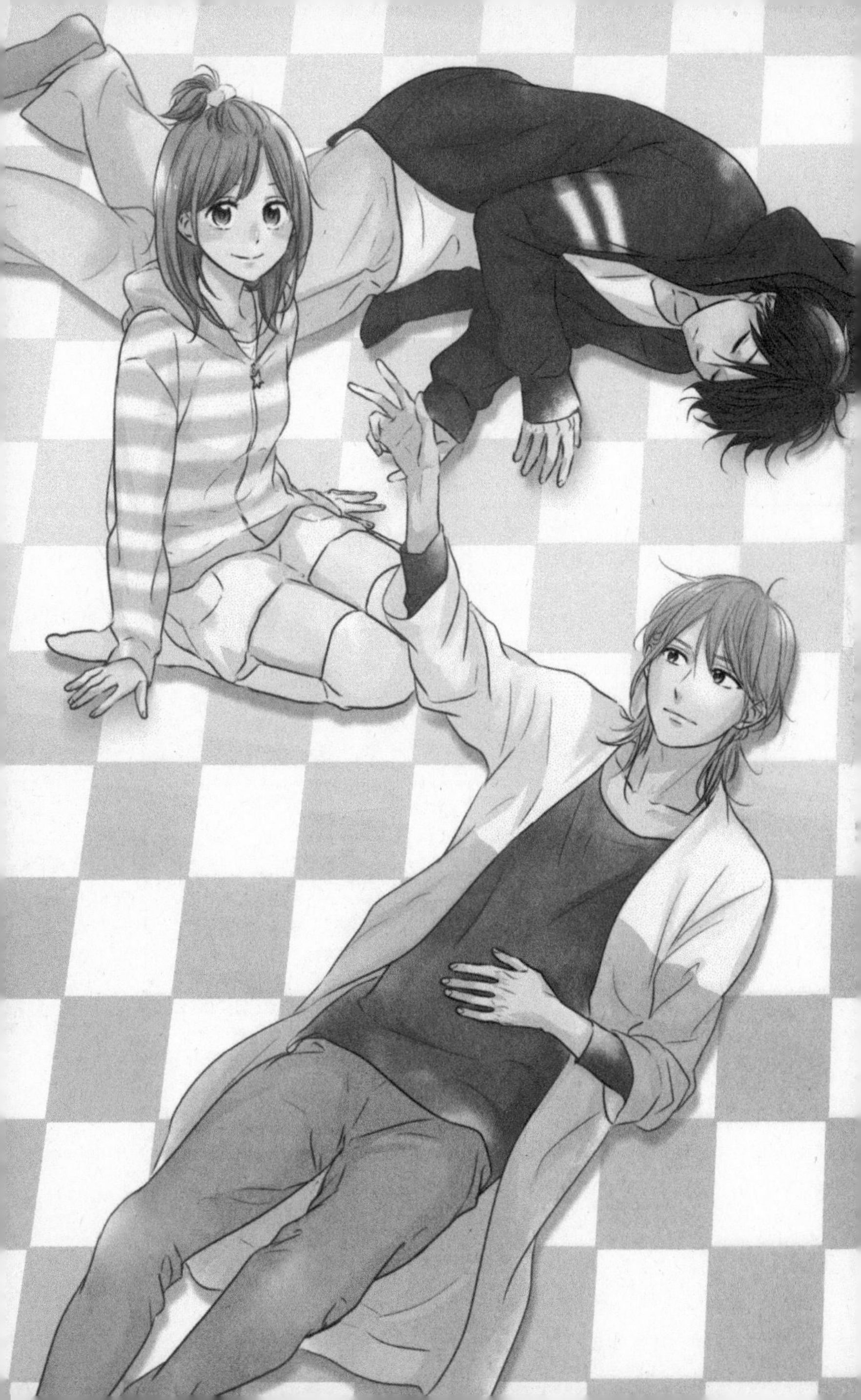

Snow White

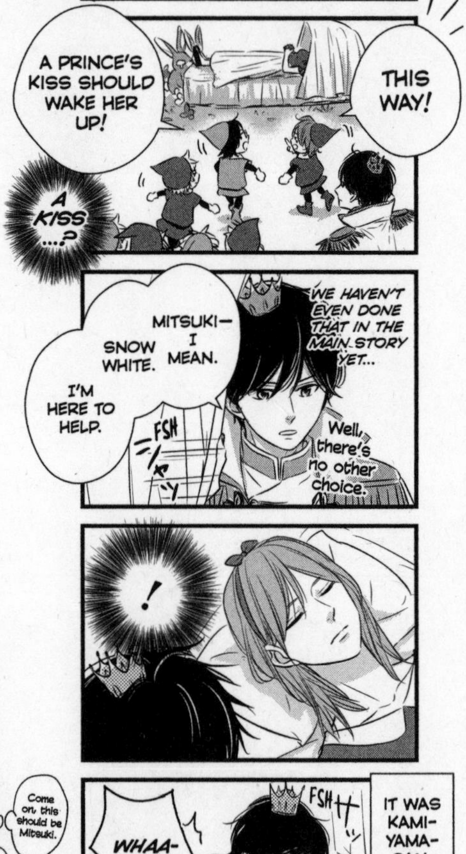
THIS WAY!
A PRINCE'S KISS SHOULD WAKE HER UP!
A KISS ...?
WE HAVEN'T EVEN DONE THAT IN THE MAIN STORY YET...
MITSUKI— I MEAN.
SNOW WHITE.
I'M HERE TO HELP.
FSH
Well, there's no other choice.
!
IT WAS KAMI-YAMA-SAN.
FSH
WHAA-AAT!!!
I'M SORRY. I CAN'T.

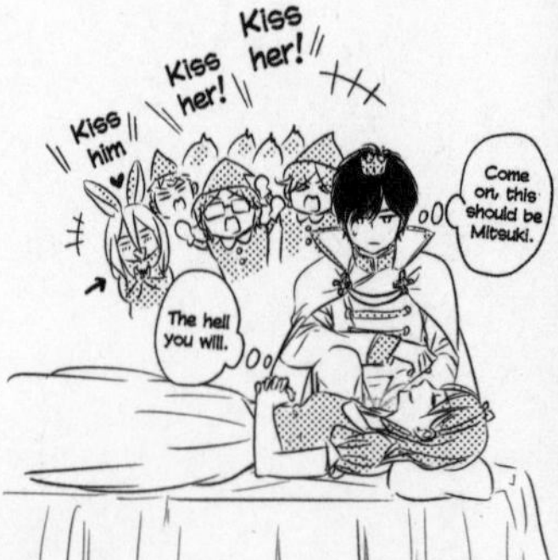
Kiss her!
Kiss her!
Kiss him ♥
Come on, this should be Mitsuki.
The hell you will.

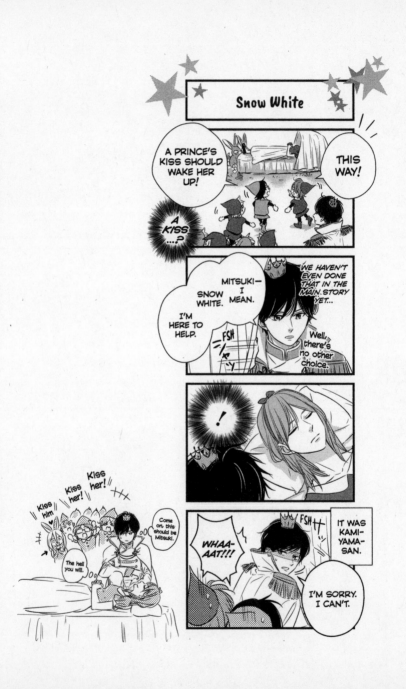

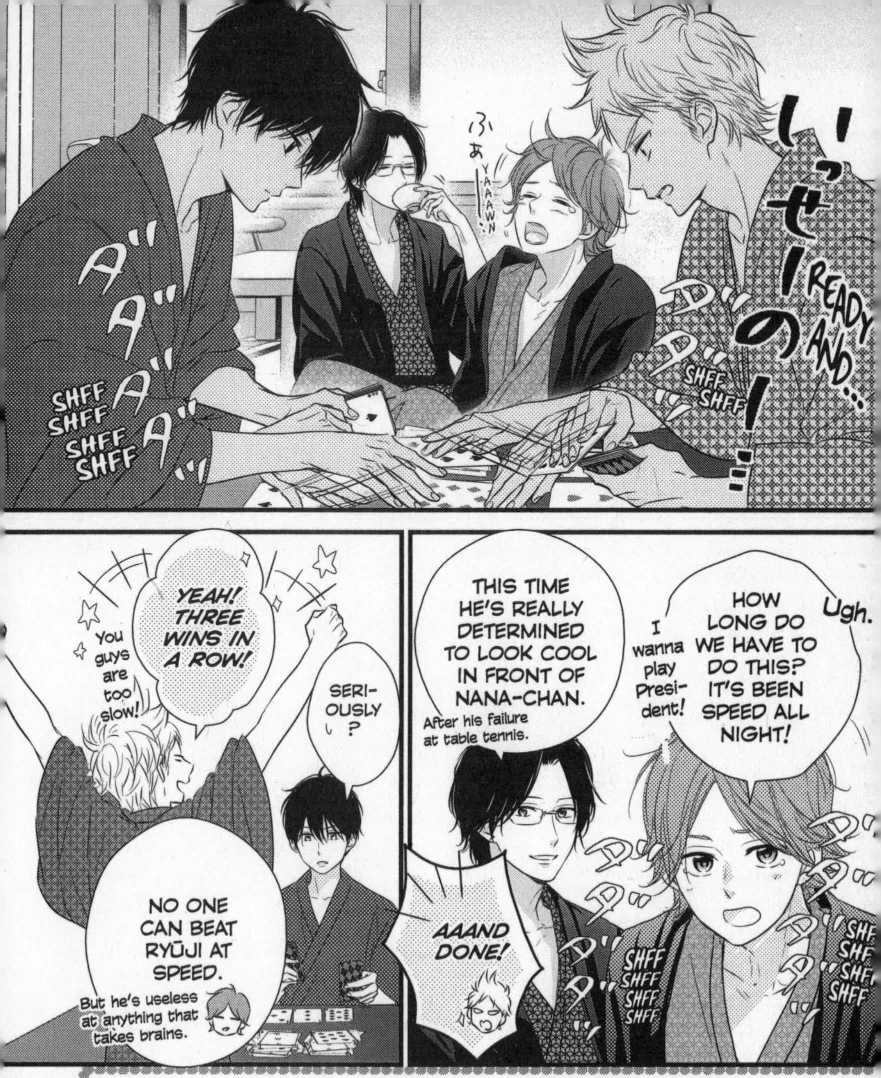
いっせーの…!!
READY AND...
ダダ
SHFF SHFF
ふあ
YAAAWN
ダダダダ
SHFF SHFF SHFF SHFF
Ugh.
HOW LONG DO WE HAVE TO DO THIS? IT'S BEEN SPEED ALL NIGHT!
I wanna play President!
THIS TIME HE'S REALLY DETERMINED TO LOOK COOL IN FRONT OF NANA-CHAN.
After his failure at table tennis.
AAAND DONE!
SHFF SHFF SHFF SHFF
SHFF SHFF SHFF SHFF
YEAH! THREE WINS IN A ROW!
You guys are too slow!
SERI-OUSLY ?
NO ONE CAN BEAT RYŪJI AT SPEED.
But he's useless at anything that takes brains.

The third thing is...going to be another character. Aya-chan

I don't really put myself into my characters very much, and especially with *Waiting for Spring*, I think of the characters as close friends or my children. But Aya-chan is the one exception, and there are parts of him that I do project myself onto. Of course, I don't have nearly as high stats as he does (ha ha). And I think it's because I have Aya-chan that I can draw the characters better than before, and I love them even more.

(People ask me who my favorite is, but after all this time, I really can't choose. So I'm a fan of the whole set. I hope you'll still look kindly on this group of characters that means so much to me.)

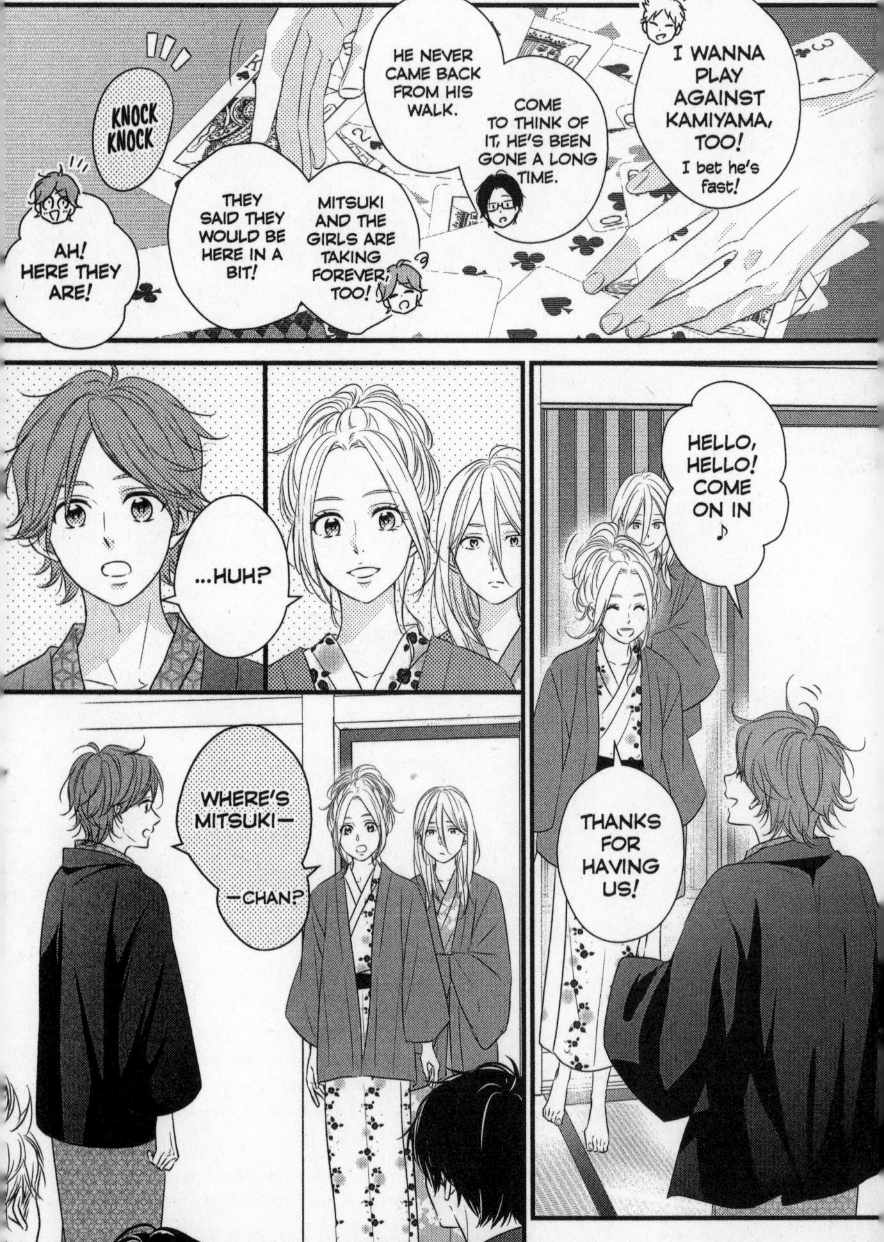
I WANNA PLAY AGAINST KAMIYAMA, TOO! I bet he's fast!
COME TO THINK OF IT, HE'S BEEN GONE A LONG TIME.
HE NEVER CAME BACK FROM HIS WALK.
MITSUKI AND THE GIRLS ARE TAKING FOREVER, TOO!
THEY SAID THEY WOULD BE HERE IN A BIT!
KNOCK KNOCK
AH! HERE THEY ARE!
HELLO, HELLO! COME ON IN ♪
THANKS FOR HAVING US!
...HUH?
WHERE'S MITSUKI—
—CHAN?

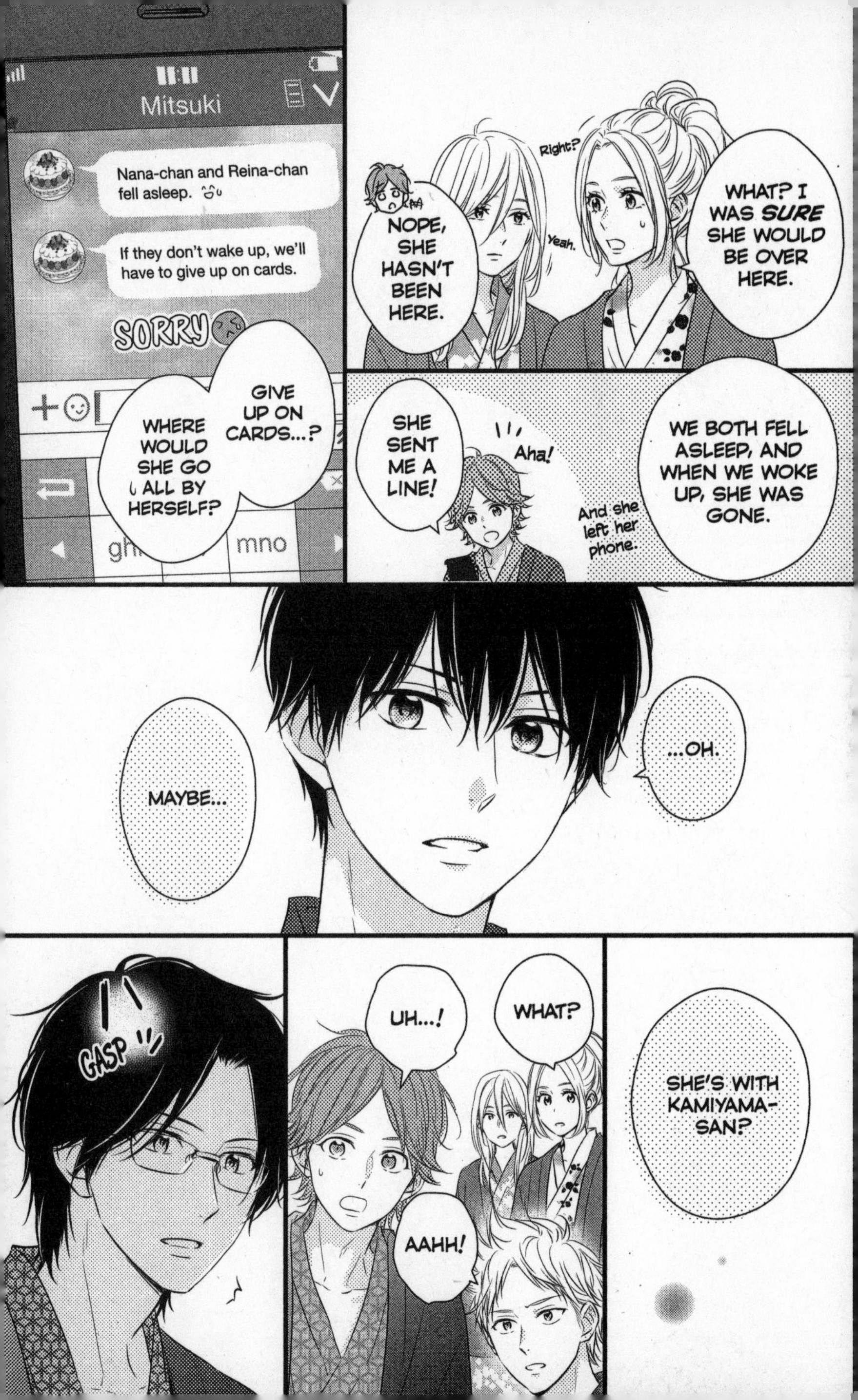
WHAT? I WAS *SURE* SHE WOULD BE OVER HERE.
Right?
Yeah.
NOPE, SHE HASN'T BEEN HERE.
WE BOTH FELL ASLEEP, AND WHEN WE WOKE UP, SHE WAS GONE.
And she left her phone.
Aha!
SHE SENT ME A LINE!
11:11
Mitsuki
Nana-chan and Reina-chan fell asleep.
If they don't wake up, we'll have to give up on cards.
SORRY
GIVE UP ON CARDS...?
WHERE WOULD SHE GO ALL BY HERSELF?
mno
...OH.
MAYBE...
SHE'S WITH KAMIYAMA-SAN?
WHAT?
UH...!
AAHH!
GASP

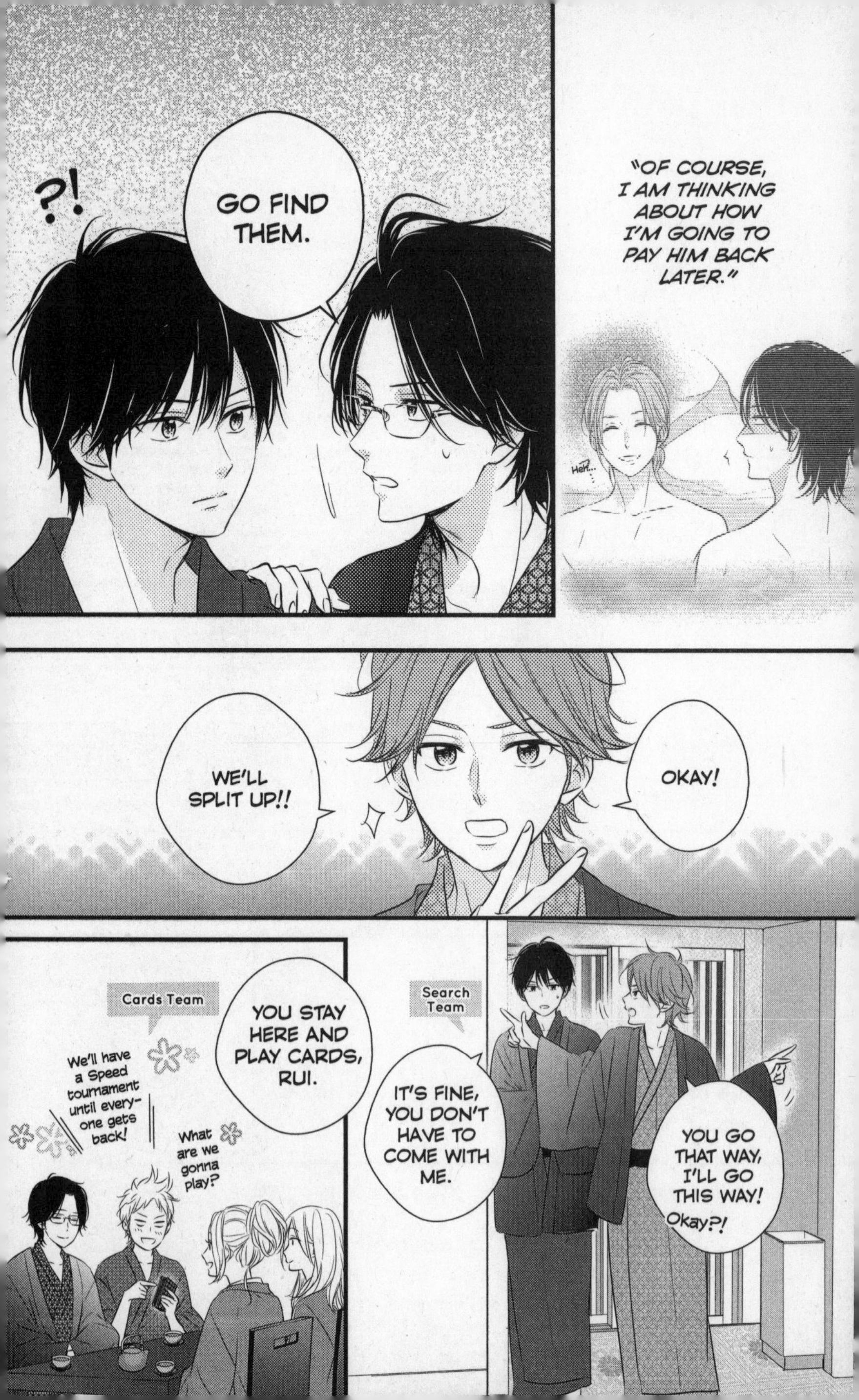
"OF COURSE, I AM THINKING ABOUT HOW I'M GOING TO PAY HIM BACK LATER."
Heh...
?!
GO FIND THEM.
OKAY!
WE'LL SPLIT UP!!
Search Team
YOU GO THAT WAY, I'LL GO THIS WAY!
Okay?!
IT'S FINE, YOU DON'T HAVE TO COME WITH ME.
YOU STAY HERE AND PLAY CARDS, RUI.
Cards Team
We'll have a Speed tournament until every-one gets back!
What are we gonna play?

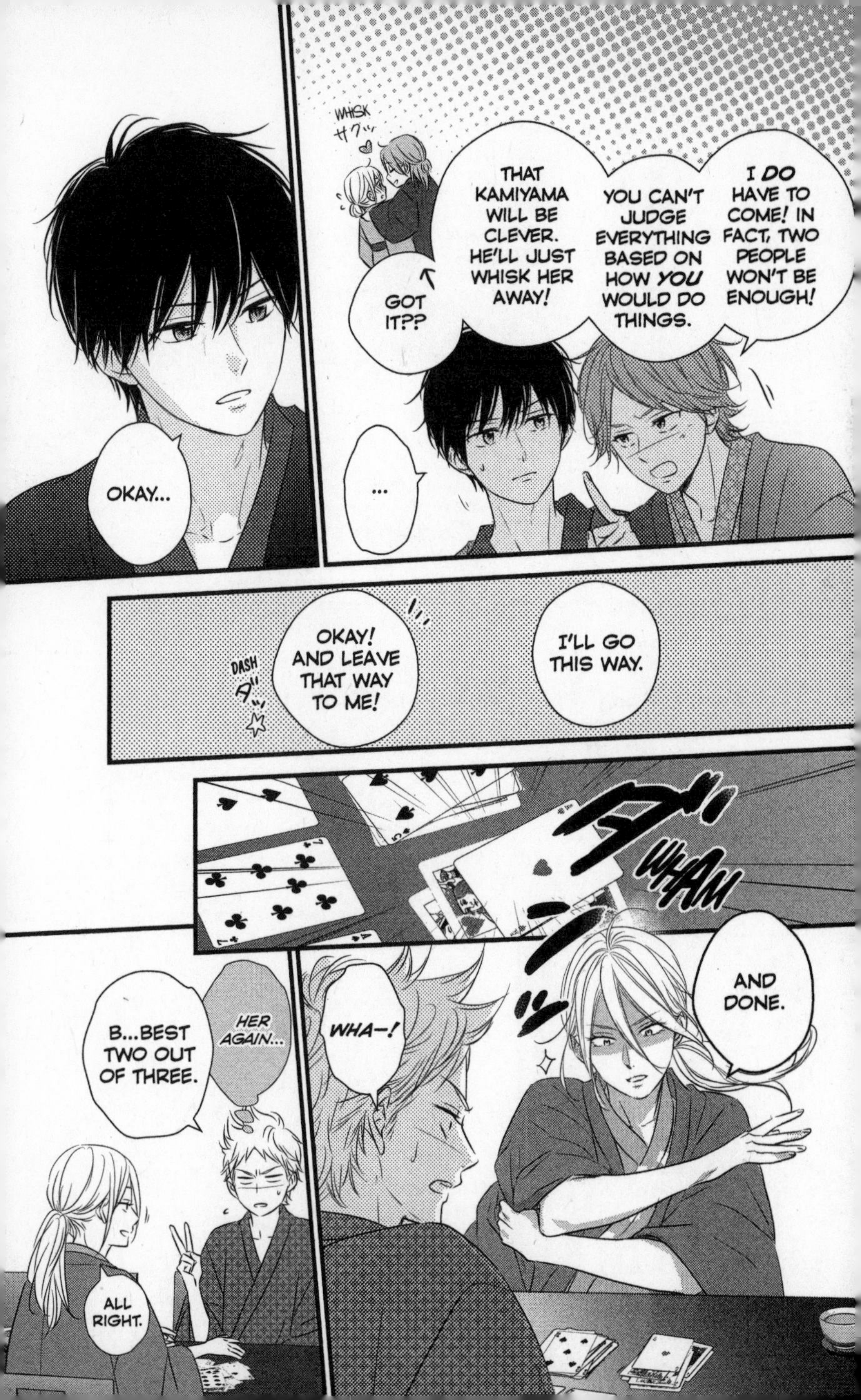
I DO HAVE TO COME! IN FACT, TWO PEOPLE WON'T BE ENOUGH!
YOU CAN'T JUDGE EVERYTHING BASED ON HOW YOU WOULD DO THINGS.
THAT KAMIYAMA WILL BE CLEVER. HE'LL JUST WHISK HER AWAY!
WHISK
サクッ
GOT IT??
...
OKAY...
I'LL GO THIS WAY.
OKAY! AND LEAVE THAT WAY TO ME!
DASH
WHAM
AND DONE.
WHA-!
HER AGAIN...
B...BEST TWO OUT OF THREE.
ALL RIGHT.

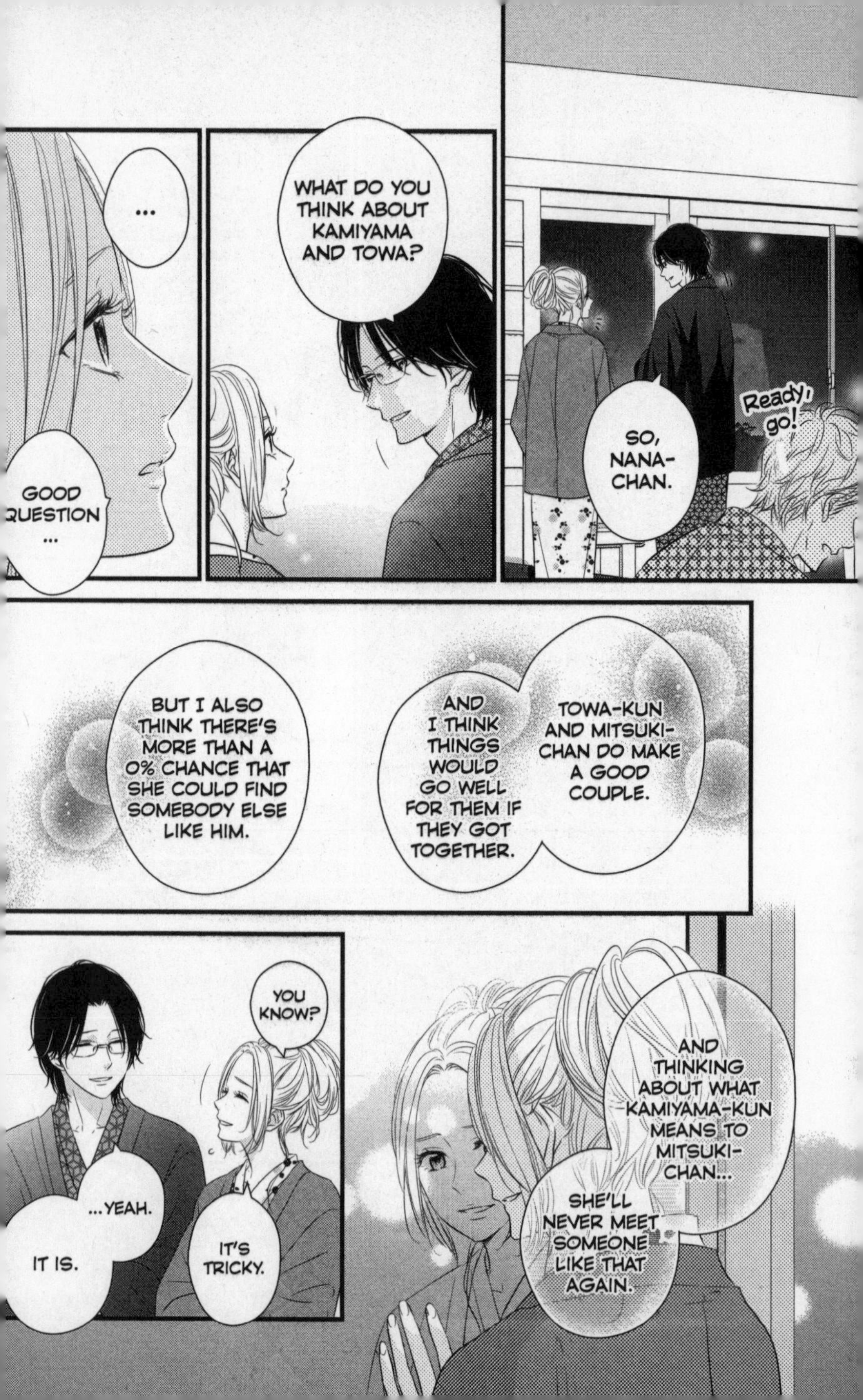
Ready, go!
SO, NANA-CHAN.
WHAT DO YOU THINK ABOUT KAMIYAMA AND TOWA?
...
GOOD QUESTION ...
TOWA-KUN AND MITSUKI-CHAN DO MAKE A GOOD COUPLE.
AND I THINK THINGS WOULD GO WELL FOR THEM IF THEY GOT TOGETHER.
BUT I ALSO THINK THERE'S MORE THAN A 0% CHANCE THAT SHE COULD FIND SOMEBODY ELSE LIKE HIM.
AND THINKING ABOUT WHAT KAMIYAMA-KUN MEANS TO MITSUKI-CHAN...
SHE'LL NEVER MEET SOMEONE LIKE THAT AGAIN.
YOU KNOW?
...YEAH.
IT'S TRICKY.
IT IS.

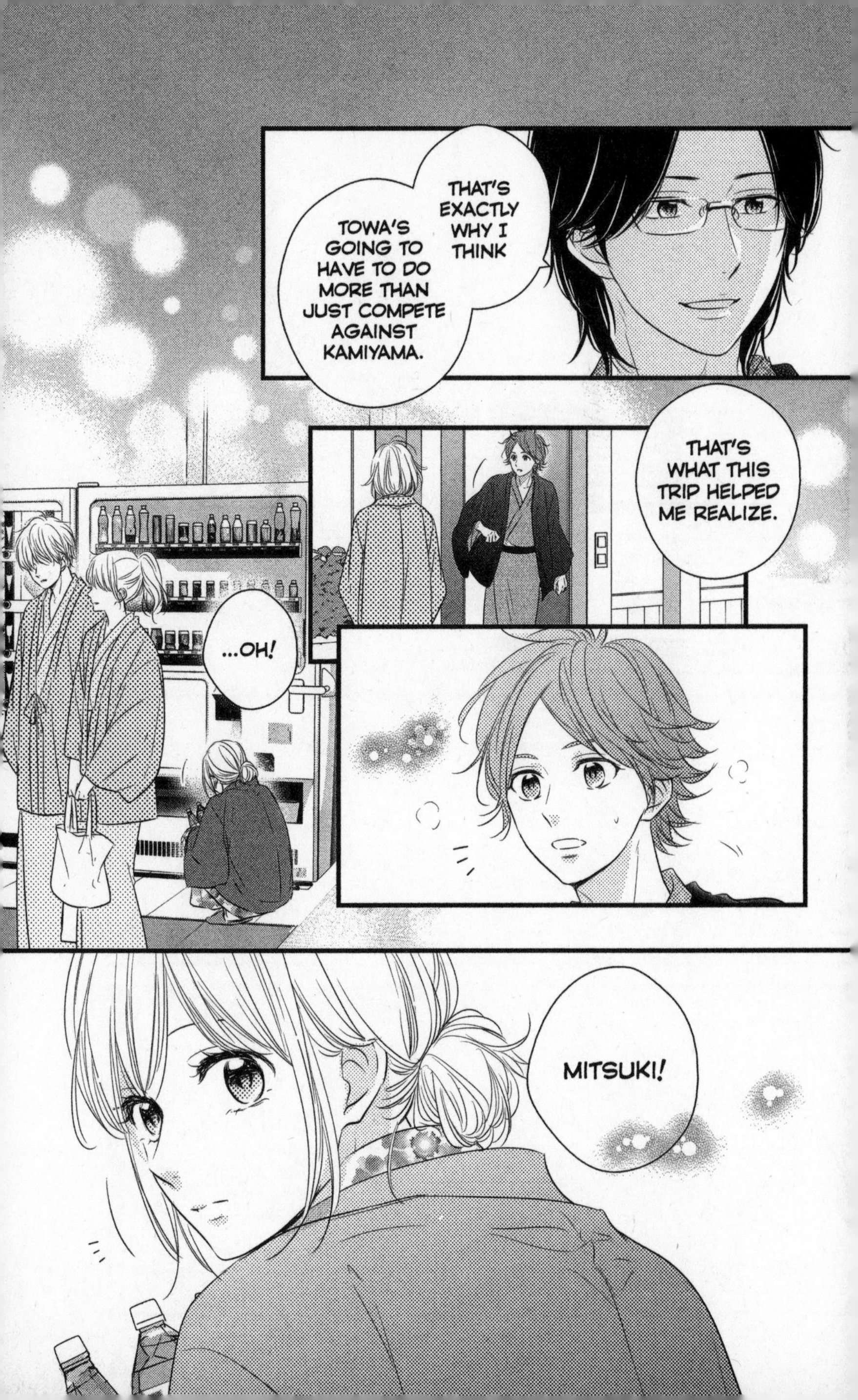
THAT'S EXACTLY WHY I THINK TOWA'S GOING TO HAVE TO DO MORE THAN JUST COMPETE AGAINST KAMIYAMA.
THAT'S WHAT THIS TRIP HELPED ME REALIZE.
...OH!
MITSUKI!

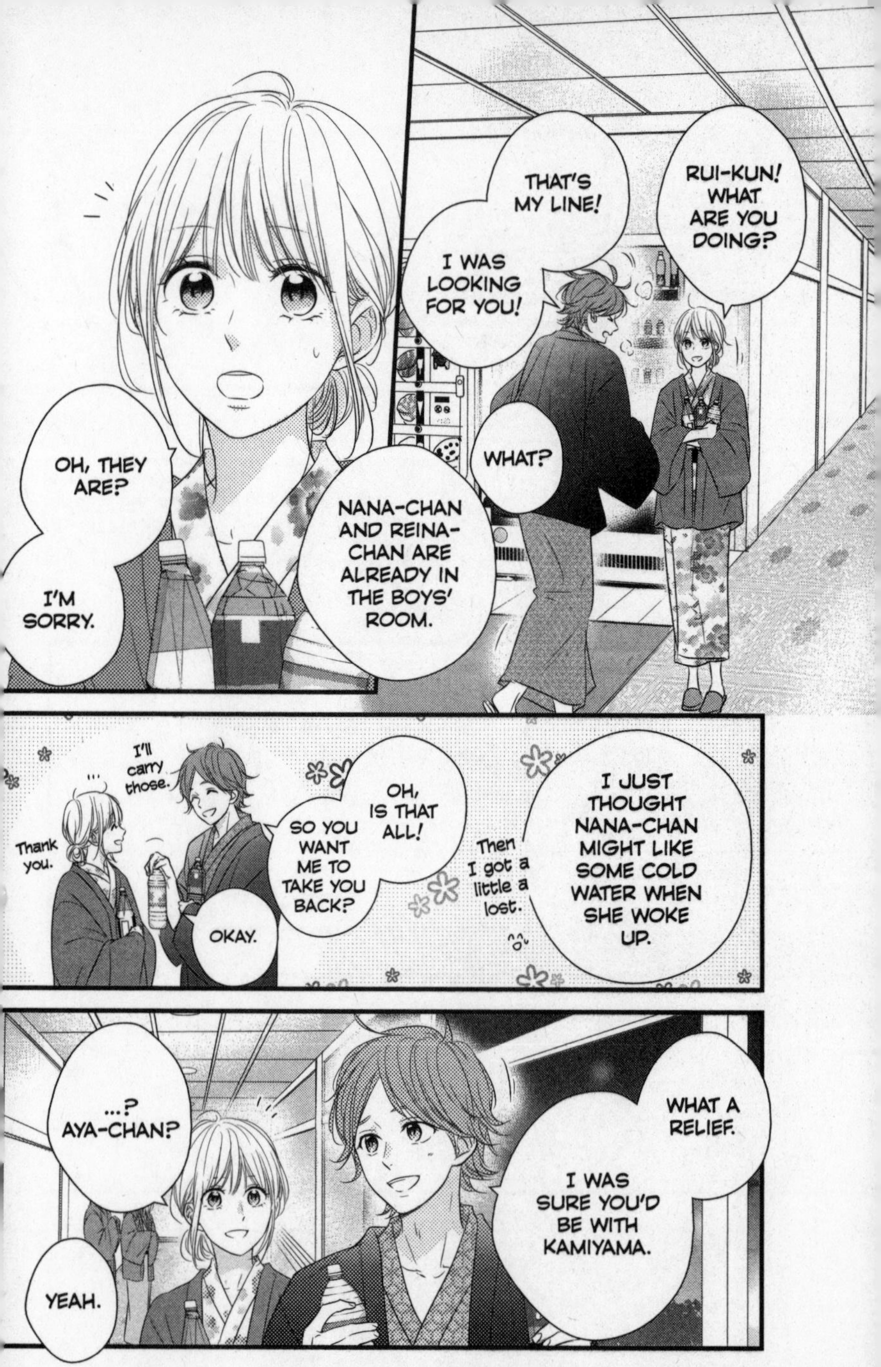
RUI-KUN! WHAT ARE YOU DOING?
THAT'S MY LINE!
I WAS LOOKING FOR YOU!
WHAT?
NANA-CHAN AND REINA-CHAN ARE ALREADY IN THE BOYS' ROOM.
OH, THEY ARE?
I'M SORRY.
I JUST THOUGHT NANA-CHAN MIGHT LIKE SOME COLD WATER WHEN SHE WOKE UP.
Then I got a little a lost.
OH, IS THAT ALL!
SO YOU WANT ME TO TAKE YOU BACK?
OKAY.
I'll carry those.
...
Thank you.
WHAT A RELIEF.
I WAS SURE YOU'D BE WITH KAMIYAMA.
...? AYA-CHAN?
YEAH.

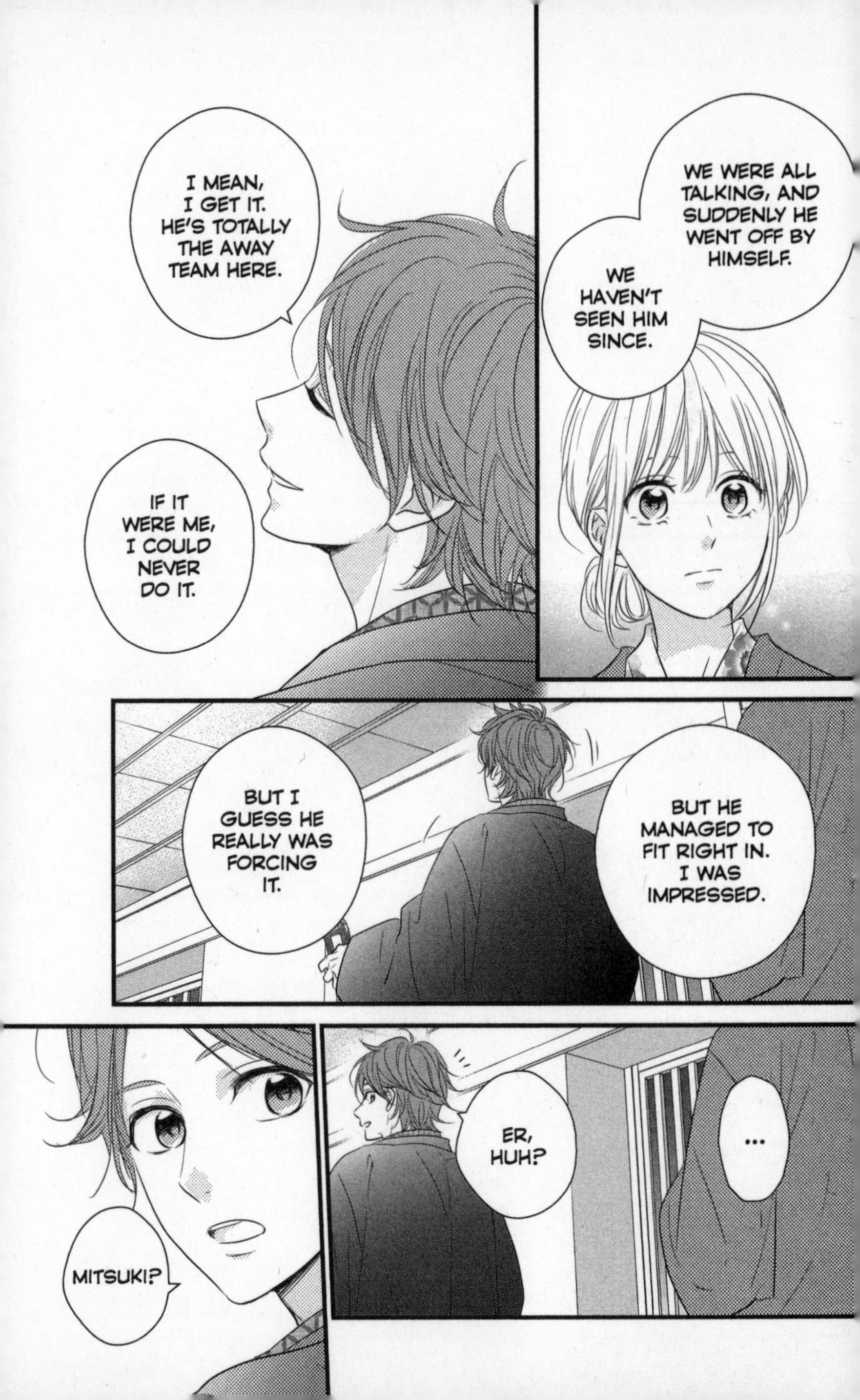
WE WERE ALL TALKING, AND SUDDENLY HE WENT OFF BY HIMSELF.
WE HAVEN'T SEEN HIM SINCE.
I MEAN, I GET IT. HE'S TOTALLY THE AWAY TEAM HERE.
IF IT WERE ME, I COULD NEVER DO IT.
BUT HE MANAGED TO FIT RIGHT IN. I WAS IMPRESSED.
BUT I GUESS HE REALLY WAS FORCING IT.
...
ER, HUH?
MITSUKI?

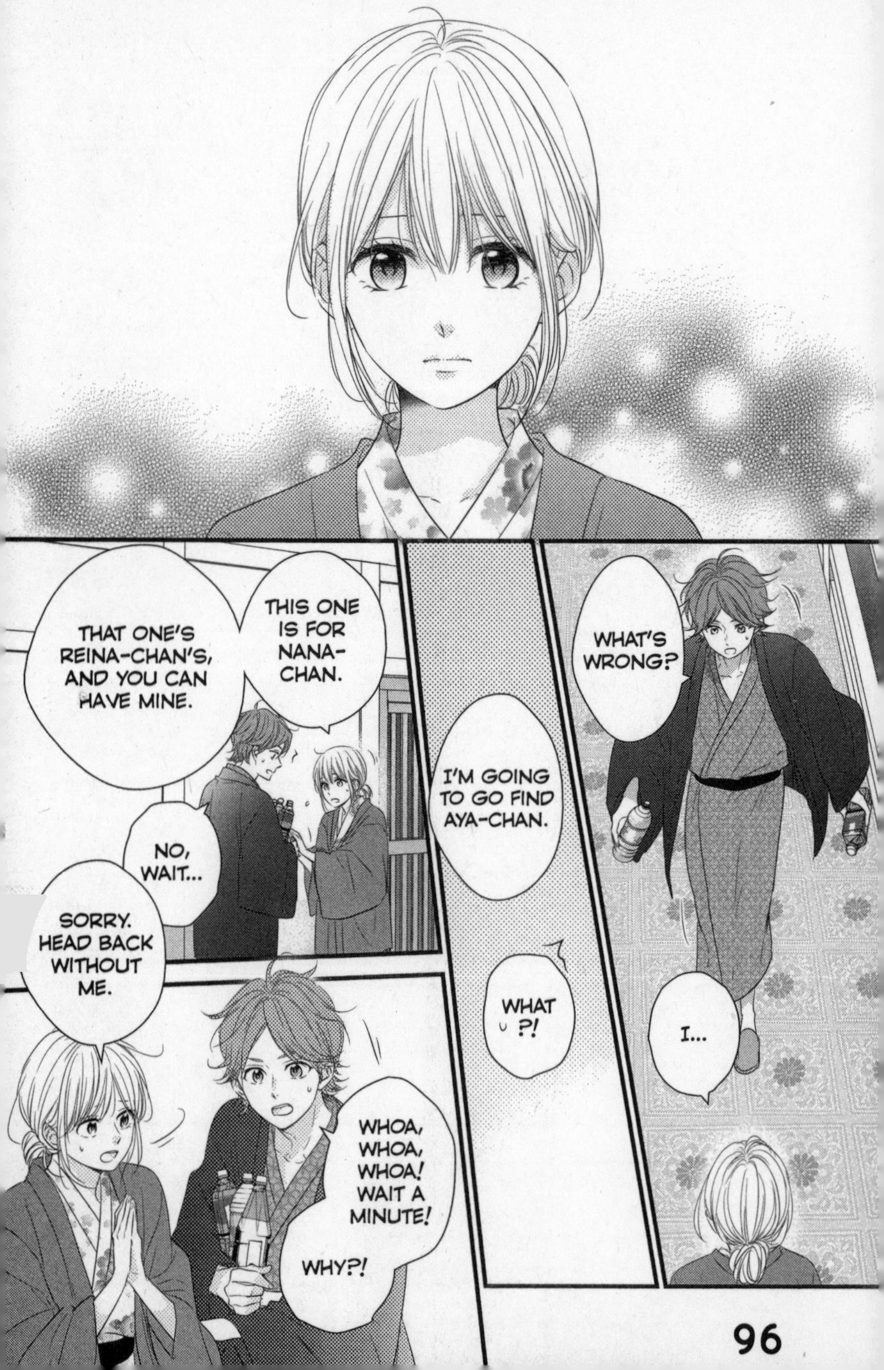
WHAT'S WRONG?
I...
I'M GOING TO GO FIND AYA-CHAN.
WHAT ?!
THIS ONE IS FOR NANA-CHAN.
THAT ONE'S REINA-CHAN'S, AND YOU CAN HAVE MINE.
NO, WAIT...
SORRY. HEAD BACK WITHOUT ME.
WHOA, WHOA, WHOA! WAIT A MINUTE!
WHY?!

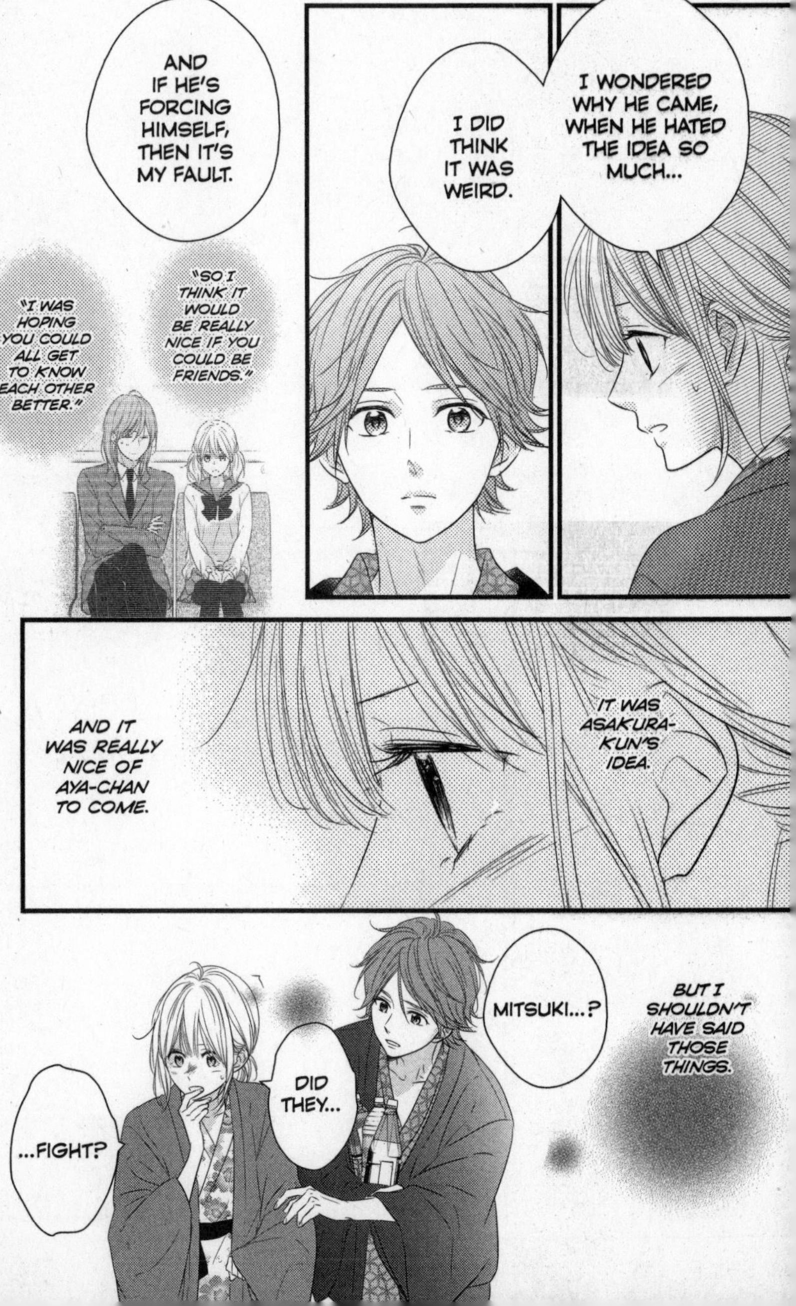
I WONDERED WHY HE CAME, WHEN HE HATED THE IDEA SO MUCH...
I DID THINK IT WAS WEIRD.
AND IF HE'S FORCING HIMSELF, THEN IT'S MY FAULT.
"SO I THINK IT WOULD BE REALLY NICE IF YOU COULD BE FRIENDS."
"I WAS HOPING YOU COULD ALL GET TO KNOW EACH OTHER BETTER."
IT WAS ASAKURA-KUN'S IDEA.
AND IT WAS REALLY NICE OF AYA-CHAN TO COME.
BUT I SHOULDN'T HAVE SAID THOSE THINGS.
MITSUKI...?
DID THEY...
...FIGHT?

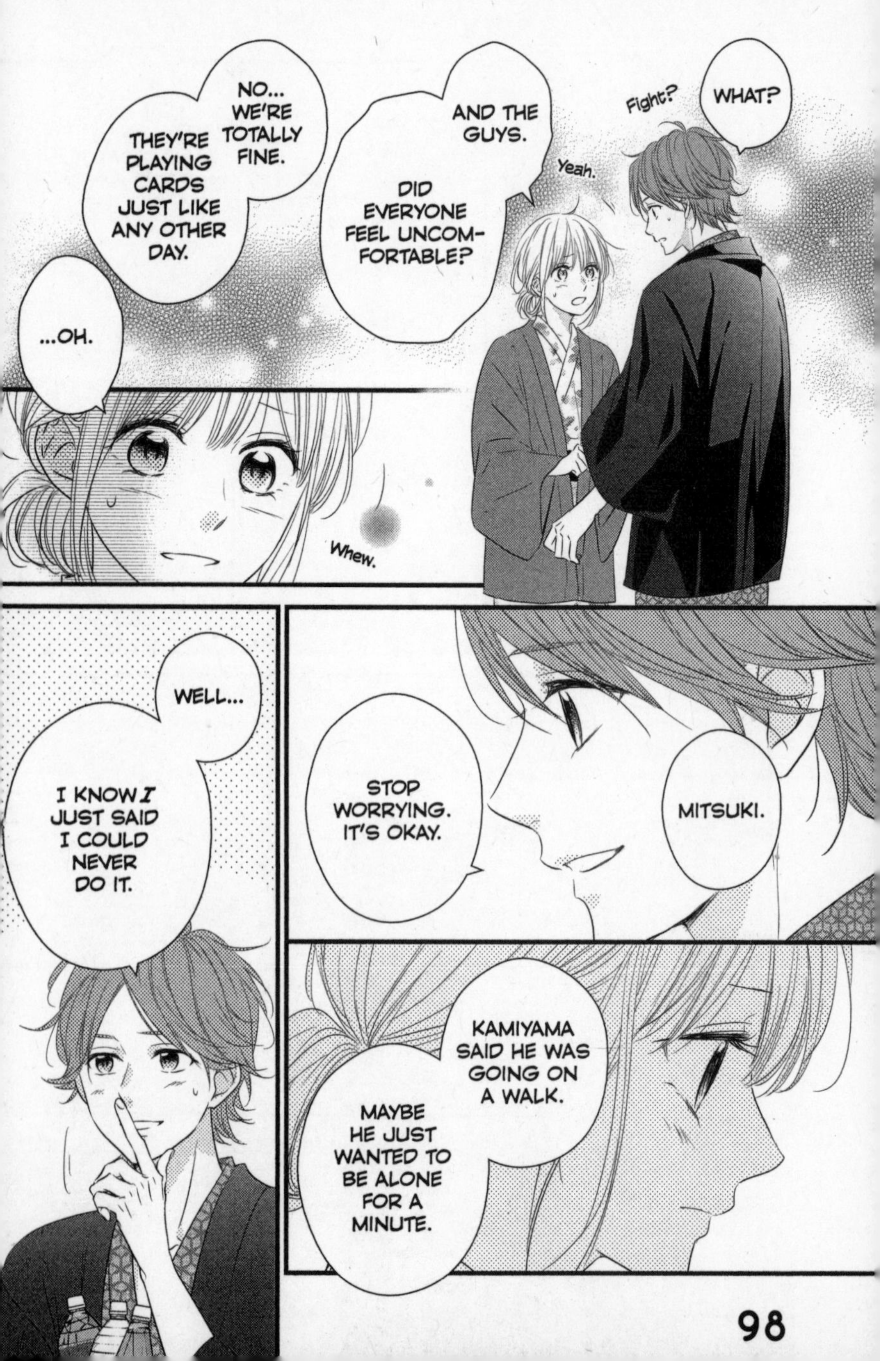
WHAT?
Fight?
Yeah.
AND THE GUYS.
DID EVERYONE FEEL UNCOMFORTABLE?
NO... WE'RE TOTALLY FINE.
THEY'RE PLAYING CARDS JUST LIKE ANY OTHER DAY.
...OH.
Whew.
MITSUKI.
STOP WORRYING. IT'S OKAY.
KAMIYAMA SAID HE WAS GOING ON A WALK.
MAYBE HE JUST WANTED TO BE ALONE FOR A MINUTE.
WELL...
I KNOW *I* JUST SAID I COULD NEVER DO IT.

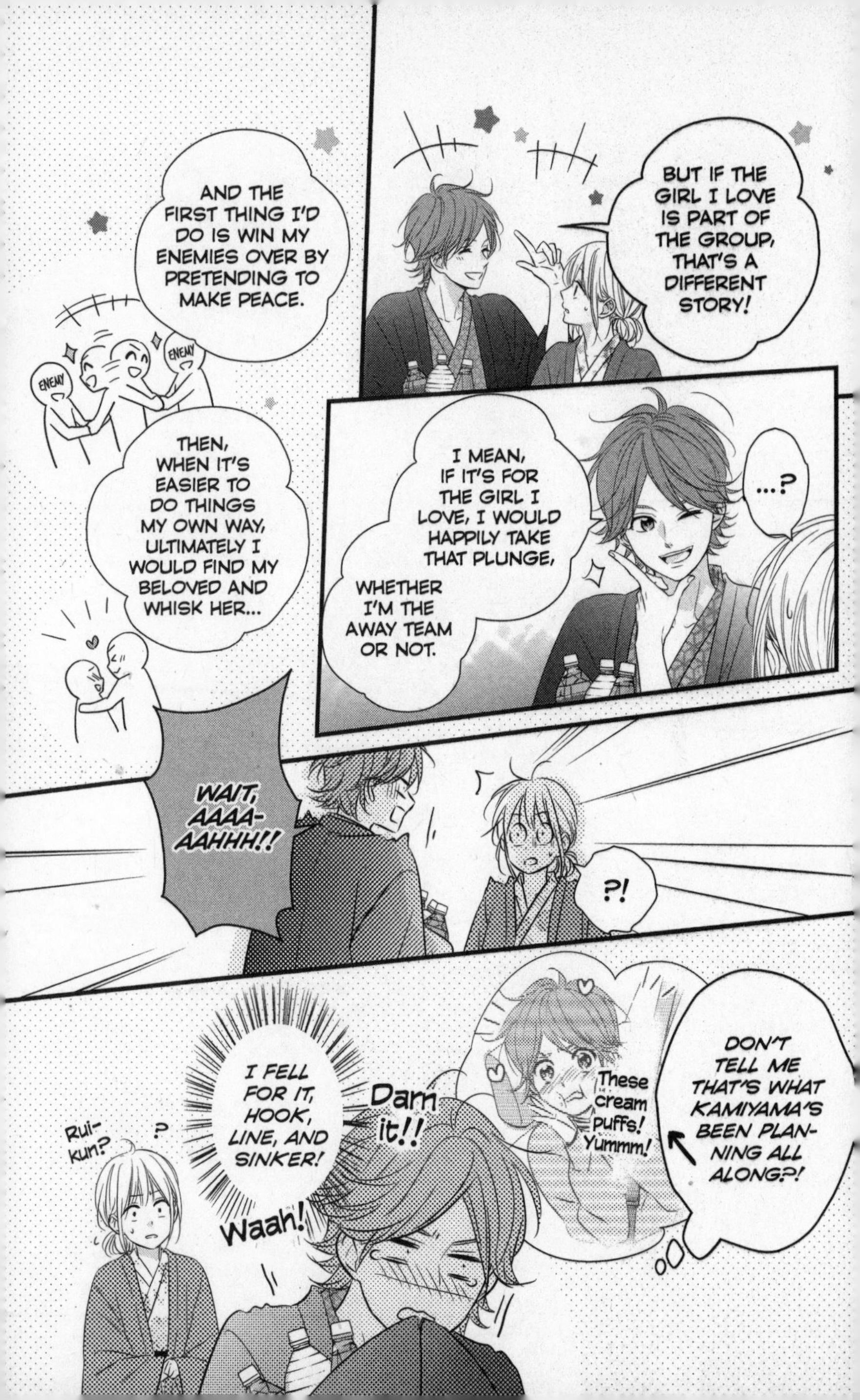

AND THE FIRST THING I'D DO IS WIN MY ENEMIES OVER BY PRETENDING TO MAKE PEACE.
ENEMY
ENEMY
THEN, WHEN IT'S EASIER TO DO THINGS MY OWN WAY, ULTIMATELY I WOULD FIND MY BELOVED AND WHISK HER...
BUT IF THE GIRL I LOVE IS PART OF THE GROUP, THAT'S A DIFFERENT STORY!
...?
I MEAN, IF IT'S FOR THE GIRL I LOVE, I WOULD HAPPILY TAKE THAT PLUNGE,
WHETHER I'M THE AWAY TEAM OR NOT.
WAIT, AAAA-AAHHH!!
?!
DON'T TELL ME THAT'S WHAT KAMIYAMA'S BEEN PLAN-NING ALL ALONG?!
These cream puffs! Yummm!
Darn it!!
I FELL FOR IT, HOOK, LINE, AND SINKER!
Waah!
Rui-kun?
?

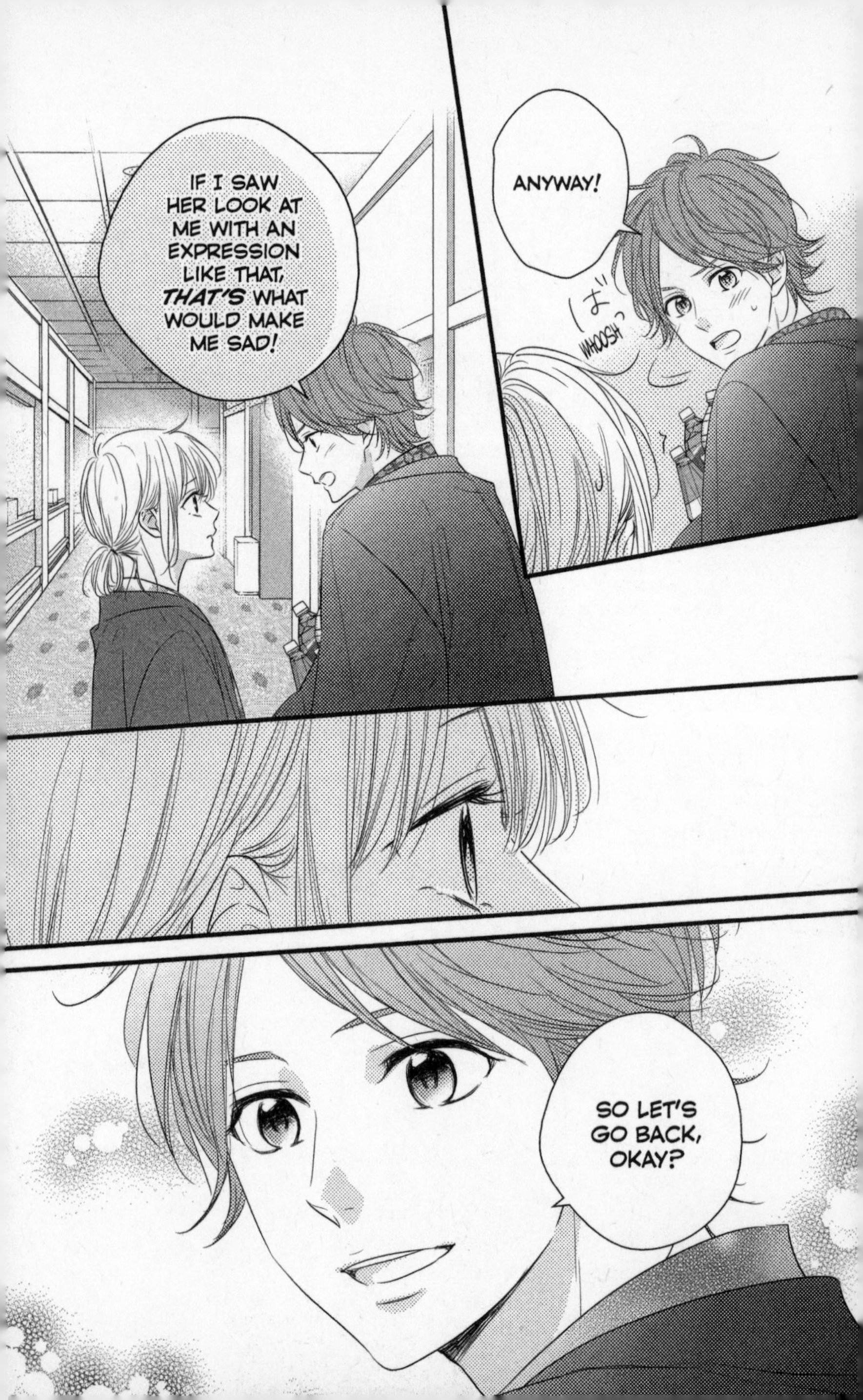
ANYWAY!
ばっ
WHOOSH
IF I SAW HER LOOK AT ME WITH AN EXPRESSION LIKE THAT, ***THAT'S*** WHAT WOULD MAKE ME SAD!
SO LET'S GO BACK, OKAY?

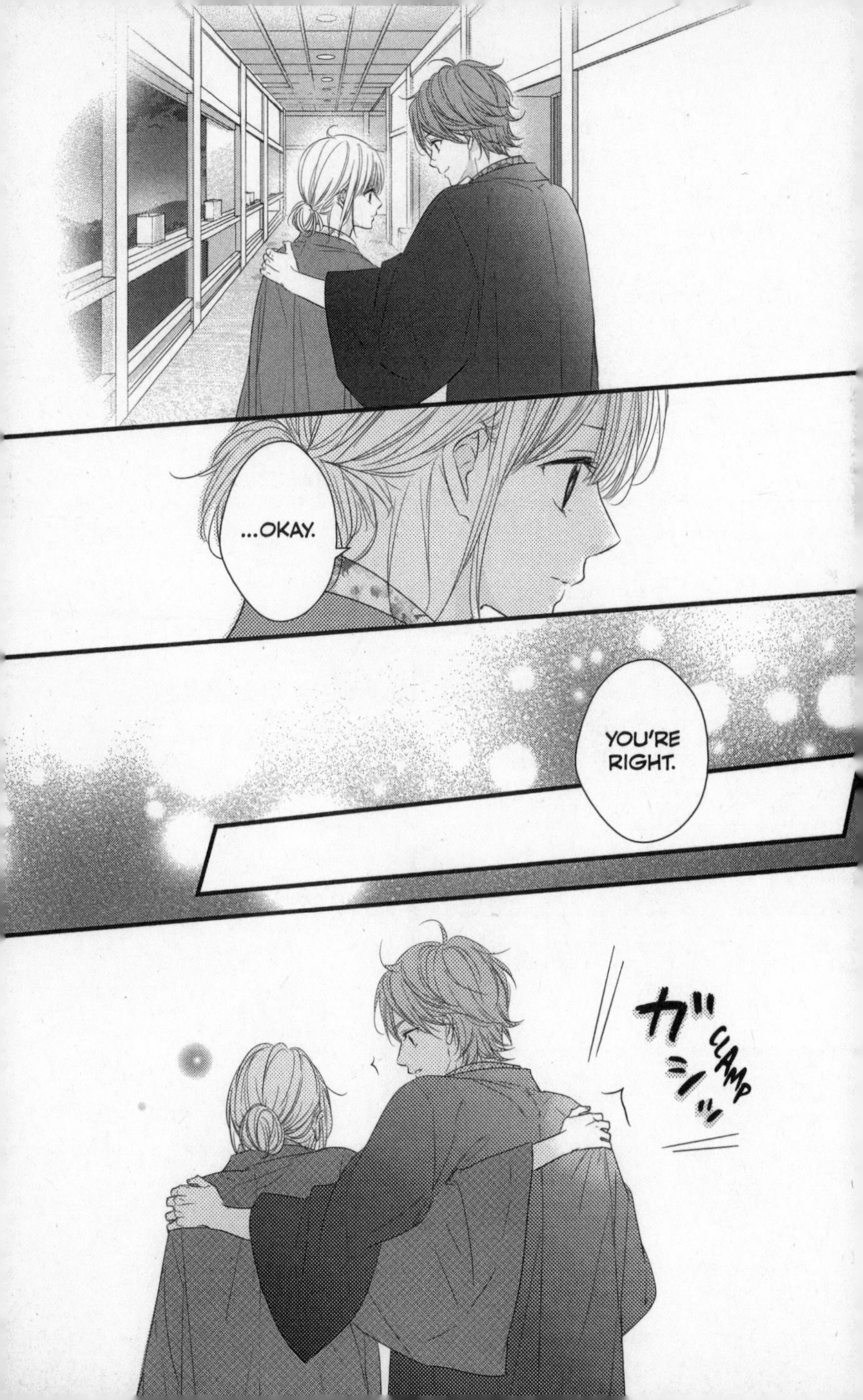
...OKAY.
YOU'RE RIGHT.
ガシッ
CLAMP

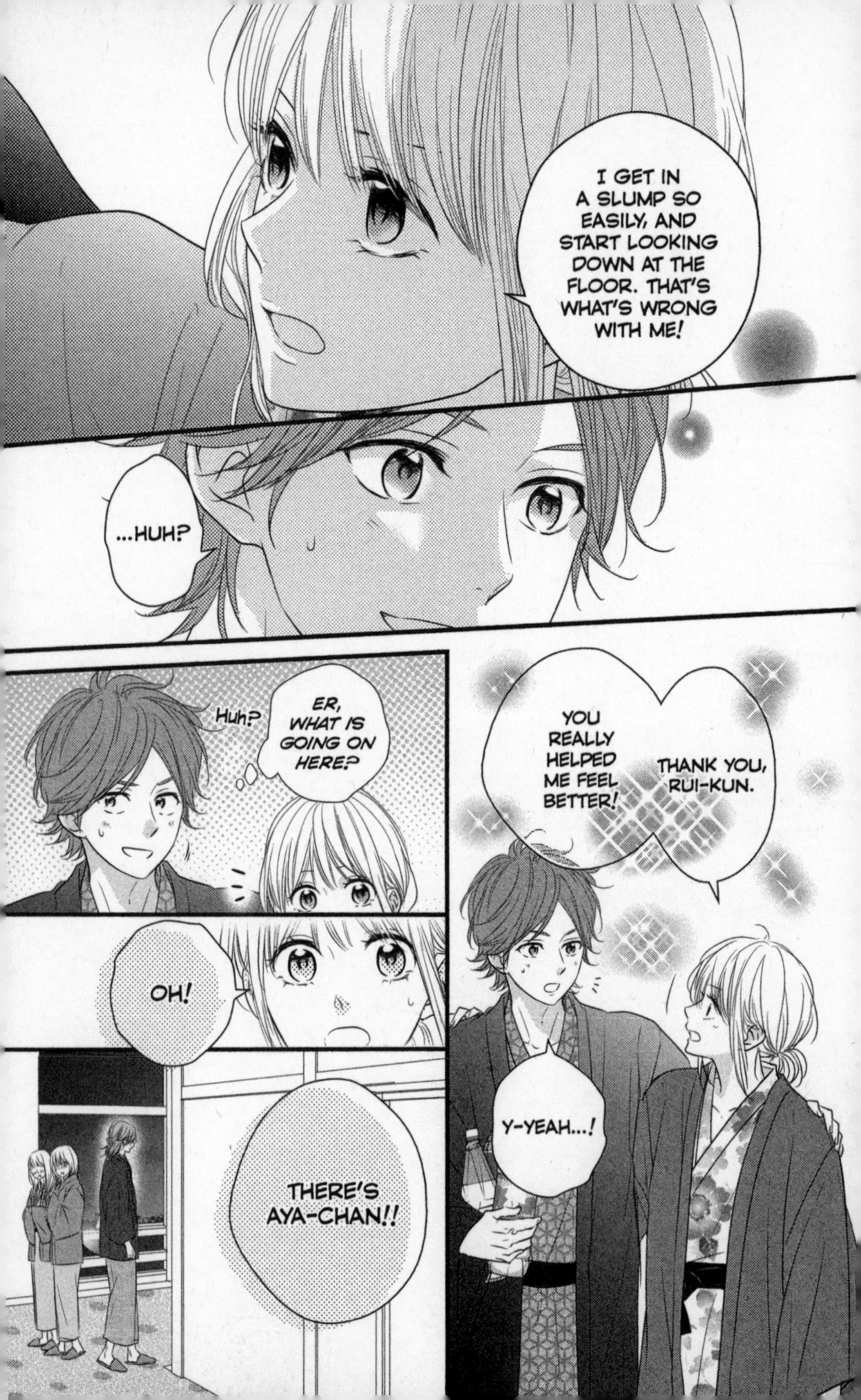
I GET IN A SLUMP SO EASILY, AND START LOOKING DOWN AT THE FLOOR. THAT'S WHAT'S WRONG WITH ME!
...HUH?
THANK YOU, RUI-KUN.
YOU REALLY HELPED ME FEEL BETTER!
Y-YEAH...!
ER, WHAT IS GOING ON HERE?
Huh?
OH!
THERE'S AYA-CHAN!!

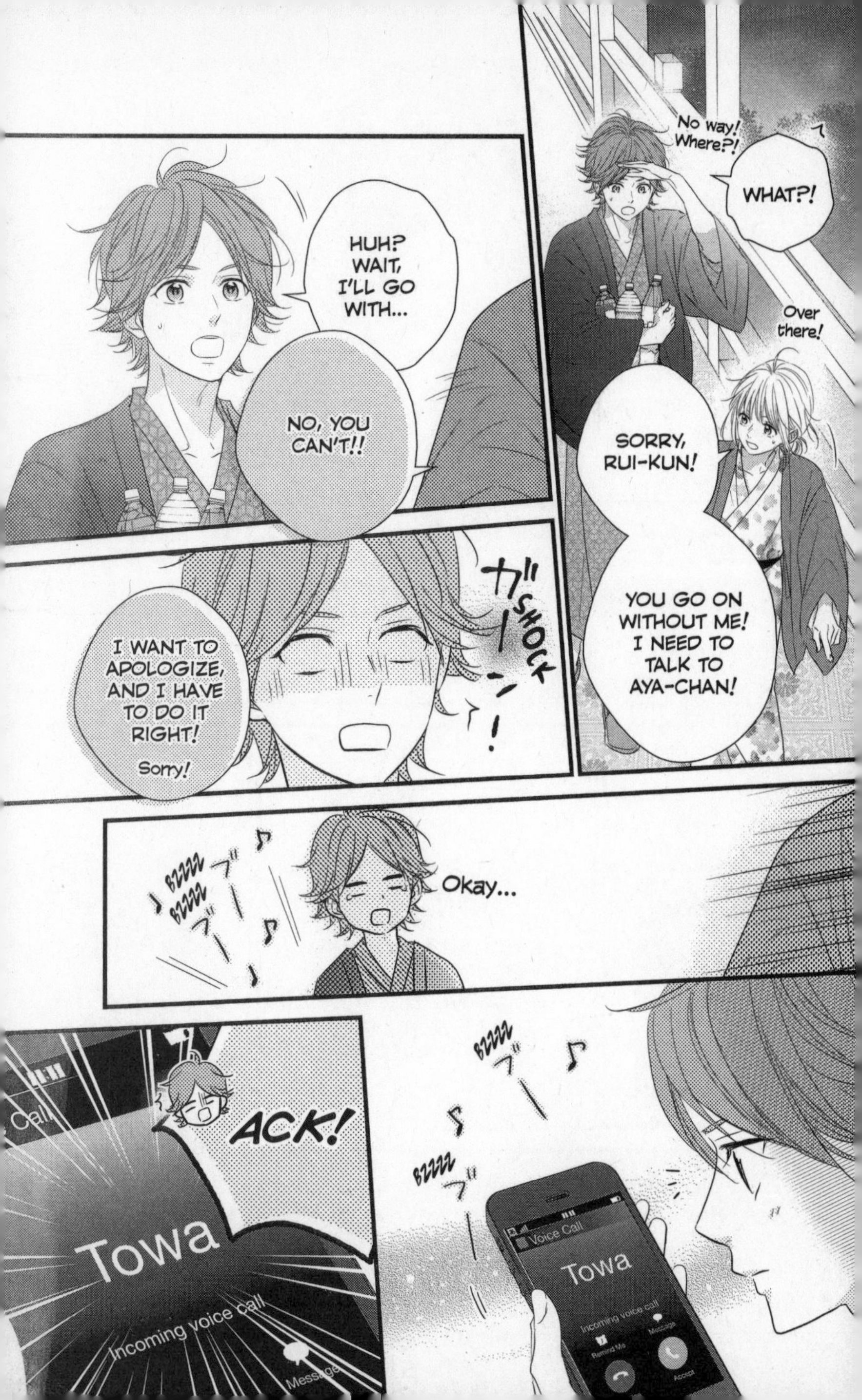
WHAT?!
No way! Where?!
Over there!
SORRY, RUI-KUN!
YOU GO ON WITHOUT ME! I NEED TO TALK TO AYA-CHAN!
HUH? WAIT, I'LL GO WITH...
NO, YOU CAN'T!!
ガ SHOCK
I WANT TO APOLOGIZE, AND I HAVE TO DO IT RIGHT!
Sorry!
Okay...
BZZZZ ブー
BZZZZ ブー
BZZZZ ブー
BZZZZ ブー
Voice Call
Towa
Incoming voice call
Message
Accept
ACK!
Call
Towa
Incoming voice call
Message

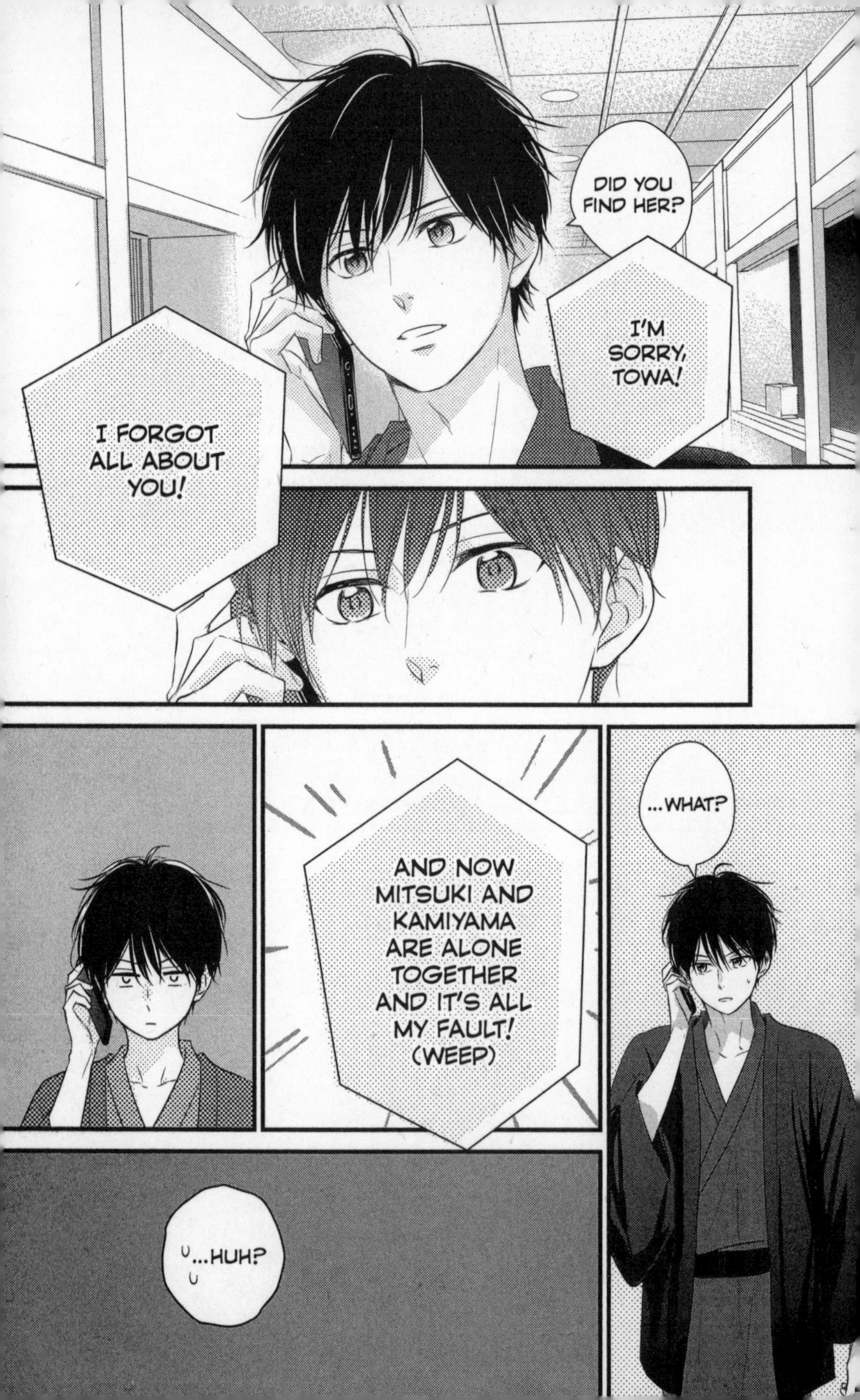
DID YOU FIND HER?
I'M SORRY, TOWA!
I FORGOT ALL ABOUT YOU!
...WHAT?
AND NOW MITSUKI AND KAMIYAMA ARE ALONE TOGETHER AND IT'S ALL MY FAULT! (WEEP)
...HUH?

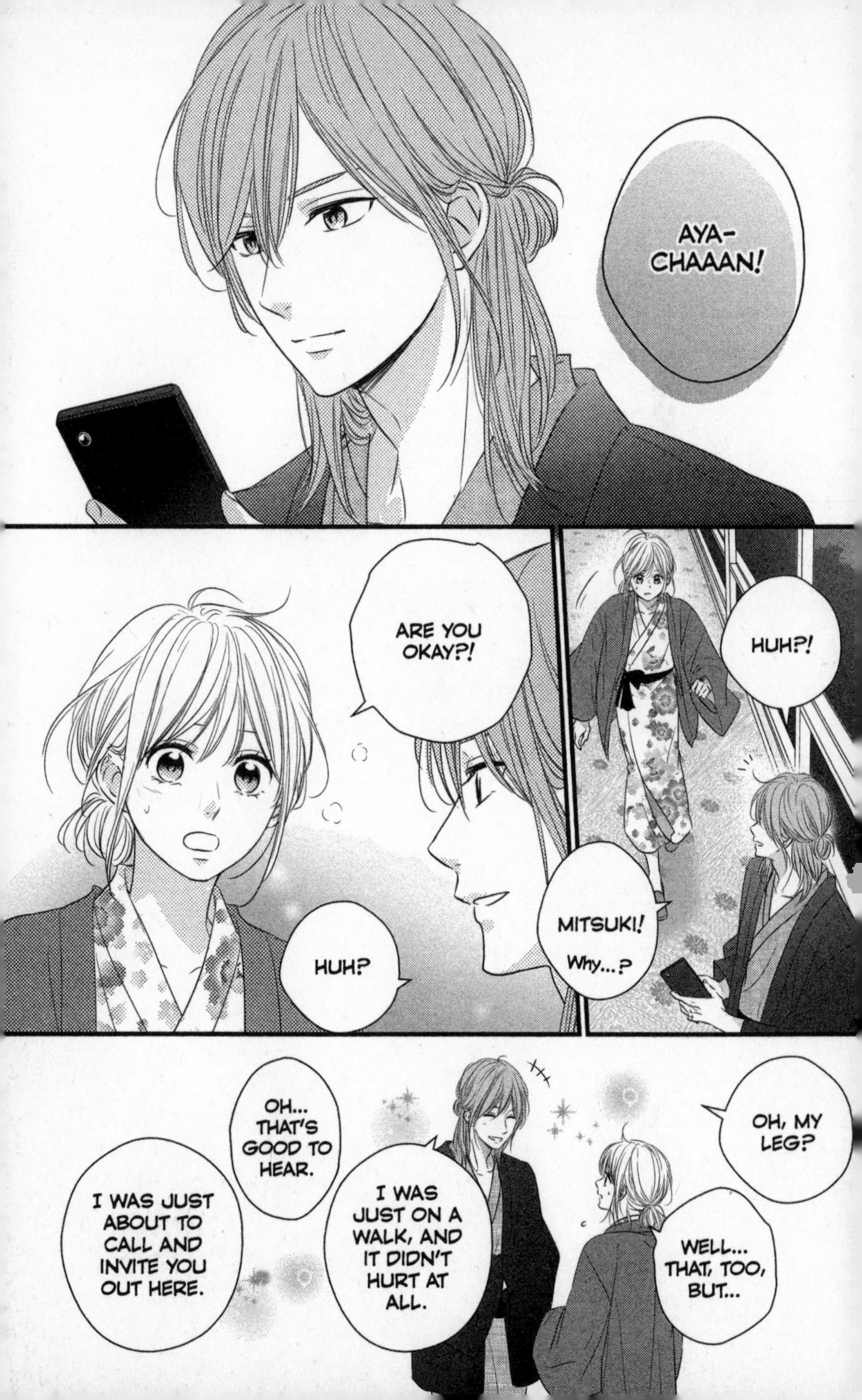
AYA-CHAAAN!
HUH?!
MITSUKI!
Why...?
ARE YOU OKAY?!
HUH?
OH, MY LEG?
WELL... THAT, TOO, BUT...
I WAS JUST ON A WALK, AND IT DIDN'T HURT AT ALL.
OH... THAT'S GOOD TO HEAR.
I WAS JUST ABOUT TO CALL AND INVITE YOU OUT HERE.

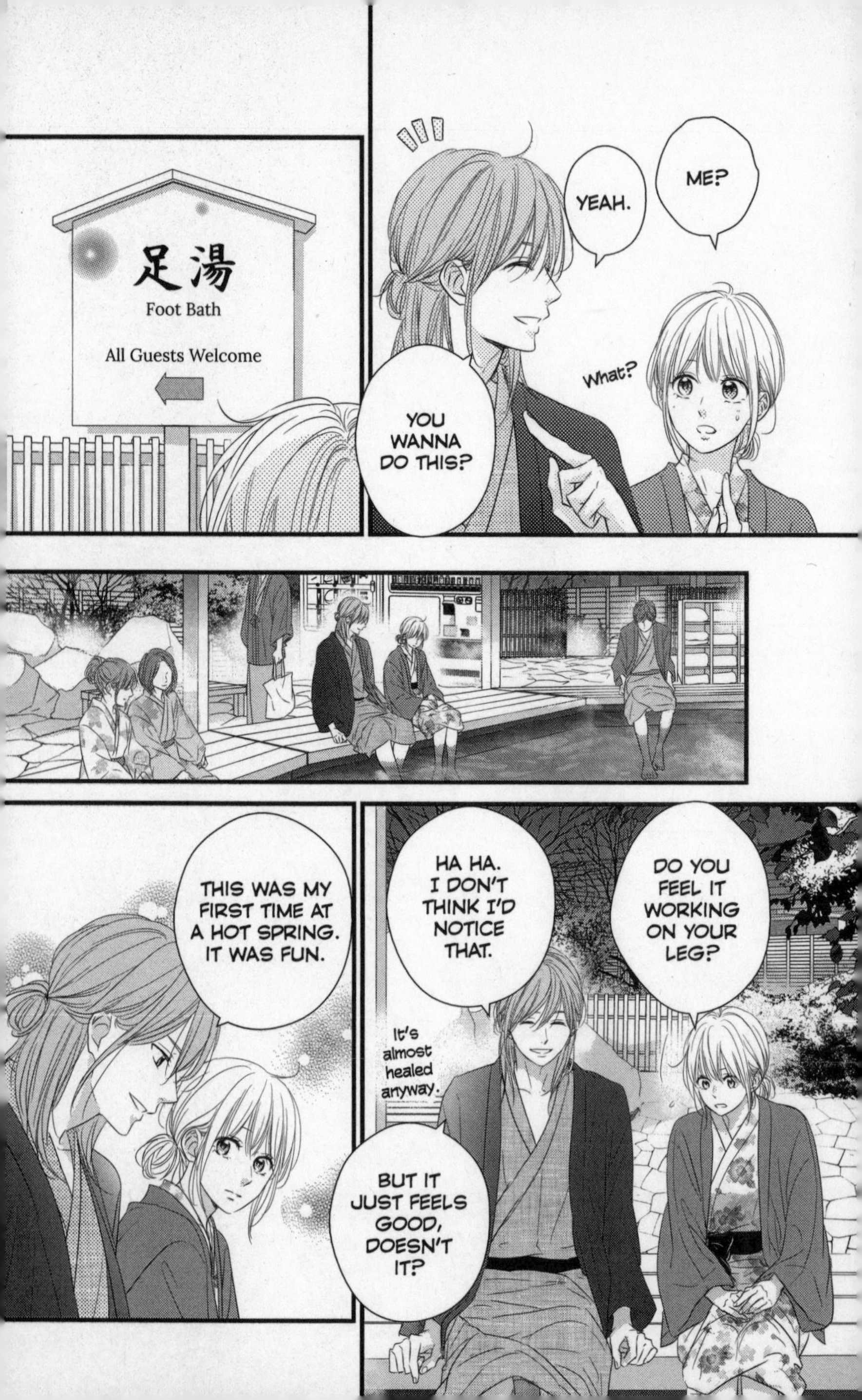
ME?
YEAH.
What?
YOU WANNA DO THIS?
足湯
Foot Bath
All Guests Welcome
DO YOU FEEL IT WORKING ON YOUR LEG?
HA HA. I DON'T THINK I'D NOTICE THAT.
It's almost healed anyway.
BUT IT JUST FEELS GOOD, DOESN'T IT?
THIS WAS MY FIRST TIME AT A HOT SPRING. IT WAS FUN.

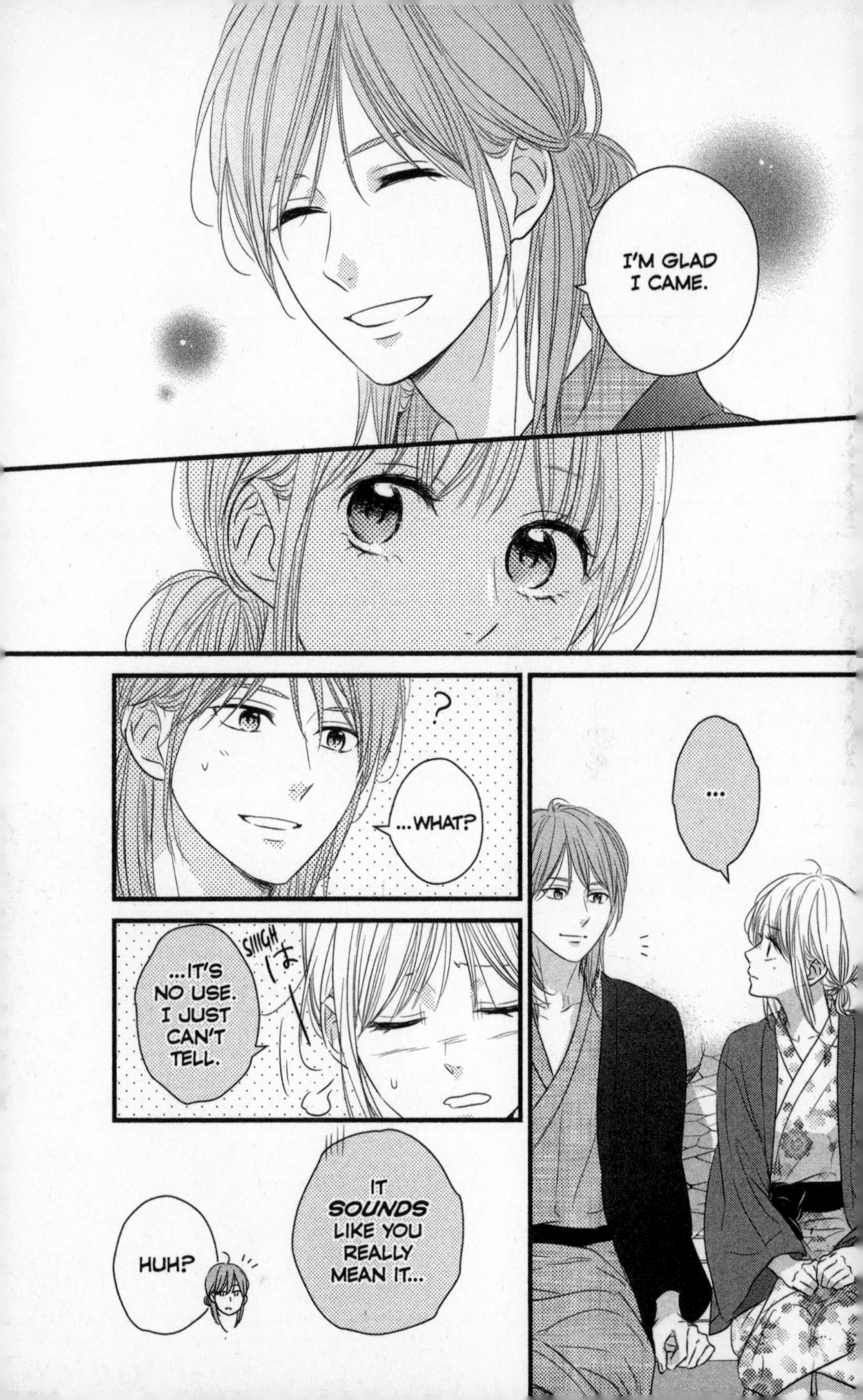
I'M GLAD I CAME.
...
?
...WHAT?
SIIGH
は
...IT'S NO USE. I JUST CAN'T TELL.
IT SOUNDS LIKE YOU REALLY MEAN IT...
HUH?

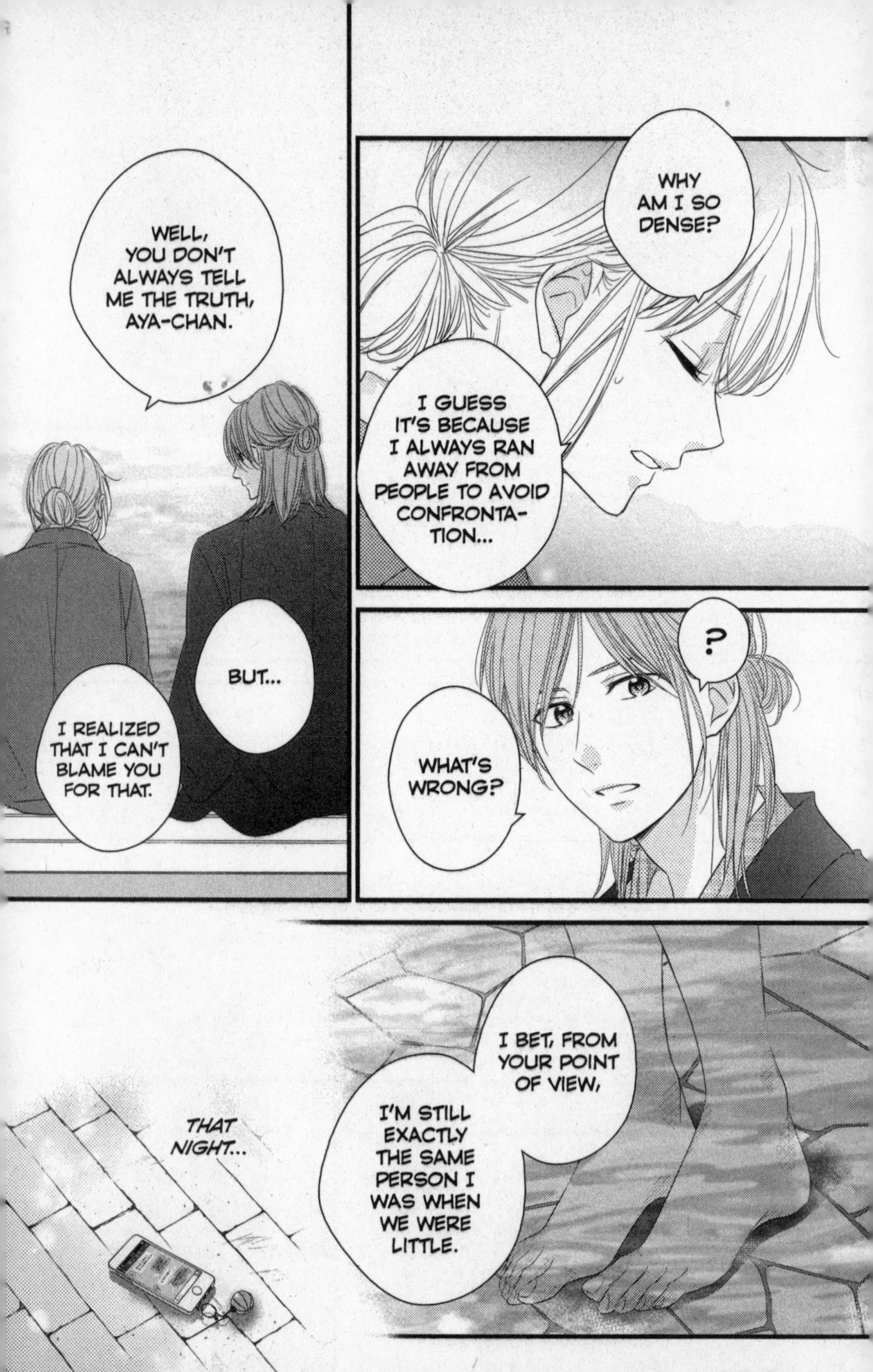
WHY AM I SO DENSE?
I GUESS IT'S BECAUSE I ALWAYS RAN AWAY FROM PEOPLE TO AVOID CONFRONTA-TION...
?
WHAT'S WRONG?
WELL, YOU DON'T ALWAYS TELL ME THE TRUTH, AYA-CHAN.
BUT...
I REALIZED THAT I CAN'T BLAME YOU FOR THAT.
I BET, FROM YOUR POINT OF VIEW,
I'M STILL EXACTLY THE SAME PERSON I WAS WHEN WE WERE LITTLE.
THAT NIGHT...

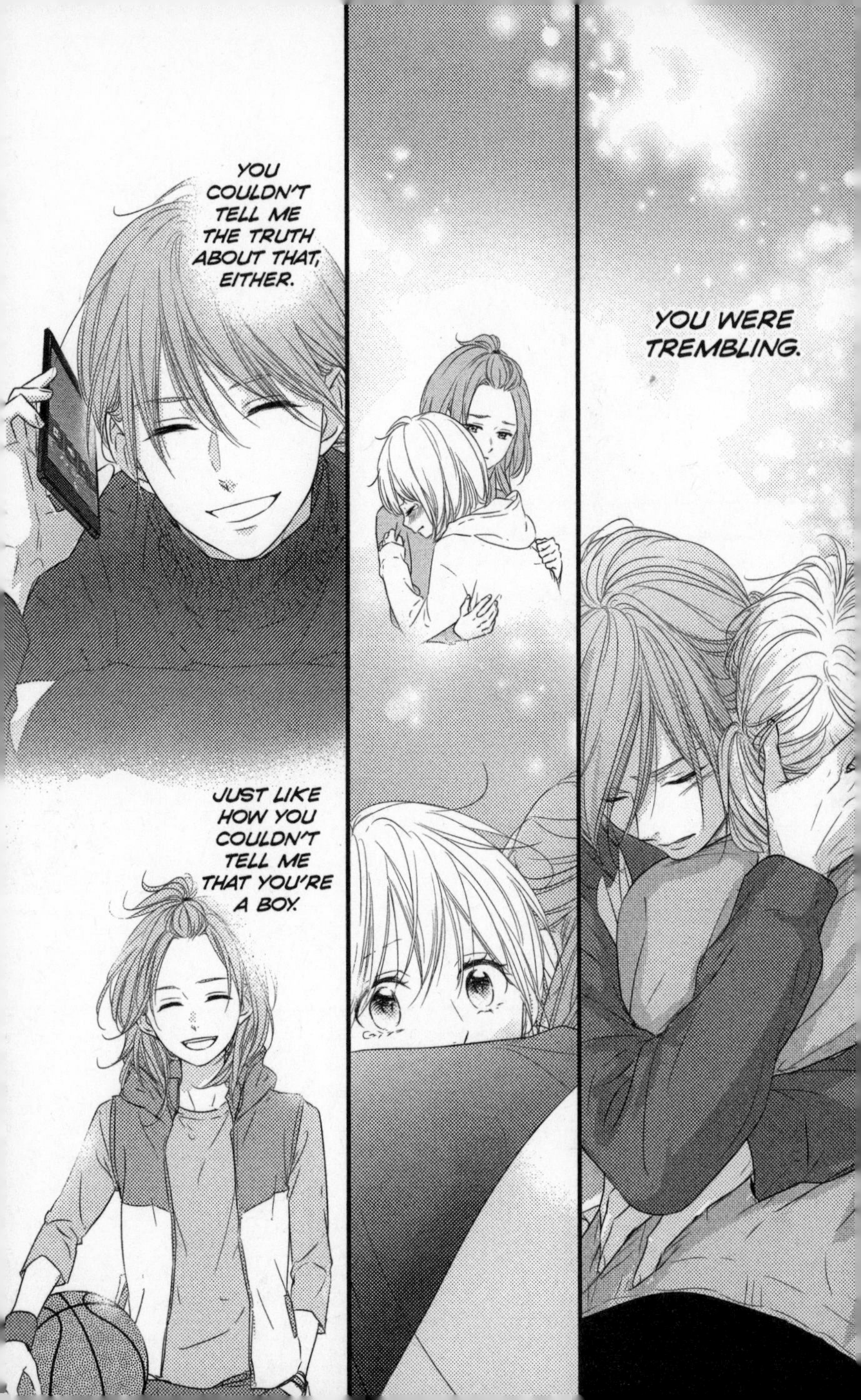
YOU WERE TREMBLING.
YOU COULDN'T TELL ME THE TRUTH ABOUT THAT, EITHER.
JUST LIKE HOW YOU COULDN'T TELL ME THAT YOU'RE A BOY.

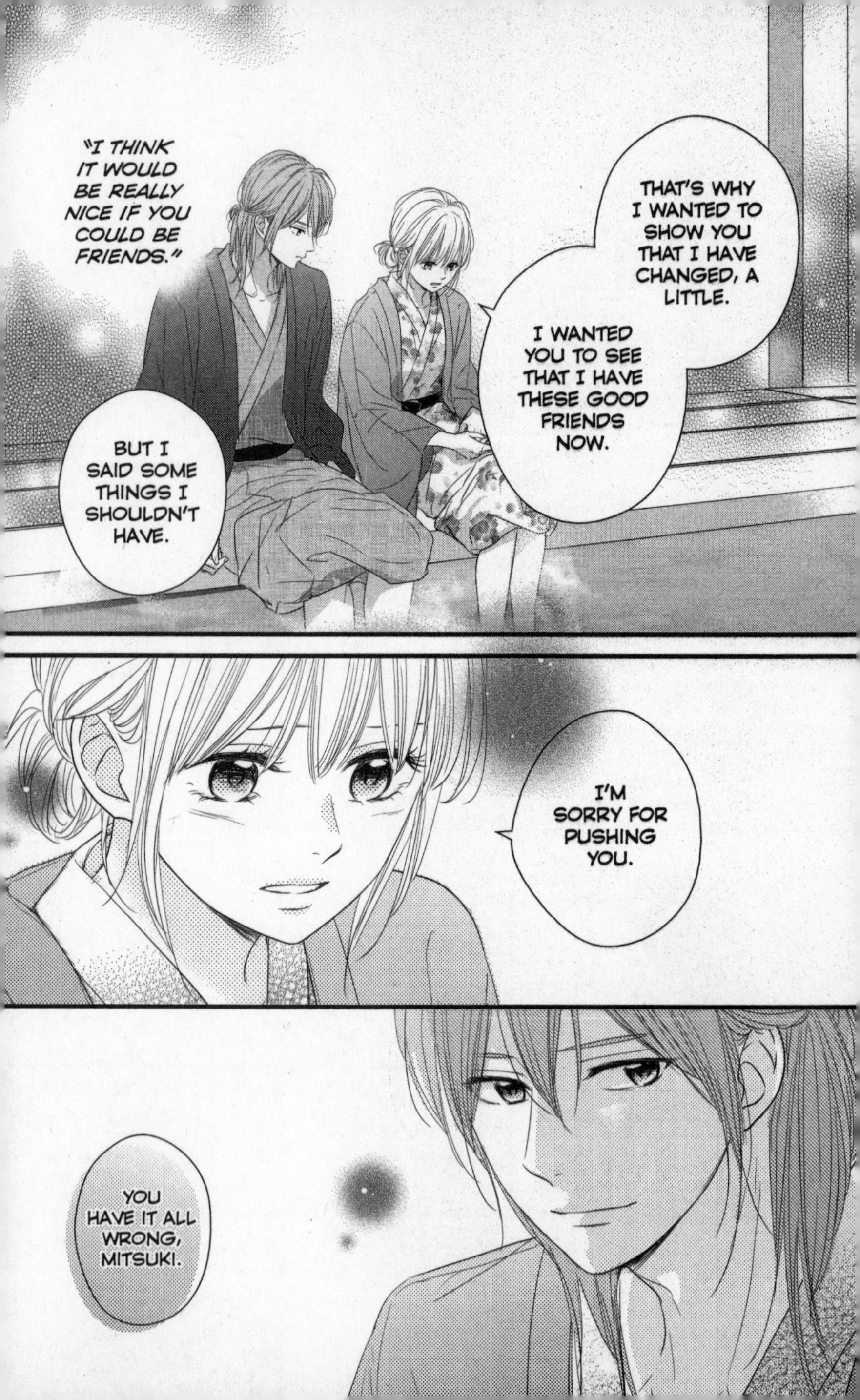
THAT'S WHY I WANTED TO SHOW YOU THAT I HAVE CHANGED, A LITTLE.
I WANTED YOU TO SEE THAT I HAVE THESE GOOD FRIENDS NOW.
"I THINK IT WOULD BE REALLY NICE IF YOU COULD BE FRIENDS."
BUT I SAID SOME THINGS I SHOULDN'T HAVE.
I'M SORRY FOR PUSHING YOU.
YOU HAVE IT ALL WRONG, MITSUKI.

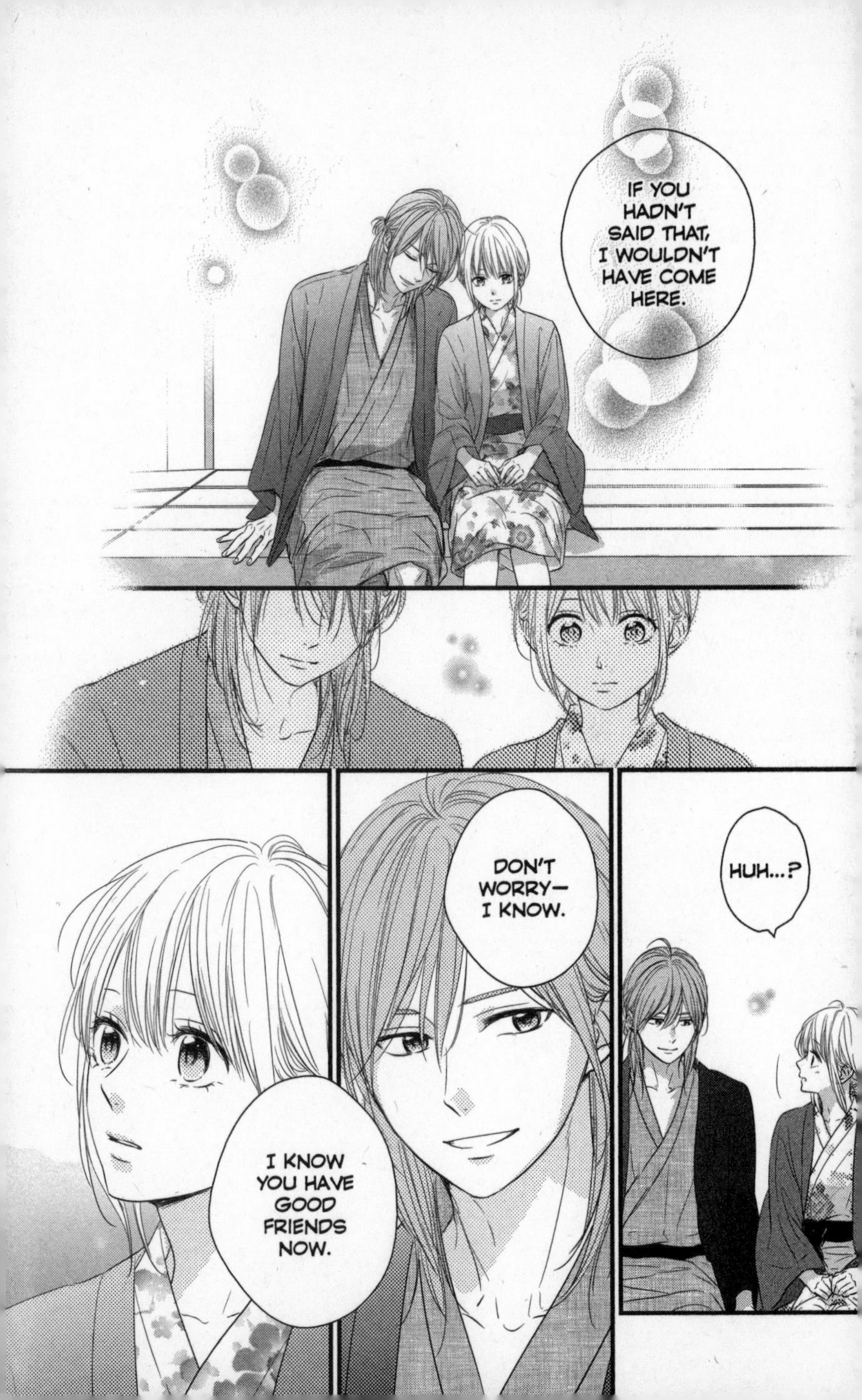
IF YOU HADN'T SAID THAT, I WOULDN'T HAVE COME HERE.
HUH...?
DON'T WORRY— I KNOW.
I KNOW YOU HAVE GOOD FRIENDS NOW.

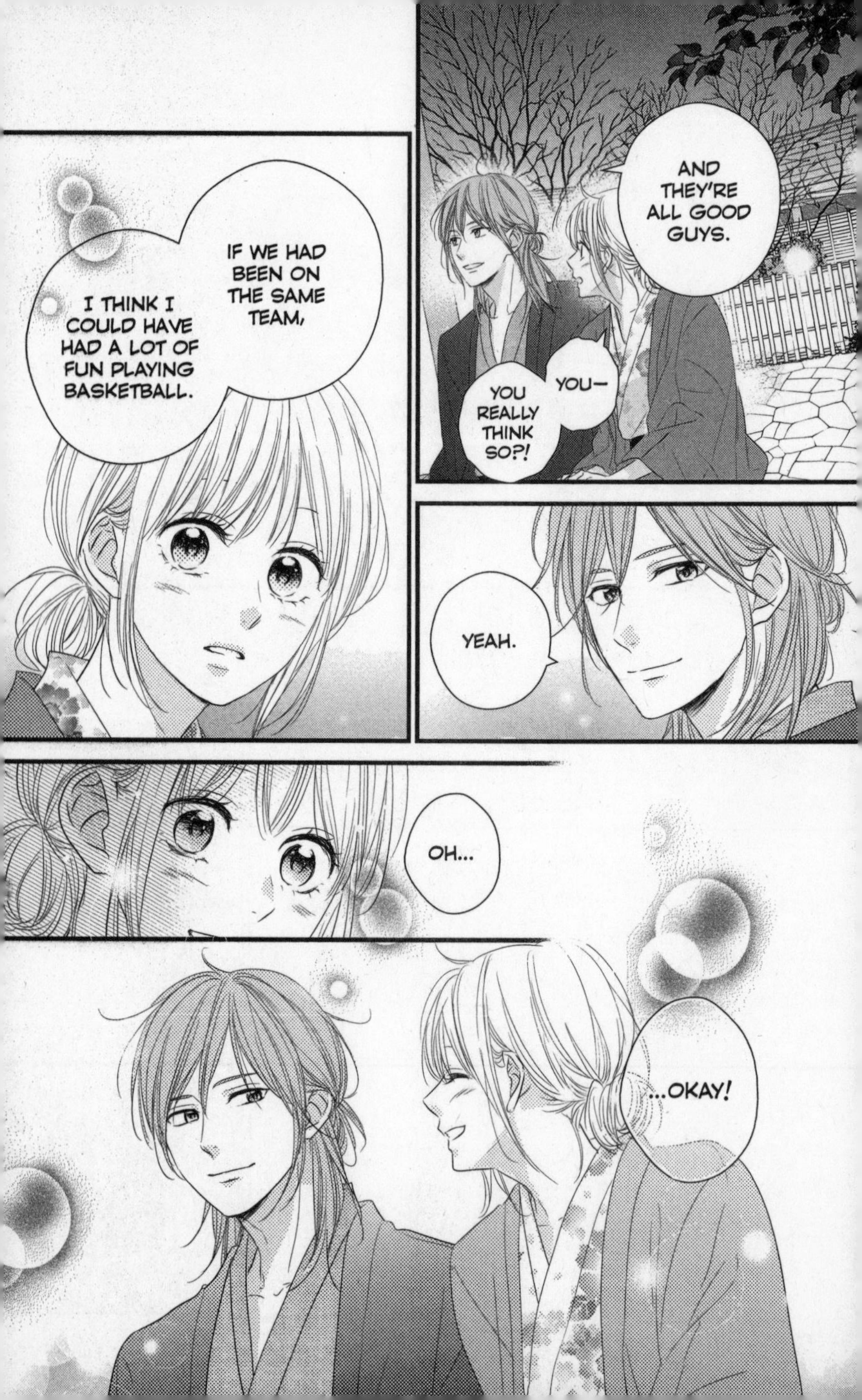
AND THEY'RE ALL GOOD GUYS.
YOU— YOU REALLY THINK SO?!
YEAH.
IF WE HAD BEEN ON THE SAME TEAM,
I THINK I COULD HAVE HAD A LOT OF FUN PLAYING BASKETBALL.
OH...
...OKAY!

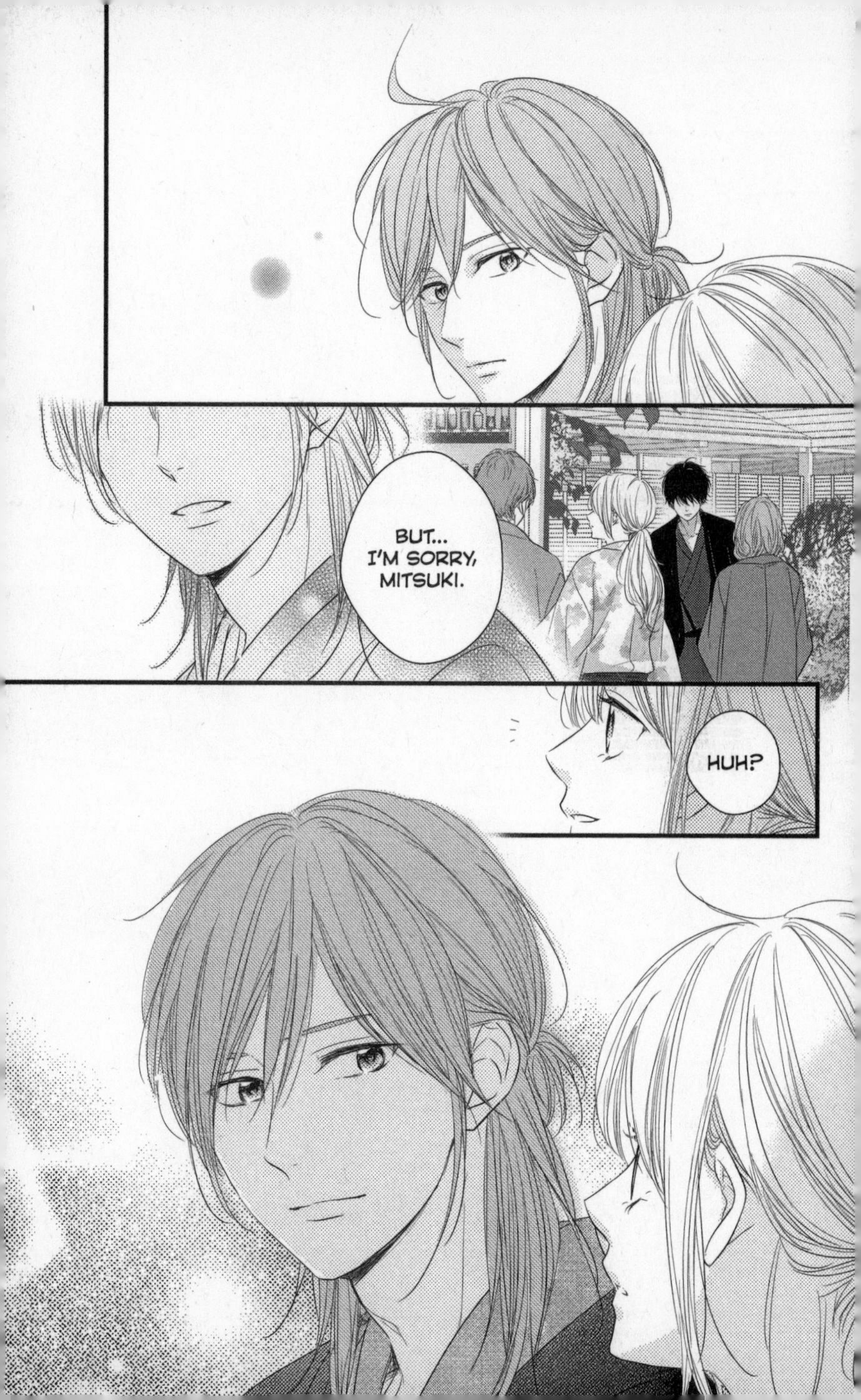
BUT... I'M SORRY, MITSUKI.
HUH?

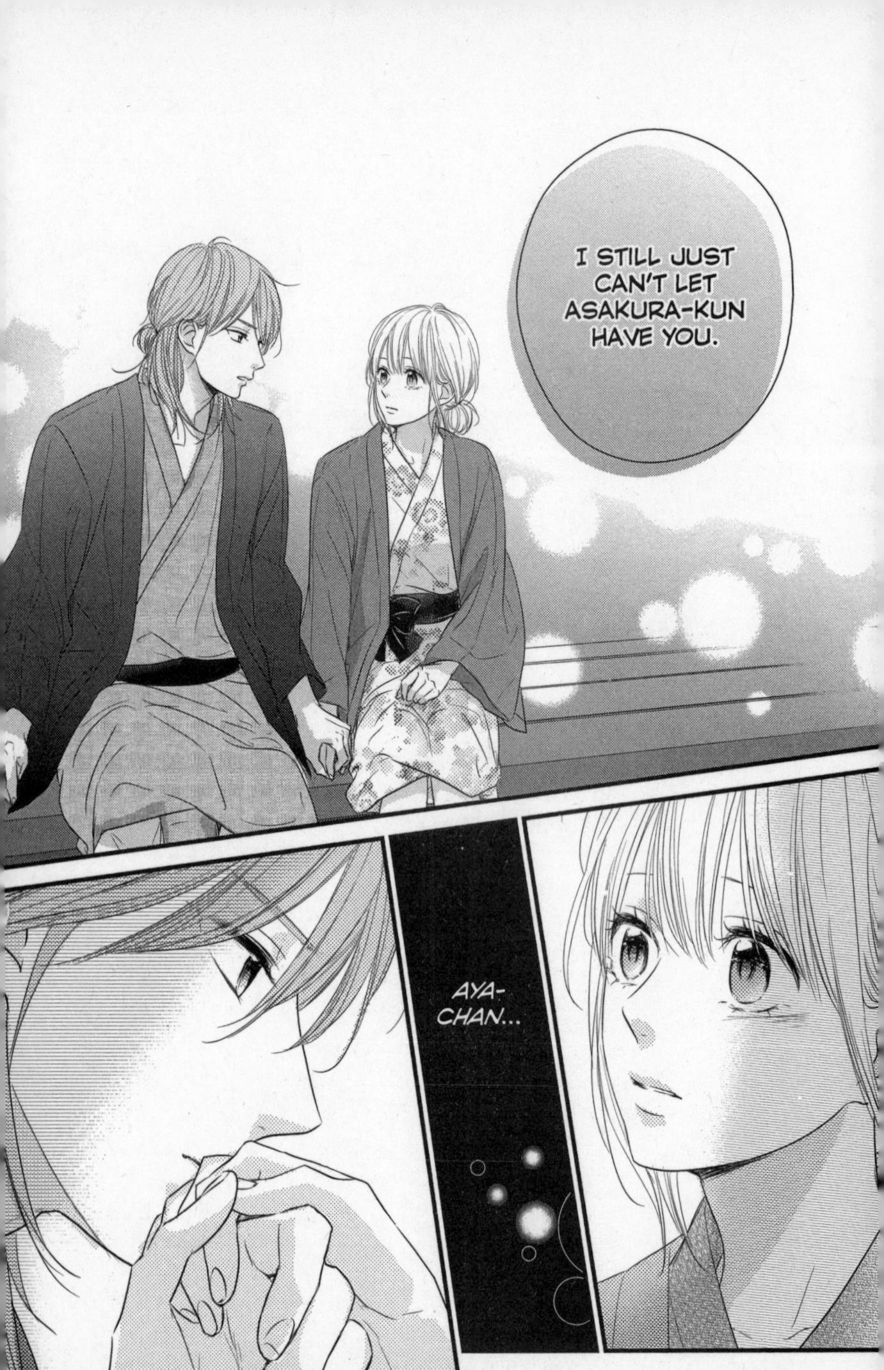
I STILL JUST CAN'T LET ASAKURA-KUN HAVE YOU.
AYA-CHAN...

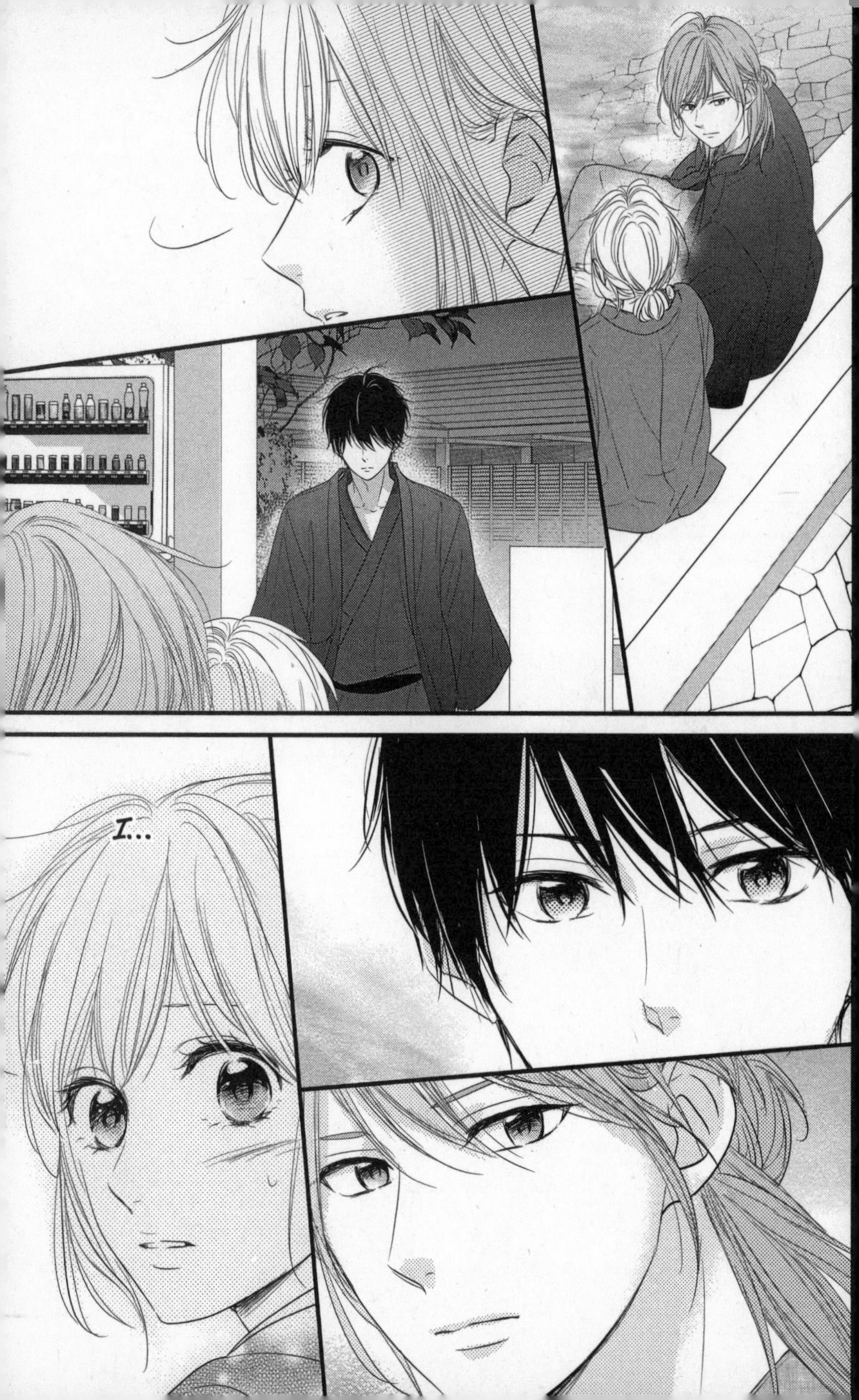
I...

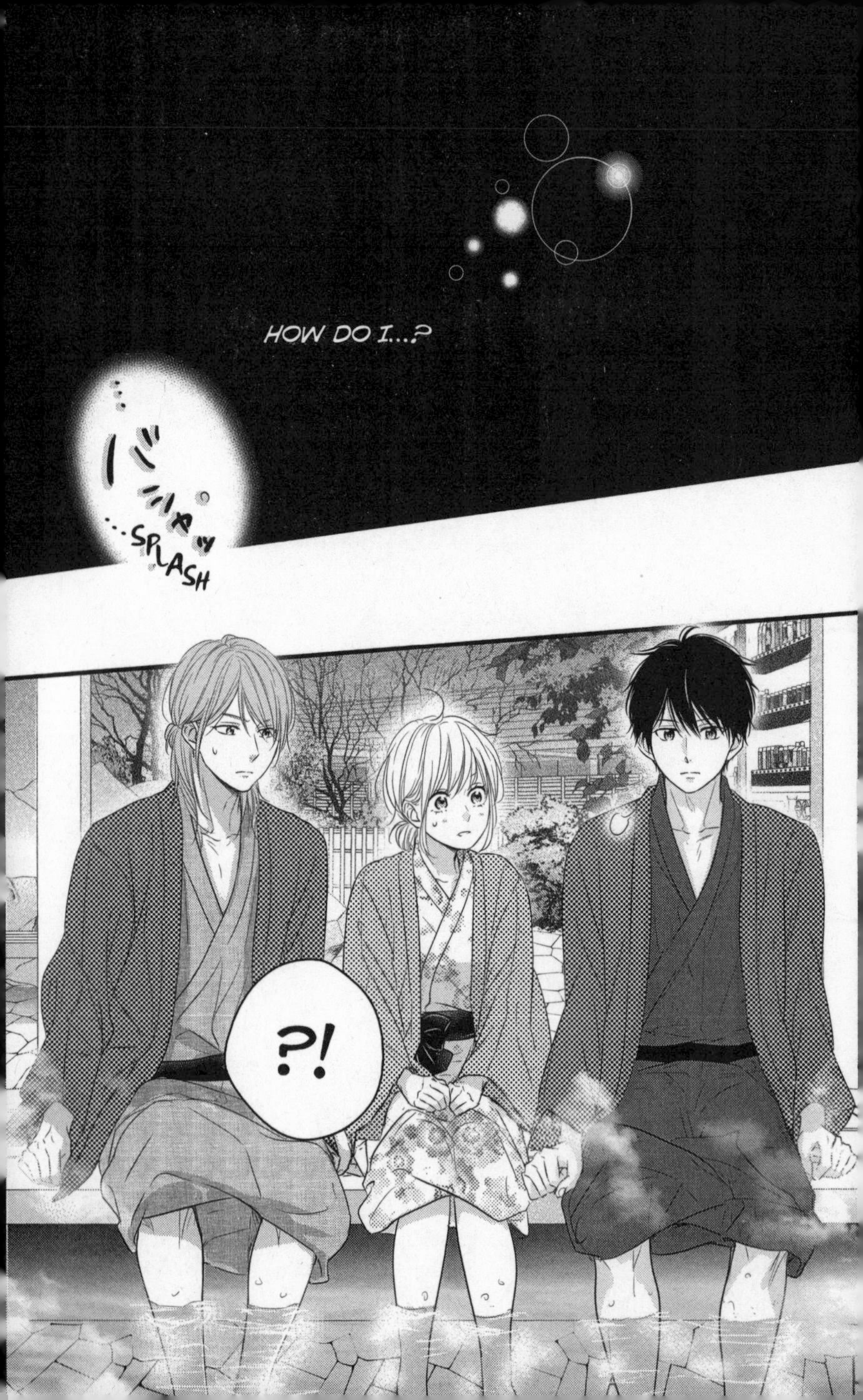
HOW DO I...?
...バシャッ
...SPLASH
?!

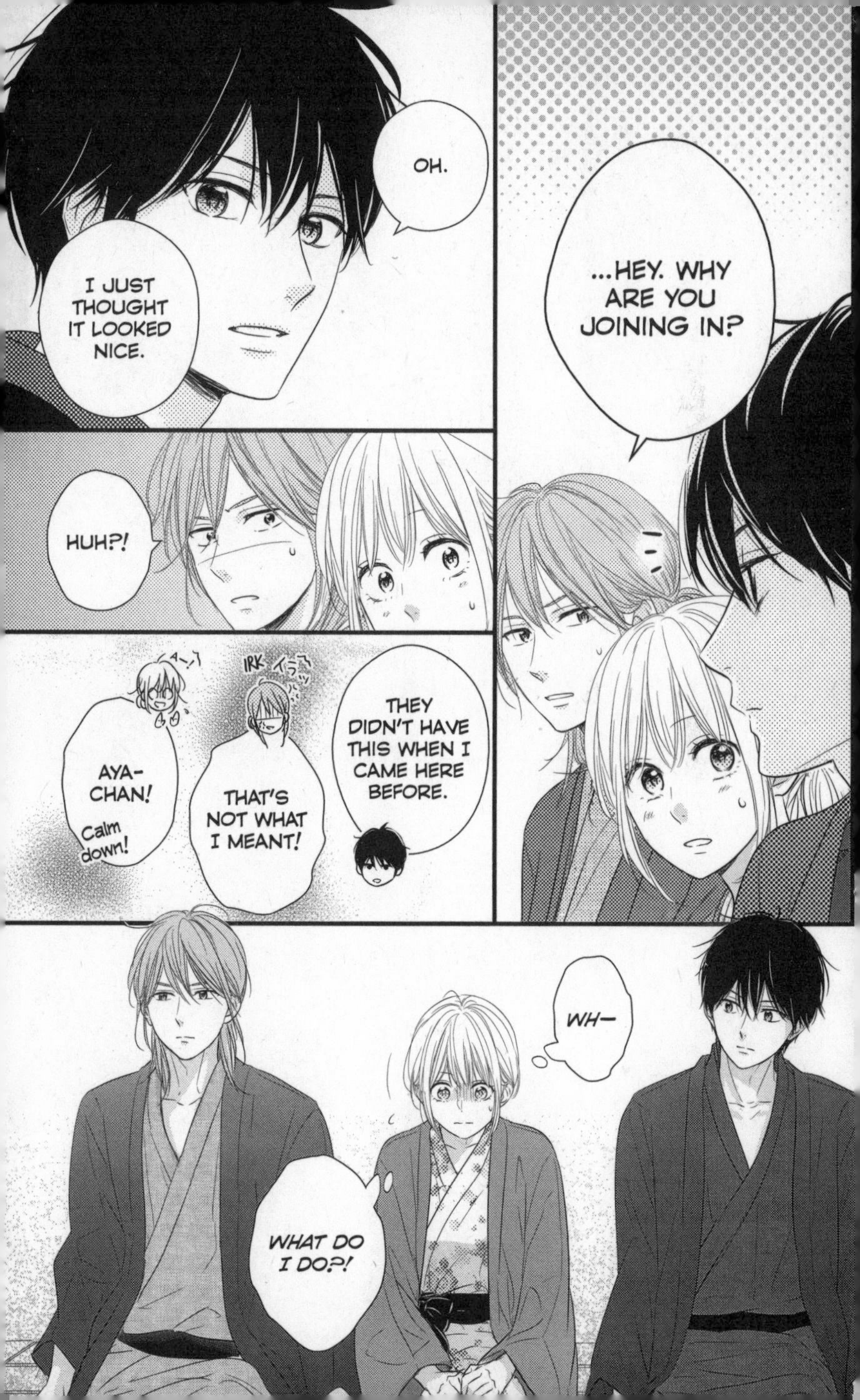
...HEY. WHY ARE YOU JOINING IN?
OH.
I JUST THOUGHT IT LOOKED NICE.
HUH?!
THEY DIDN'T HAVE THIS WHEN I CAME HERE BEFORE.
IRK
THAT'S NOT WHAT I MEANT!
AYA-CHAN!
Calm down!
WH—
WHAT DO I DO?!

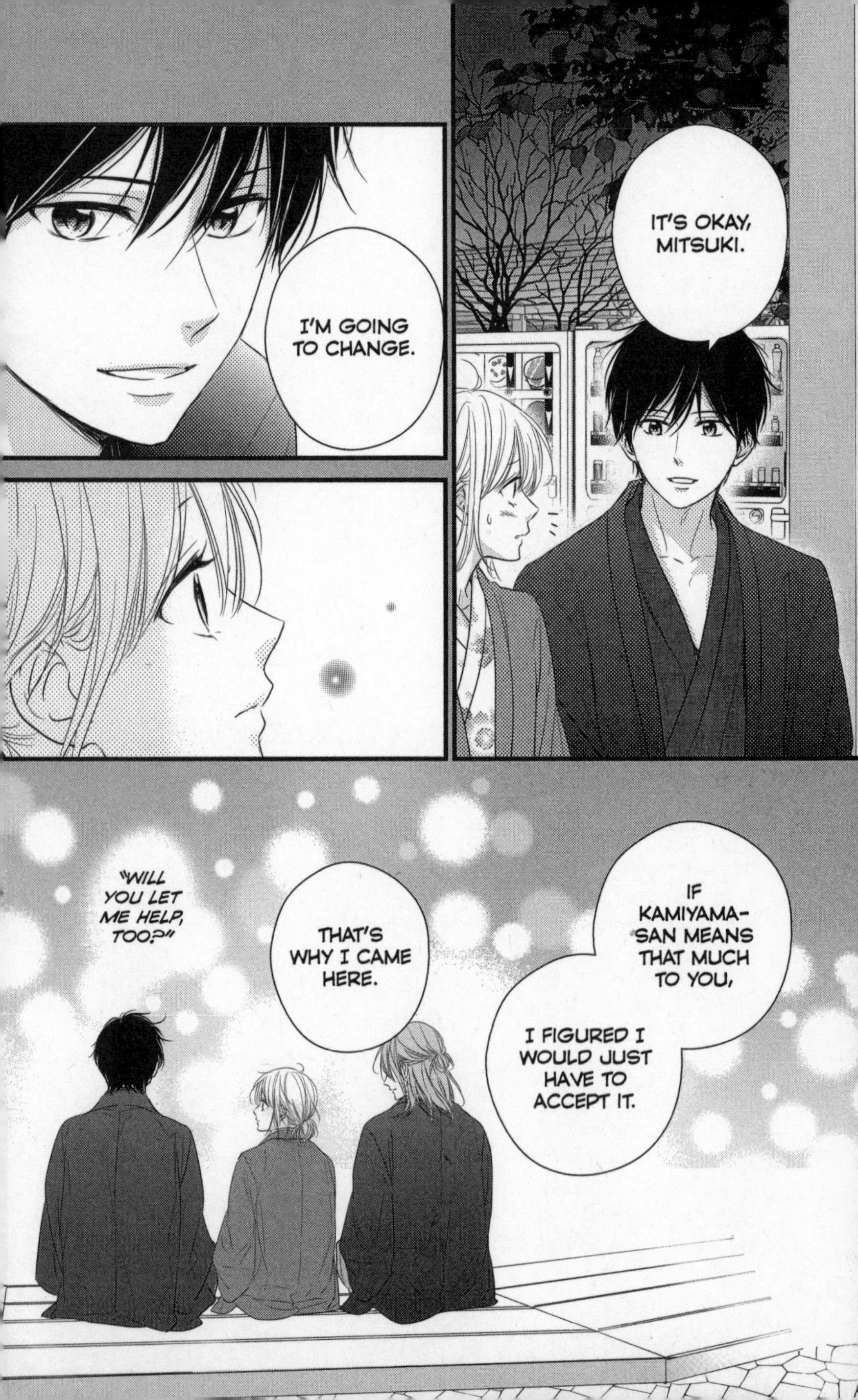
IT'S OKAY, MITSUKI.
I'M GOING TO CHANGE.
IF KAMIYAMA-SAN MEANS THAT MUCH TO YOU,
I FIGURED I WOULD JUST HAVE TO ACCEPT IT.
THAT'S WHY I CAME HERE.
"WILL YOU LET ME HELP, TOO?"

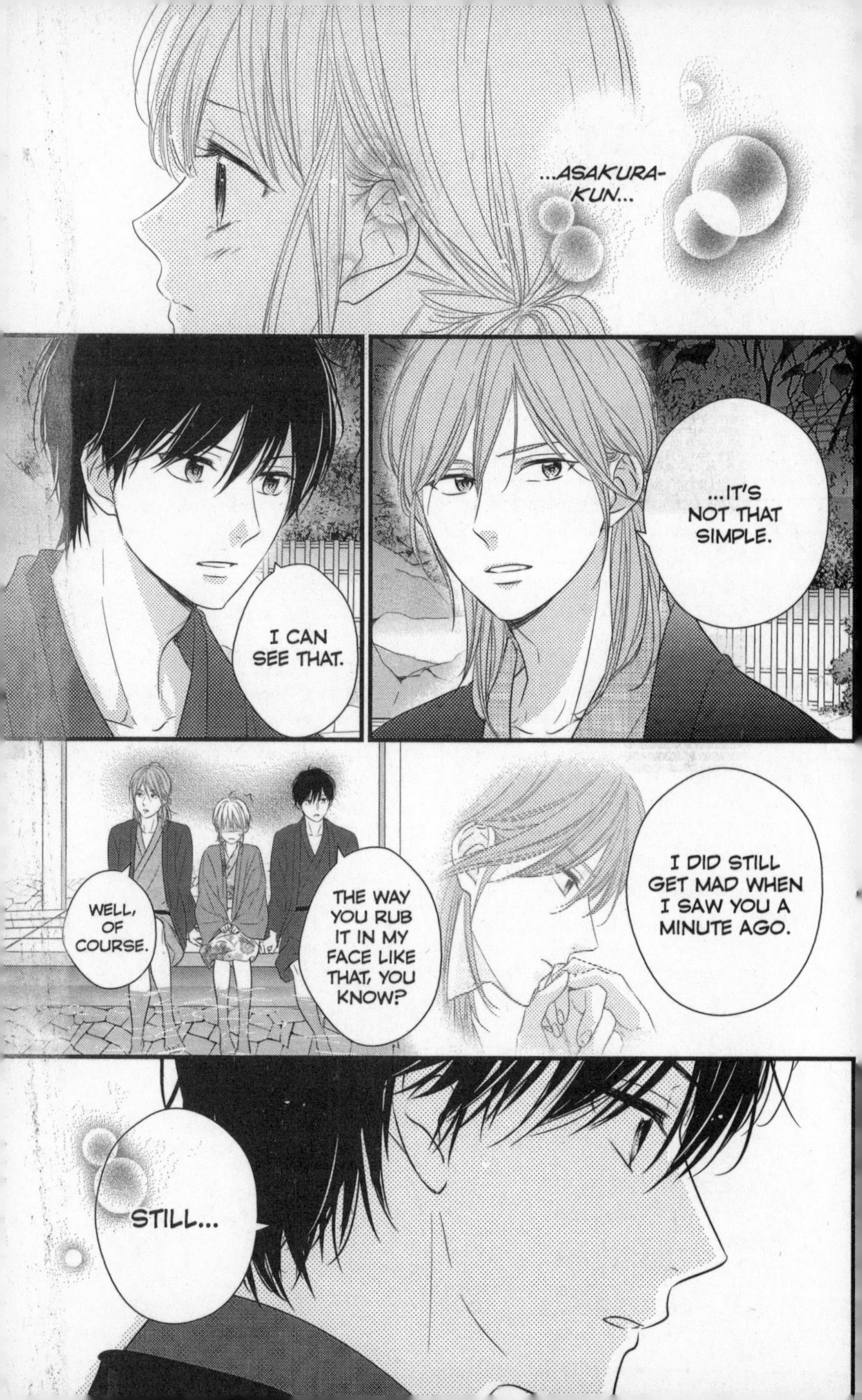
...ASAKURA-KUN...
...IT'S NOT THAT SIMPLE.
I CAN SEE THAT.
I DID STILL GET MAD WHEN I SAW YOU A MINUTE AGO.
THE WAY YOU RUB IT IN MY FACE LIKE THAT, YOU KNOW?
WELL, OF COURSE.
STILL...

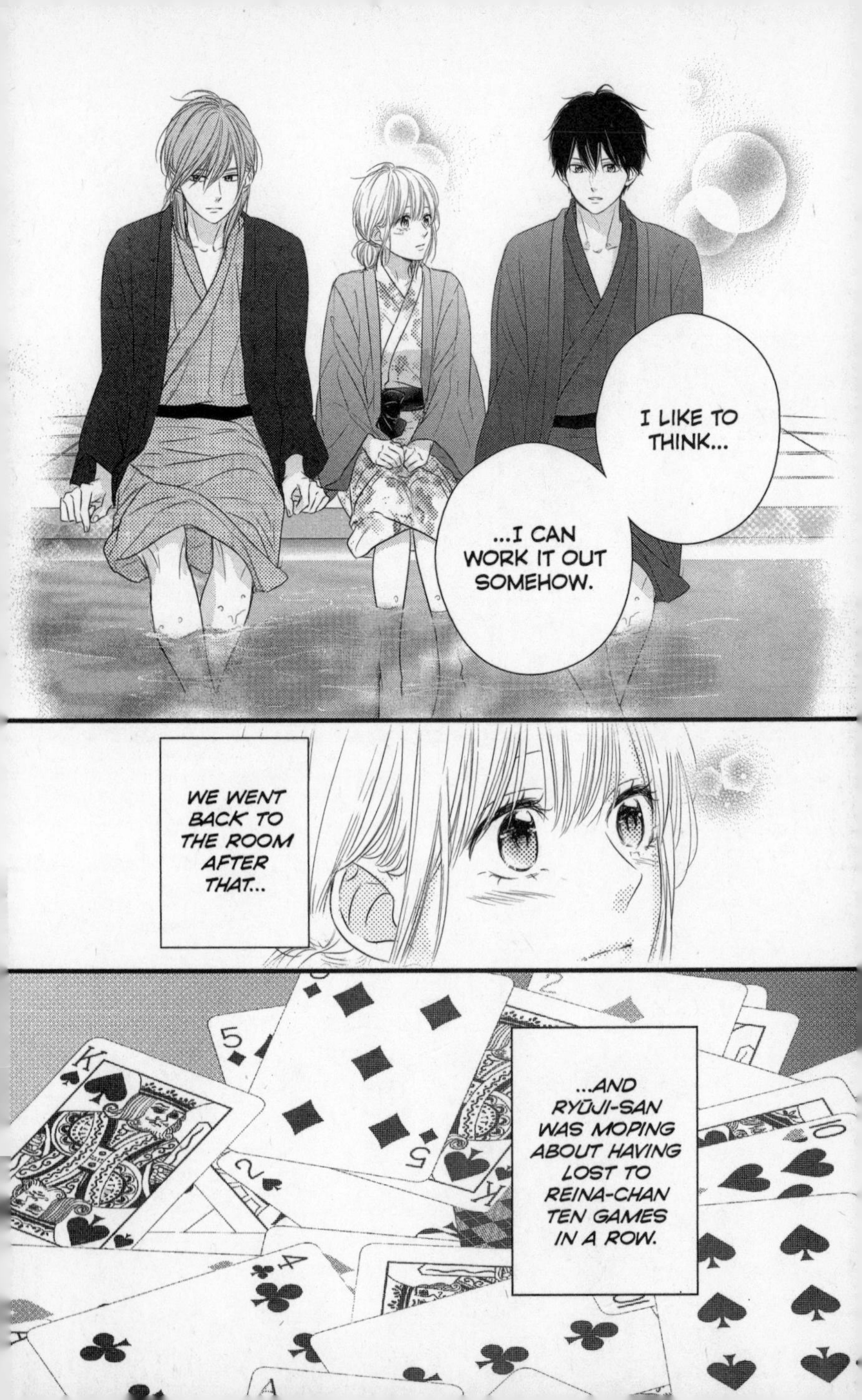
I LIKE TO THINK...
...I CAN WORK IT OUT SOMEHOW.
WE WENT BACK TO THE ROOM AFTER THAT...
...AND RYŪJI-SAN WAS MOPING ABOUT HAVING LOST TO REINA-CHAN TEN GAMES IN A ROW.

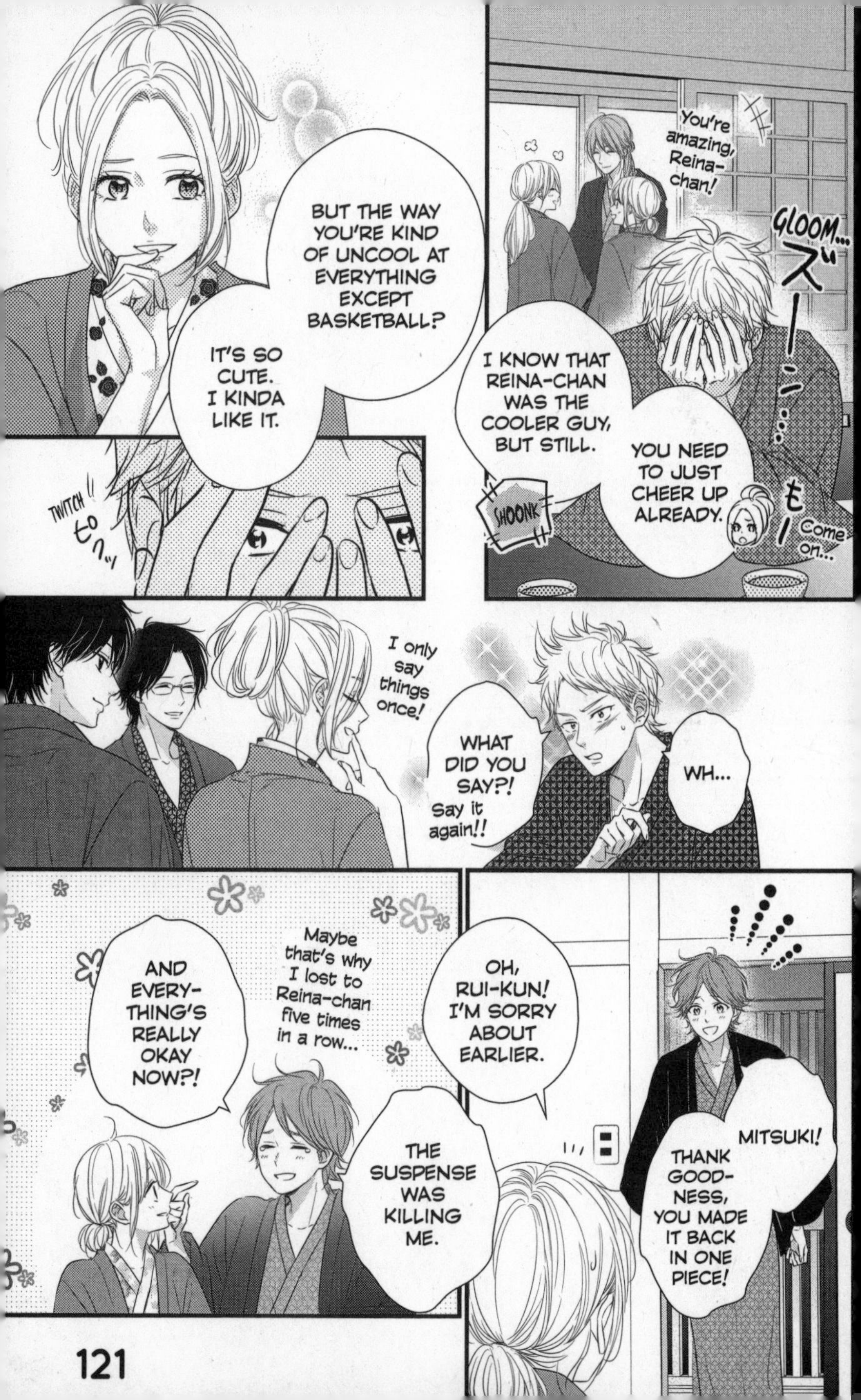

You're amazing, Reina-chan!
GLOOM...
I KNOW THAT REINA-CHAN WAS THE COOLER GUY, BUT STILL.
SHOONK
YOU NEED TO JUST CHEER UP ALREADY.
Come on...
BUT THE WAY YOU'RE KIND OF UNCOOL AT EVERYTHING EXCEPT BASKETBALL?
IT'S SO CUTE. I KINDA LIKE IT.
TWITCH!!
WH...
WHAT DID YOU SAY?!
Say it again!!
I only say things once!
MITSUKI!
THANK GOODNESS, YOU MADE IT BACK IN ONE PIECE!
OH, RUI-KUN! I'M SORRY ABOUT EARLIER.
THE SUSPENSE WAS KILLING ME.
Maybe that's why I lost to Reina-chan five times in a row...
AND EVERYTHING'S REALLY OKAY NOW?!

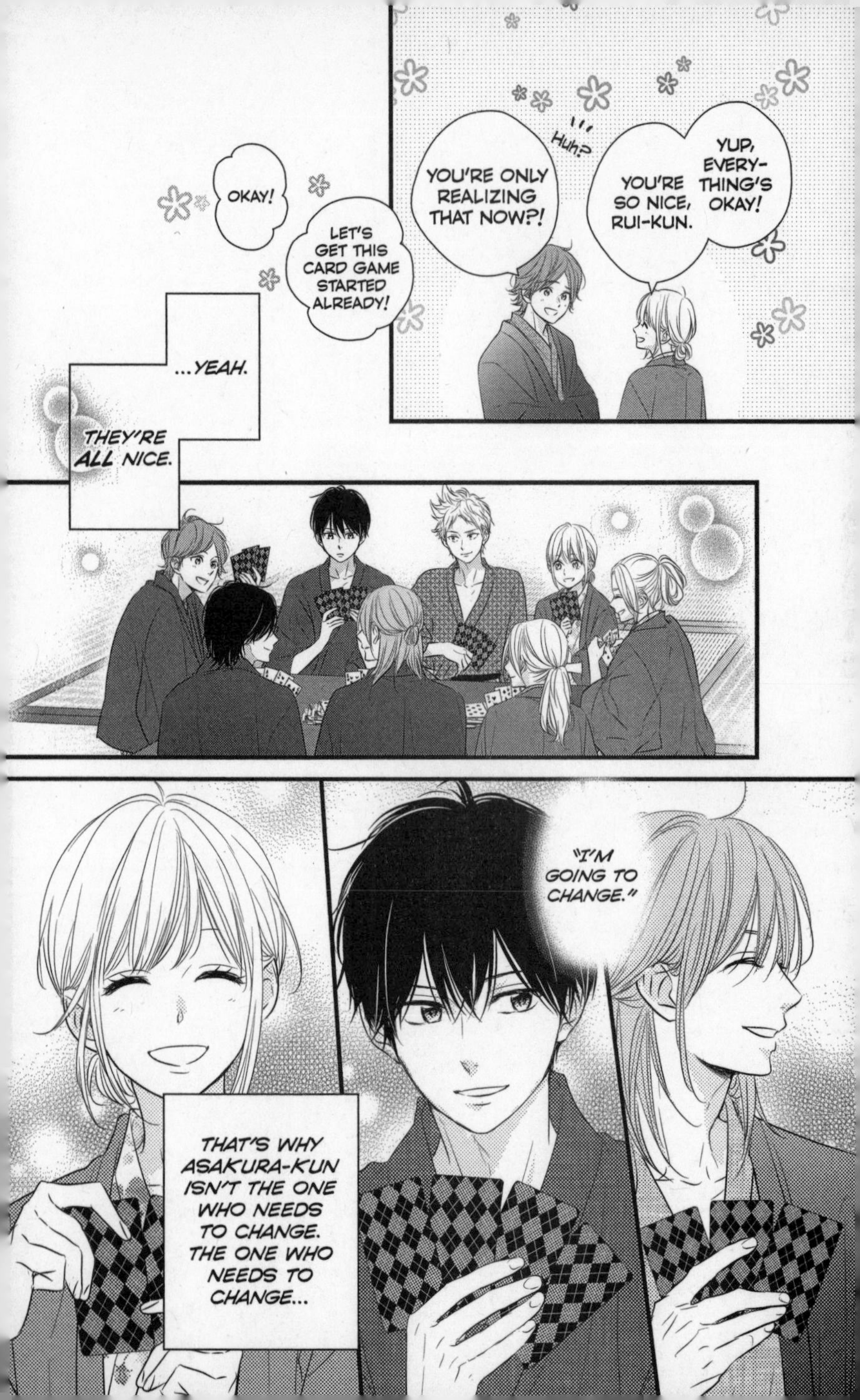
YUP, EVERY-THING'S OKAY!
YOU'RE SO NICE, RUI-KUN.
Huh?
YOU'RE ONLY REALIZING THAT NOW?!
LET'S GET THIS CARD GAME STARTED ALREADY!
OKAY!
...YEAH.
THEY'RE ALL NICE.
"I'M GOING TO CHANGE."
THAT'S WHY ASAKURA-KUN ISN'T THE ONE WHO NEEDS TO CHANGE. THE ONE WHO NEEDS TO CHANGE...

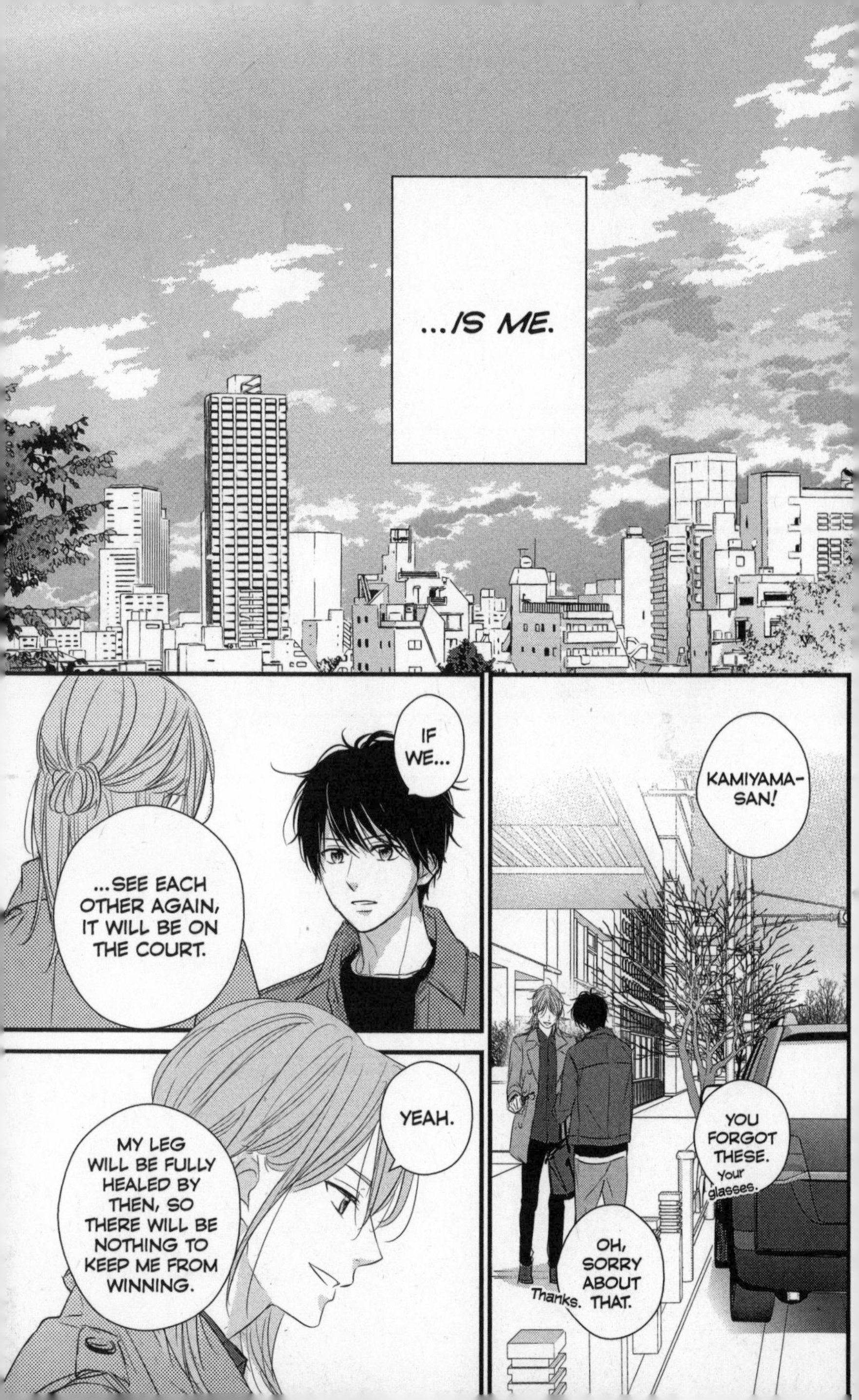
...IS ME.
KAMIYAMA-SAN!
YOU FORGOT THESE.
Your glasses.
OH, SORRY ABOUT THAT.
Thanks.
IF WE...
...SEE EACH OTHER AGAIN, IT WILL BE ON THE COURT.
YEAH.
MY LEG WILL BE FULLY HEALED BY THEN, SO THERE WILL BE NOTHING TO KEEP ME FROM WINNING.

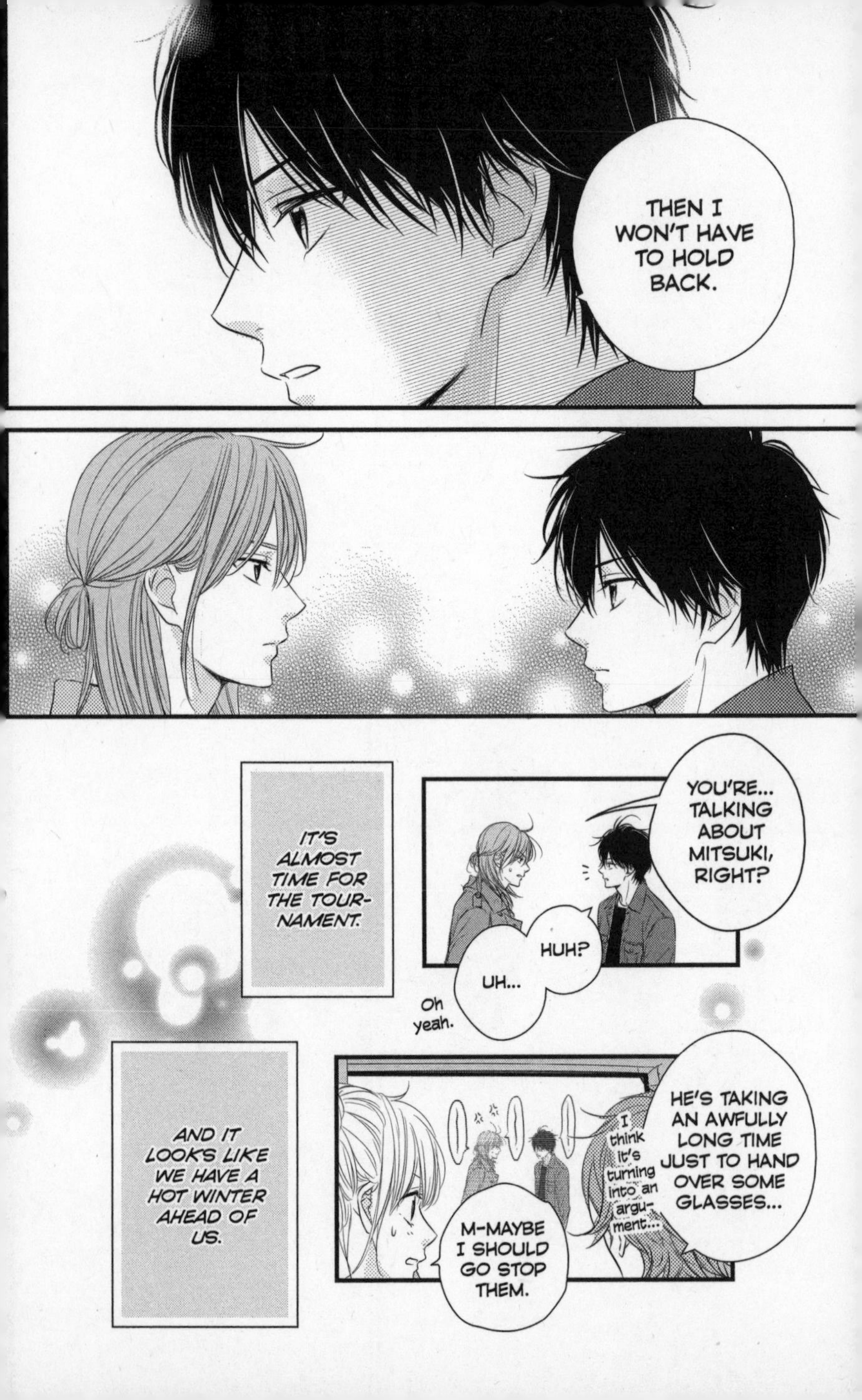
THEN I WON'T HAVE TO HOLD BACK.
YOU'RE... TALKING ABOUT MITSUKI, RIGHT?
HUH?
UH...
Oh yeah.
IT'S ALMOST TIME FOR THE TOURNAMENT.
HE'S TAKING AN AWFULLY LONG TIME JUST TO HAND OVER SOME GLASSES...
I think it's turning into an argument...
M-MAYBE I SHOULD GO STOP THEM.
AND IT LOOKS LIKE WE HAVE A HOT WINTER AHEAD OF US.

period 44: "A Pure Winter Night"

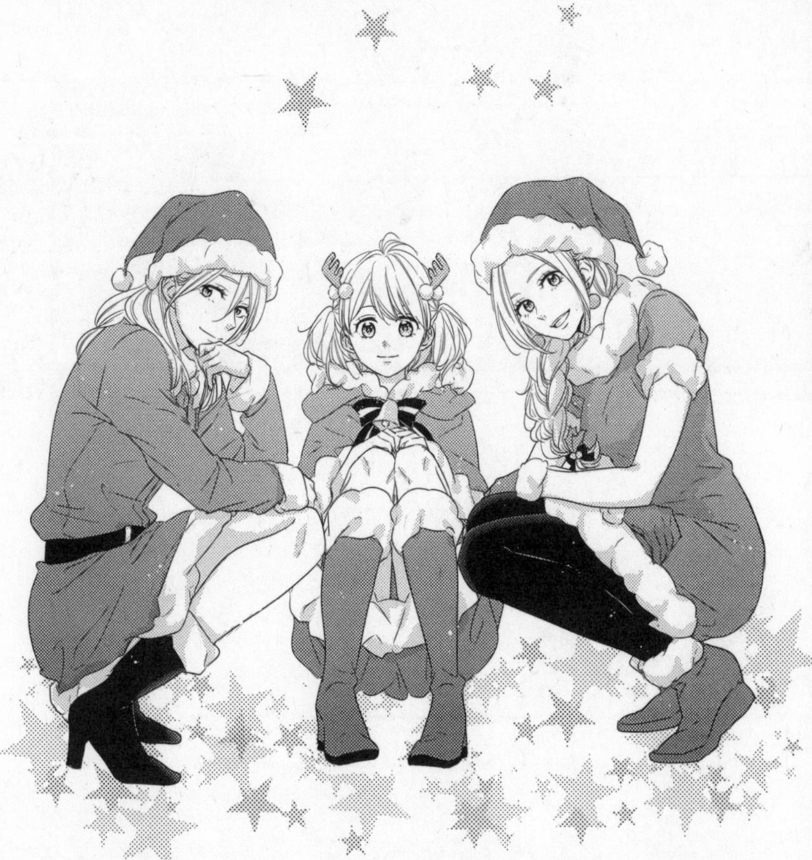

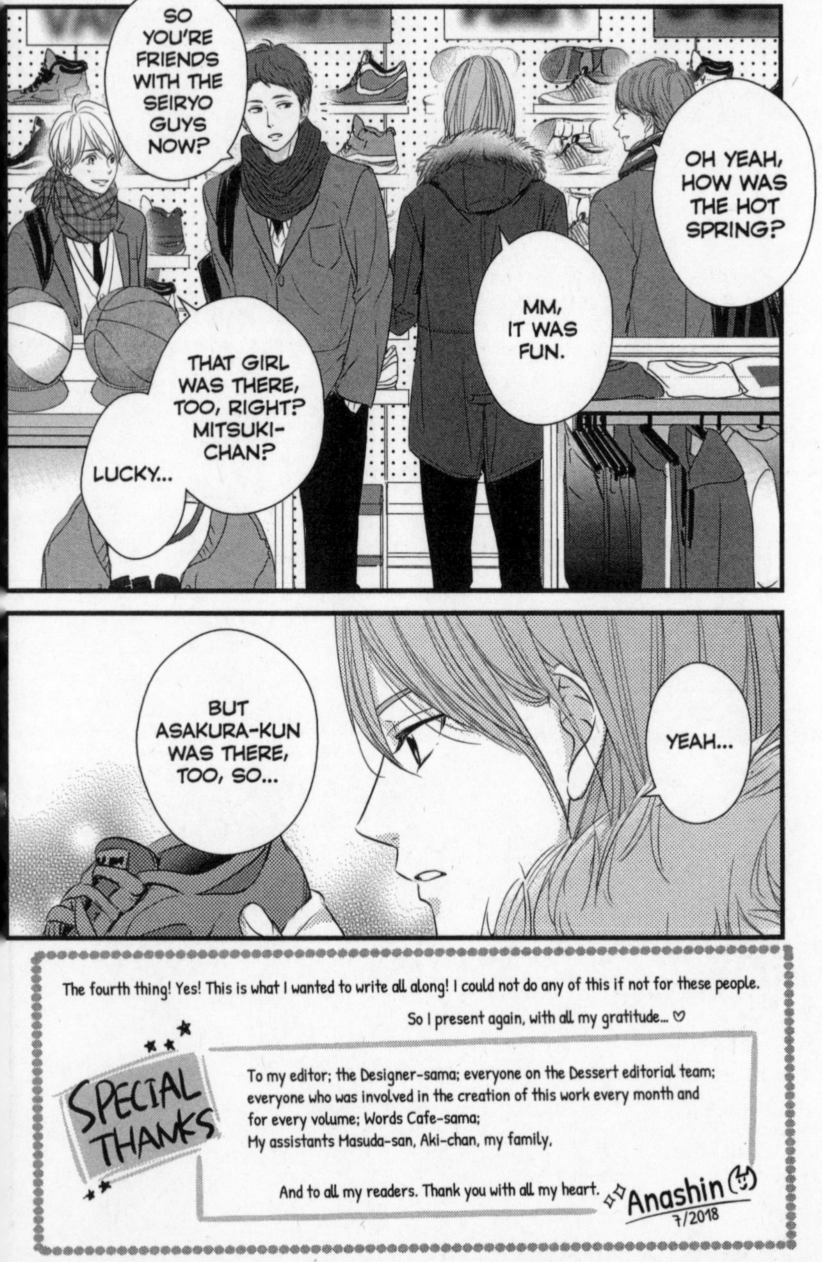
OH YEAH, HOW WAS THE HOT SPRING?
MM, IT WAS FUN.
SO YOU'RE FRIENDS WITH THE SEIRYO GUYS NOW?
THAT GIRL WAS THERE, TOO, RIGHT? MITSUKI-CHAN?
LUCKY...
BUT ASAKURA-KUN WAS THERE, TOO, SO...
YEAH...

The fourth thing! Yes! This is what I wanted to write all along! I could not do any of this if not for these people.

So I present again, with all my gratitude... ♡

SPECIAL THANKS

To my editor; the Designer-sama; everyone on the Dessert editorial team; everyone who was involved in the creation of this work every month and for every volume; Words Cafe-sama;
My assistants Masuda-san, Aki-chan, my family,

And to all my readers. Thank you with all my heart.

Anashin
7/2018

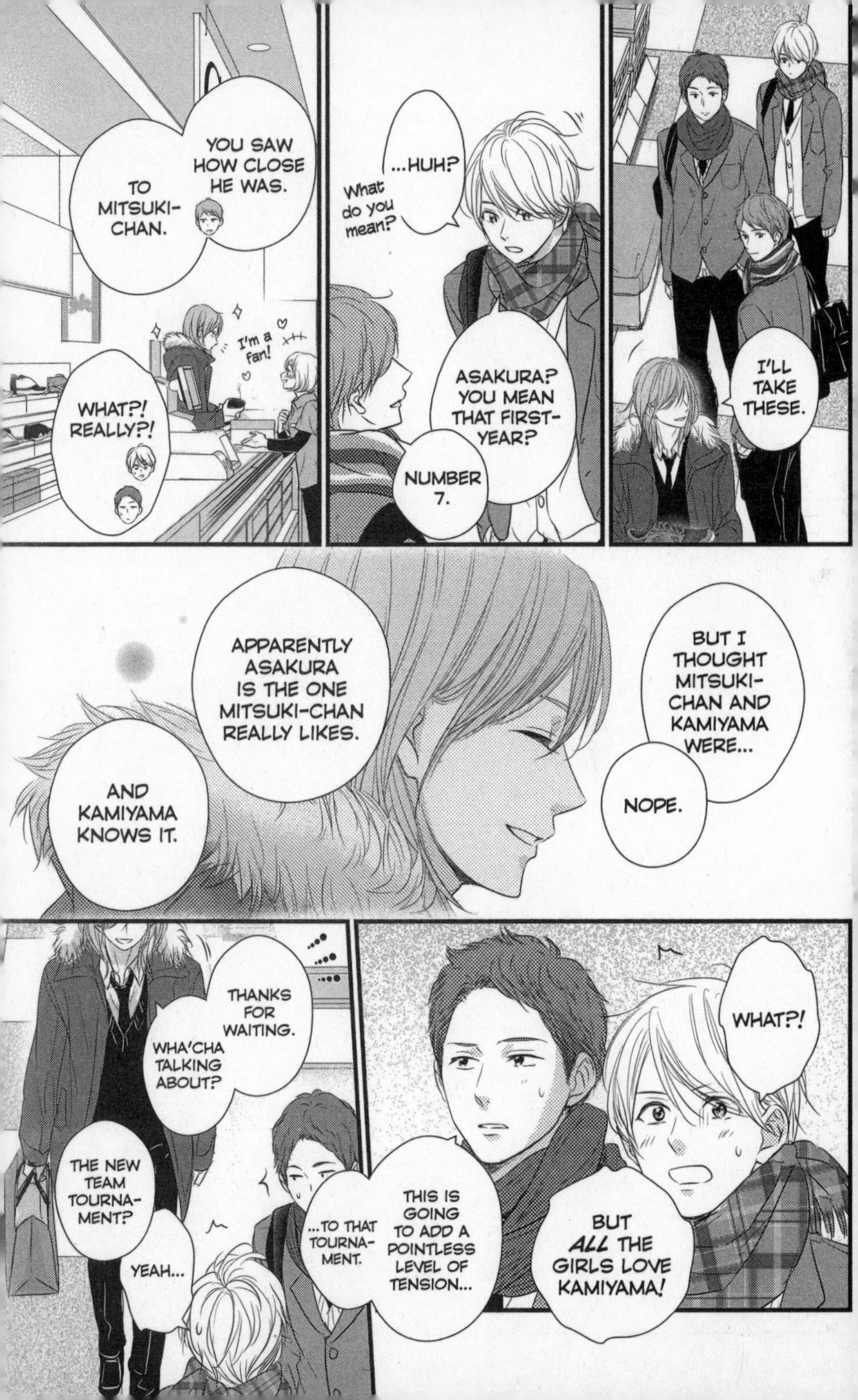
I'LL TAKE THESE.
...HUH?
What do you mean?
ASAKURA? YOU MEAN THAT FIRST-YEAR?
NUMBER 7.
YOU SAW HOW CLOSE HE WAS.
TO MITSUKI-CHAN.
I'm a fan!
WHAT?! REALLY?!
BUT I THOUGHT MITSUKI-CHAN AND KAMIYAMA WERE...
NOPE.
APPARENTLY ASAKURA IS THE ONE MITSUKI-CHAN REALLY LIKES.
AND KAMIYAMA KNOWS IT.
WHAT?!
BUT *ALL* THE GIRLS LOVE KAMIYAMA!
THIS IS GOING TO ADD A POINTLESS LEVEL OF TENSION...
...TO THAT TOURNAMENT.
THANKS FOR WAITING.
WHA'CHA TALKING ABOUT?
THE NEW TEAM TOURNAMENT?
YEAH...

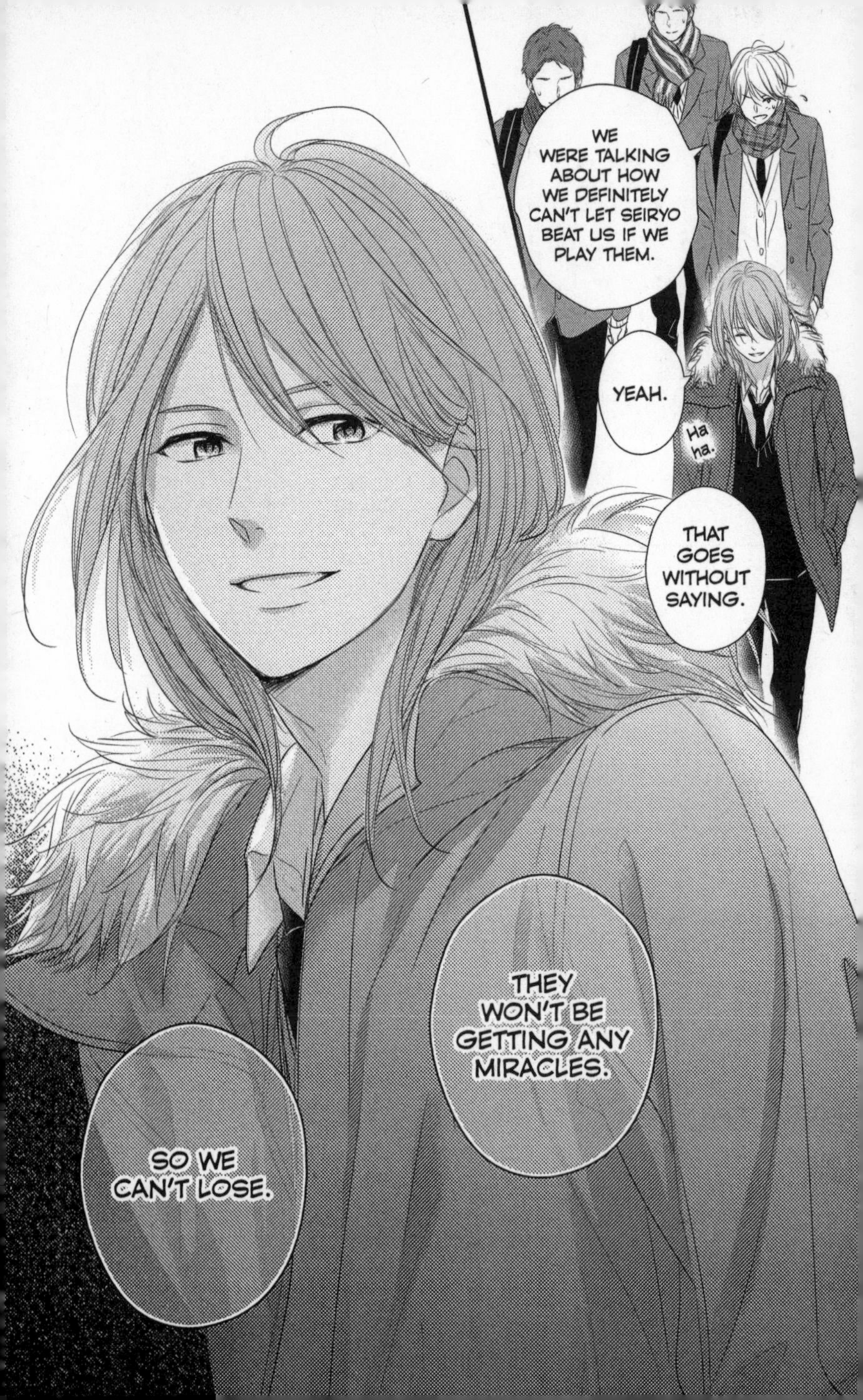
WE WERE TALKING ABOUT HOW WE DEFINITELY CAN'T LET SEIRYO BEAT US IF WE PLAY THEM.
YEAH.
Ha ha.
THAT GOES WITHOUT SAYING.
THEY WON'T BE GETTING ANY MIRACLES.
SO WE CAN'T LOSE.

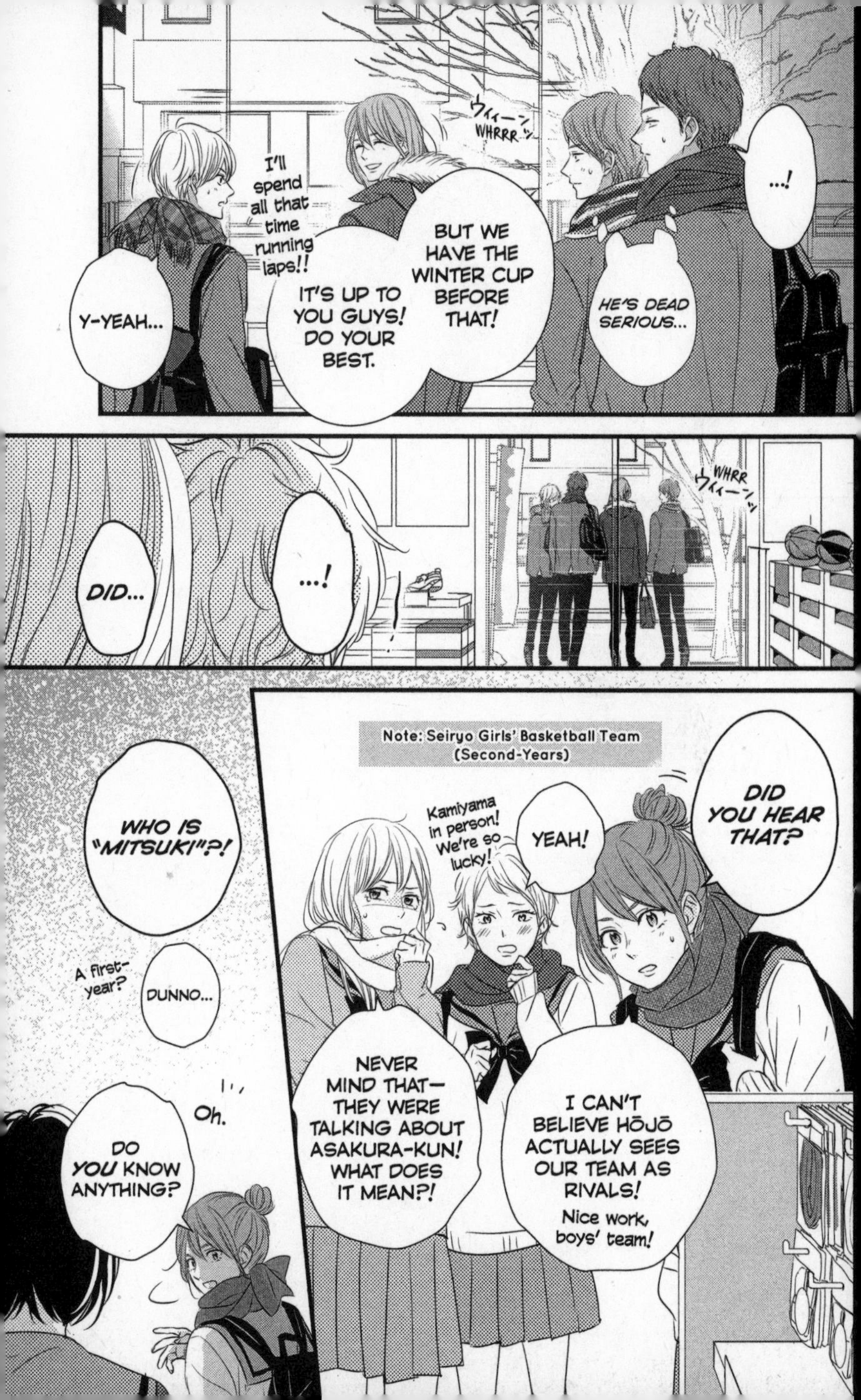
...!
HE'S DEAD SERIOUS...
WHRRR
BUT WE HAVE THE WINTER CUP BEFORE THAT!
I'll spend all that time running laps!!
IT'S UP TO YOU GUYS! DO YOUR BEST.
Y-YEAH...
WHRR
...!
DID...
Note: Seiryo Girls' Basketball Team (Second-Years)
DID YOU HEAR THAT?
YEAH!
Kamiyama in person! We're so lucky!
I CAN'T BELIEVE HŌJŌ ACTUALLY SEES OUR TEAM AS RIVALS!
Nice work, boys' team!
NEVER MIND THAT—THEY WERE TALKING ABOUT ASAKURA-KUN! WHAT DOES IT MEAN?!
WHO IS "MITSUKI"?!
DUNNO...
A first-year?
Oh.
DO YOU KNOW ANYTHING?

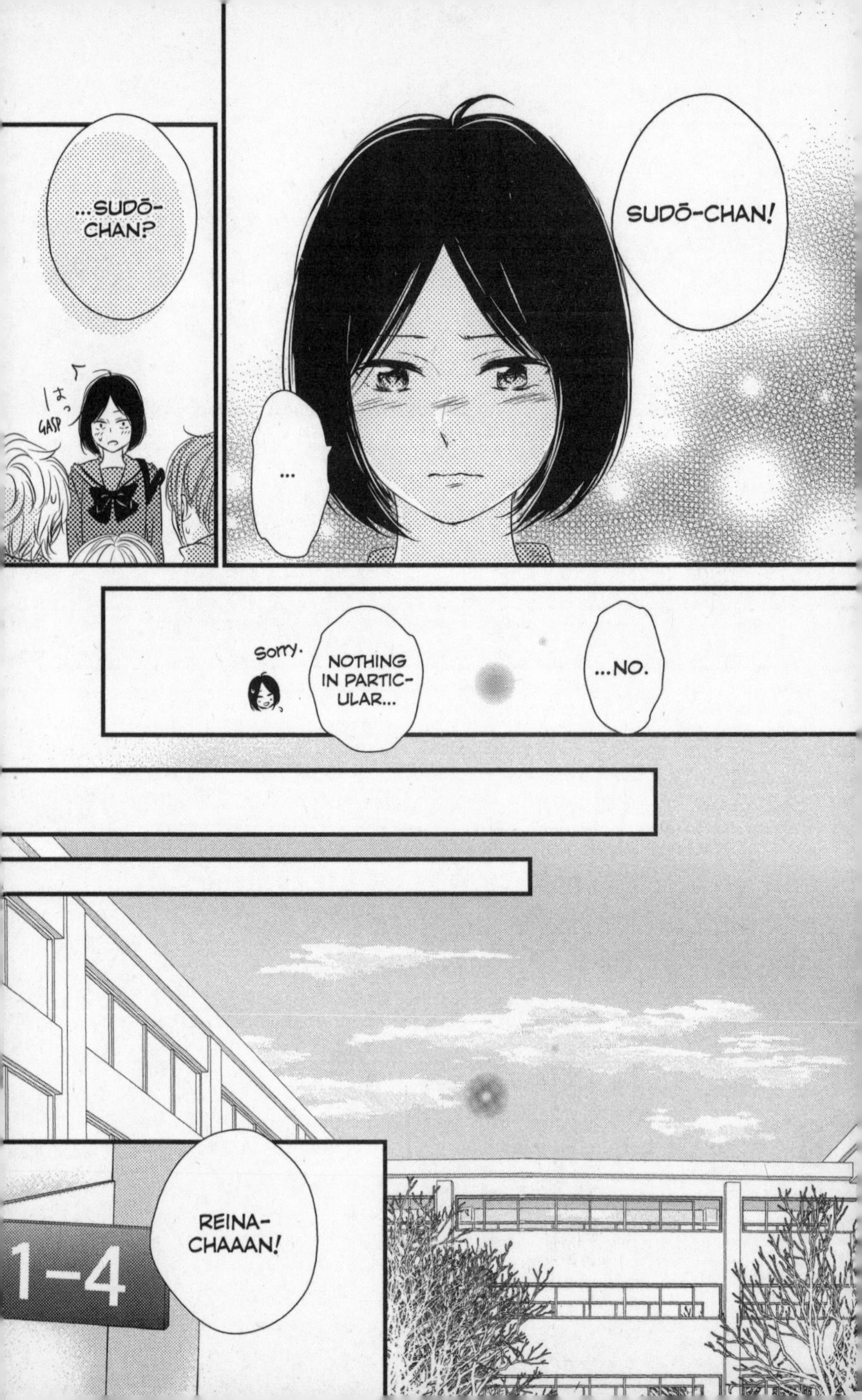
SUDŌ-CHAN!
...
...SUDŌ-CHAN?
はっ GASP
...NO.
NOTHING IN PARTIC-ULAR...
Sorry.
REINA-CHAAAN!
1-4

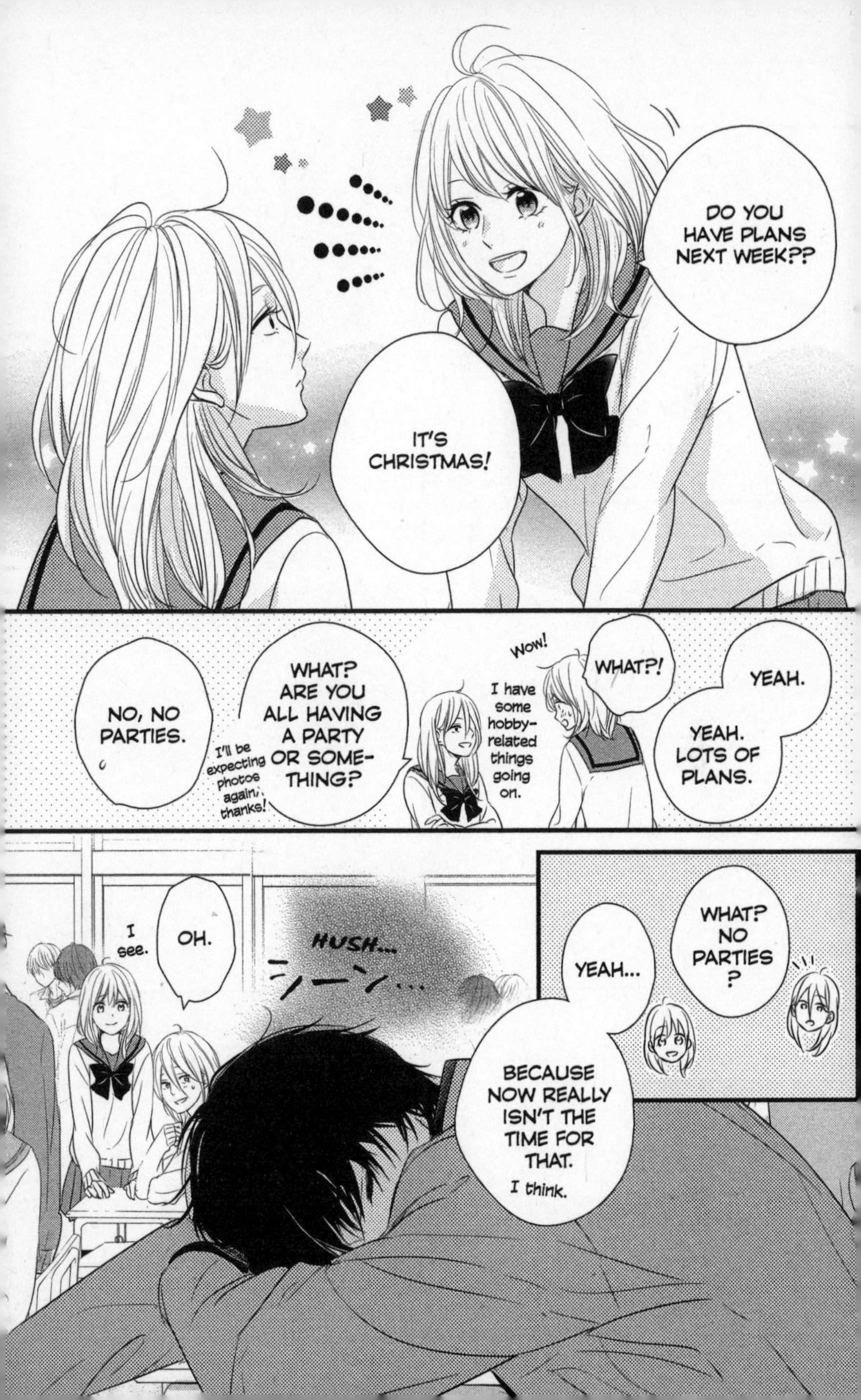
DO YOU HAVE PLANS NEXT WEEK??
IT'S CHRISTMAS!
YEAH.
YEAH. LOTS OF PLANS.
WHAT?!
Wow!
I have some hobby-related things going on.
WHAT? ARE YOU ALL HAVING A PARTY OR SOME-THING?
I'll be expecting photos again, thanks!
NO, NO PARTIES.
WHAT? NO PARTIES?
YEAH...
BECAUSE NOW REALLY ISN'T THE TIME FOR THAT.
I think.
HUSH...
OH.
I see.

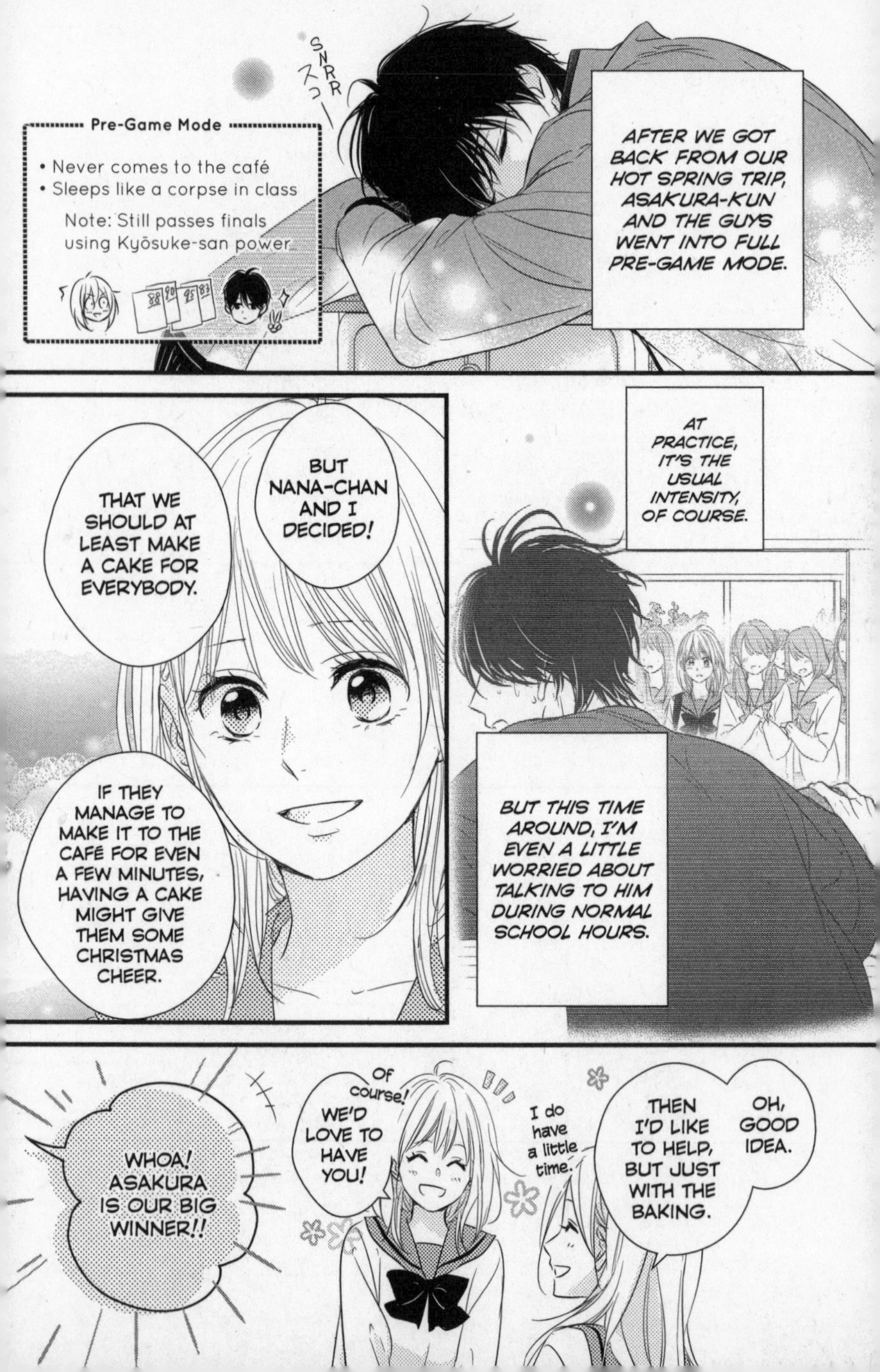
AFTER WE GOT BACK FROM OUR HOT SPRING TRIP, ASAKURA-KUN AND THE GUYS WENT INTO FULL PRE-GAME MODE.
SNRR
Pre-Game Mode
• Never comes to the café
• Sleeps like a corpse in class
Note: Still passes finals using Kyōsuke-san power
88 90 95 83
AT PRACTICE, IT'S THE USUAL INTENSITY, OF COURSE.
BUT THIS TIME AROUND, I'M EVEN A LITTLE WORRIED ABOUT TALKING TO HIM DURING NORMAL SCHOOL HOURS.
BUT NANA-CHAN AND I DECIDED!
THAT WE SHOULD AT LEAST MAKE A CAKE FOR EVERYBODY.
IF THEY MANAGE TO MAKE IT TO THE CAFÉ FOR EVEN A FEW MINUTES, HAVING A CAKE MIGHT GIVE THEM SOME CHRISTMAS CHEER.
OH, GOOD IDEA.
THEN I'D LIKE TO HELP, BUT JUST WITH THE BAKING.
I do have a little time.
Of course!
WE'D LOVE TO HAVE YOU!
WHOA! ASAKURA IS OUR BIG WINNER!!

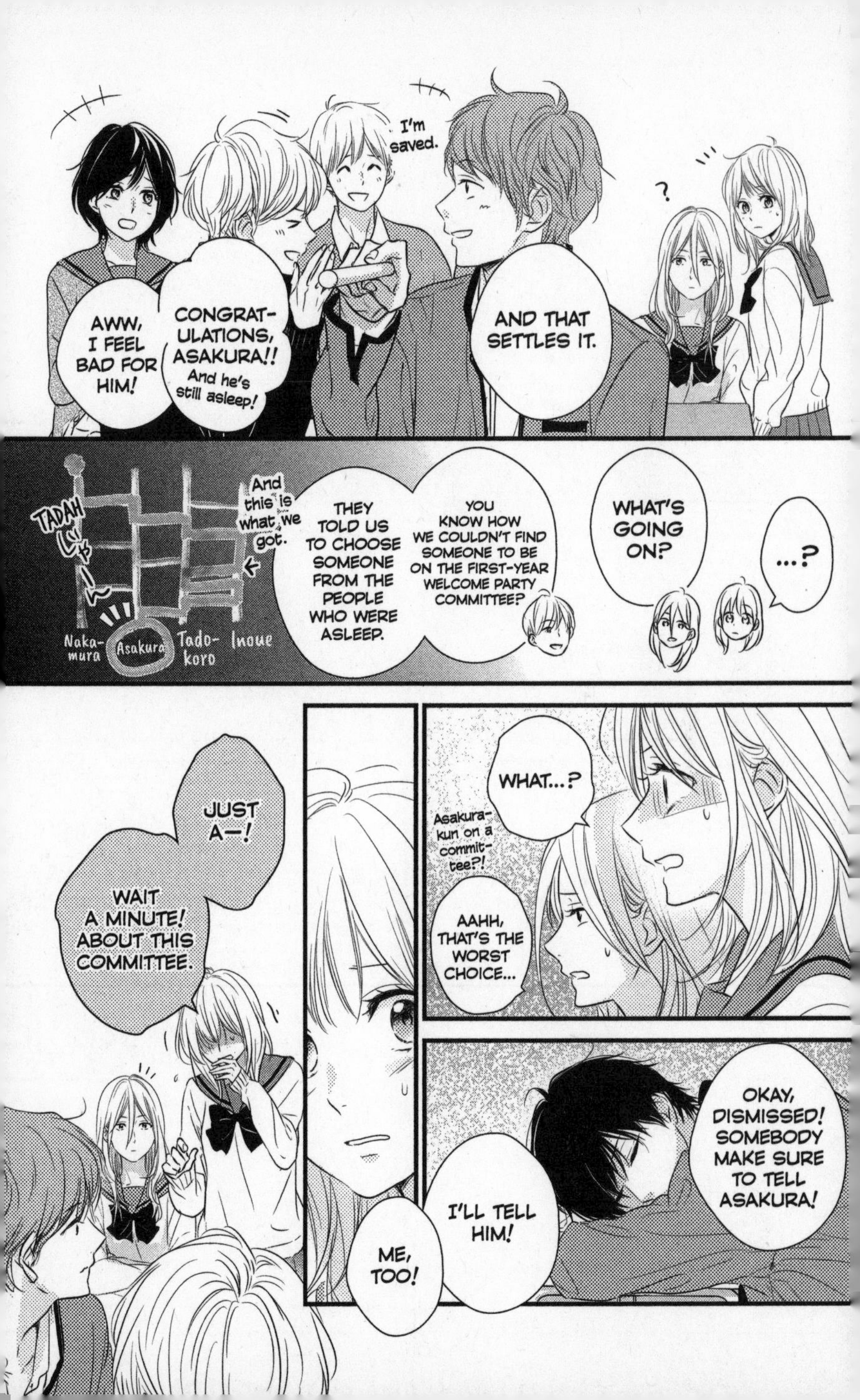
AND THAT SETTLES IT.
I'm saved.
CONGRAT-ULATIONS, ASAKURA!!
And he's still asleep!
AWW, I FEEL BAD FOR HIM!
...?
WHAT'S GOING ON?
YOU KNOW HOW WE COULDN'T FIND SOMEONE TO BE ON THE FIRST-YEAR WELCOME PARTY COMMITTEE?
THEY TOLD US TO CHOOSE SOMEONE FROM THE PEOPLE WHO WERE ASLEEP.
And this is what we got.
TADAH
じゃ〜ん
Nakamura
Asakura
Tadokoro
Inoue
WHAT...?
Asakura-kun on a committee?!
AAHH, THAT'S THE WORST CHOICE...
OKAY, DISMISSED! SOMEBODY MAKE SURE TO TELL ASAKURA!
I'LL TELL HIM!
ME, TOO!
JUST A—!
WAIT A MINUTE! ABOUT THIS COMMITTEE.

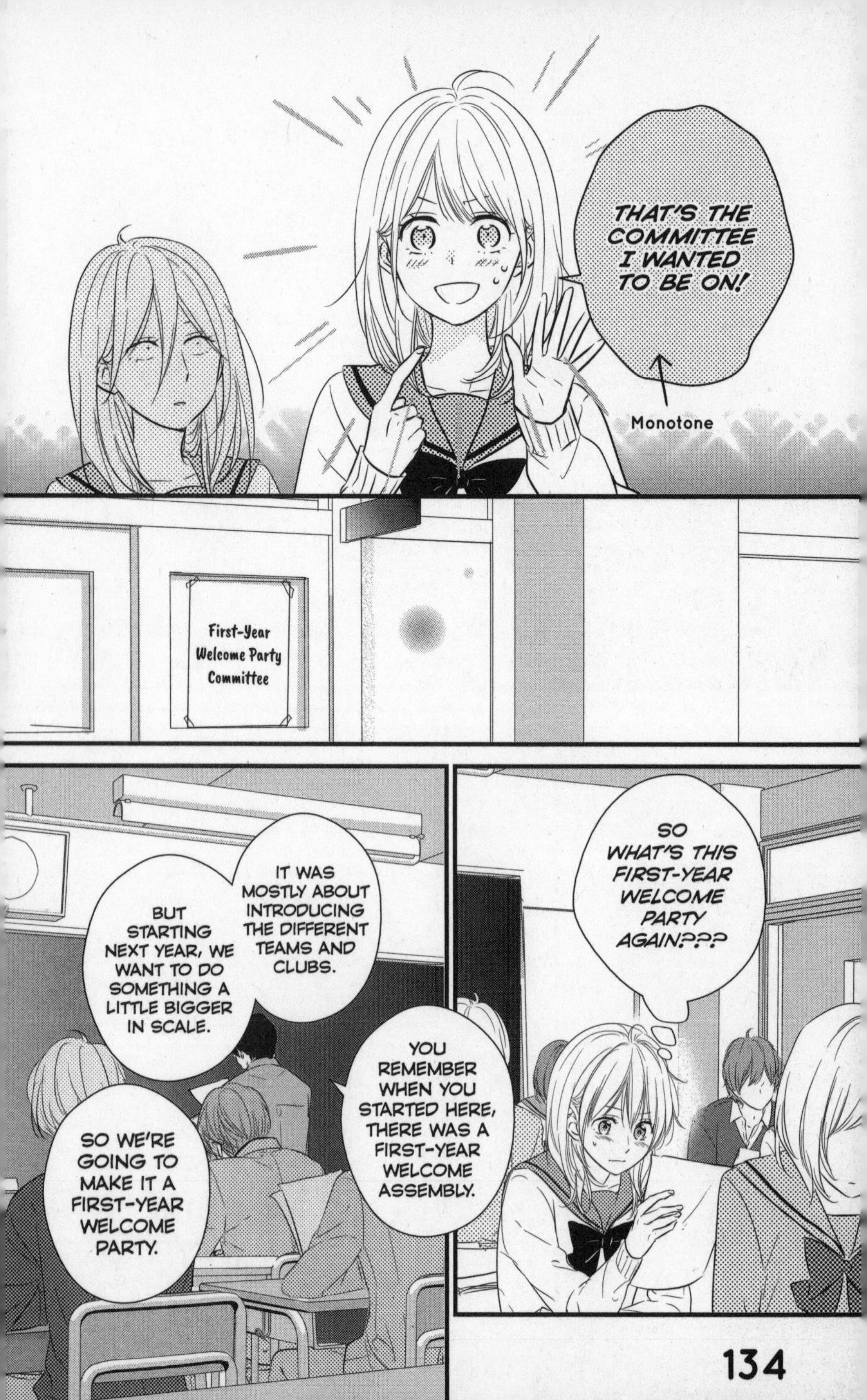
THAT'S THE COMMITTEE I WANTED TO BE ON!
Monotone
First-Year Welcome Party Committee
SO WHAT'S THIS FIRST-YEAR WELCOME PARTY AGAIN???
YOU REMEMBER WHEN YOU STARTED HERE, THERE WAS A FIRST-YEAR WELCOME ASSEMBLY.
IT WAS MOSTLY ABOUT INTRODUCING THE DIFFERENT TEAMS AND CLUBS.
BUT STARTING NEXT YEAR, WE WANT TO DO SOMETHING A LITTLE BIGGER IN SCALE.
SO WE'RE GOING TO MAKE IT A FIRST-YEAR WELCOME PARTY.

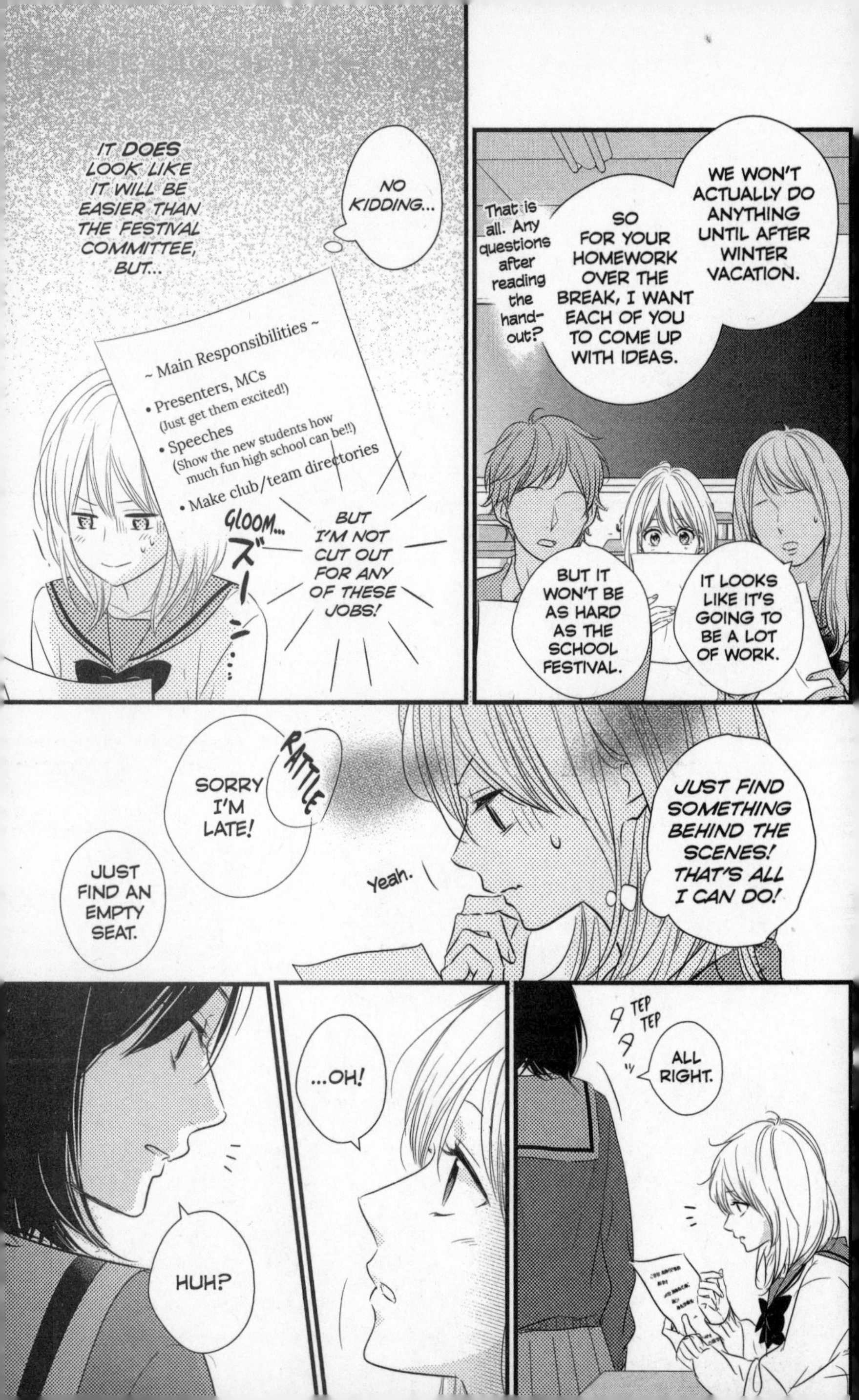
WE WON'T ACTUALLY DO ANYTHING UNTIL AFTER WINTER VACATION.
SO FOR YOUR HOMEWORK OVER THE BREAK, I WANT EACH OF YOU TO COME UP WITH IDEAS.
That is all. Any questions after reading the hand-out?
IT LOOKS LIKE IT'S GOING TO BE A LOT OF WORK.
BUT IT WON'T BE AS HARD AS THE SCHOOL FESTIVAL.
NO KIDDING...
IT DOES LOOK LIKE IT WILL BE EASIER THAN THE FESTIVAL COMMITTEE, BUT...
~ Main Responsibilities ~
• Presenters, MCs (Just get them excited!)
• Speeches (Show the new students how much fun high school can be!!)
• Make club/team directories
BUT I'M NOT CUT OUT FOR ANY OF THESE JOBS!
GLOOM...
ズーン…
JUST FIND SOMETHING BEHIND THE SCENES! THAT'S ALL I CAN DO!
Yeah.
RATTLE
SORRY I'M LATE!
JUST FIND AN EMPTY SEAT.
TEP TEP
ALL RIGHT.
...OH!
HUH?

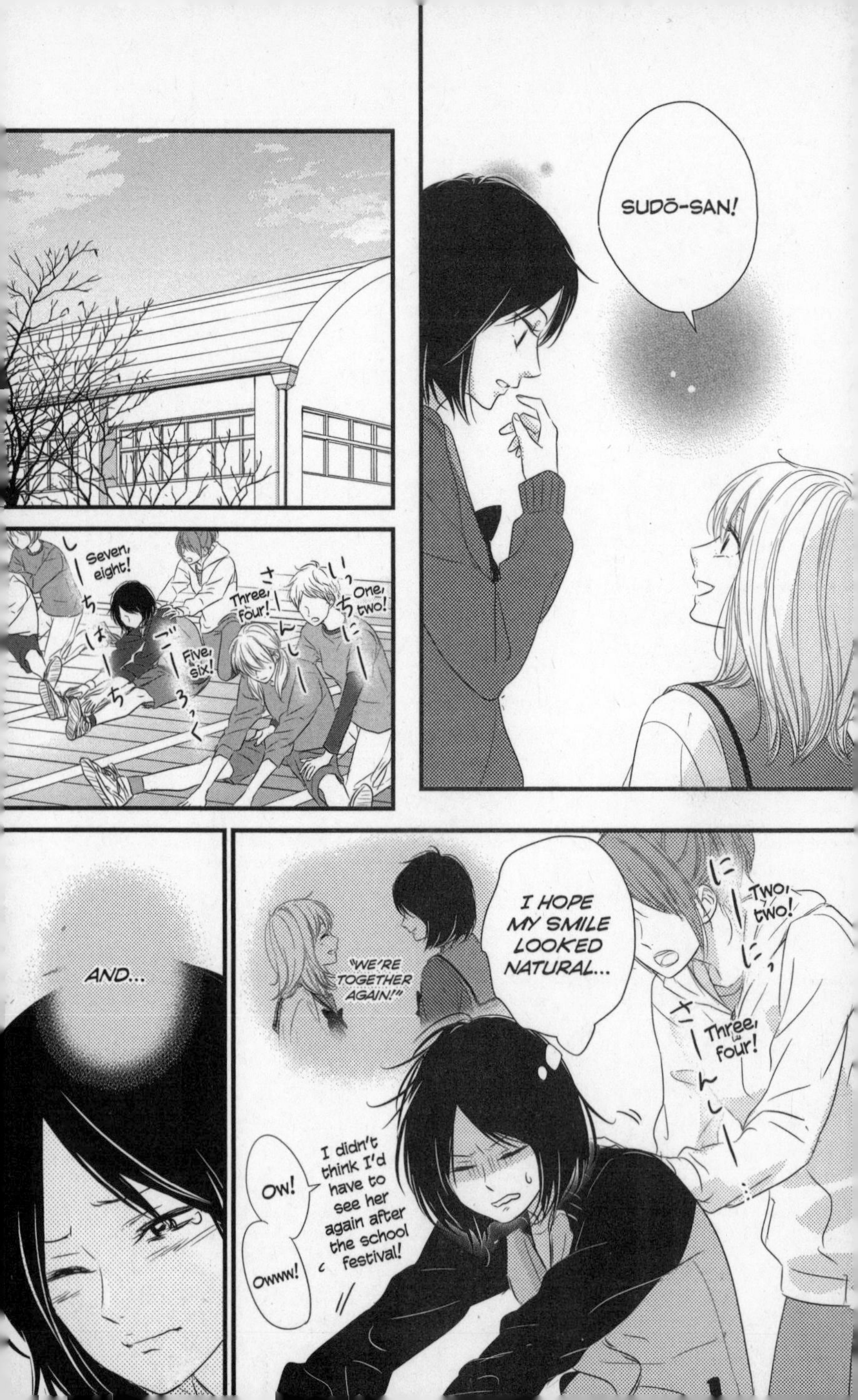
SUDŌ-SAN!
いっちにー
One, two!
さーんしー
Three, four!
ごーろっく
Five, six!
しーちはーち
Seven, eight!
にーにっ
Two, two!
I HOPE MY SMILE LOOKED NATURAL...
"WE'RE TOGETHER AGAIN!"
さーんしー
Three, four!
I didn't think I'd have to see her again after the school festival!
Ow!
Owww!
AND...

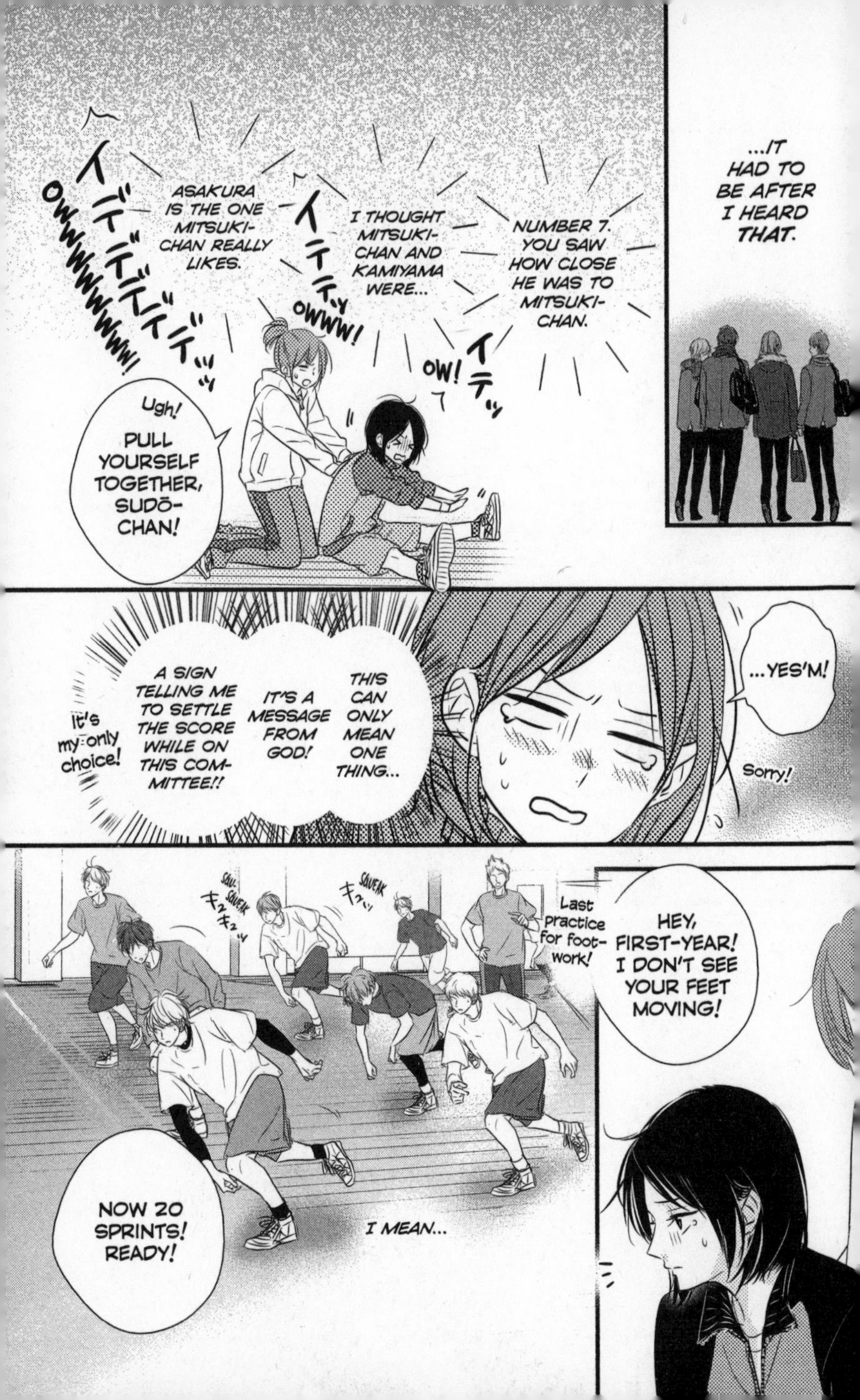
...IT HAD TO BE AFTER I HEARD THAT.
NUMBER 7. YOU SAW HOW CLOSE HE WAS TO MITSUKI-CHAN.
I THOUGHT MITSUKI-CHAN AND KAMIYAMA WERE...
ASAKURA IS THE ONE MITSUKI-CHAN REALLY LIKES.
イテッ
OW!
イテテッ
OWWW!
イデデデデデッ
OWWWWWWWW!
Ugh!
PULL YOURSELF TOGETHER, SUDŌ-CHAN!
...YES'M!
Sorry!
THIS CAN ONLY MEAN ONE THING...
IT'S A MESSAGE FROM GOD!
A SIGN TELLING ME TO SETTLE THE SCORE WHILE ON THIS COMMITTEE!!
It's my only choice!
HEY, FIRST-YEAR! I DON'T SEE YOUR FEET MOVING!
Last practice for footwork!
キュッ
SQUEAK
キュキュッ
SQU-SQUEAK
NOW 20 SPRINTS! READY!
I MEAN...

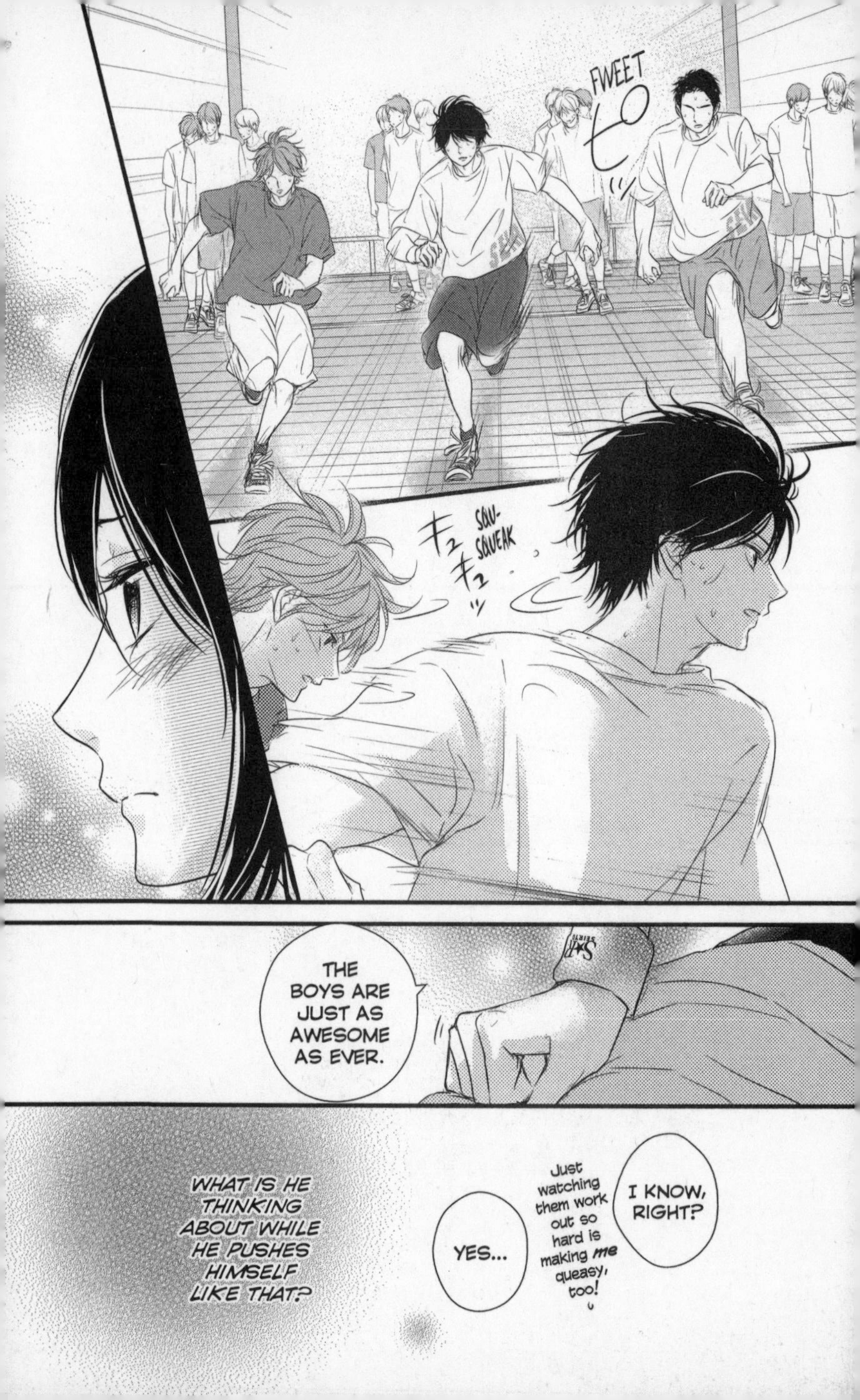
FWEET
SQU-SQUEAK
THE BOYS ARE JUST AS AWESOME AS EVER.
I KNOW, RIGHT?
Just watching them work out so hard is making me queasy, too!
YES...
WHAT IS HE THINKING ABOUT WHILE HE PUSHES HIMSELF LIKE THAT?

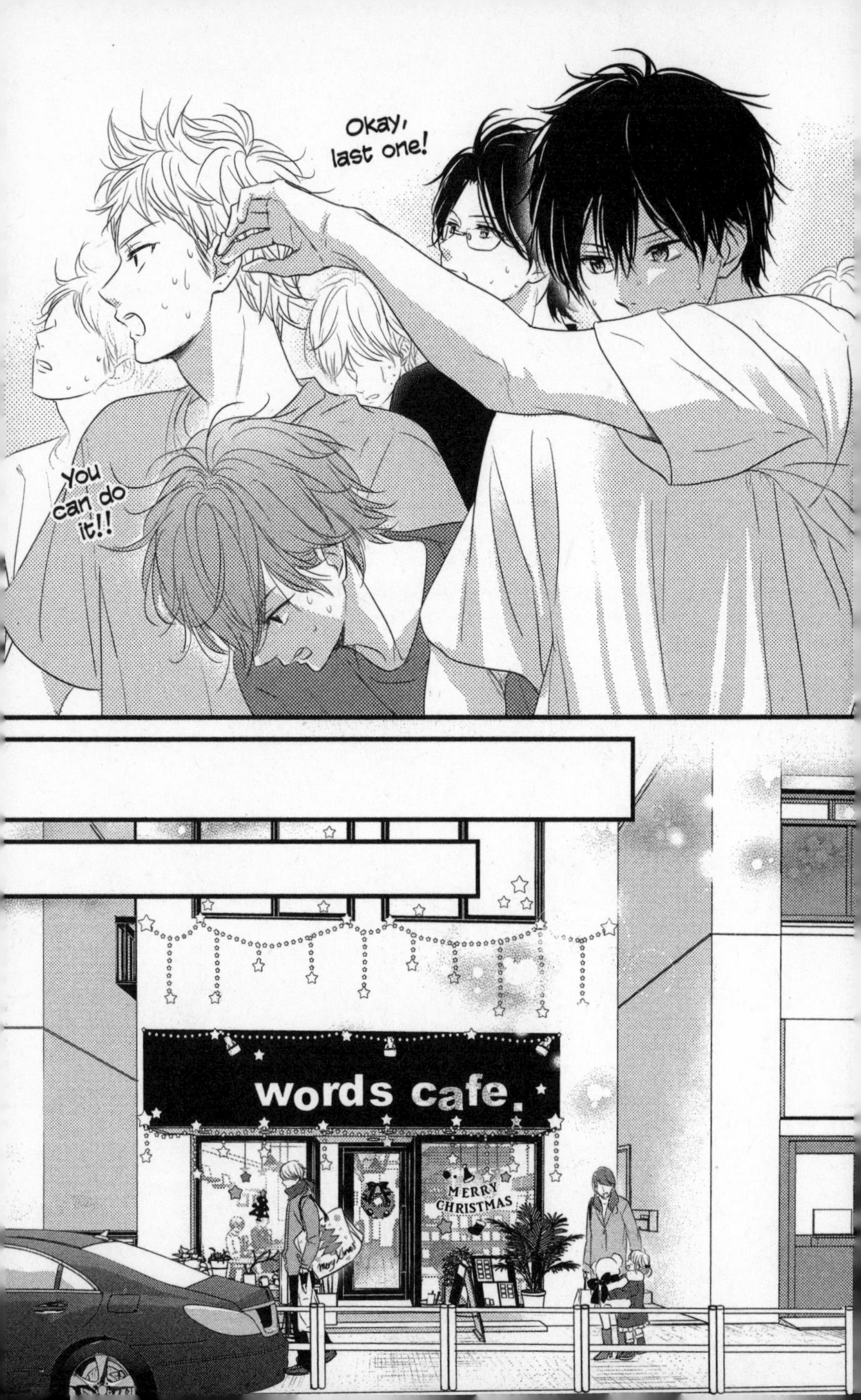
Okay, last one!
You can do it!!
words cafe.
MERRY CHRISTMAS

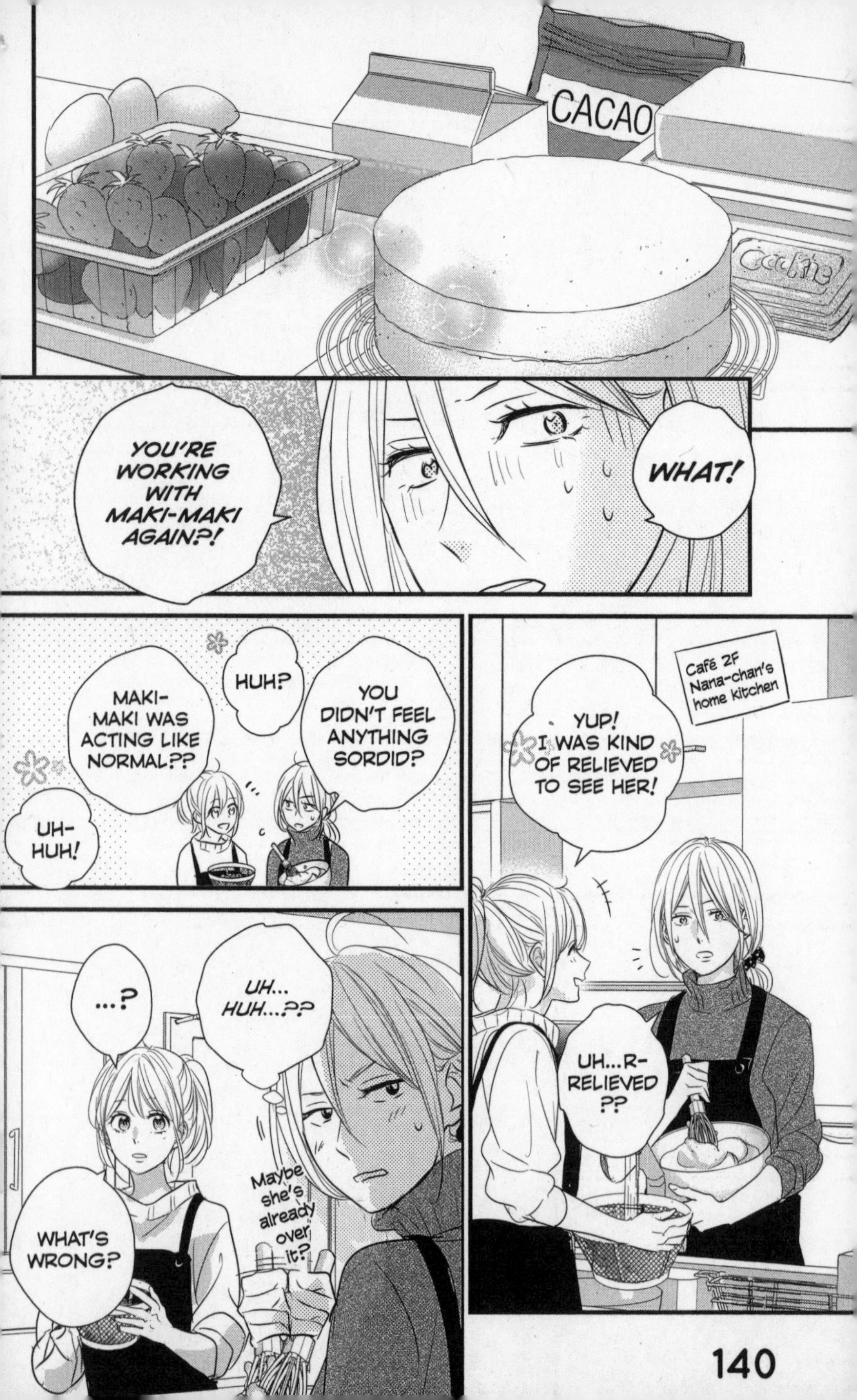
CACAO
WHAT!
YOU'RE WORKING WITH MAKI-MAKI AGAIN?!
Café 2F Nana-chan's home kitchen
YUP! I WAS KIND OF RELIEVED TO SEE HER!
UH...R-RELIEVED??
YOU DIDN'T FEEL ANYTHING SORDID?
HUH?
MAKI-MAKI WAS ACTING LIKE NORMAL??
UH-HUH!
UH... HUH...??
...?
Maybe she's already over it?
WHAT'S WRONG?

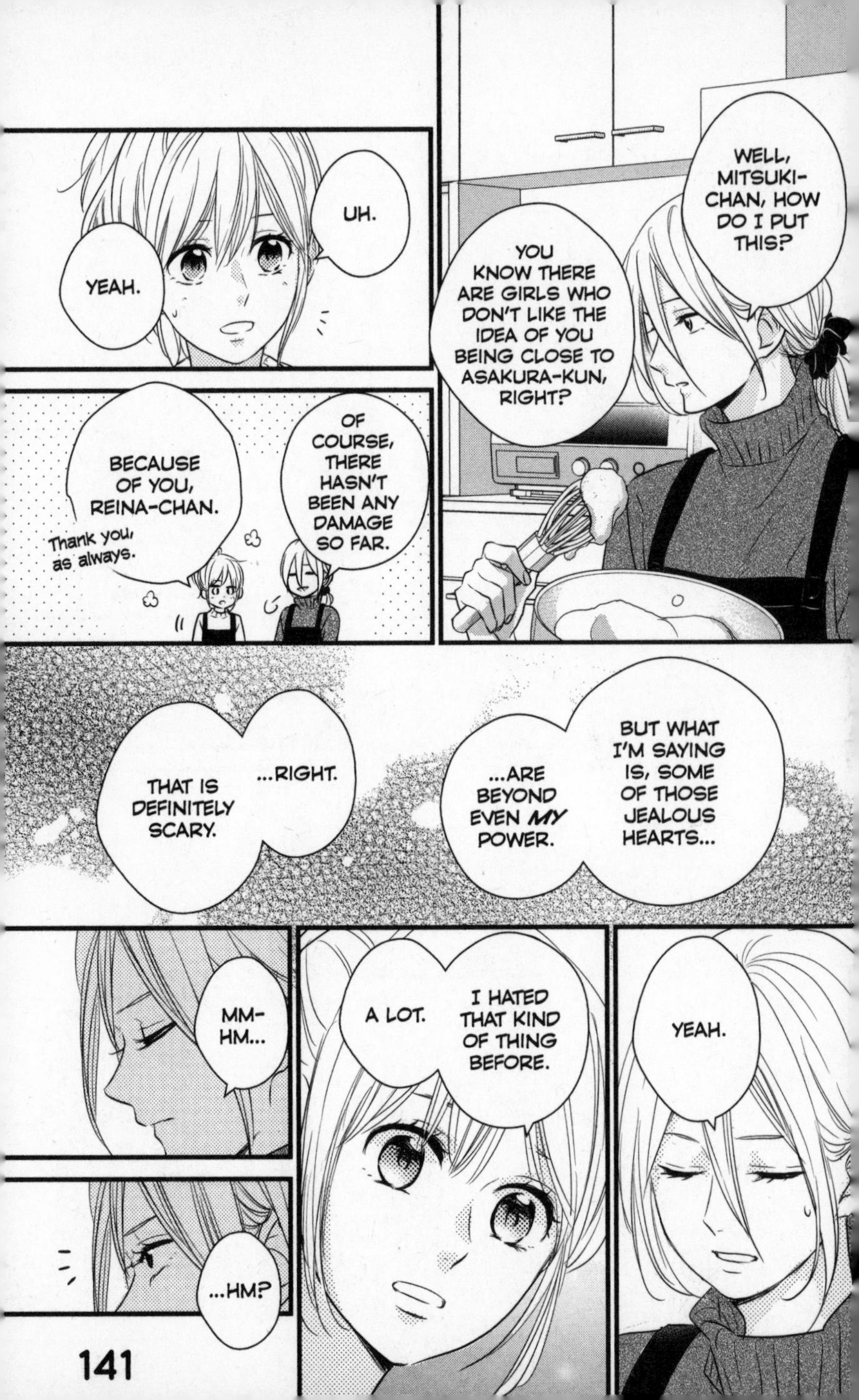
WELL, MITSUKI-CHAN, HOW DO I PUT THIS?
YOU KNOW THERE ARE GIRLS WHO DON'T LIKE THE IDEA OF YOU BEING CLOSE TO ASAKURA-KUN, RIGHT?
UH.
YEAH.
OF COURSE, THERE HASN'T BEEN ANY DAMAGE SO FAR.
BECAUSE OF YOU, REINA-CHAN.
Thank you, as always.
BUT WHAT I'M SAYING IS, SOME OF THOSE JEALOUS HEARTS...
...ARE BEYOND EVEN *MY* POWER.
...RIGHT.
THAT IS DEFINITELY SCARY.
YEAH.
I HATED THAT KIND OF THING BEFORE.
A LOT.
MM-HM...
...HM?

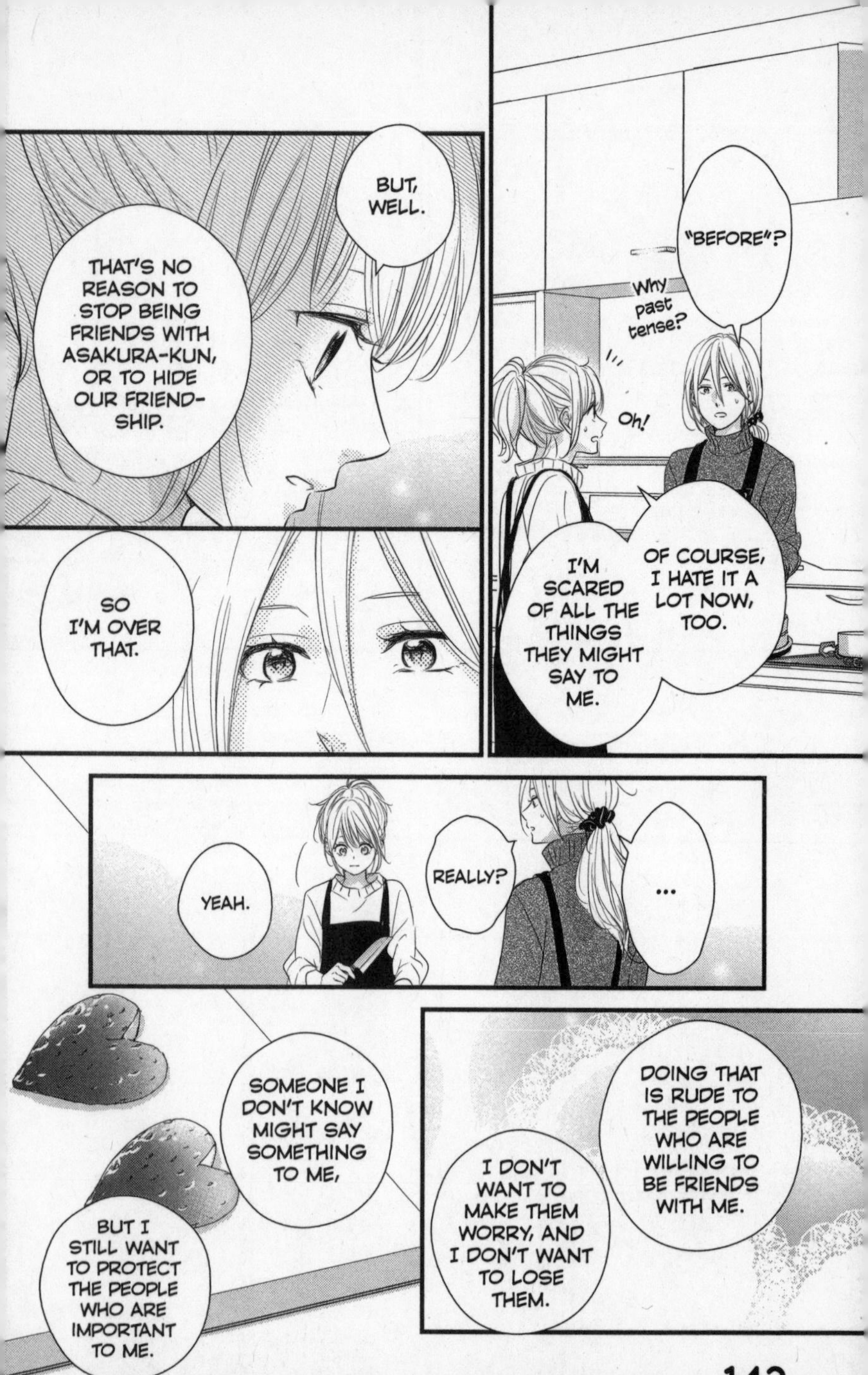
"BEFORE"?
Why past tense?
Oh!
OF COURSE, I HATE IT A LOT NOW, TOO.
I'M SCARED OF ALL THE THINGS THEY MIGHT SAY TO ME.
BUT, WELL.
THAT'S NO REASON TO STOP BEING FRIENDS WITH ASAKURA-KUN, OR TO HIDE OUR FRIEND-SHIP.
SO I'M OVER THAT.
...
REALLY?
YEAH.
DOING THAT IS RUDE TO THE PEOPLE WHO ARE WILLING TO BE FRIENDS WITH ME.
I DON'T WANT TO MAKE THEM WORRY, AND I DON'T WANT TO LOSE THEM.
SOMEONE I DON'T KNOW MIGHT SAY SOMETHING TO ME,
BUT I STILL WANT TO PROTECT THE PEOPLE WHO ARE IMPORTANT TO ME.

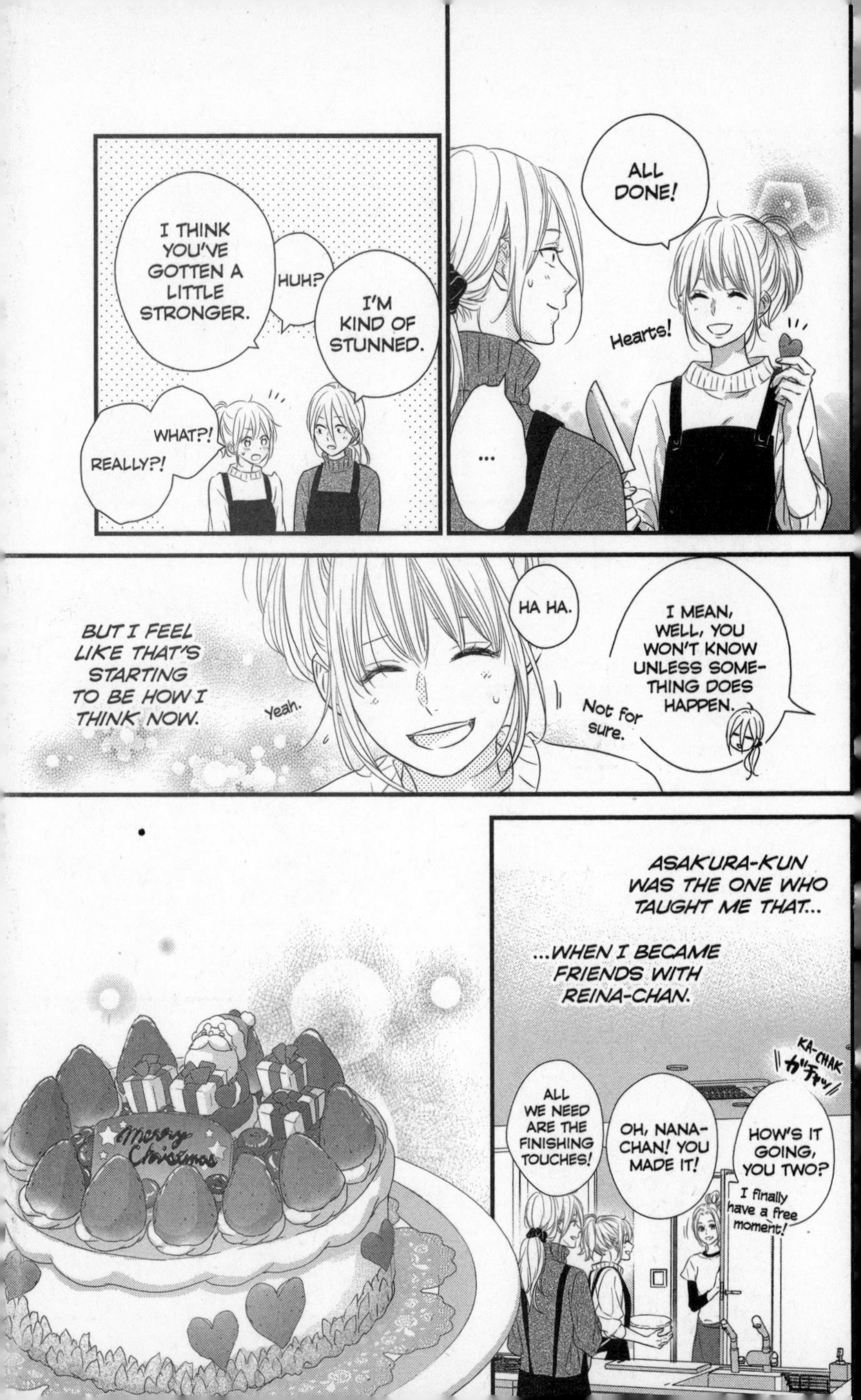
ALL DONE!
Hearts!
...
I THINK YOU'VE GOTTEN A LITTLE STRONGER.
HUH?
I'M KIND OF STUNNED.
WHAT?! REALLY?!
I MEAN, WELL, YOU WON'T KNOW UNLESS SOME-THING DOES HAPPEN.
Not for sure.
HA HA.
Yeah.
BUT I FEEL LIKE THAT'S STARTING TO BE HOW I THINK NOW.
ASAKURA-KUN WAS THE ONE WHO TAUGHT ME THAT...
...WHEN I BECAME FRIENDS WITH REINA-CHAN.
KA-CHAK ガチャッ
HOW'S IT GOING, YOU TWO?
I finally have a free moment!
OH, NANA-CHAN! YOU MADE IT!
ALL WE NEED ARE THE FINISHING TOUCHES!
Merry Christmas

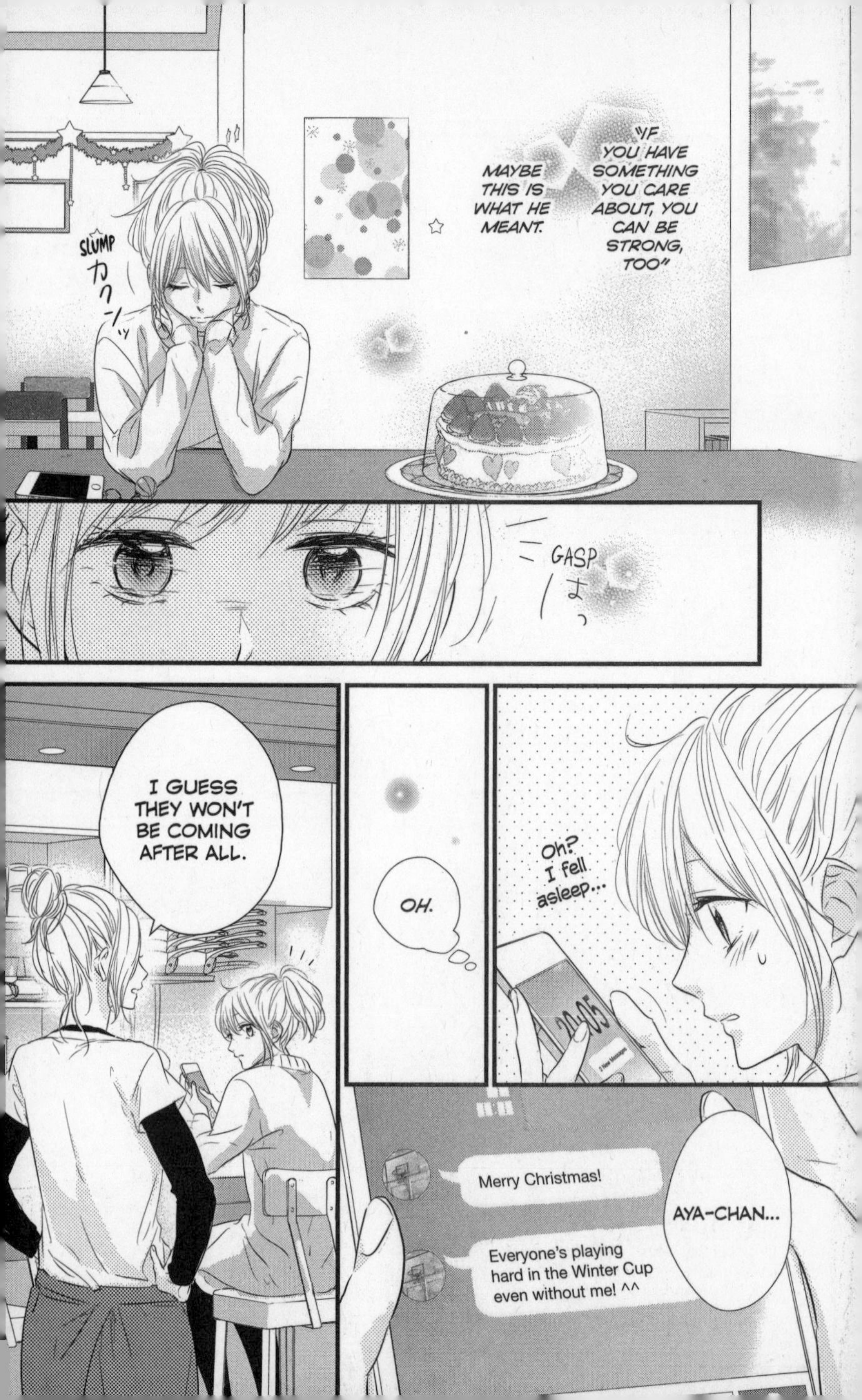
"IF YOU HAVE SOMETHING YOU CARE ABOUT, YOU CAN BE STRONG, TOO"
MAYBE THIS IS WHAT HE MEANT.
SLUMP
GASP
Oh? I fell asleep...
OH.
Merry Christmas!
Everyone's playing hard in the Winter Cup even without me! ^^
AYA-CHAN...
I GUESS THEY WON'T BE COMING AFTER ALL.

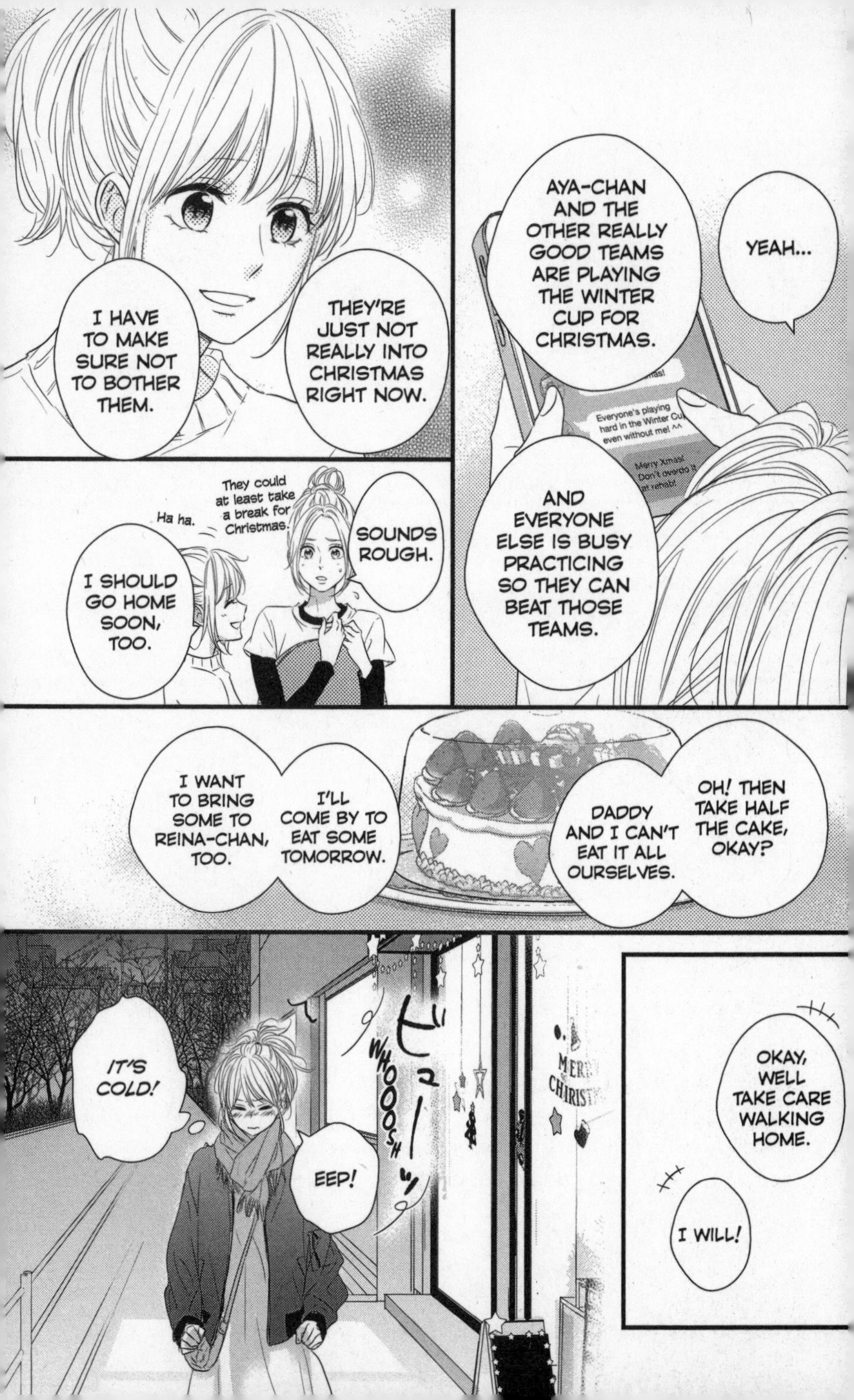
YEAH...
AYA-CHAN AND THE OTHER REALLY GOOD TEAMS ARE PLAYING THE WINTER CUP FOR CHRISTMAS.
Everyone's playing hard in the Winter Cu even without me! ^^
Merry Xmas! Don't overdo it at rehab!
AND EVERYONE ELSE IS BUSY PRACTICING SO THEY CAN BEAT THOSE TEAMS.
THEY'RE JUST NOT REALLY INTO CHRISTMAS RIGHT NOW.
I HAVE TO MAKE SURE NOT TO BOTHER THEM.
SOUNDS ROUGH.
They could at least take a break for Christmas.
Ha ha.
I SHOULD GO HOME SOON, TOO.
OH! THEN TAKE HALF THE CAKE, OKAY?
DADDY AND I CAN'T EAT IT ALL OURSELVES.
I'LL COME BY TO EAT SOME TOMORROW.
I WANT TO BRING SOME TO REINA-CHAN, TOO.
OKAY, WELL TAKE CARE WALKING HOME.
I WILL!
ビューッ
WHOOOOSH
EEP!
IT'S COLD!

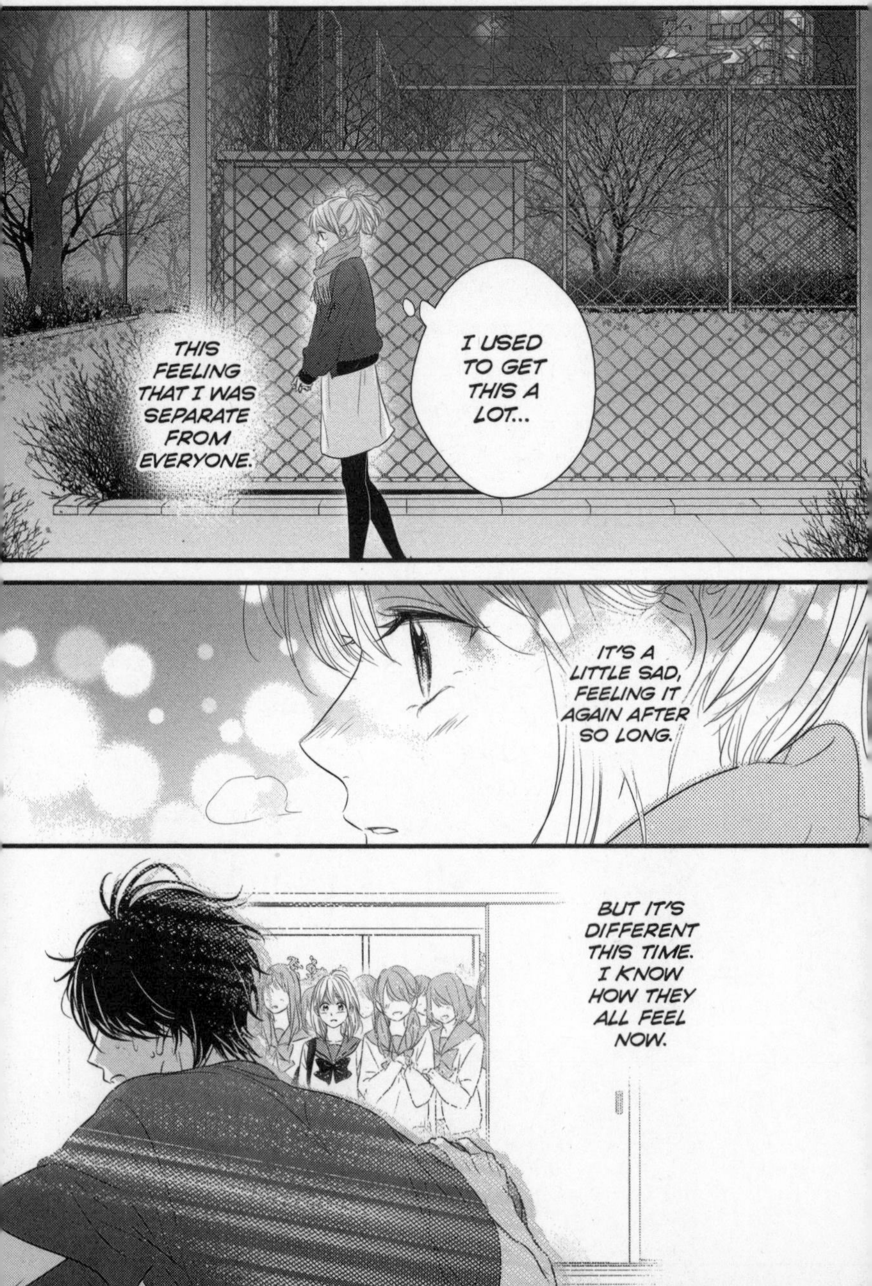
I USED TO GET THIS A LOT...
THIS FEELING THAT I WAS SEPARATE FROM EVERYONE.
IT'S A LITTLE SAD, FEELING IT AGAIN AFTER SO LONG.
BUT IT'S DIFFERENT THIS TIME. I KNOW HOW THEY ALL FEEL NOW.

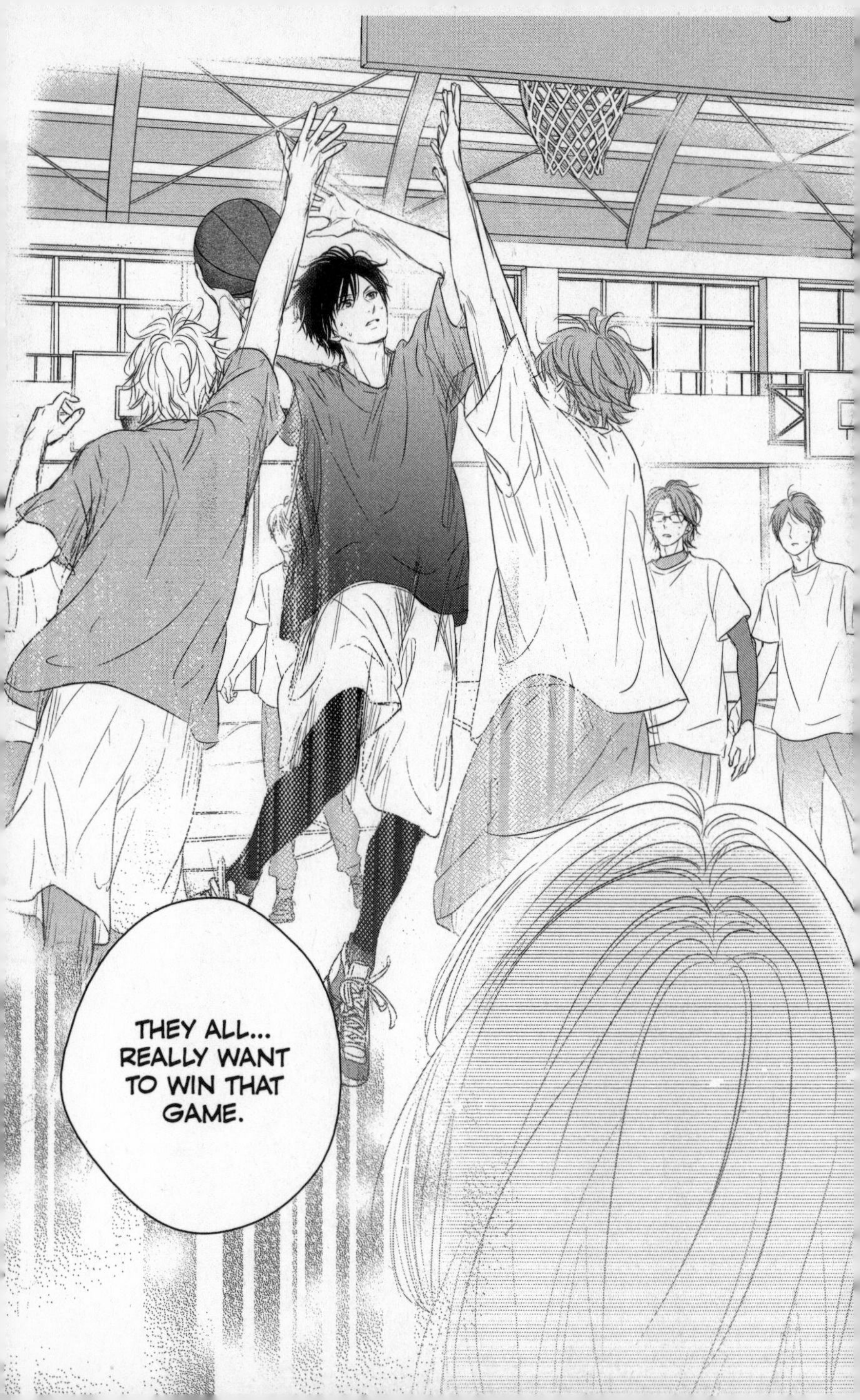
THEY ALL... REALLY WANT TO WIN THAT GAME.

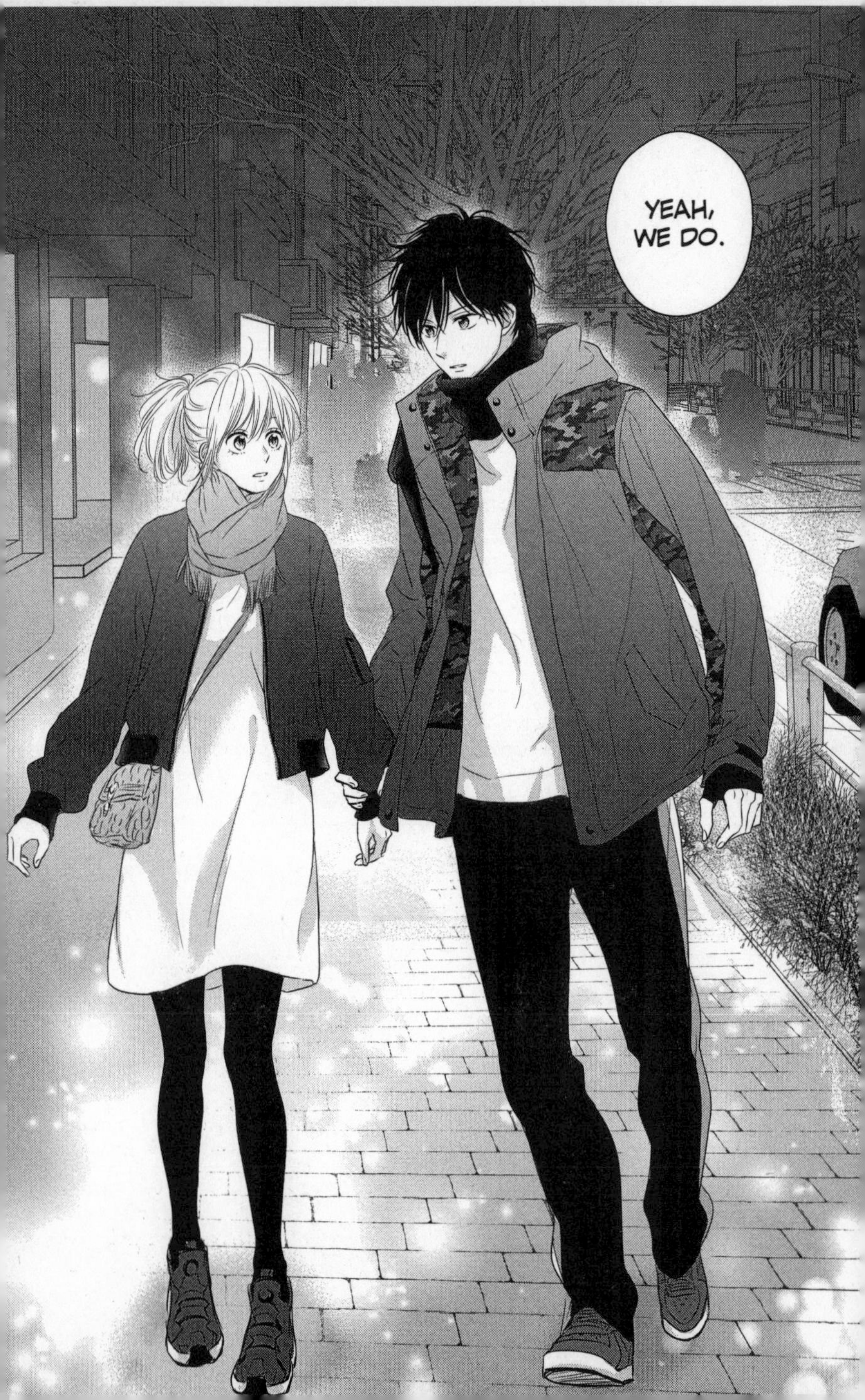
YEAH, WE DO.

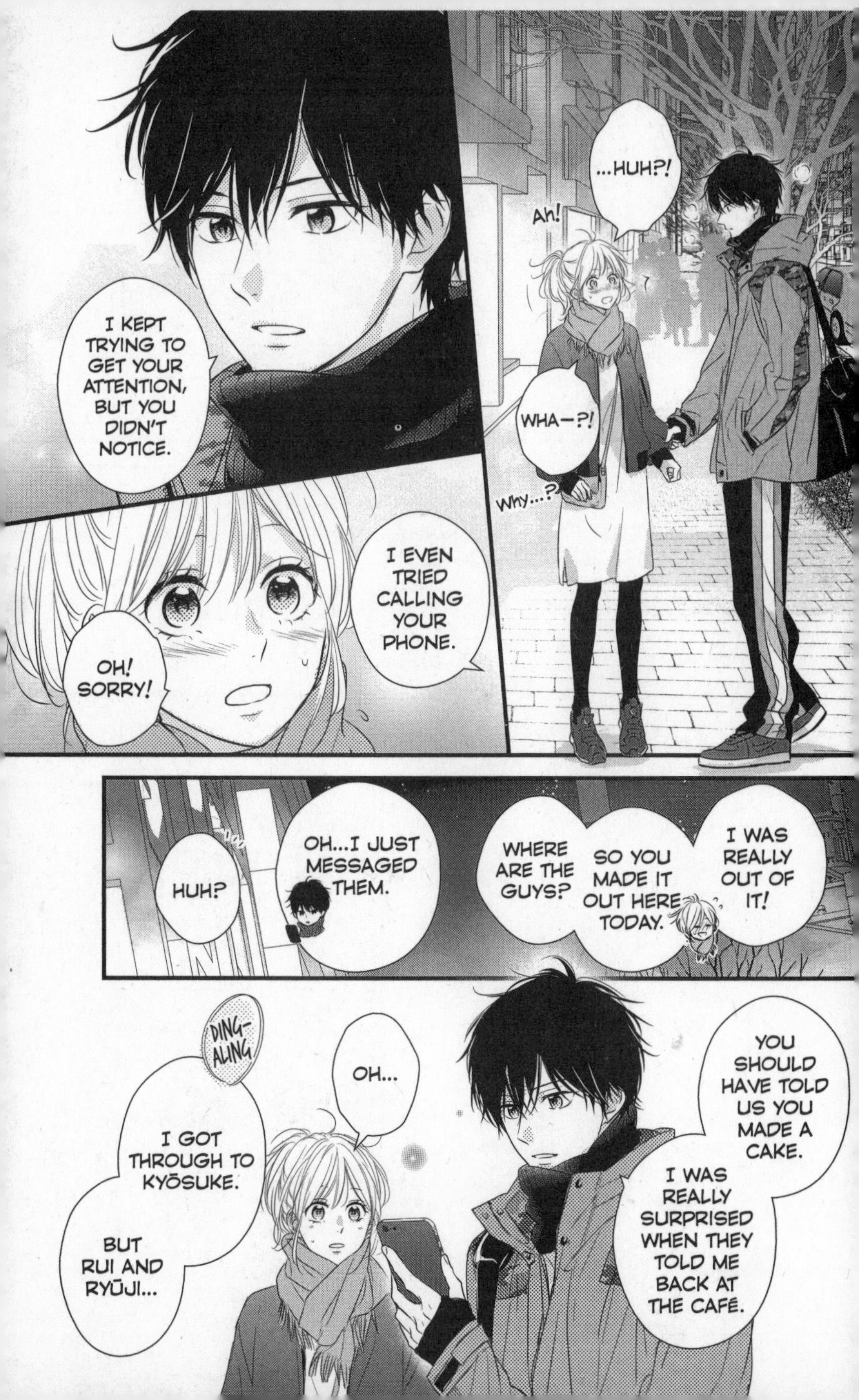
...HUH?!
Ah!
WHA—?!
Why...?
I KEPT TRYING TO GET YOUR ATTENTION, BUT YOU DIDN'T NOTICE.
I EVEN TRIED CALLING YOUR PHONE.
OH! SORRY!
I WAS REALLY OUT OF IT!
SO YOU MADE IT OUT HERE TODAY.
WHERE ARE THE GUYS?
OH...I JUST MESSAGED THEM.
HUH?
YOU SHOULD HAVE TOLD US YOU MADE A CAKE.
I WAS REALLY SURPRISED WHEN THEY TOLD ME BACK AT THE CAFÉ.
OH...
DING-ALING
I GOT THROUGH TO KYŌSUKE.
BUT RUI AND RYŪJI...

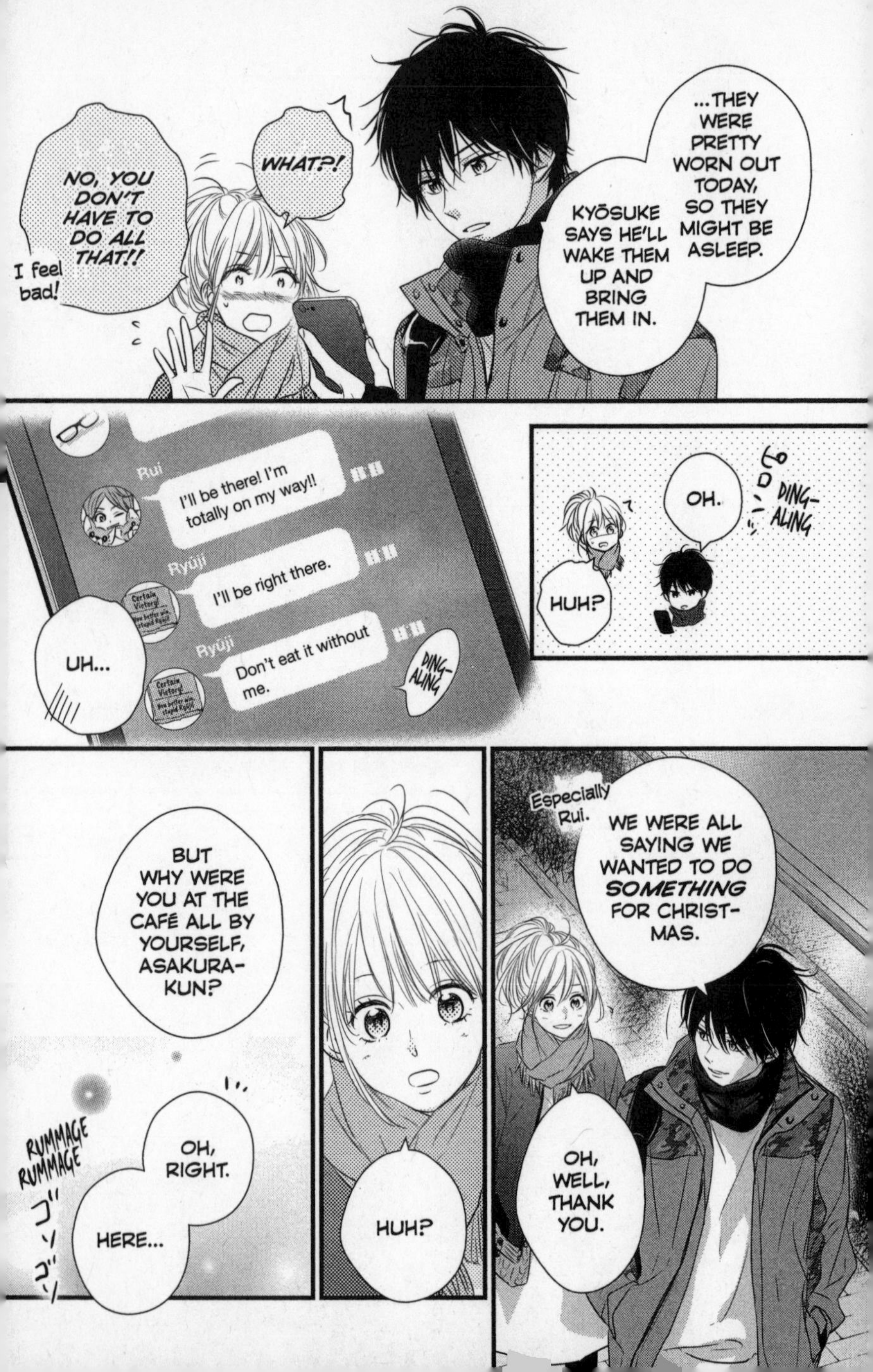
...THEY WERE PRETTY WORN OUT TODAY, SO THEY MIGHT BE ASLEEP.
KYŌSUKE SAYS HE'LL WAKE THEM UP AND BRING THEM IN.
WHAT?!
NO, YOU DON'T HAVE TO DO ALL THAT!!
I feel bad!
DING-ALING
OH.
HUH?
Rui
I'll be there! I'm totally on my way!!
Ryūji
I'll be right there.
Ryūji
Don't eat it without me.
DING-ALING
UH...
Especially Rui.
WE WERE ALL SAYING WE WANTED TO DO *SOMETHING* FOR CHRIST-MAS.
OH, WELL, THANK YOU.
HUH?
BUT WHY WERE YOU AT THE CAFÉ ALL BY YOURSELF, ASAKURA-KUN?
RUMMAGE RUMMAGE
ゴソゴソ
OH, RIGHT.
HERE...

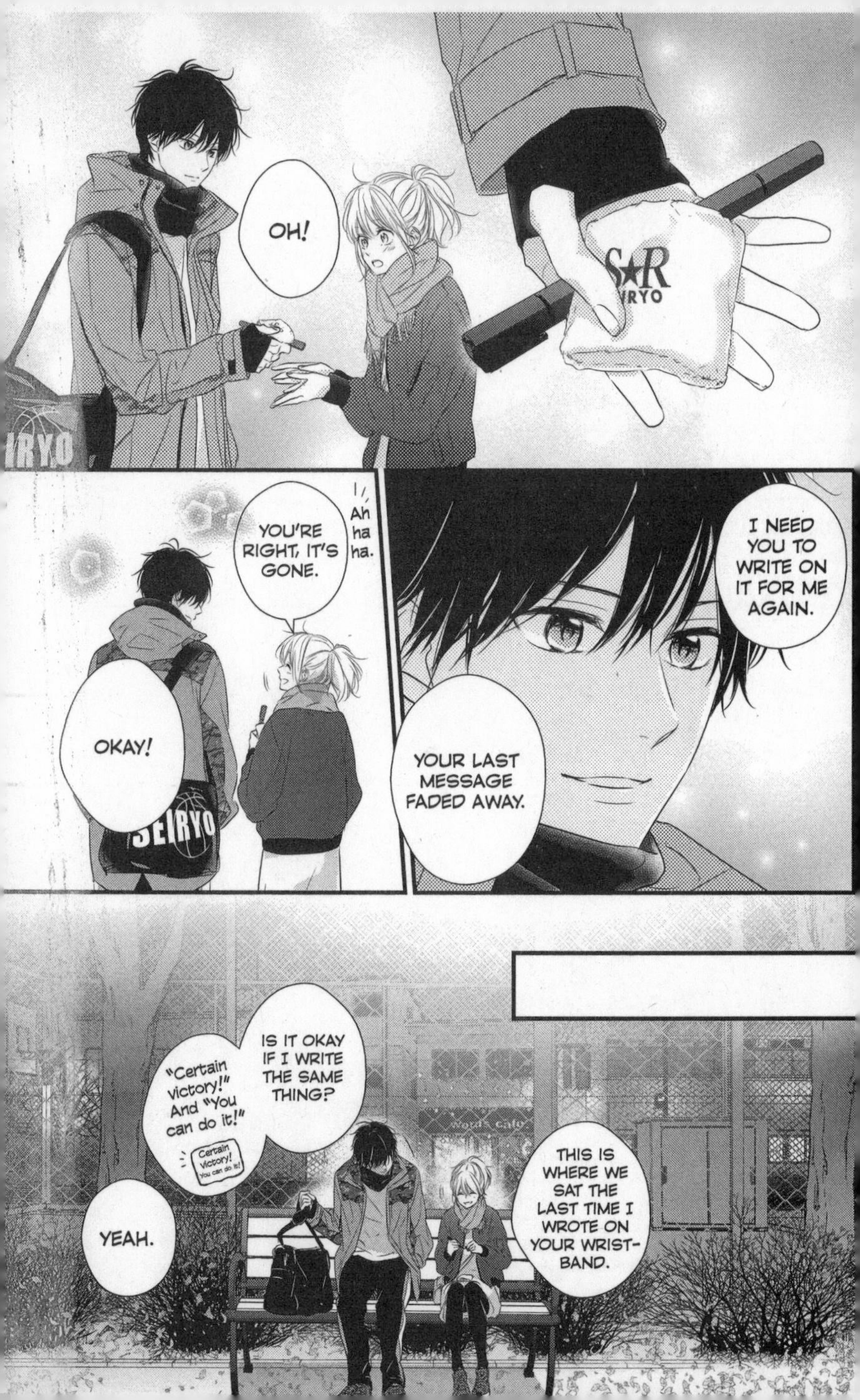
OH!
S★R SEIRYO
I NEED YOU TO WRITE ON IT FOR ME AGAIN.
YOUR LAST MESSAGE FADED AWAY.
Ah ha ha.
YOU'RE RIGHT, IT'S GONE.
OKAY!
SEIRYO
THIS IS WHERE WE SAT THE LAST TIME I WROTE ON YOUR WRIST-BAND.
IS IT OKAY IF I WRITE THE SAME THING?
"Certain victory!" And "You can do it!"
Certain Victory! You can do it!
YEAH.

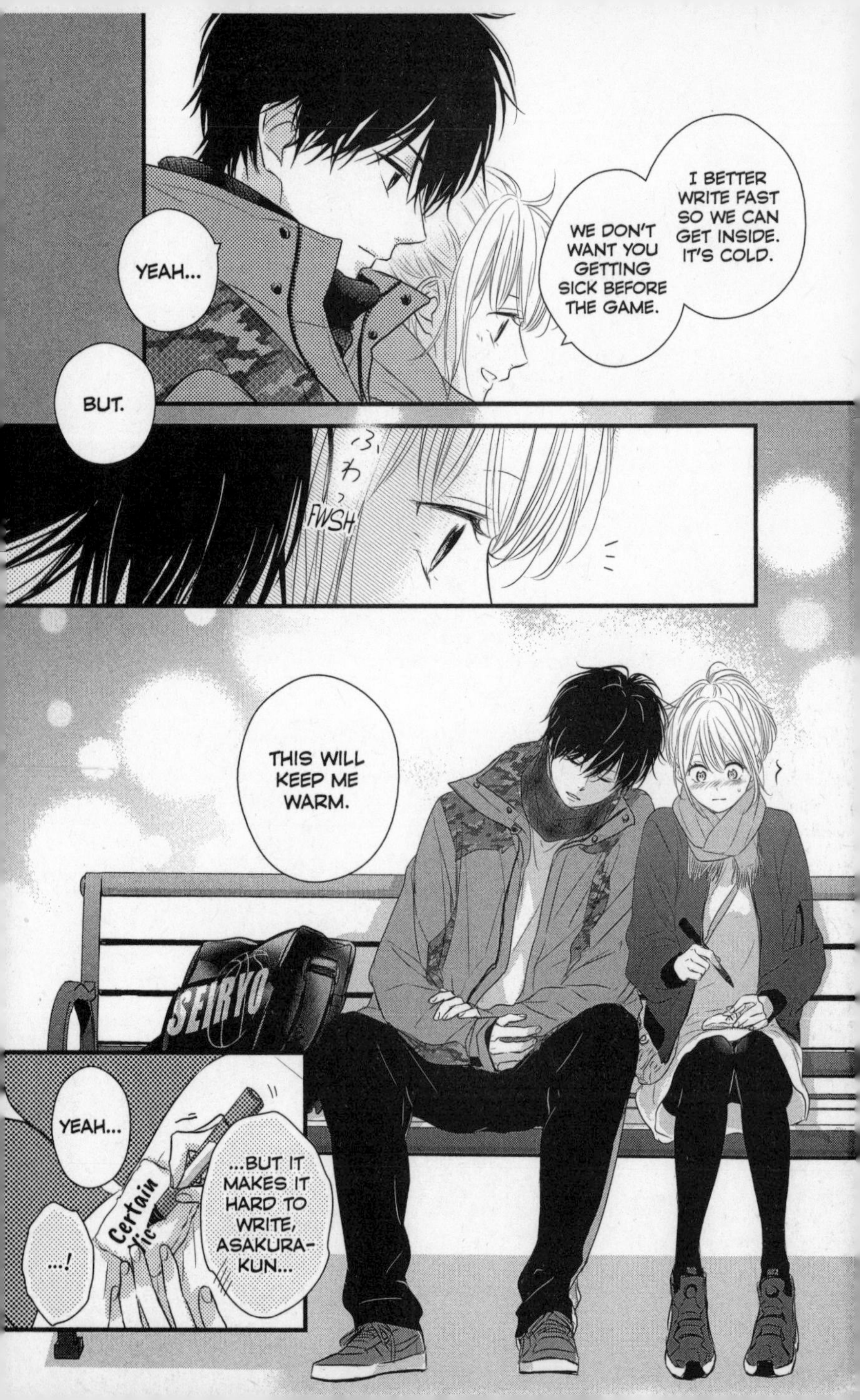
I BETTER WRITE FAST SO WE CAN GET INSIDE. IT'S COLD.
WE DON'T WANT YOU GETTING SICK BEFORE THE GAME.
YEAH...
BUT.
ふわっ
FWSH
THIS WILL KEEP ME WARM.
SEIRYO
YEAH...
...BUT IT MAKES IT HARD TO WRITE, ASAKURA-KUN...
Certain
...!

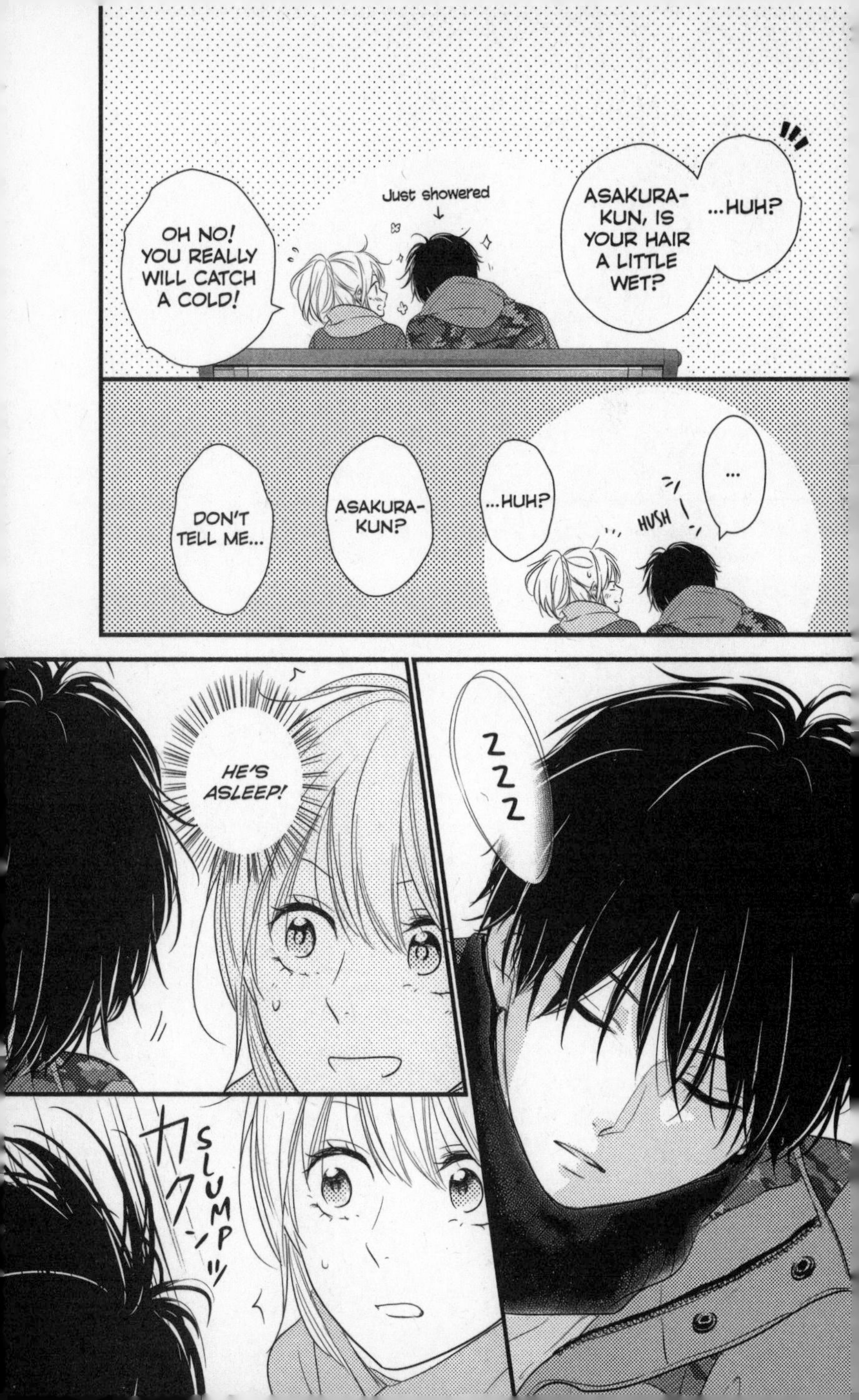
...HUH?
ASAKURA-KUN, IS YOUR HAIR A LITTLE WET?
Just showered ↓
OH NO! YOU REALLY WILL CATCH A COLD!
...
HUSH
...HUH?
ASAKURA-KUN?
DON'T TELL ME...
ZZZ
HE'S ASLEEP!
SLUMP

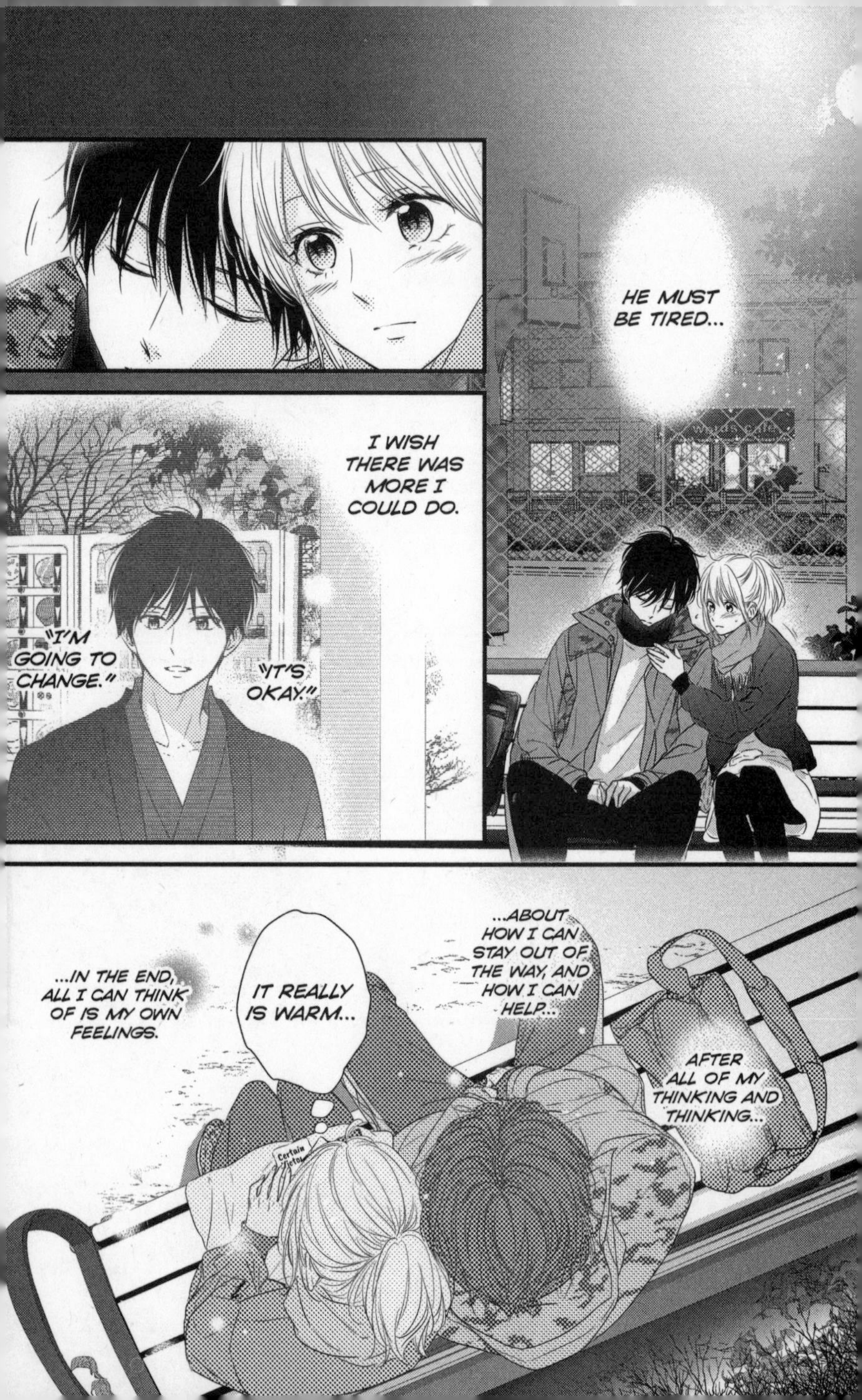
HE MUST BE TIRED...
I WISH THERE WAS MORE I COULD DO.
"IT'S OKAY."
"I'M GOING TO CHANGE."
AFTER ALL OF MY THINKING AND THINKING...
...ABOUT HOW I CAN STAY OUT OF THE WAY, AND HOW I CAN HELP...
IT REALLY IS WARM...
...IN THE END, ALL I CAN THINK OF IS MY OWN FEELINGS.

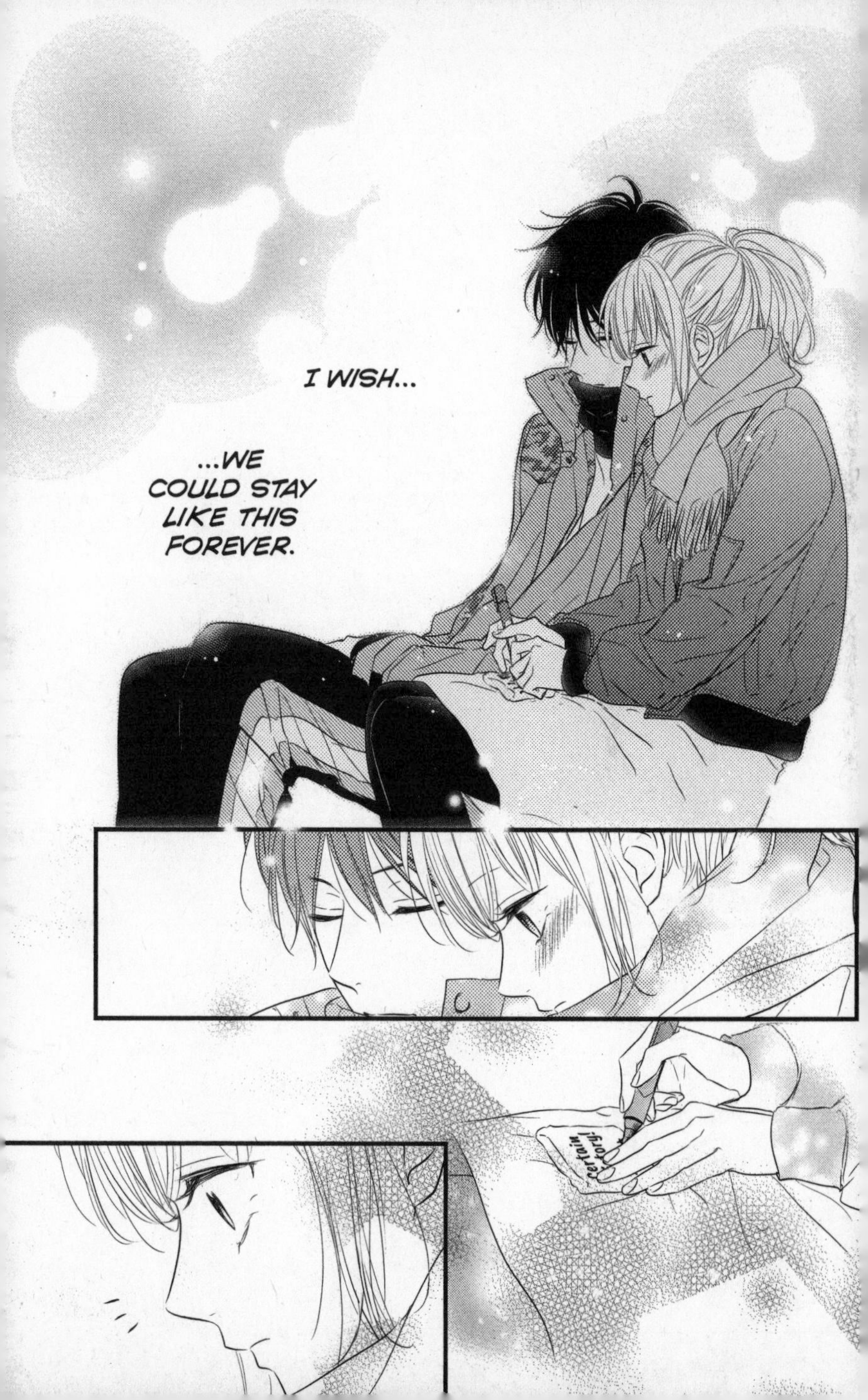
I WISH...
...WE COULD STAY LIKE THIS FOREVER.

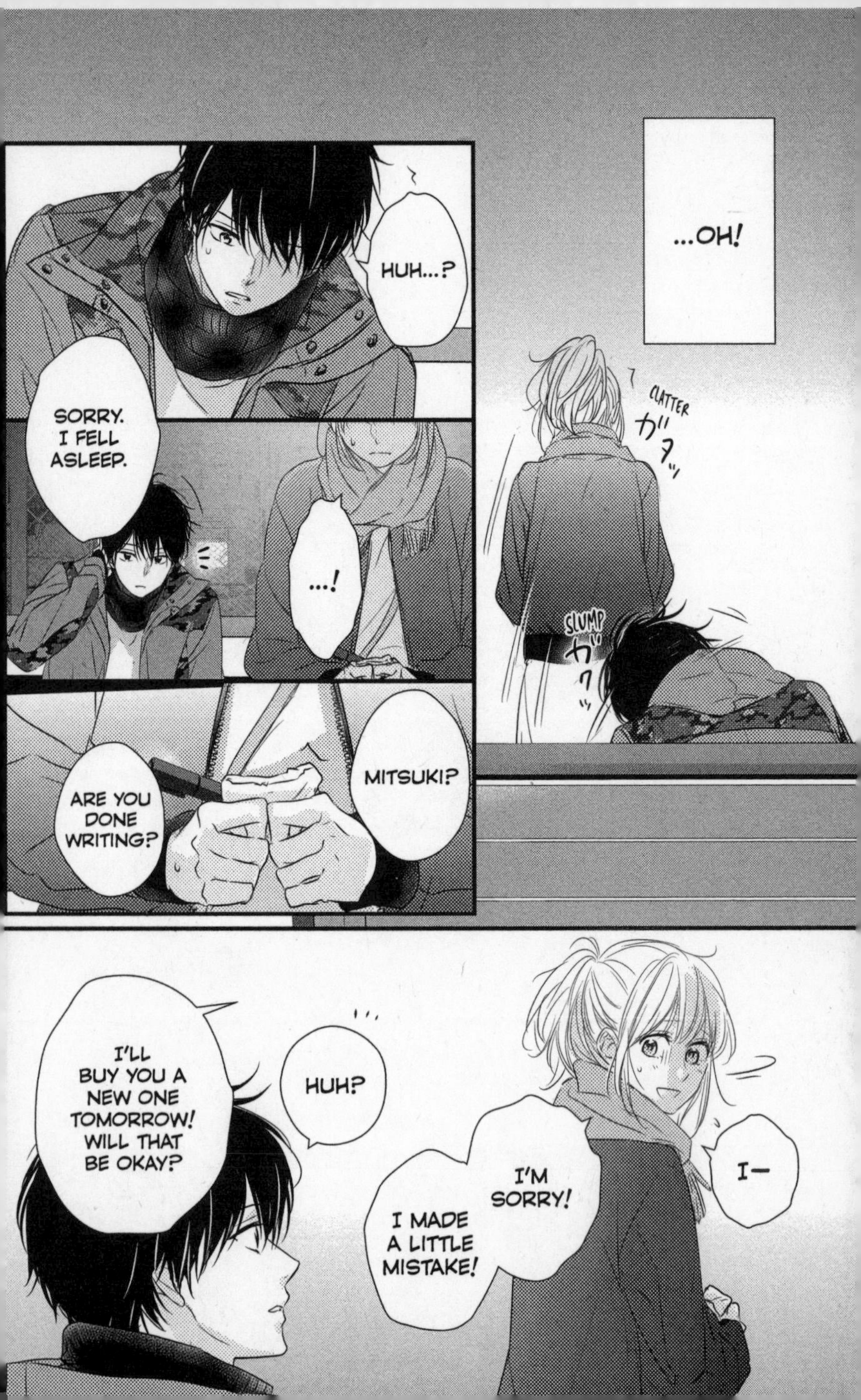
...OH!
CLATTER
ガタッ
SLUMP
ガクッ
HUH...?
SORRY. I FELL ASLEEP.
...!
MITSUKI?
ARE YOU DONE WRITING?
I—
I'M SORRY!
I MADE A LITTLE MISTAKE!
HUH?
I'LL BUY YOU A NEW ONE TOMORROW! WILL THAT BE OKAY?

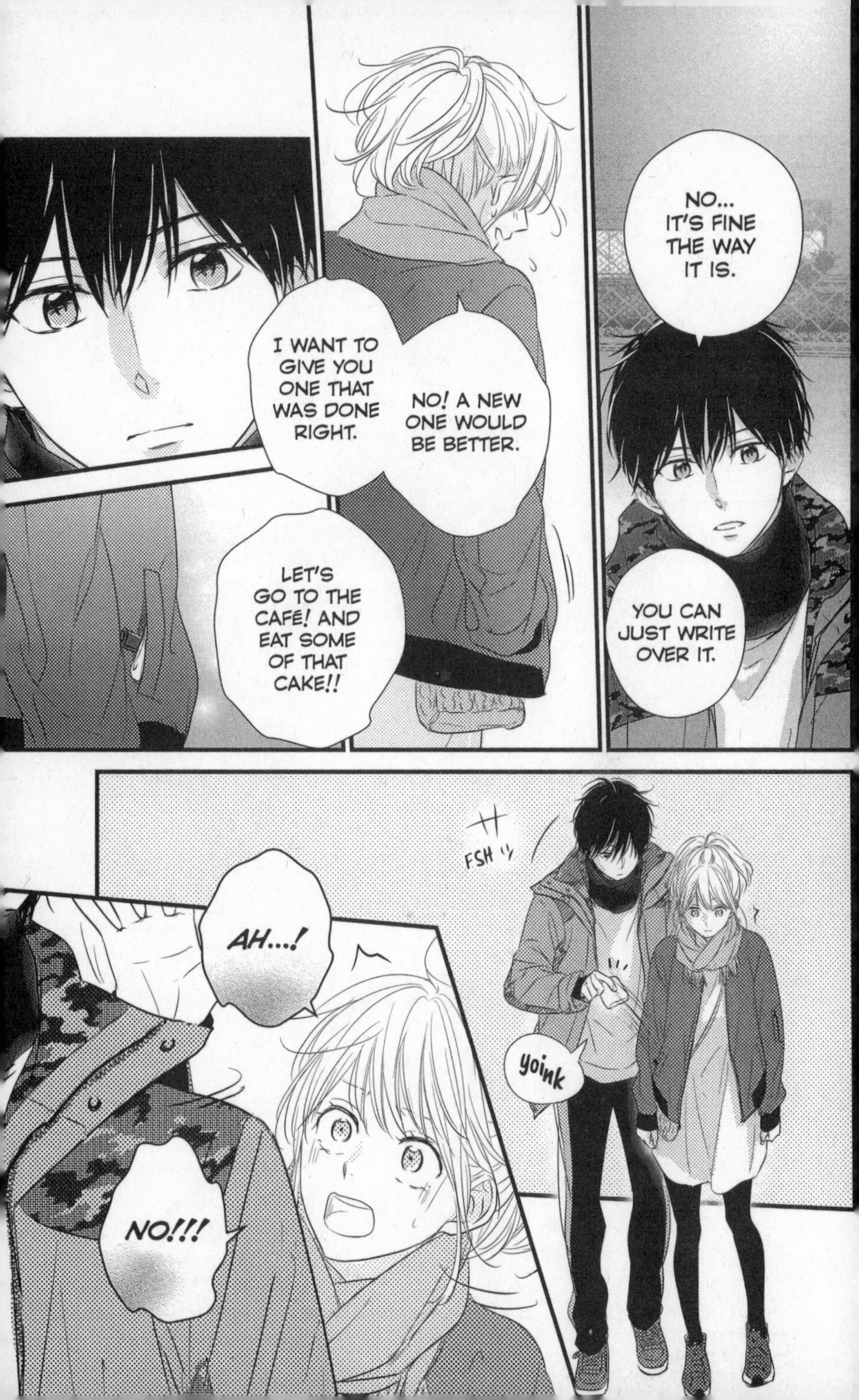
NO... IT'S FINE THE WAY IT IS.
YOU CAN JUST WRITE OVER IT.
NO! A NEW ONE WOULD BE BETTER.
I WANT TO GIVE YOU ONE THAT WAS DONE RIGHT.
LET'S GO TO THE CAFÉ! AND EAT SOME OF THAT CAKE!!
FSH
yoink
AH...!
NO!!!

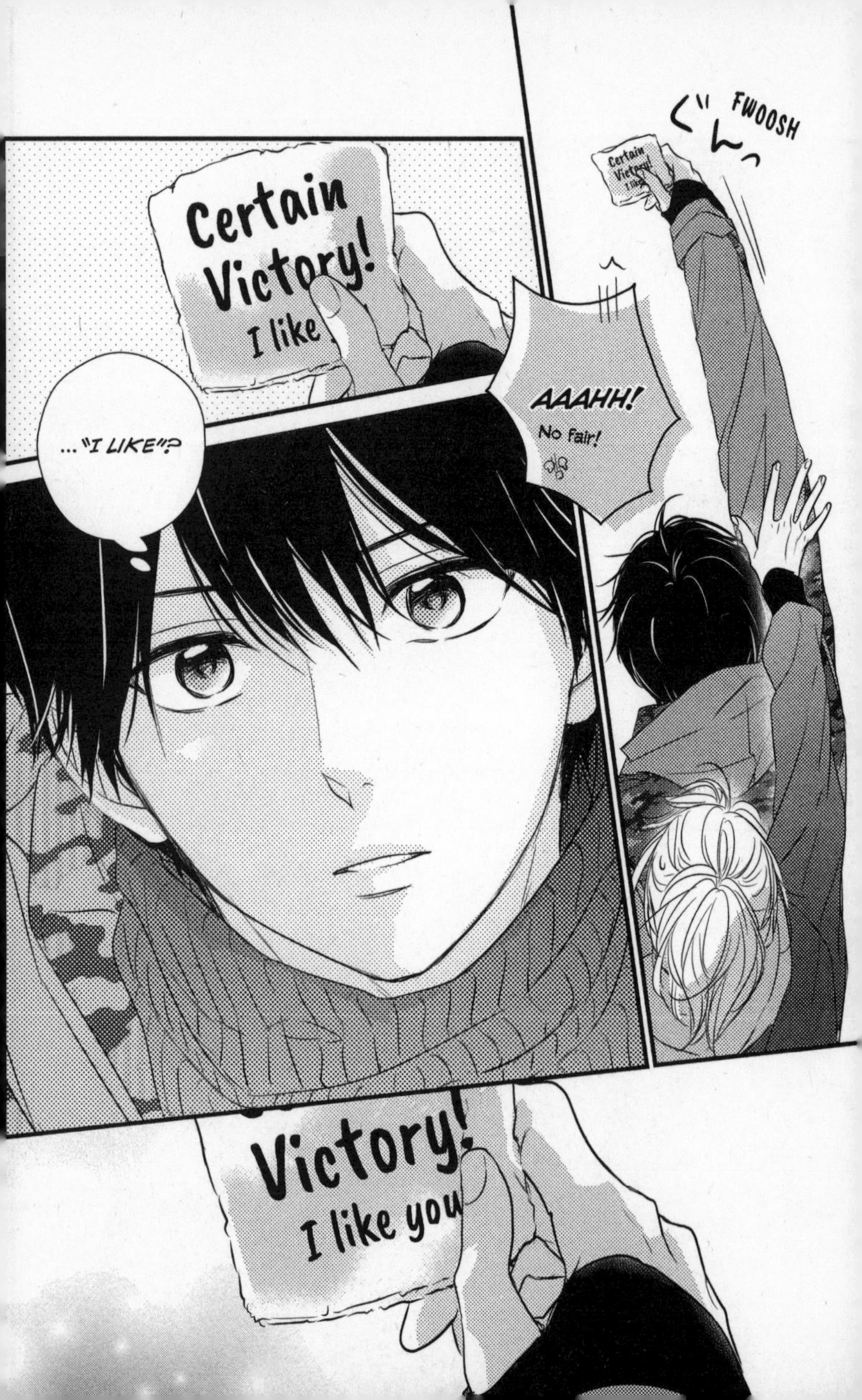

FWOOSH
Certain Victory! I like
AAAHH!
No fair!
Certain Victory! I like
..."I LIKE"?
Victory! I like you

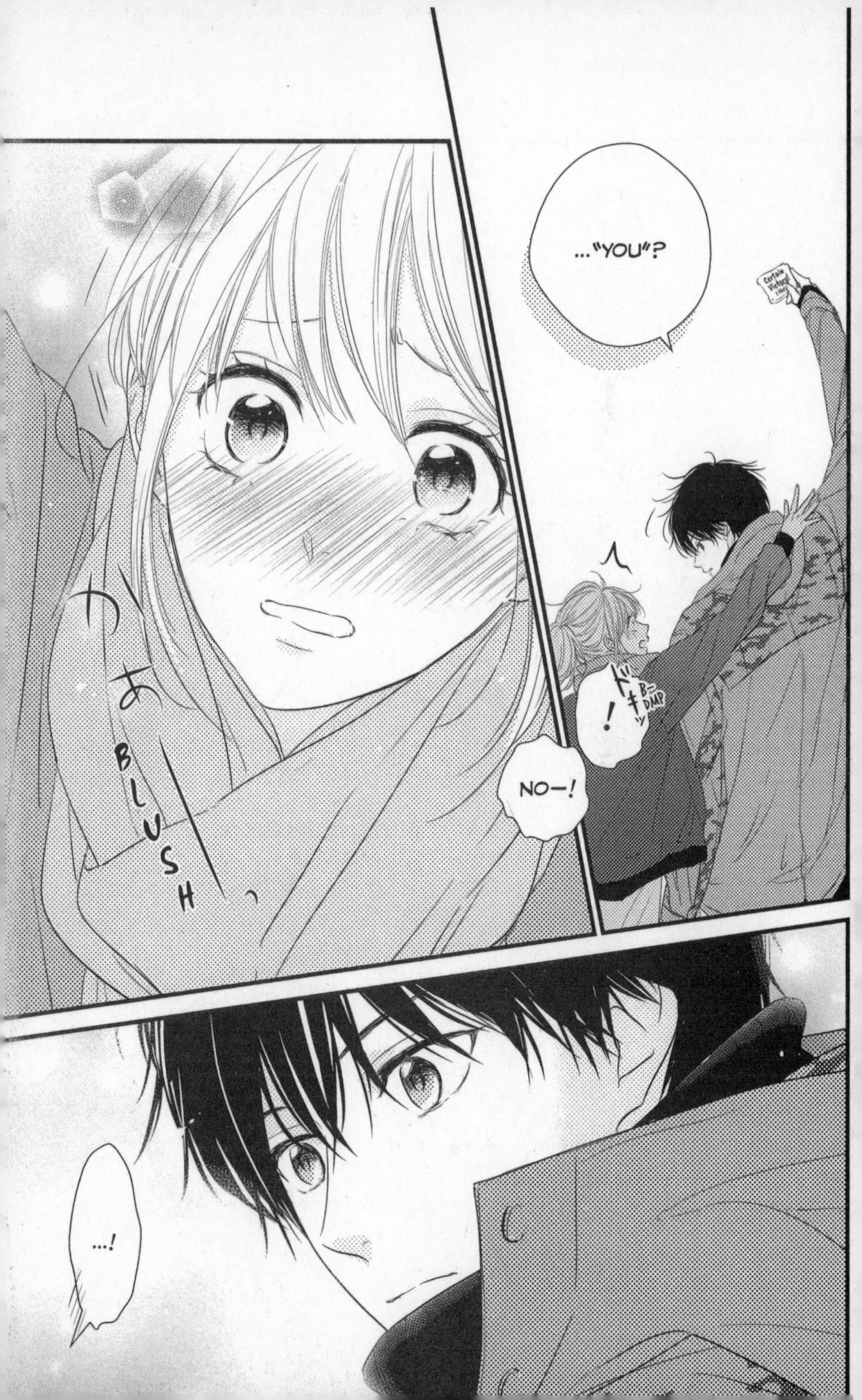

..."YOU"?
Certain Victory!
B-DMP
NO—!
BLUSH
...!

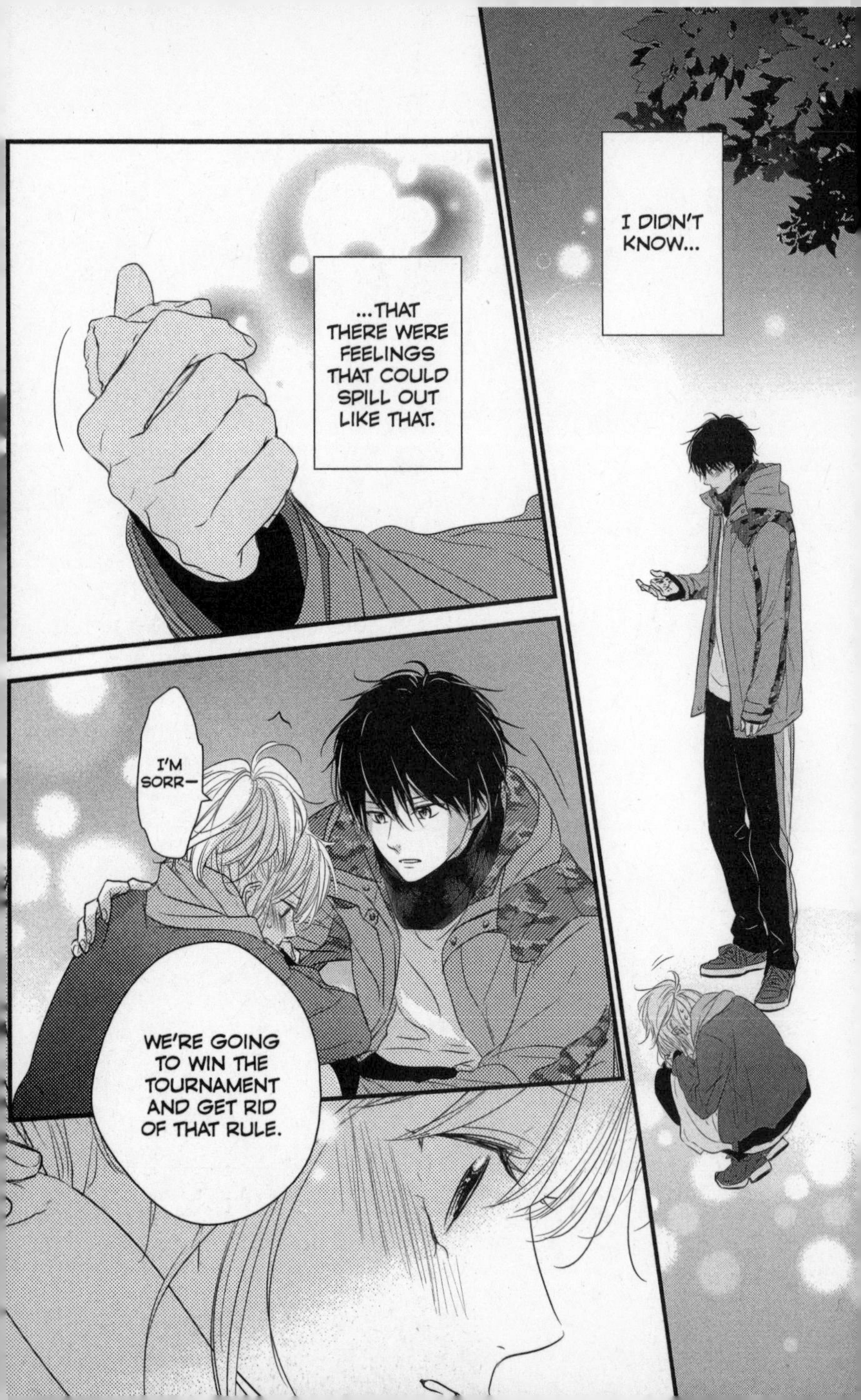
I DIDN'T KNOW...
...THAT THERE WERE FEELINGS THAT COULD SPILL OUT LIKE THAT.
I'M SORR—
WE'RE GOING TO WIN THE TOURNAMENT AND GET RID OF THAT RULE.

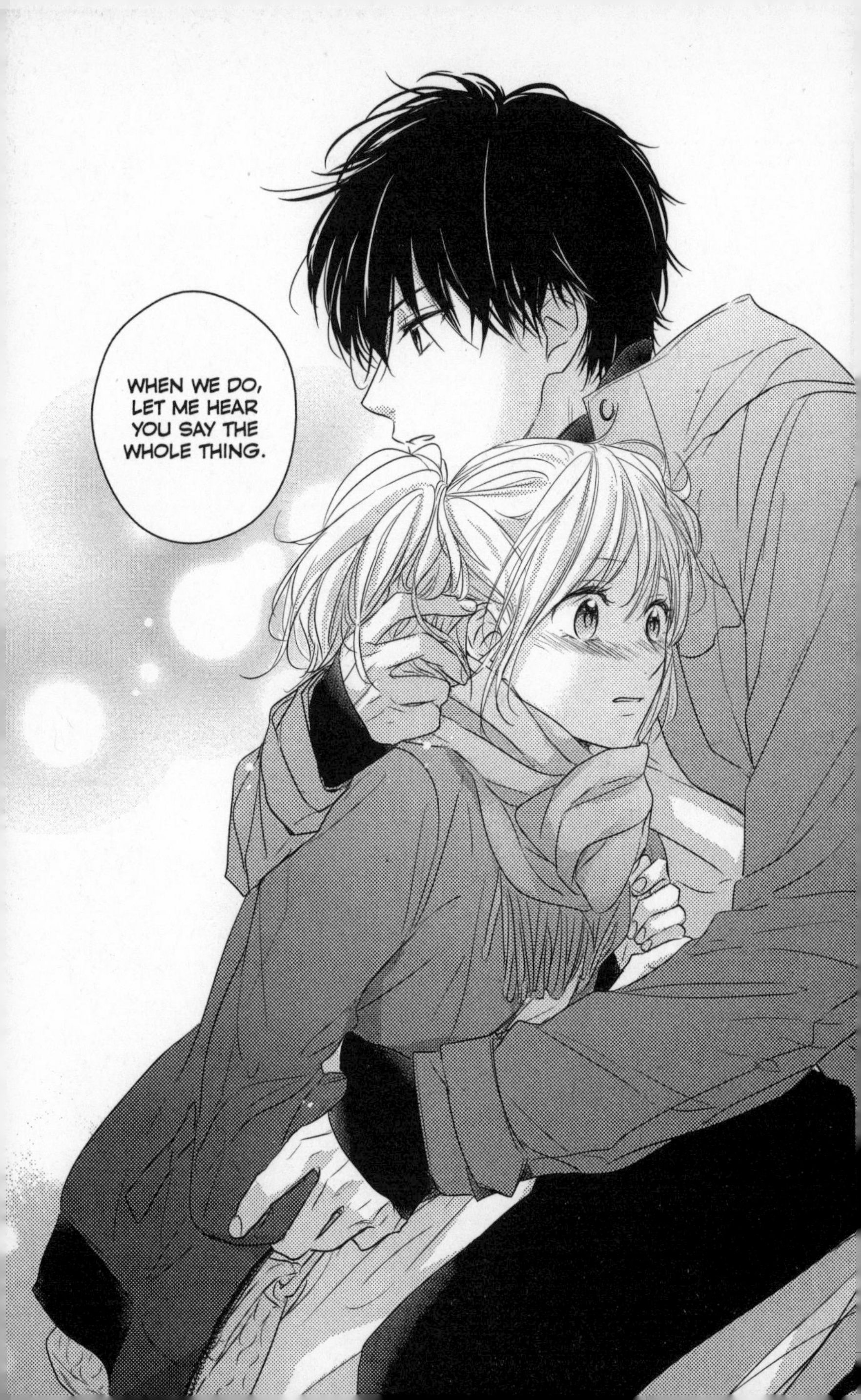
WHEN WE DO, LET ME HEAR YOU SAY THE WHOLE THING.

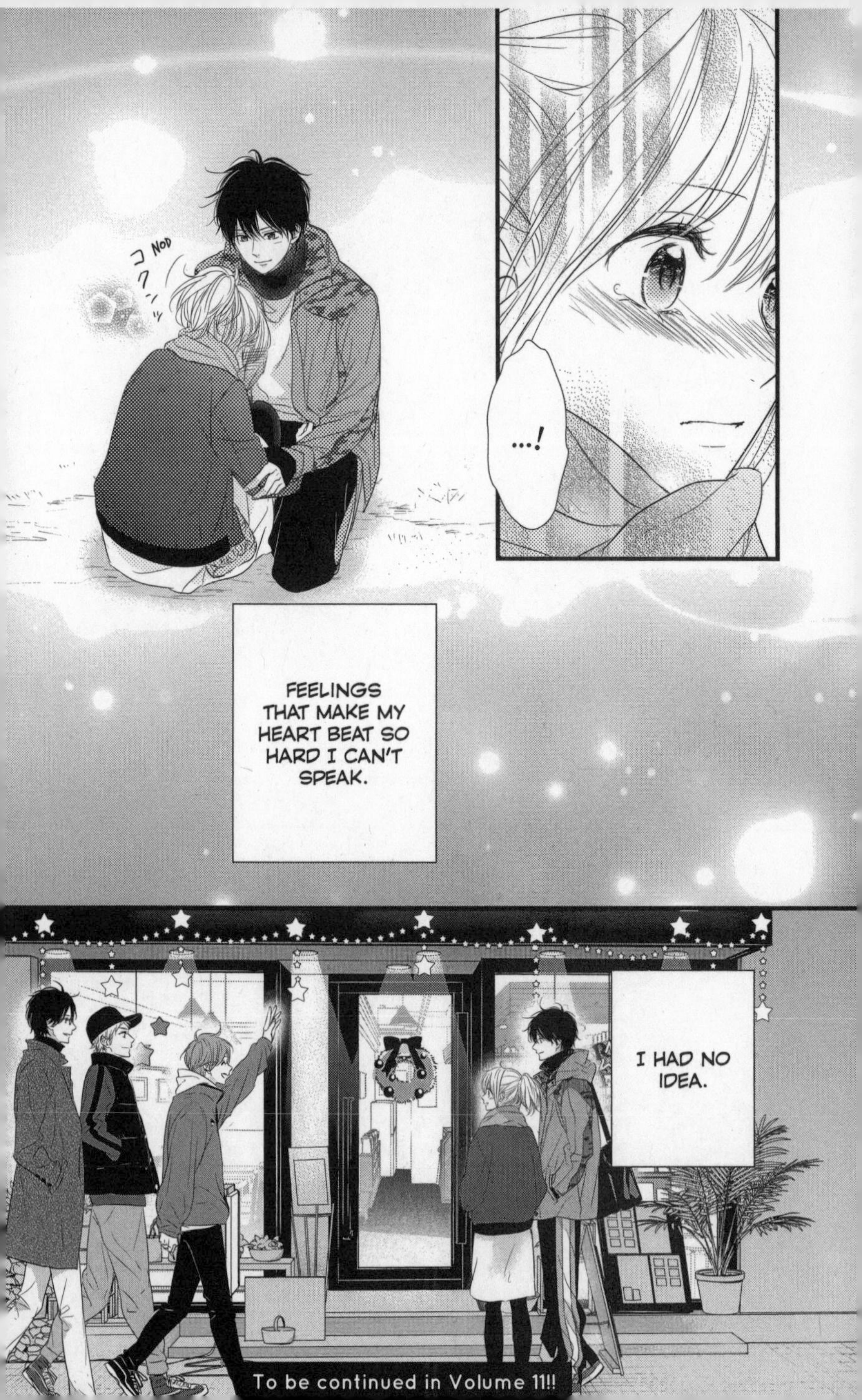
...!
コクンッ
NOD
FEELINGS THAT MAKE MY HEART BEAT SO HARD I CAN'T SPEAK.
I HAD NO IDEA.
To be continued in Volume 11!!

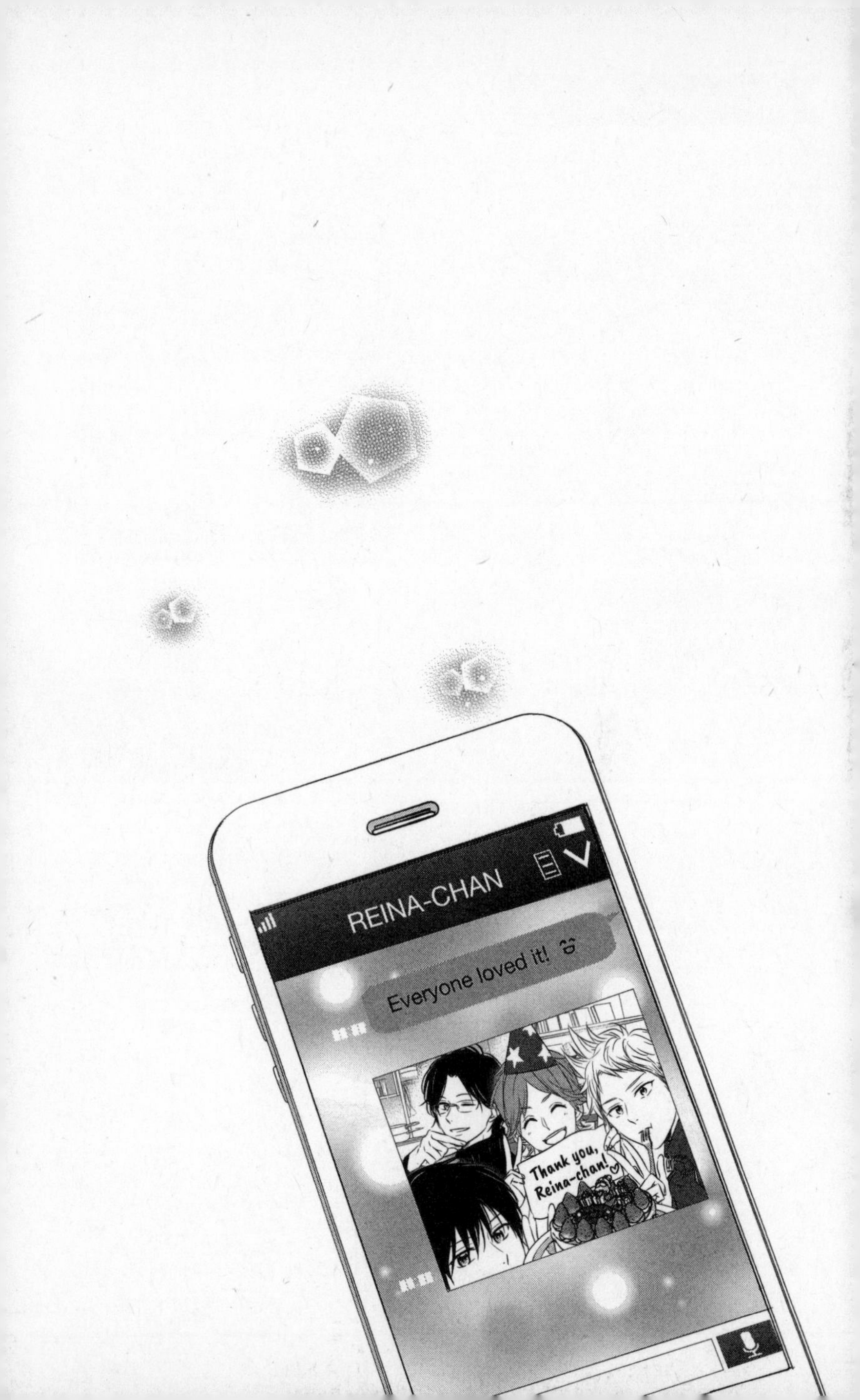
REINA-CHAN
Everyone loved it!
Thank you, Reina-chan!

Bonus Extra Manga

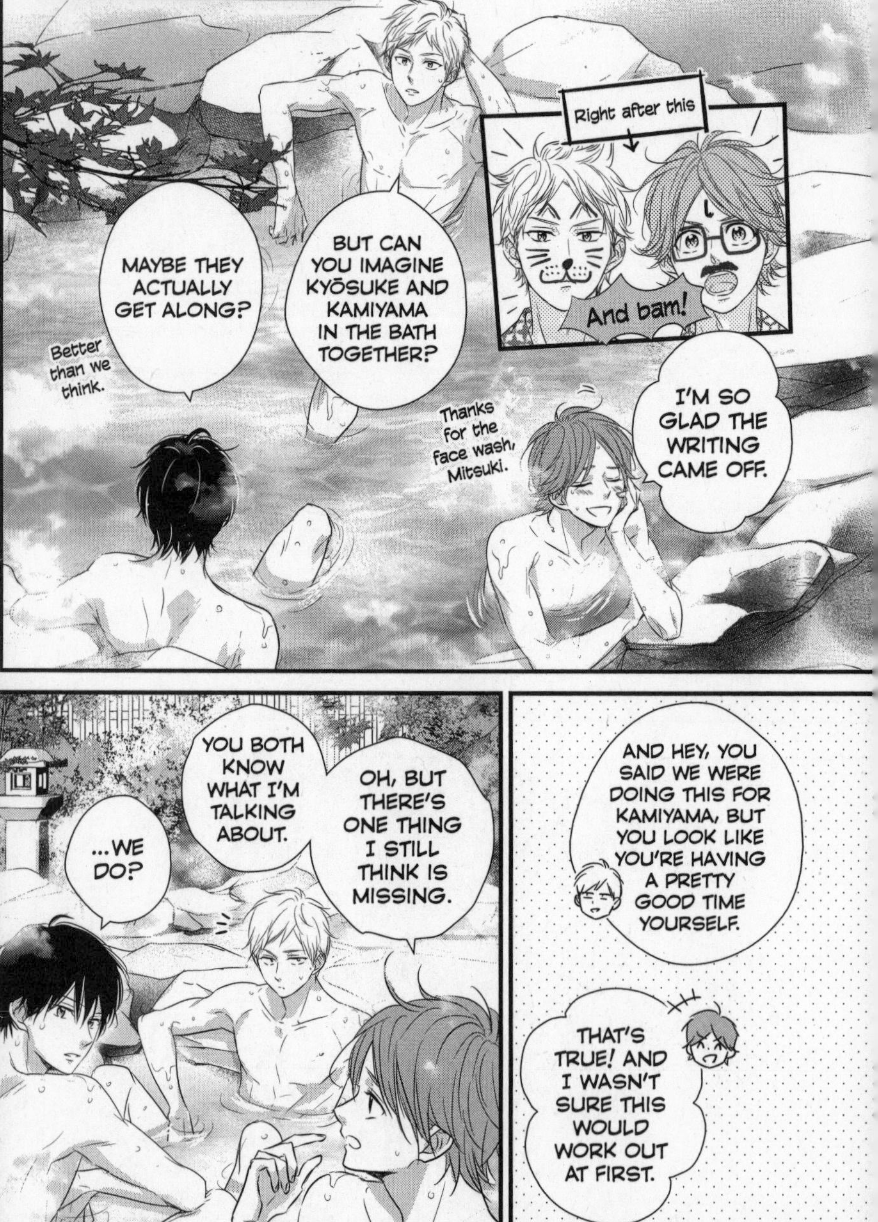
Right after this
And bam!
BUT CAN YOU IMAGINE KYŌSUKE AND KAMIYAMA IN THE BATH TOGETHER?
MAYBE THEY ACTUALLY GET ALONG?
Better than we think.
I'M SO GLAD THE WRITING CAME OFF.
Thanks for the face wash, Mitsuki.
AND HEY, YOU SAID WE WERE DOING THIS FOR KAMIYAMA, BUT YOU LOOK LIKE YOU'RE HAVING A PRETTY GOOD TIME YOURSELF.
THAT'S TRUE! AND I WASN'T SURE THIS WOULD WORK OUT AT FIRST.
OH, BUT THERE'S ONE THING I STILL THINK IS MISSING.
YOU BOTH KNOW WHAT I'M TALKING ABOUT.
...WE DO?

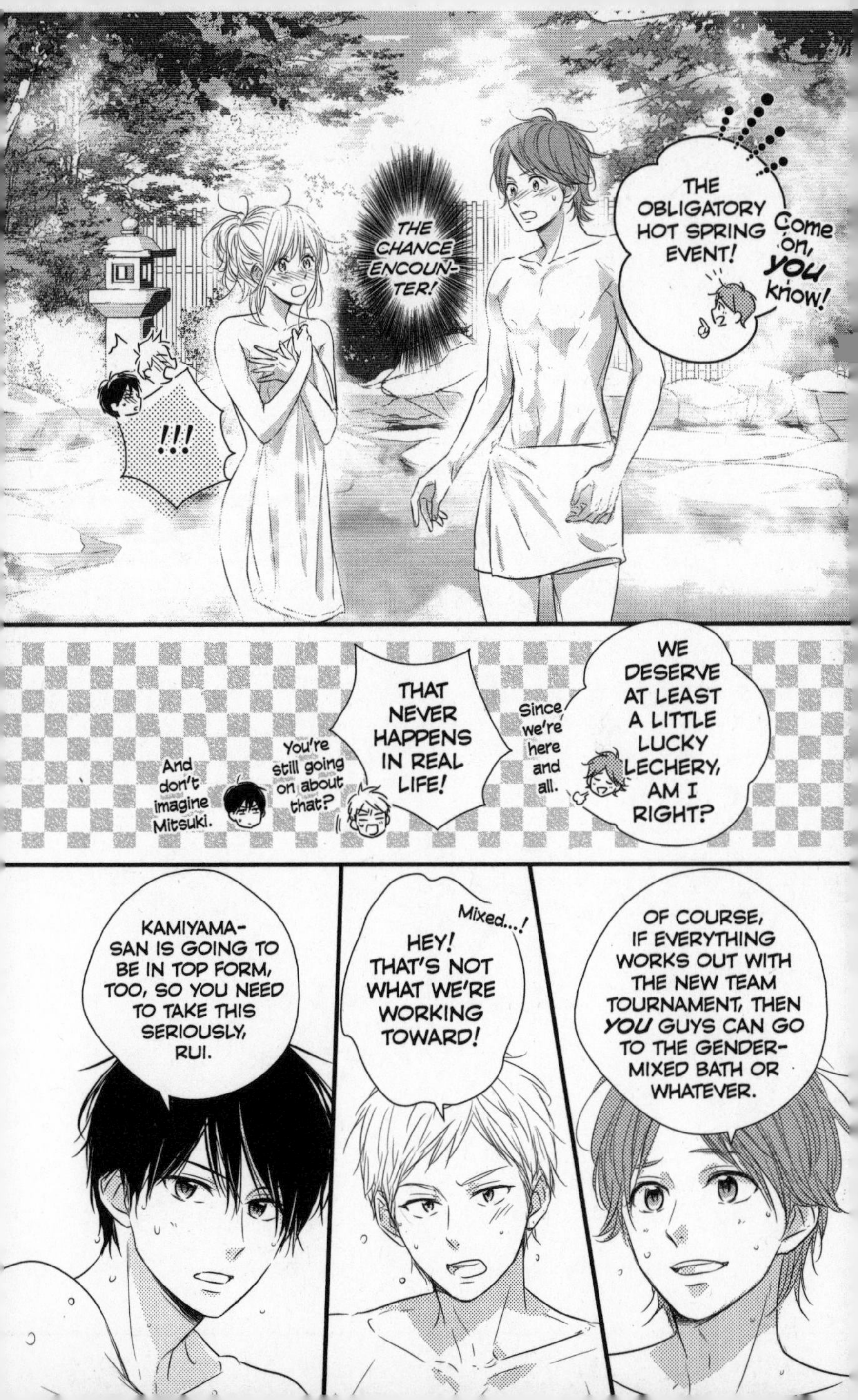
THE OBLIGATORY HOT SPRING EVENT!
Come on, YOU know!
THE CHANCE ENCOUNTER!
!!!
WE DESERVE AT LEAST A LITTLE LUCKY LECHERY, AM I RIGHT?
Since we're here and all.
THAT NEVER HAPPENS IN REAL LIFE!
You're still going on about that?
And don't imagine Mitsuki.
OF COURSE, IF EVERYTHING WORKS OUT WITH THE NEW TEAM TOURNAMENT, THEN YOU GUYS CAN GO TO THE GENDER-MIXED BATH OR WHATEVER.
Mixed...!
HEY! THAT'S NOT WHAT WE'RE WORKING TOWARD!
KAMIYAMA-SAN IS GOING TO BE IN TOP FORM, TOO, SO YOU NEED TO TAKE THIS SERIOUSLY, RUI.

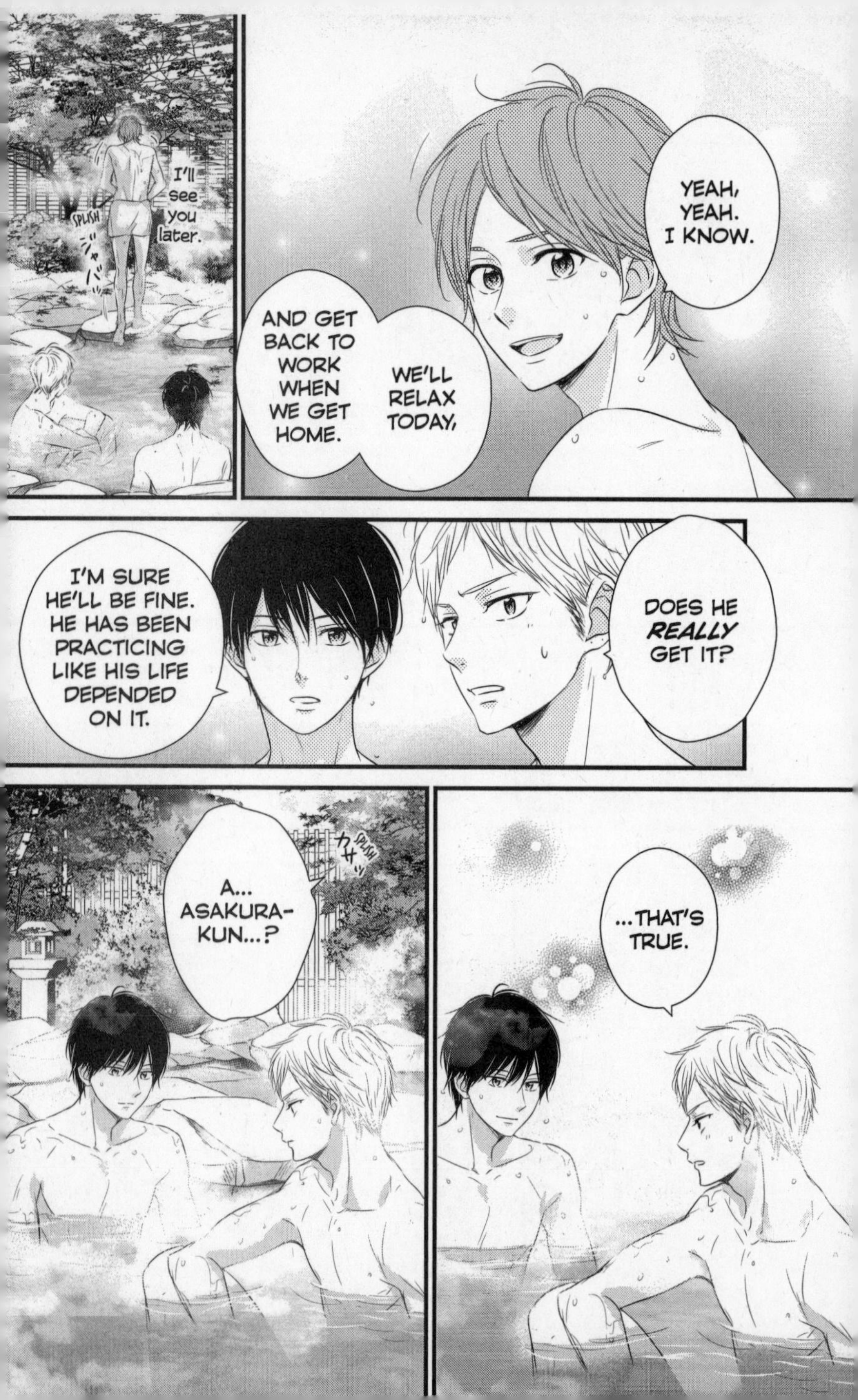
YEAH, YEAH. I KNOW.
WE'LL RELAX TODAY,
AND GET BACK TO WORK WHEN WE GET HOME.
SPLISH
I'll see you later.
DOES HE *REALLY* GET IT?
I'M SURE HE'LL BE FINE. HE HAS BEEN PRACTICING LIKE HIS LIFE DEPENDED ON IT.
...THAT'S TRUE.
SPLISH
A... ASAKURA-KUN...?

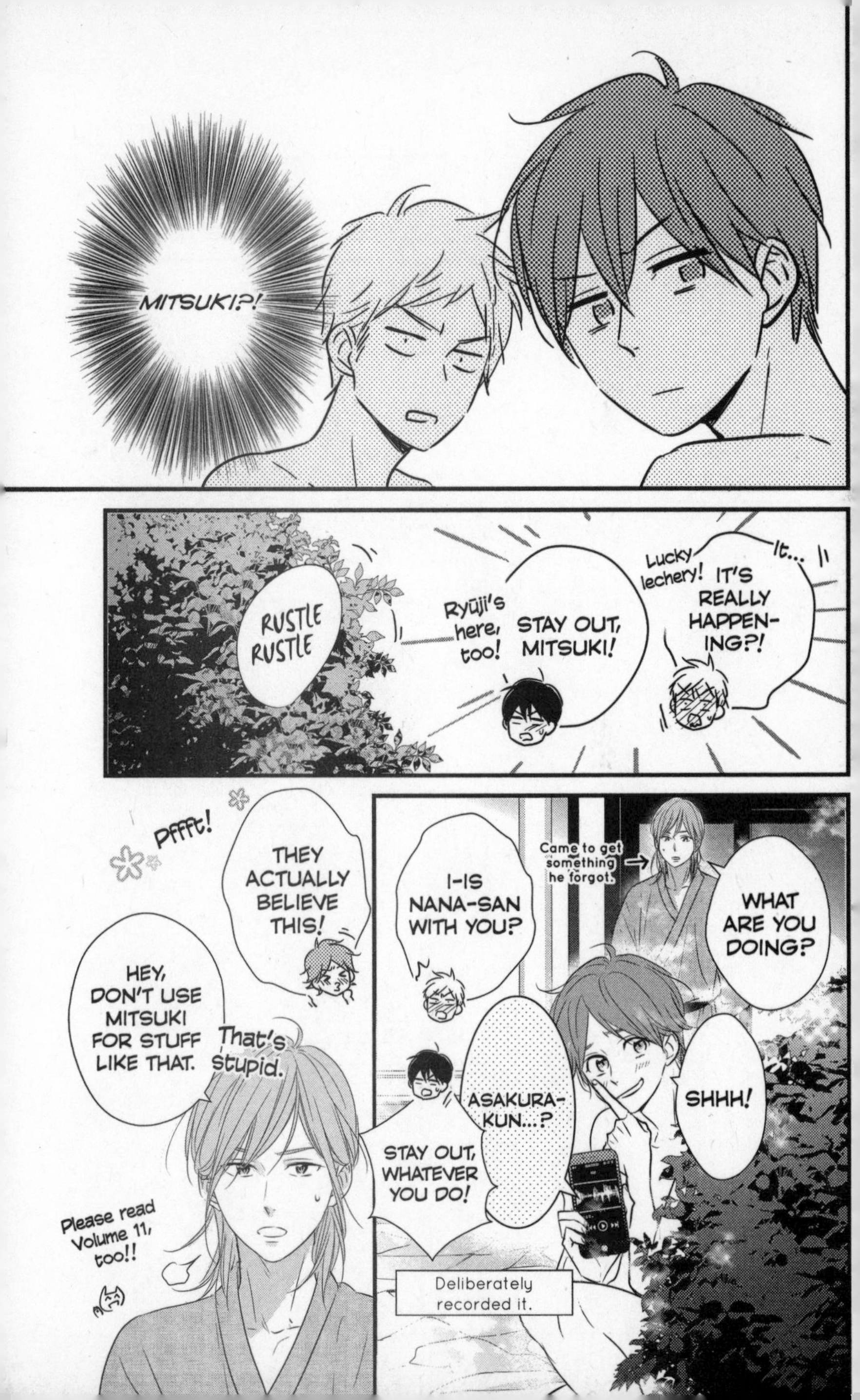
MITSUKI?!
It...
IT'S REALLY HAPPENING?!
Lucky lechery!
STAY OUT, MITSUKI!
Ryūji's here, too!
RUSTLE RUSTLE
WHAT ARE YOU DOING?
Came to get something he forgot.
I-IS NANA-SAN WITH YOU?
SHHH!
ASAKURA-KUN...?
STAY OUT, WHATEVER YOU DO!
Deliberately recorded it.
Pffft!
THEY ACTUALLY BELIEVE THIS!
HEY, DON'T USE MITSUKI FOR STUFF LIKE THAT.
That's stupid.
Please read Volume 11, too!!

Grandpa and Towa

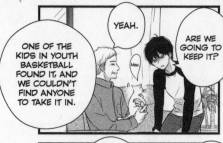

THE DAY A CAT CAME HOME.
ARE WE GOING TO KEEP IT?
YEAH.
Mew.
ONE OF THE KIDS IN YOUTH BASKETBALL FOUND IT, AND WE COULDN'T FIND ANYONE TO TAKE IT IN.
WHAT DO YOU WANT TO NAME IT?
Don't just name it Shiro* because it's white.
LET'S GIVE IT A *CUTE* NAME.
HMM... OKAY...
MILK.
...TOWA...
I LOVE IT.
THERE WAS NO ONE TO BE THE VOICE OF REASON.

*"White" in Japanese.

Grandma stopped them and named the cat Milk.

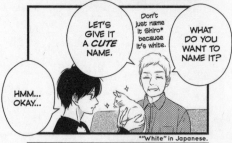

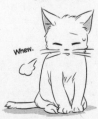

Whew.

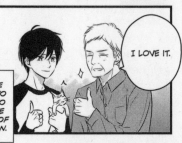

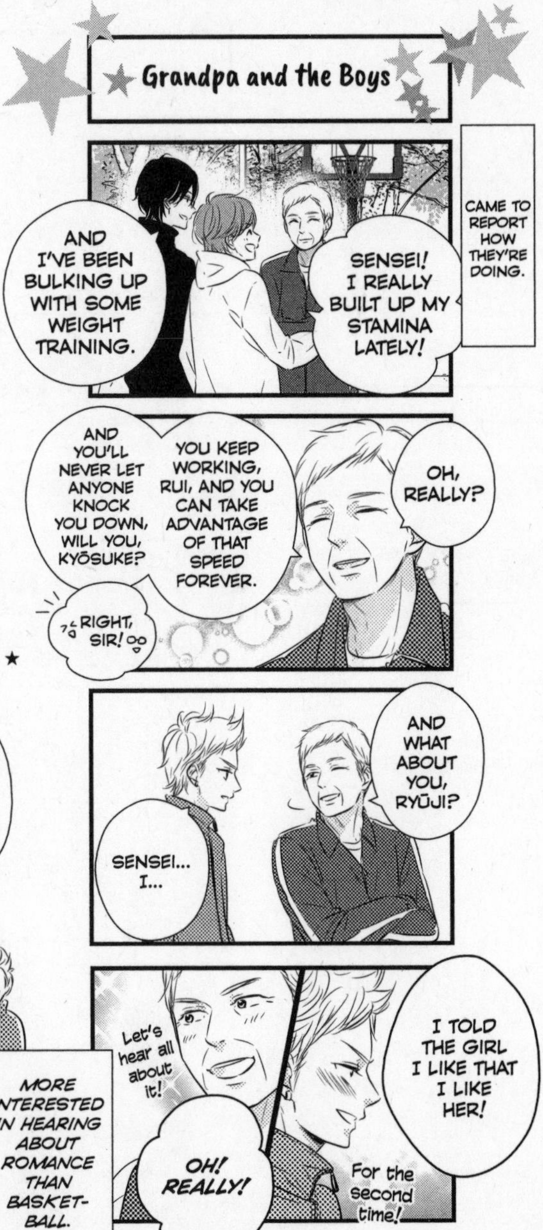
Grandpa and the Boys
CAME TO REPORT HOW THEY'RE DOING.
SENSEI! I REALLY BUILT UP MY STAMINA LATELY!
AND I'VE BEEN BULKING UP WITH SOME WEIGHT TRAINING.
OH, REALLY?
YOU KEEP WORKING, RUI, AND YOU CAN TAKE ADVANTAGE OF THAT SPEED FOREVER.
AND YOU'LL NEVER LET ANYONE KNOCK YOU DOWN, WILL YOU, KYŌSUKE?
RIGHT, SIR!
AND WHAT ABOUT YOU, RYŪJI?
SENSEI... I...
I TOLD THE GIRL I LIKE THAT I LIKE HER!
For the second time!
Let's hear all about it!
OH! REALLY!
MORE INTERESTED IN HEARING ABOUT ROMANCE THAN BASKETBALL.

★ Please read Volume 11, too ★

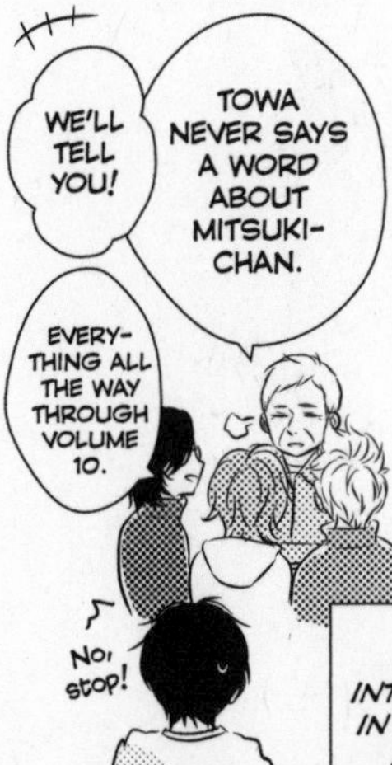
TOWA NEVER SAYS A WORD ABOUT MITSUKI-CHAN.
WE'LL TELL YOU!
EVERYTHING ALL THE WAY THROUGH VOLUME 10.
No, stop!

To be continued in Volume 11!

Translation Notes

Let's go go go, page 20

This comes from a famous phony English phrase, "*Letsura go*!" The phrase was invented by legendary manga artist, Fujio Akatsuka, in his series *Letsura Gon*, which included other phony English such as "*thank you vera macha*."

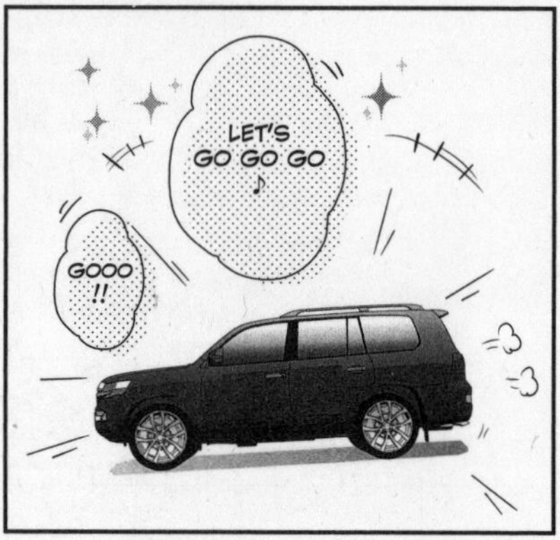
LET'S GO GO GO ♪
GOOO !!

Yukata, page 27

In addition to being the traditional attire for summer festivals, a simplified version of this casual kimono is often provided at hotels and inns to wear as pajamas. At hot springs resorts, it is perfectly acceptable to wear these yukata around the facilities.

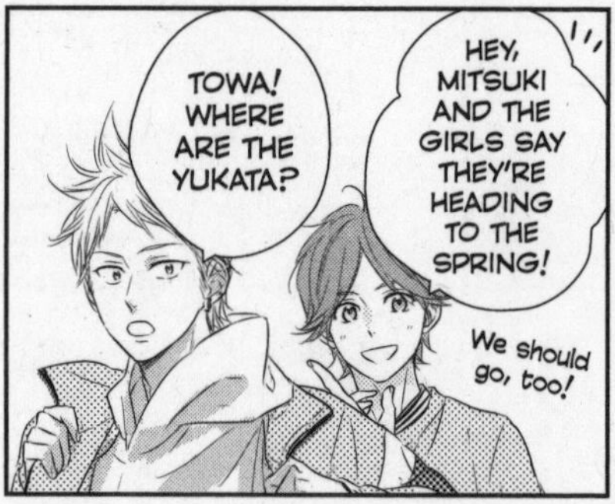
HEY, MITSUKI AND THE GIRLS SAY THEY'RE HEADING TO THE SPRING!
We should go, too!
TOWA! WHERE ARE THE YUKATA?

Could have gone to a better high school, page 79

In Japan, kids don't just go to the school they live closest to. To an extent, they have a choice of what school to attend, as long as they can get accepted. There are all kinds of factors that go into choosing a school—prestige, cutest uniforms, convenience, etc. However, to get into many schools, students have to be able to pass the entrance exam, which means the level of school someone can go to is determined in part by their ability to pass the schools' tests. This means that Kyōsuke could easily have gone to a more prestigious high school, but instead he chose to go to one his friends could attend with him.

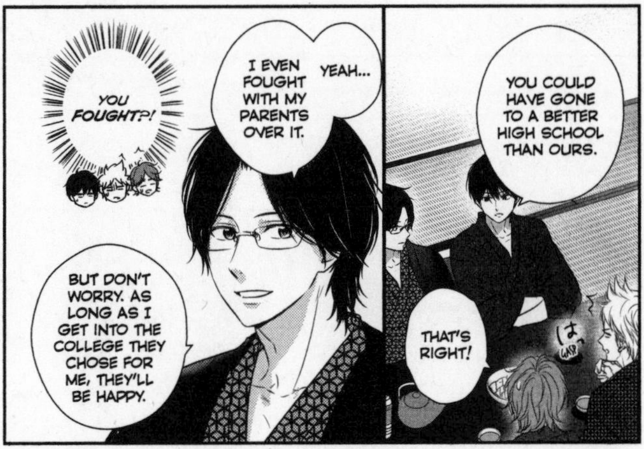
YOU COULD HAVE GONE TO A BETTER HIGH SCHOOL THAN OURS.
THAT'S RIGHT!
GASP
YEAH...
I EVEN FOUGHT WITH MY PARENTS OVER IT.
YOU FOUGHT?!
BUT DON'T WORRY. AS LONG AS I GET INTO THE COLLEGE THEY CHOSE FOR ME, THEY'LL BE HAPPY.

Ghost leg, page 133

Ghost leg, or Amida-kuji as it's known in Japan, is a way of selecting from several options in a semi-random way (like Eeny, Meeny, Miny, Moe). The different options are listed in a row at the bottom with a vertical line drawn from each one. Horizontal lines are drawn at random to connect the vertical ones. The selector chooses a vertical line and starts at the top, tracing downward until coming to a horizontal line. The horizontal line is traced to the next vertical line and the tracing continues downward, crossing all horizontal lines in its path, until it reaches one of the options at the bottom.

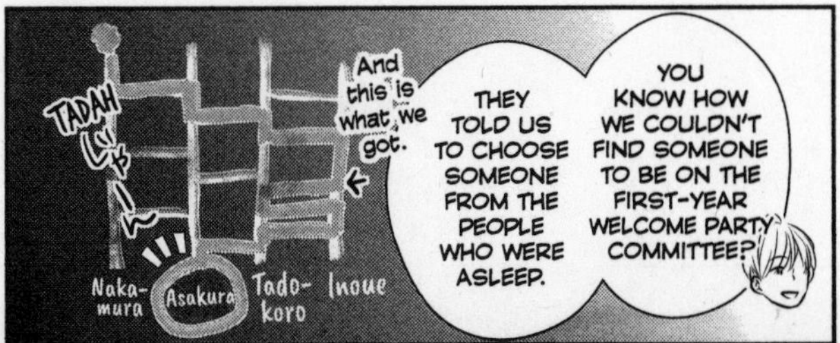
YOU KNOW HOW WE COULDN'T FIND SOMEONE TO BE ON THE FIRST-YEAR WELCOME PARTY COMMITTEE?
THEY TOLD US TO CHOOSE SOMEONE FROM THE PEOPLE WHO WERE ASLEEP.
And this is what we got.
TADAH
Nakamura
Asakura
Tadokoro
Inoue

Waiting for Spring

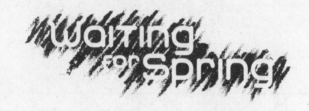

My Little Monster

OPPOSITES ATTRACT...MAYBE?

Haru Yoshida is feared as an unstable and violent "monster."
Mizutani Shizuku is a grade-obsessed student with no friends.
Fate brings these two together to form the most unlikely pair. Haru
firmly believes he's in love with Mizutani and she firmly believes
he's insane.

KC
KODANSHA

Say I Love You.

KC
KODANSHA
COMICS

Mei Tachibana has no friends — and says she doesn't need them!

But everything changes when she accidentally roundhouse kicks the most popular boy in school! However, Yamato Kurosawa isn't angry in the slightest— in fact, he thinks his ordinary life could use an unusual girl like Mei. But winning Mei's trust will be a tough task. How long will she refuse to say, "I love you"?

"An emotional and artistic tour de force! We see incredible triumph, and crushing defeat... each panel [is] a thrill!"
—Anitay

"A journey that's instantly compelling."
—Anime News Network

WELCOME TO THE BALLROOM

By Tomo Takeuchi

Feckless high school student Tatara Fujita wants to be good at something—anything. Unfortunately, he's about as average as a slouchy teen can be. The local bullies know this, and make it a habit to hit him up for cash, but all that changes when the debonair Kaname Sengoku sends them packing. Sengoku's not the neighborhood watch, though. He's a professional ballroom dancer. And once Tatara Fujita gets pulled into the world of ballroom, his life will never be the same.

KC KODANSHA COMICS

A Kodansha Comics Trade Paperback Original
Waiting for Spring volume 10 copyright © 2018 Anashin
English translation copyright © 2019 Anashin

Published in the United States by Kodansha Comics, an imprint of Kodansha USA Publishing, LLC, New York.

Publication rights for this English edition arranged through Kodansha Ltd, Tokyo.

ISBN 978-1-63236-742-6

Printed in the United States of America.

www.kodanshacomics.com

9 8 7 6 5 4 3 2 1
Translation: Alethea and Athena Nibley
Lettering: Sara Linsley
Editing: Haruko Hashimoto
Kodansha Comics edition cover design by Phil Balsman